Moral Development, Self, and Identity

Moral Development, Self, and Identity

Edited by

Daniel K. Lapsley
Ball State University

Darcia Narvaez
University of Notre Dame

LEA LAWRENCE ERLBAUM ASSOCIATES, PUBLISHERS
2004 Mahwah, New Jersey London

Camera ready copy for this book provided by the editors

Lawrence Erlbaum Associates, Inc., Publishers
10 Industrial Avenue
Mahwah, New Jersey 07430-2262

Cover design by Sean Trane Sciarrone

Library of Congress Cataloging-in-Publication Data

Moral Development, self, and identity / Daniel K. Lapsley and Darcia Narvaez, editors.
    p. cm.
Includes bibliographical references and Index.
ISBN 0-8058-4286-1 (hc : alk. Paper)
1. Moral development. I. Blasi, Augusto. II. Lapsley, Daniel K. III. Narvaez, Darcia.

BF723.M54M686 2004
155.2'5--dc22

2003059902

Books published by Lawrence Erlbaum Associates
are printed on acid-free paper, and their bindings are
chosen for strength and durability.

Printed in the United States of America
10 9 8 7 6 5 4 3 2

Contents

Preface

Augusto Blasi's writing on moral cognition, the development of self-identity, and moral personality has transformed the research agenda in moral psychology. His earliest writings on ego development, his compelling critique of the cognitive developmental hypothesis of adolescence, and his classic papers on the relation between moral cognition and behavior all indicate an abiding interest in the role of the self in human development. In later writings, this interest led Blasi to articulate a stage sequence that described identity development from the perspective of the self-as-subject. Two important novelties are evident in this work. First, contrary to traditional sentiment, Blasi approached the self from the perspective of agency and subjectivity, rather than as an object or concept. Second, the sequence of "modes of identity" that he identified stands in stark relief to the "identity status" approach to identity. Indeed, Blasi's trenchant critique has undermined confidence in the status paradigm, and it has restored the phenomenological complexity of the intentional subject to the core of identity work.

The importance of Blasi's writings on the intentional subject, the self-as-agent, and modes of identity cannot be overstated. They stand as towering achievements in social–cognitive and adolescent personality development. Yet, these notions have had particular resonance in moral psychology. Blasi's "self-model," for example, is now a standard explanation for the relation between moral cognition and moral behavior. The intentional self-as-agent, constructed with reference to moral reasons, imbued with a sense of obligation and personal responsibility, is at the very core of contemporary notions of moral identity.

For Blasi one has moral identity to the extent that the self is organized around moral commitments. One has a moral identity to the extent that moral notions are central, important, and essential to one's self-understanding. This yields a personality imbued with "good will," a moral self, a self that is characterized by a deep, central, affective, and motivational orientation toward morality. Indeed, the heart of Blasi's project in moral psychology might be put this way: to resist the tendency in moral psychology toward *fragmentation* (which denies that there is a unifying center to the personality or describes the personality in terms of functionally independent sets of traits), *secularization* (which reduces moral notions to strong will or merely adaptational functions of character), and *depersonalization* (which treats moral issues as abstractions divorced from one's personal life) and to insist, instead, on the primacy of good will in moral functioning, on the essential, responsible self-as-subject— the moral self. Blasi insists, too, that any account of moral personality must start with the fact that rationality is the core of the moral life. To have a moral identity is to have good moral reasons for the identity-defining commitments that one makes.

Blasi's understanding of moral identity is now the starting point of all discussions about the relation between self and morality; the parameters of moral personality; and the moral integration of cognition, emotion, and behavior. Moreover, his writings on moral personality are the starting point for current interest in moral excellence, the nature of moral character, and moral education, and they will command the attention of researchers, ethicists, and educators for years to come.

THE PRESENT VOLUME

This Festschrift recognizes Augusto Blasi's monumental contribution to moral, personality, and developmental psychology. It reflects the determination of his grateful colleagues to not let his retirement pass unremarked in light of his pervasive and enduring influence on the field. To this end a distinguished interdisciplinary and international panel of scholars have contributed essays to discuss key themes suggested by Gus' work and to assess its contribution to development, education, and ethics. Participants use the occasion of a Festschrift to delight in the work of the celebrant, note how his work has influenced one's thinking on a topic, and show how the celebrant's work has served as a starting point for productive lines of investigation. Along the way contributors summarize their own theoretical and empirical work on critical topics in moral psychology.

The real test of genius, as was said of Freud, is not to have the last word but to say the first word. Saying something original, compelling, and first is the hardest part. In this volume we honor Gus Blasi for doing the hardest part in developmental psychology: for showing us how to talk sensibly about the integration of self, ego, and identity with moral rationality, responsibility, and behavior.

OVERVIEW

In chapter 1 Lawrence Walker reviews several features of Blasi's work that have influenced his own research program on naturalistic conceptions of moral functioning. In particular, Walker takes up Blasi's call for research on the moral life as commonly understood by ordinary people rather than on categories suggested by strictly philosophical concerns. Walker's research program reveals at least three "gaps" in our understanding of moral functioning: (a) the role of practical realities in moral deliberation, (b) the influence of religious faith and spirituality in how people frame moral issues, and (c) the role of intuitions and automaticity in moral functioning. Moreover, Walker describes a sophisticated methodology for identifying the cluster of personality traits that attach to an empirically derived typology of moral exemplars.

The next three chapters take up the motivational and social relational features of moral self-identity. In chapter 2 Roger Bergman reviews the work of prominent developmental theorists with respect to how the moral self is conceptualized, and he concludes that Blasi's understanding of moral identity offers the best answer to the question, "Why be moral?" Our moral commitments take on motivational power to the extent that the self identifies with them.

In chapter 3 F. Clark Power discusses two strands of his research on the self as a moral agent. One strand is his influential work on how collective norms emerge within just communities. A second strand is his work on the assessment and meaning of moral self-worth. The two strands are not independent in the sense that moral self-worth is perhaps mediated by one's experience of community. Indeed, Power suggests that it is the experience of community that sustains moral commitment.

Robert Atkins and Daniel Hart extend this theme in chapter 4. In their view the constituents of moral identity are rooted in stable configurations of personality and social influence. Moral identity is not something that one achieves all by oneself; it is deeply conditioned by social relationships and social institutions. In particular, much like Power, Atkins and Hart emphasize the importance of school-based experiences on the formation of moral identity. Schools provide (a) opportunities for adolescents to interact with caring teachers who model prosocial community standards, (b) opportunities for youngsters to explore moral lines of prosocial action and to enact moral commitments in the form of community service, and (c) provide the sort of moral atmosphere that emphasizes the communitarian basis of democratic citizenship. Atkins and Hart describe empirical findings from their analysis of data from the National Study of Youth to show that voluntary community service and a sense of school attachment are related to moral identity in adolescents. These three chapters illustrate not only the motivational role of moral identity in personality but also the social relational and communitarian grounds of its formation.

The next four chapters offer cautionary perspectives on moral self-identity. In chapter 5 David Moshman argues that a moral identity is an explicit theory about oneself as a moral agent who acts on the basis of moral beliefs and values. An identity is the result of an ongoing creative process whose nature changes with experience. Every moral identity is a unique coordination of moral and personal commitments. Although driven by rational processes, an identity can be true or false, the latter occurring when the self manipulates evidence about personal behavior. Indeed, it is the disconcerting tendency of individuals to assimilate, distort, deny, and rationalize moral iniquity that is the focus of Moshman's chapter. He illustrates the heinous consequences of false moral identity in a case study of the El Mozote massacre in El Salvador in 1981. Here a military commander, armed with a self-image as a righteous moral agent defending the welfare of the Salvadoran people against evil Communism, is capable of implementing a scorched earth policy that ordered soldiers to brutally rape, kill, and impale villagers of all ages. It would not be difficult to multiply examples of false moral identity closer to home, especially since the events of September 11, 2001.

In chapter 6 Larry Nucci's problem with the notion of moral self is not that it is sometimes false, but that it is ill conceived as a basis for moral action. In his view it is entirely likely that one can act for moral reasons quite irrespective of whether one has a moral identity. Moreover, it is inappropriate, in his view, to reduce complex and highly contextualized moral judgments to a simple matter of whether an action is consistent with a moral self-conception. Indeed, maintaining self-consistency as a basis of moral action looks a lot like ethical egoism. There are also gaps in our understanding of the early developmental sources of moral identity, and there are grounds for doubting whether a tight connection between morality and self-identity is even desirable. Nucci argues instead for a contextualized view of moral identity that requires a richer appreciation of how moral and nonmoral factors are evaluated, how agents conceptualize social practices, and how one's position within social hierarchies influences moral appraisal. More than other theorists, Nucci cautions us to reject a static notion of moral identity. Moral identity must be open textured, and open to moral improvement and disequilibration, because only in this way can we avoid the sort of false moral identity which Moshman decries.

Mordecai Nisan provides another critical analysis of Blasi's notion of moral identity in chapter 7. Although recognizing its many strengths, Nisan also wonders if it is sufficient to account for the particularistic aspect of persons and the criticisms of the cognitive approach to morality more generally. He draws a useful distinction between two kinds of moral judgments, one more implicative of the self than the other. Evaluative judgments entail the application of moral standards in a universal and impartial manner. These judgments are considered obligatory, inflexible, and impersonal. Evaluative judgments attend to the morality of the right, not the good, and are intended to tame the 'beast' within. Choice judgments, in contrast, have to do with one's status as a moral person, leaving room for consideration of personal circumstances. These choices are less rigid, incorporating the whole of the person's values. Judgments of choice are personal weighings of directions that contain both positive and negative features. Finally, judgments of choice focus on personal wholeness. They are deeply linked to moral identity, reflecting core aspects of identity such as agency and continuity.

In chapter 8 Bill Puka provides a keen analysis of altruism and character and their respective relation to morality and moral functioning. In his view character fails to capture important features of the moral personality, and it hardly seems to be the right word to describe altruists or moral exemplars. He provides the first commentary on Blasi's critique of Batson's long-term study of altruism, and he presses a trenchant attack on the notion of character. It is wrong, he notes, to associate character with virtues. Moreover, both concepts are "pre-empirical" notions "fashioned during times of fantastical superstition, spurious observation, and false wisdom." Character and virtues are the psychological analogue and contemporaries of the four elements of physical reality (earth, wind, fire, and water); they predate phlogiston and phlegm, bile and vital—all physical categories of explanation long ago refuted by the advance of the empirical sciences. Yet, character and virtues have endured in ethics and moral psychology. Puka concludes with a subtle analysis of Blasi's ingenious approach to character, will, and integrity, and he suggests that attempts to integrate it with alternative accounts will pay important dividends.

In chapter 9 we (Daniel K. Lapsley and Darcia Narvaez) present an integrative approach to the moral personality. We argue that social–cognitive theory provides at least six critical resources when pressed into the service of moral psychology, not the least of which is its ability to anticipate novel facts about moral personological and moral cognitive functioning. The social–cognitive model of moral personality advanced here touts schema accessibility as a general principle of moral knowledge activation. It draws attention to individual differences in moral chronicity, and it insists that the tacit, implicit, and automatic features of social cognition find a place in the explanation of moral functioning. Finally, we make a case for a possible developmental grounding of the moral personality by invoking the literatures of early, generalized event representations and autobiographical memory. The capacity for event representation, according to this view, is the social–cognitive foundation of character.

Citing the failure of most individuals to reach the highest stages in both Piaget's and Kohlberg's models, Wolfgang Edelstein and Tobias Krettenauer examine the precursors to postformal reasoning and postconventional moral reasoning in chapter 10. They observe that human progress from simpler to more complex societies has provided the demand characteristics required to stimulate more complex problem-solving abilities. Yet, they suggest that the conditions for growth into the highest stages of reasoning and of moral judgment are enriched environments like those provided by higher education. Using a longitudinal study of ego development, which has a similar growth curve to that of moral judgment development, they provide evidence for the disjunction hypothesis in which non-normative experience is required for higher stage attainment.

The next three chapters explore the notion of moral self and identity from cultural (Wren & Mendoza), cross-cultural (Keller), and sociohistorical (Nunner-Winkler) perspectives. In chapter 11 Thomas Wren and Carmen Mendoza explore the various modalities by which the self is socially constructed, and they note that such a construction is made difficult when the racial and ethnic heritage of an individual is complex. According to Wren and Mendoza, when one exists within multiple social worlds, one's moral orientation and personal sense of coherence are ongoing projects. Referring to several case studies, they describe the difficulties of situating one's identity in a multicultural life and the constant reorganizations that it requires.

Similarly, Monika Keller explores the emergence and developmental grounding of the moral self in Western (Icelandic) and Chinese adolescents in chapter 12. In her view the self in adolescence is closely interconnected with relationships and the experience of intimacy. Close friendship is critical to self-definition, and this appears to be a universal feature of adolescent development. Yet, one's cultural and societal context also influences the meaning of self-in-relationship. Indeed, Keller's empirical work shows that the role of moral consistency and moral feelings in the emergence of the moral self does indeed show interesting variation in Western and Chinese adolescents.

In chapter 13 Gertrud Nunner-Winkler provides empirical support for the claim that the structure of moral motivation shows not just cultural or cross-cultural variation but socio-historical, intergenerational variation as well. In a provocative thesis Nunner-Winkler tests the notion that societal and personality structures coevolve and that sociohistorical change from command authority in the organization of society toward egalitarian, democratic processes is mirrored in a shift away from "superego control" to "egosyntonic" types of conformity motives that entail volitional commitment. All three chapters remind us that a full understanding of moral psychological processes must not neglect culture, context, and history.

It is fitting that Augusto Blasi provides the concluding chapter to this volume. Here Gus offers a personal reflection on how his work has come to focus on the cognitive basis of morality and on the personal agentic capacities of the self, which he calls the "two anchor points" of his intellectual project. He reviews the main themes of his position and uses the occasion to respond to some of the issues raised in this volume. We are confident that the field of moral psychology will be productively engaged with the problematic that Gus has set before it and that a generation of grateful scholars will welcome his contribution with justifiable admiration.

1

Gus in the Gap: Bridging the Judgment–Action Gap in Moral Functioning

Lawrence J. Walker
University of British Columbia

Gus Blasi's contributions to the field of moral psychology have been hugely significant, and a Festschrift is more than appropriate and timely. It is a privilege to contribute to this volume honoring him, especially because his thinking on several issues has been very influential in my own research over the years; it is a joy to join in recognizing someone whose personal and professional life has so clearly exemplified the aspects of moral identity and personality that he has studied in his own work.

I entitled my chapter, "Gus in the Gap," because more than anyone else in contemporary psychology Gus Blasi has been responsible not only for identifying and explaining the significance of the gap between moral judgment and action but also for helping to bridge this gap that has so befuddled the field. The judgment–action gap has been a recurrent conundrum for us, both as scholars seeking to understand moral functioning and as individual moral agents striving to live the good life. This gap is revelatory of some importunate aspects of the human condition; as the Apostle Paul cogently noted, "For what I do is not the good I want to do; no, the evil I do not want to do—this I keep on doing" (Romans 7:19).

1

Blasi's (1980) comprehensive review of the relation between moral reasoning and behavior, published in the *Psychological Bulletin*, is a citation classic and remains the definitive work on the issue over 20 years later. Published at the time when Kohlberg's (1969, 1981, 1984) cognitive–developmental model was in ascendance, this review made two extremely important points that need to be held in dynamic tension, perhaps reflecting the ambiguity of the "glass half full or half empty" phenomenon: First, despite the familiar findings that (at least superficially) identical behaviors can be supported by different moral criteria and that the same moral criteria can lead to quite different moral behaviors, this review established the clear significance of reasoning in moral functioning by demonstrating that higher moral reasoning was indeed predictive of better behavior across a wide variety of domains, although the strength of this relationship varied considerably for arguably good reasons. Blasi's conclusion in this regard was substantiated by subsequent meta-analyses of research on the judgment–action relationship (Arnold, 1989; Buchanan, 1992). The persistent myth that moral thinking and moral behavior are independent and unrelated dimensions was convincingly debunked. Second, his review clearly established that moral cognition alone plays a somewhat modest role in explaining the variability in moral action (explaining roughly 10% of the variance), implying that a more comprehensive conceptual framework is necessary to make adequate sense of the scope and complexity of moral functioning. In other words, there is more to morality than mere cognition.

THE SELF MODEL

For the last 2 decades, Blasi (1983, 1984, 1993, 1995) systematically and thoughtfully advanced the self model as a way to understand moral psychology more fully. This model uses self-identity as the central explanatory concept in moral functioning, and it is intended to integrate moral cognition and moral personality within a framework that better explicates moral behavior. Perhaps surprisingly, until Blasi's initiative, the role of the self had been by-and-large ignored in the study of moral functioning. This situation becomes somewhat easier to comprehend when it is realized that the predominant research paradigm has been the analysis of responses to hypothetical moral dilemmas in which the self, of course, is not particularly engaged or relevant. This is obviously not the case in everyday moral situations.

The self model points to three major components of moral functioning. The first component, the *moral self*, focuses on the significance and salience of moral values in one's self-identity. For some individuals, moral considerations are abundant in everyday living because morality is rooted at the core of their being; whereas for other people, moral standards and values are not particularly salient in their daily activities and self-concept. This has been evident in our own research (Walker, Pitts, Hennig, & Matsuba, 1995) in which participants have been asked to reveal and discuss a recent moral dilemma from their own experience—some people could readily proffer several from that day, whereas others were stymied and had to reach back in their memory for a situation decades earlier with moral overtones. Morality seems to have differing degrees of centrality in people's awareness and lives. Similarly, one of the distinguishing characteristics in Colby and Damon's (1992) case-study analysis of the life stories of a sample of moral exemplars was the exceptional uniting of self and morality in their personality, with minimal distinction between their personal and moral goals. Moral goals were seen as inherent to the realization of personal goals and vice versa. This reflects Blasi's (1995) argument that "the highest degree of moral integration is achieved when one's moral understanding and concerns become a part of one's sense of identity" (p. 229). Further evidence regarding this component of the moral self was reported by Hart and Fegley (1995) who systematically examined the self-concepts of a sample of adolescents displaying exceptional levels of prosocial behavior. These prosocial adolescents, in comparison to a matched group, made self-attributions that were more likely to include moral traits and goals, and their actual self-descriptions were more likely to incorporate their ideal selves. All of this evidence supports Blasi's contention regarding the significance of the moral self-concept in moral functioning.

The second component of Blasi's self model refers to individuals' sense of personal *responsibility* for moral action, or what could also be understood as a process of moral engagement (Haste, 1990). It is one thing to formulate a judgment that arbitrates which course of action is the morally right one to do; it is something else (and something additional) to come to the realization that one is morally obligated to undertake that action. This sense of personal responsibility is an important aspect of the connection between judgment and action because it implicates the self in action and because it reflects a personal sense of moral worth (thereby connecting the judgment of responsibility to one's self-definition; Kohlberg & Candee, 1984). The developmental antecedents of this motivation for action have not yet been empirically examined to any extent and represent a fruitful area for future research. Kohlberg and Diessner (1991) suggested that this sense of personal responsibility for moral action may have its roots in a developmental process of moral attachment—the formation of specific relationships to other people, such as parents and friends—that contributes to a variety of moral dispositions, such as empathy, guilt, and commitment. This suggestion clearly implicates affective processes in the origins of the felt sense of personal responsibility.

The third component in Blasi's self model is *self-consistency* or integrity. In Blasi's conceptualization, a fundamental motive in personality functioning is psychological self-consistency, a motive that can only be satisfied by congruence between judgment and action. It is this sense of the self's integrity that is at stake in moral action. In my own research (to be discussed later in this chapter; Walker & Hennig, 2003; Walker & Pitts, 1998; Walker et al., 1995), notions surrounding integrity were found to be central both to people's conceptions of moral character and to their handling of everyday moral problems. Unfortunately, the field's preoccupation with hypothetical scenarios, in which integrity is obviously not a particularly salient factor, has contributed to the failure to adequately examine this aspect of moral functioning. Blasi's acute observation that self-consistency is a powerful and compelling motive in personality functioning reflects our deeply felt and expressed need to appear, in our own eyes and those of others, to be highly moral (sometimes even in the face of overwhelming evidence to the contrary). Thus, our own sense of integrity perhaps is often fallaciously maintained by an arsenal of distorting rationalizations and defense mechanisms. Bandura (1999, 2002) identified several processes by which we selectively disengage from moral self-sanctions, such as the cognitive reconstrual of immoral behavior (with moral justifications, exonerating comparisons, and sanitizing language), the minimizing of personal causal agency in immoral behavior (through the displacement and diffusion of responsibility), the distortion and disregard of harmful consequences, and the blaming and devaluing of victims. Blasi (1995) argued that such processes of moral self-deception should be less likely to be operative for those at more mature levels of moral development and for whom morality is central to their self-definition, but there is as yet little available evidence in that regard. Given the compelling power of the motivation to perceive oneself as a moral person with integrity and to be regarded by others in that way, and the risk that it can be maintained by self-deceiving rationalizations and defense mechanisms, it strongly suggests that the field of moral psychology would benefit greatly from the systematic study of the role of the self in moral functioning—as Blasi so eloquently argued—research that would bring us closer to bridging the judgment–action gap.

Over the last few years, many researchers, myself among them, have decried the rationalistic emphasis that has characterized contemporary moral psychology and have advocated instead for a focus on moral character and moral personality (Campbell & Christopher, 1996; Punzo, 1996; Walker & Hennig, 1997). Blasi (1984, 1999), perhaps surprisingly given his personological intellectual heritage (having studied with Jane Loevinger), was resolute in retaining the cognitive core for morality. Repeatedly, and most helpfully for those of us prone to be swept away by bandwagon movements, he argued that we must not ignore the rational element in morality. As noted in his 1980 article, the significance of cognition in moral functioning is twofold: the creation of meaning and the determination of truth. Moral action is intentional action—it is the result of reasons, reasons that determine its moral quality (Blasi, 1999). If we ignore moral cognition we risk destroying the moral nature of the phenomenon itself, reducing it to an issue of emotionality and losing the objective foundation on which morality must stand (Blasi, 1984, 1995). Blasi (1984) identified the difficulty of the issue as follows:

> If moral identity is based on natural impulses, egoistic or social, one loses the cognitive basis of morality; if cognition and reason are stressed as establishing moral motives, one risks losing the person as the center of morality. It would appear, then, that the only hope of grounding morality on the essential self without losing morality's reason is to hypothesize that the self's very identity is constructed, at least in part, under the influence of moral reasons. (p. 138)

In the self model, it is assumed that moral knowledge does indeed have some inherent motivation force—given its truth value—and that a basic motive arising from a moral identity is consistency between one's appraisal of truth and action.

NEGATIVE CONSEQUENCES OF PHILOSOPHICAL CONSTRAINTS

One of the more formative of Blasi's writings for my own work and, I suspect, for that of many others was his 1990 chapter titled, "How Should Psychologists Define Morality? Or, the Negative Side Effects of Philosophy's Influence on Psychology." Here he made some acute observations about the negative consequences of a reliance on a particular philosophical tradition in the psychological study of moral development, a pattern perhaps best exemplified by Kohlberg's (1981) explicit reliance on the formalist tradition in moral philosophy. Note that neither Blasi nor I hold that philosophy's overall influence on moral psychology has been negative; contrarily, philosophy has played an essential and positive role in informing the enterprise. Unfortunately, there is a considerable body of psychological research regarding morality that is characterized by philosophical naïveté, a situation that contributes to its triviality. Nevertheless, philosophical perspectives do have the potential to be constraining, and we need to be mindful of their negative side effects. These negative consequences include (a) a narrowing of the moral domain (e.g., by a single emphasis on justice with minimal attention to other aspects of morality such as

1982, forcefully argued, or supererogatory obligations), (b) a
tion of the moral agent and moral functioning (e.g., by a fo-
with minimal consideration of the affective, behavioral, and
components), and (c) a failure to take a phenomenological
perspective that reflects people's ordinary experiences and understanding of
morality—a philosophically driven approach to moral psychology defines for
people what morality is and is not open to their lived conceptions of it. "Psychologists may risk missing a large portion of ... people's moral life when they
are rigidly guided by definitions constructed within specific philosophical theories" (Blasi, 1990, p. 45). In response to this conceptual skew, Blasi noted the
need for the field to study and meaningfully incorporate into its purview "phenomena that, according to common understanding and ordinary language,
many would consider to be moral or morally relevant" (p. 40).

CONCEPTIONS AND EXPERIENCES OF MORALITY

In response to this expressed need, my colleagues and I have conducted a series
of studies over the last several years that have examined, in an exploratory way,
ordinary people's conceptions and experiences of morality. At this juncture in
the development of the field, moral psychology needs to be more closely based
on how people experience and understand morality day by day than on the tight
constraints of philosophical considerations (which do, of course, have their
role). In one study (Walker et al., 1995), we conducted extensive open-ended
interviews with participants from across the adult lifespan, exploring their
conceptions of morality, their handling of a number of actual moral problems
from their personal experience, and their identification of morally exemplary
individuals. Our intent here was to expand the boundaries and chart the landscape of the moral domain in a way that would redirect both conceptual and
empirical attention to some significant aspects of moral functioning that have
until now been minimally examined. There were several pertinent findings
from this project for the current discussion.

An examination of the content of participants' actual moral dilemmas revealed that people frequently confront moral problems in everyday life that are
not well tapped by standard measures of moral reasoning, especially those
problems involving relational and intrapsychic issues. Relational issues involve particular obligations to spouses, parents, children, and friends, and they
represent aspects of morality that are not well tapped by models of moral psychology that emphasize justice. Intrapsychic moral issues were also relatively
frequent in people's experience and pertain more to the pursuit of ideals and
the maintenance of one's sense of moral self. These intrapsychic, character-

ological issues similarly have not been well tapped by models of moral psychology that have focused on the interpersonal aspects of morality (e.g., rights, responsibilities, and welfare). These relational and intrapsychic moral problems are ones that are commonly confronted in everyday life and thus are ones to which researchers should more closely attend.

In their reported handling of moral problems, many people in this project voiced types of moral reasoning to which our models of moral development have paid scant attention. For example, in describing important factors in resolving moral issues and evaluating their actions, many people expressed concerns regarding practical considerations and outcomes. Note that they were making prescriptive judgments in this regard, not simply describing what they might have thought. These practical considerations and outcomes were ones that people held to be valid factors within a moral framework. Such practical considerations are relatively rare in response to hypothetical dilemmas and when expressed are considered immature (low stage), but in dealing with difficult moral problems in everyday life, people did assert the moral relevance of psychological reality, reflecting Flanagan's (1991) notion that ethical theories must recognize that people are legitimately partial to their own projects and that our theories must take account of psychological reality. He stated, "No ethical conception … can reasonably demand a form of impersonality, abstraction, or impartiality which ignores the constraints laid down by the universal psychological features" (pp. 100–101). This is not to imply that morality should be reduced to self-interest but rather that our models of moral functioning need to account for the role of practical realities in everyday functioning.

Many people also voiced notions of religion, faith, and spirituality in resolving real-life moral problems. For these people, morality and spirituality were not really separate and distinct domains, rather their moral framework was firmly embedded in their faith—their values and goals, their thinking through moral problems, and their choice of various social behaviors and relationships were all governed by their faith. Their moral framework was framed by their religious beliefs, which were integral to their identity. Blasi (1990) earlier argued that for many people morality only acquires meaning within the context of religious experience. The fields of moral psychology and moral education have paid minimal accord to the significance of spirituality perhaps in deference to an antagonistic academic climate and to the perceived requirement that moral education programs be uncontaminated by religious influence. Nevertheless, it is important to recognize that for many people the moral and spiritual domains are inextricably intertwined and that our models of moral functioning must take account of such relationships.

A third theme in people's everyday moral experience was their reliance on intuition in resolving moral issues and evaluating their actions. Understandably, notions of intuition, automaticity, and habitual responding are anathematized by the rationalistic models that have dominated moral psychology, but they are persistent themes in people's self-awareness and require some accounting. Many people stressed the validity of intuition in handling moral problems despite acknowledging its fallibility (although they also asserted the fallibility of other strategies for resolving moral issues). Recently, Haidt (2001) proposed a social intuitionist model that posits that intuition is actually the default process in moral functioning and that claims, in direct challenge to rationalist models in moral psychology, that a deliberate process of moral deliberation is, when activated at all, likely an ex post facto process intended more for impression management and social persuasion than for actual decision making. Likewise, in other moral philosophical traditions such as Confucianism (Walker & Moran, 1991), for example, the personal cultivation of a moral sense is emphasized, a moral sense that allows one to intuit automatically what is right in a situation without any real reflection (and indeed resorting to such moral deliberation would be regarded as indicative of moral immaturity). In any case, it is important to recognize the significance of intuitions that are evoked in many moral situations prior to any extensive cognitive processing.

A final aspect of this project involved asking participants to identify moral exemplars and justify their nominations. This was an attempt to approach moral functioning without involving the problem solving of moral conflicts and thus was reasonably expected to be more character than cognition based. The Kohlbergian view (1981, 1984) portrays morally exemplary individuals primarily by virtue of their principled, high-stage reasoning ability. However, in our project it was found that participants' identification of moral exemplars was justified more frequently on the basis of moral character traits and virtues (e.g., caring and compassion, self-sacrifice, consistency, honesty, and open-mindedness) than by references to principled moral judgment. A content analysis of the types of moral exemplars identified revealed that, although the somewhat predictable categories were found (e.g., humanitarians, revolutionaries, and social activists), the most frequent categories were not public figures but rather family members and friends—individuals who were known personally because, for many participants, integrity was a particularly valued and critical indicator of moral excellence, a characteristic best assessed by direct interaction. Many participants expressed an explicit distrust of the public persona of many historical and highly visible people. This notion of integrity is, of course, foundational in Blasi's (1993, 1995) understanding of the moral self.

1. GUS IN THE GAP

Some of the other highly valued charac
are ones that have as yet received mini
gether contribute to a fuller conception
   A second series of projects (Walker &
has also responded to Blasi's (1990) a
guage and common understandings abo
digm and findings are presented, som
projects may be helpful. The intention
notions of moral excellence—ones err
everyday language—would reveal so
that are operative and salient in everyday ......g

resented in contemporary moral development theory and research. This intention accords with an emerging trend in moral philosophy (Flanagan, 1991;
Johnson, 1996; Thomas, 1989) that argues that ethical theories should be constrained by an empirically informed account of how people understand morality as well as by what moral ideals are realistically attainable in terms of
psychological processes, an approach Flanagan labels *psychological realism.*
Similarly, our intention accords with a trend in psychology that regards implicit (lay) psychological theories as important in their own right because people's notions regarding psychological functioning are operative in everyday
functioning and because these implicit theories serve as needed complements
to philosophically derived explicit theories. When there is a disjunction between the findings yielded by empirically driven and philosophically driven
research there should be some impetus to rethink our understanding of those
aspects of moral functioning and to account for the discrepant perspectives.
   In the first project in this series (Walker & Pitts, 1998), conceptions of moral
excellence were compared with those of religious and spiritual excellence.
This comparison was prompted, in part, by Blasi's (1990) suggestion that for
many people morality is framed by their religious beliefs as well as by our finding (Walker et al., 1995) of the significance of faith and spirituality in many
people's actual moral decision making and by Colby and Damon's (1992) finding that many of the moral exemplars in their case-study analysis attributed
their core value commitments to their religious faith. Thus, it seems appropriate to compare people's understanding of these domains.
   Simply described, the research paradigm for this project involved a sequence of three studies. In the initial study, participants generated, in a
free-listing procedure, the attributes that they believed to be descriptive of a
highly moral, highly religious, and highly spiritual person. Once these
descriptors were distilled into nonredundant lists using an established set of
judgment rules, participants in the second study rated the prototypicality of

igh prototypicality ratings designate attributes that people
characteristic of the exemplar, and low ratings designate at-
re less or uncharacteristic. Some of the attributes were unique to
types of exemplars, whereas other attributes were shared among
or example, *just* was a unique attribute for the moral exemplar, *tradi-
l* was unique to the religious exemplar, and *peaceful* was unique to the
iritual exemplar, and so on. Other attributes were shared: for example,
hard-working was common to the moral and religious exemplars, *devout* was
common to the religious and spiritual exemplars, *truthful* was common to the
moral and spiritual exemplars, and *caring* was common to all three. When concepts are overlapping but not synonymous (as in this case), prototype theory
holds that the relative prototypicality ratings for shared versus unique attributes informs the relation in people's understanding among these concepts.

The findings indicated that these concepts are related but in an asymmetrical pattern. For the moral exemplar, unique attributes had higher
prototypicality ratings than did the attributes shared with the religious and spiritual exemplars. This implies that moral virtues are somewhat independent of
religious and spiritual ones; in other words, to be a moral person one does not
need to manifest characteristics that are central to religion and spirituality. In
contrast, for both the religious and spiritual exemplars, shared attributes (with
each other and with the moral exemplar) had higher ratings than did the unique
attributes, implying that notions of religion and spirituality are more strongly
related to each other and that they are somewhat embedded in notions of morality. In other words, central to what it means to be a religious or spiritual person
is the embodiment of moral virtues, consistent with the fact that moral guidelines have always been a primary component of religious imperatives.

The lengthy lists of descriptors attributed to these exemplars, although
somewhat informative, are also rather unmanageable. The purpose of the third
study in this project was to derive parsimonious typologies of the attributes of
each of these exemplars implicit in people's understanding. Participants in this
third study were asked to freely sort the most prototypic attributes for each exemplar into groups. This similarity-sort procedure did not constrain for participants the number of groups or the number of attributes per group. Data
reduction techniques (i.e., multidimensional scaling and hierarchical cluster
analysis) were then used to discern the latent structure—the dimensions and
themes—of these implicit typologies. Given the present focus, discussion will
center only on the typology for the moral exemplar.

Multidimensional scaling (literally) maps attributes relative to each other,
on the basis of an appropriate number of orthogonal dimensions, as a function
of their similarity in the sorts. The interpretive process attempts to identify the
implicit dimensional axes around which attributes are configured. Examina-

tion of the multidimensional scaling solution suggested that the attributes of the moral exemplar were organized along the two dimensions of a *self–other* orientation and an *external–internal* orientation. The first (and more important) self–other dimension was anchored at the *self* pole by attributes reflecting personal agency and at the *other* pole by attributes reflecting a focus on care for others. This dimension reflects a tension between the themes of agency and communion in a basic naturalistic understanding of morality (agency and communion are often considered the fundamental constructs in the understanding of interpersonal behavior; Wiggins, 1991). The second external–internal dimension was anchored at the *external* pole by attributes reflecting an orientation to external moral guidelines and standards and at the *internal* pole by attributes reflecting a reliance on personal strength and the internal workings of conscience. Again, this dimension illustrates the tension between the social and the individual in the understanding of morality.

The other data reduction technique used with these sorts was hierarchical cluster analysis, a technique that generates clusters of attributes based on their patterns of association. This analysis yielded a typology of six distinct clusters of attributes for the moral exemplar, and again the interpretive task was to provide appropriate labels that capture the essence of the attributes comprising each cluster. The typology of clusters (or themes) for the moral exemplar were (a) *principled–idealistic*, (b) *dependable–loyal*, (c) *has integrity*, (d) *caring–trustworthy*, (e) *fair*, and (f) *confident*. The principled–idealistic cluster, the most prototypic cluster of attributes for the moral exemplar, signals the significance of strongly held values and principles and the maintenance of high standards and ideals. This cluster, along with the *fair* cluster, resonates with some of the themes in Kohlberg's model, and so he was at least partially correct in his caricature of moral excellence. The dependable–loyal, has integrity, and caring–trustworthy clusters confirm that people regard other-oriented compassion and care, interpersonal sensitivity, thoughtful and considerate action, and the nurturing of relationships through faithfulness and reliability as important aspects of moral functioning. Note the salience of integrity in people's conceptions, which is consistent with the central role it is accorded in Blasi's model. Finally, the confident cluster reiterates the agentic qualities that are essential in the pursuit of moral goals and social action. Perhaps the acute sense of morality (the principled–idealistic cluster), when joined by a strong sense of self and personal agency (the confident cluster), contributes to the formation of integrity that people regard as essential to moral character.

This project sought to uncover people's ordinary understandings and implicit personality theory of moral functioning. It appears that this approach has identified a range of moral virtues and aspects of the moral personality that have, until now, been minimized in moral psychology and that now warrant serious conceptual and empirical attention. There is, however, one questionable implication from this research project that should be flagged, and that is whether or not there is a single prototype for moral excellence. The dimensions and clusters of attributes for the moral exemplar yielded in this last study may entail an amalgamation of attributes that would be impossible, even incoherent, for a single person to embody. This issue provided the impetus for the second project along these lines (Walker & Hennig, 2003).

The suggestion pursued here is that moral maturity can be exemplified in quite divergent ways—think, for example, of Martin Luther King, Jr. versus Mother Teresa versus Oskar Schindler, all moral heroes who are recognized for quite different collections of virtues. In Flanagan's (1991) *Varieties of Moral Personality*, he argued that "ethical goodness is realized in a multiplicity of ways" (p. 332). So the main questions here were as follows: How do personality traits cluster for different types of moral exemplarity? What traits are common across these divergent types—suggestive of the core of morality—and what traits are peculiar to each? In this study (Walker & Hennig, 2003), we explored three types of moral exemplarity—just, brave, and caring—because they are salient in both philosophical thought and everyday experience, but there may be other important types that could be considered as well.

As in our previous project, participants in an initial study generated the attributes of the three different types of moral exemplarity (just, brave, and caring) in a free-listing procedure. These attributes were distilled into nonredundant descriptor lists to be used in the subsequent studies. As might be expected, some attributes were unique to each type of moral exemplar, whereas others were shared in common. This indicates that the concepts overlap but are hardly synonymous. At this point it is helpful to explore the meaning of these descriptors that were found to be common to all of these divergent types of moral exemplars, because these could be considered the core traits of moral excellence. Salient in the attributions made regarding all of these exemplars were traits reflecting honesty, dependability, and self-control. A large number of terms entailed traits of an interpersonal nature that reflect a positive communal emotionality and sociability, clearly an other-oriented orientation. Other themes include personal agency, positivity, emotional stability, and openness. These common denominators across types of moral exemplarity are clearly ones that are foundational for moral functioning and warrant further conceptual and empirical scrutiny.

One of the limitations of our previous research (Walker & Pitts, 1998) that compared naturalistic conceptions of moral, religious, and spiritual exemplars is that it relied exclusively on the list of attributes spontaneously generated by ordinary people (Hart, 1998). One way to overcome this limitation is to have participants, in addition to providing prototypicality ratings for the lists of attributes, rate each type of moral exemplar using the template of a standard personality inventory that purports to capture the fundamental dimensions of personality. In the Walker and Pitts' study the primary dimension (the self–other dimension) underlying people's implicit typology of moral excellence referenced the tension between notions of agency and communion (or dominance and nurturance). This suggests the particular relevance of the interpersonal circumplex in tapping people's understanding of the personality of different types of moral exemplars. In this second study, we used the *Revised Interpersonal Adjectives Scale–Big Five* (IASR–B5; Wiggins, 1995) because it is well-validated and taps not only the personality dimensions of dominance and nurturance (around the interpersonal circumplex) but also the three other dimensions of the Five-Factor Model (conscientiousness, emotional stability, and openness) that currently dominates the study of personality structure. Thus, in this second study, participants provided not only prototypicality ratings for the descriptor lists for each type of moral exemplar but also ratings for the 124 items of the IASR–B5.

In simplified language, the analysis of the personality attributions of these three different types of moral exemplars revealed quite disparate personality profiles. The brave exemplar was most closely associated with dominance (or, in the language of the Five-Factor Model, extraversion), tending toward the positive pole of this dimension (as agentic, forceful, and self-confident). The care exemplar was regarded as the least agentic, but it was strongly associated with the nurturance (or agreeableness) dimension, being solidly at the positive pole of this dimension (as warm, agreeable, nurturant, and sympathetic). The just exemplar presented a more complex personality profile: not as strongly oriented to the dominance and nurturance dimensions as the brave and caring exemplars, respectively, but having a moderate blend of both dimensions. Actually, the just exemplar was more strongly typified by the three other fundamental dimensions of personality described by the Five-Factor Model—conscientiousness, emotional stability, and openness. This reflects the perception that a highly just person has an objective and careful orientation; is calm, stable, and levelheaded; and is open-minded and reflective.

The third study in this project attempted to understand how people would organize the multifarious collection of attributes into a manageable typology for each type of exemplar. As in the previous project, participants were asked to sort the most prototypic of the attributes for each exemplar into groups and data reduction techniques (multidimensional scaling and cluster analysis) were used to identify the dimensions and themes in their implicit typologies.

For the just exemplar, a five-cluster solution was yielded by the cluster analysis and these clusters were labeled as follows: (a) *honest*, (b) *fair*, (c) *princi-*

pled, (d) *rational*, and (e) *conscientious*. Being honest and trustworthy in one's relationships with others was seen as integral to being a just person, but this virtue has received scant research attention or been denigrated to a "good boy–good girl" mentality. Being fair and objective certainly resonates with Kohlberg's depiction of moral maturity, as does the principled cluster which also references notions of integrity. Notions of rationality and conscientiousness (thoughtful and levelheaded) round out the conception of a just person. Multidimensional scaling indicated that these attributes could be organized around two dimensions: a *character* dimension and a *particularity* dimension. The character dimension was anchored at one pole by attributes that represent the core of moral character and anchored at the other pole by attributes that are, in contrast, more cognitive. This dimension highlights the tension between the characterological and cognitive aspects of exemplarity in terms of justice. The particularity dimension was anchored at one pole by attributes that get exemplified in relationships with particular people and anchored at the other pole by attributes that represent greater universality, illustrating the recurrent tension between strict objectivity and partiality to those with whom one is in relation.

For the brave exemplar, a five-cluster solution was most appropriate and these clusters were labeled as follows: (a) *intrepid*, (b) *confident*, (c) *heroic–strong*, (d) *dedicated*, and (e) *self-sacrificial*. The intrepid cluster referenced notions of courage and lack of fear. These agentic notions are similarly reflected in the confident and heroic–strong clusters that entail traits of decisiveness, self-assuredness, and strength. All of these resonate with the findings of the second study that indicated that the brave exemplar was profiled by personality attributions emphasizing dominance or extraversion. The understanding of the brave exemplar was rounded out by themes of dedication and self-sacrifice. Multidimensional scaling indicated that the attributes for the brave exemplar could be organized around the two orthogonal dimensions: a *selfless* dimension and an *agentic* dimension. The selfless dimension was anchored at one pole by attributes that reflect a lack of concern for self and at the other pole by attributes that are more self-focused. The agentic dimension was anchored at one pole by traits indicative of personal agency and initiative and at the other pole by ones that were considerably less agentic in tone.

For the care exemplar, a three-cluster solution was most appropriate and these clusters were labeled as follows: (a) *loving–empathic*, (b) *altruistic*, and (c) *honest–dependable*. The loving–empathic cluster references traits of other-oriented positive emotionality (interpersonal warmth, empathy, and attentiveness), which is consistent with the personality profile yielded in the second study that clearly characterized the care exemplar as nurturant. The altruistic cluster pointed to attributes that are somewhat more behavioral than emotive, such as being helpful, generous, and sharing. The attributes of the honest–dependable cluster mirror, to some extent, the honest and conscientious clusters for the just exemplar. The other data reduction technique, multidimensional scaling, indicated that the attributes for the care exemplar could be represented by a genuine dimension and an emotive dimension. The attributes at one pole of the genuine dimension reflect traits of interpersonal sincerity, whereas attributes at the other pole reflected self-denial and perhaps (although not necessarily) a lack of authenticity. This negative pole of the genuine dimension is suggestive of other findings that indicate that there may be maladaptive forms of self-sacrificial care (Hennig & Walker, 2003). The emotive dimension was anchored at one pole by traits indicative of positive emotionality and at the other pole by attributes that are again more behavioral.

Despite the evidence from the first study of this project that people do identify a set of core virtues across different types of moral exemplars, the findings of this third study strongly suggest that the personality trait attributions regarding just, brave, and caring exemplars are quite disparate in that there was minimal overlap across types of exemplars in the typologies (dimensions and clusters) that were derived. Each typified a relatively distinct moral personality. It is quite possible, indeed probable, that not all moral traits are necessarily compatible and may in some cases be antithetical.

The intent of this series of two projects (Walker & Hennig, 2003; Walker & Pitts, 1998) was to respond to Blasi's (1990) call that the field attend to common understandings of moral functioning. The findings of these projects cast light on a wider range of moral virtues that has typically been the focus in dominant models of moral psychology, and they also challenge the notion of a single conception of moral excellence. The study of naturalistic conceptions of moral functioning is not without its limitations, however. One limitation concerns the adequacy and comprehensiveness of the natural language approach (Block, 1995) with its reliance on trait-term descriptions of personality functioning. Such trait terms have limited explanatory power in expressing complex aspects of moral functioning. Furthermore, they represent naïve understandings that, although revelatory of aspects of moral functioning that are important in everyday life but inadequately represented in contemporary models, still need to be augmented by the studied insights of philosophers and psychologists that may not be apparent to ordinary people. The major limitation to the study of naturalistic conceptions of moral functioning is that it simply describes people's conceptions, not the actual psychological and moral functioning of moral exemplars. Do real moral paragons evidence the range of moral virtues derived from natural language concepts?

MORAL PERSONALITY

As noted earlier, Blasi (especially his 1993 chapter) eloquently advanced the notion of the moral personality and challenged the field to provide a more full-bodied account of moral functioning—to augment (not replace) the current emphasis on moral cognition by the inclusion of an appreciation of moral personality and character. Two centuries of modernity have bequeathed to the field of moral psychology a legacy that is rich in its emphasis on moral rationality and impoverished in terms of its appreciation of moral personality and the intrapsychic aspects of moral character. The origins of this apparent conceptual skew can be traced to the influential formalist moral philosophers of the Enlightenment Era (e.g., Immanuel Kant) who advocated a dualist conception of human nature—reason versus passion—with reason regarded as providing the solid basis for moral understandings and with the passions (emotions and desires, personality, and personal projects) regarded as corrupting biases that must be overcome if one is to attain to the standard of autonomous moral rationality. Contrary to this view that regards personality as a corrupting bias to the purity of moral reason, I contend that personality is the flesh and blood vivifying the bare bones of cognition.

One way to examine the development of moral character and personality is through the analysis of the psychological functioning of people who have been identified as leading morally exemplary lives. The landmark study of this type was conducted by Colby and Damon (1992) who studied a small sample of people who evidenced extraordinary commitment to moral ideals and causes over an extended period of time. Their case study analysis yielded some valuable insights regarding various aspects of the moral personality, but note that theirs was a small select sample (with no comparison group), their method was assisted autobiographical interview with no standard measures of psychological functioning, and the analyses were solely qualitative.

In a recent study conducted with Kyle Matsuba (Matsuba & Walker, in press), we attempted to provide a more systematic assessment of the psychological functioning of moral exemplars. The moral exemplars in this case were 40 young adults who had been nominated by social service agencies because of their extraordinary moral commitment as volunteers; a matched comparison group was also recruited. In an attempt to provide a comprehensive appraisal of their psychological functioning, the choice of measures reflected McAdams' (1995) framework of three broad levels in the assessment of personality: (a) dispositional traits, (b) contextualized concerns such as developmental tasks and personal strivings, and (c) integrative narratives of the self. Thus, participants responded to several questionnaires and a lengthy life-narrative interview.

At the level of dispositional traits, participants completed a questionnaire reflecting the Five-Factor Model of personality. Although all five factors are relevant to moral functioning (as was evident in the Walker & Hennig, 2003, study), agreeableness and conscientiousness are considered the classic dimensions of character (McCrae & John, 1992) and thus are most relevant here. Not surprising then, the exemplar group was found to rate themselves higher on agreeableness than the comparison group, implicating the role of personality dispositions in moral functioning.

At the level of contextualized concerns in assessing personality functioning, we included various measures of developmental tasks and personal strivings. The findings revealed that, in contrast to the comparison group, the exemplar group was more mature in their identity development (reflecting a stronger commitment to values and a greater stability), they evidenced more mature faith development (reflecting the process by which they make meaning in life), and they used somewhat more advanced moral reasoning (confirming its critical role in moral functioning).

At the third level of personality assessment, we examined themes in individual's life narratives. Given our findings regarding the salience of both dominance and nurturance dimensions in the attributions of the personality of various types of moral exemplars (Walker & Hennig, 2003), our expectation here was that the exemplars' life narratives would be characterized by more themes of agency and communion than would be found for comparison individuals. This expectation was partly supported in that more agentic themes were found in exemplars' life stories.

Thus, this research on moral exemplars revealed that variables indicative of all three levels of personality assessment distinguished exemplars from comparison individuals (despite matching on demographic variables), providing a beginning picture of the scope of the moral personality. However, keep in mind that moral excellence can be exemplified in different ways and it is important for our understanding of moral functioning to determine what is distinctive about different types of moral exemplars as well as what may be the common core (paralleling our research on people's conceptions of different types of moral exemplars; Walker & Hennig, 2003).

In research I currently have underway (Walker, 2003), I am examining the personalities—through extensive interviews and several questionnaire measures—of two quite different types of moral exemplarity: bravery and care. The sample is comprised of Canadians, from across the country, who have received similar national awards in recognition of either their acts of bravery or of extraordinary care. Those who have received a decoration for bravery (e.g., the Star of Courage or the Medal of Bravery) have "risked their lives to save or protect others," whereas those who have been decorated for caring (the Caring Canadian Award) have "given extraordinary help or care to individuals, families or groups, or supported community service or humanitarian causes" (Governor General of Canada, 2003). These two types of extraordinary moral exemplars will be contrasted with matched comparison groups. It is anticipated that the eventual findings of this research will help us move toward a more comprehensive understanding of moral functioning and development that meaningfully integrates cognition, personality, and action. Once the field has some sense of the psychological functioning of moral exemplars, then the research agenda can focus on the formative factors in the development of such moral character.

CONCLUSION

Blasi is foremost among the very few scholars in the field of moral psychology whose conceptual work does justice to the complexity of moral functioning. He thoughtfully integrated moral cognition and moral personality in a model that goes a considerable distance in bridging the judgment–action gap; particularly significant in this model are the self-mechanisms of self-identity and self-consistency that he so carefully explicated. His further arguments that we need to balance philosophically constrained theories of moral functioning with common understandings and experiences of morality has helped to redirect conceptual and empirical attention to aspects of moral psychology that have been relatively sidelined. Some of my research provoked by his cogent arguments, as was discussed here, explored naturalistic conceptions of various types of moral exemplarity as well as the psychological functioning of actual moral exemplars. This research was intended to contribute to a more full-bodied and realistic account of moral functioning in everyday life. As is readily apparent, Blasi's seminal contributions to the field have been very formative in my own research, although I suspect that he would not approve of all the directions I have explored. What I can more confidently assert, however, is that the field of moral psychology is substantially in his debt.

REFERENCES

Arnold, M. L. (1989, April). *Moral cognition and conduct: A quantitative review of the literature*. Paper presented at the meeting of the Society for Research in Child Development, Kansas City, MO.
Bandura, A. (1999). Moral disengagement in the perpetuation of inhumanities. *Personality and Social Psychology Review, 3*, 193–209.
Bandura, A. (2002). Selective disengagement in the exercise of moral agency. *Journal of Moral Education, 31*, 101–119.

Blasi, A. (1980). Bridging moral cognition and moral action: A critical review of the literature. *Psychological Bulletin, 88,* 1–45.

Blasi, A. (1983). Moral cognition and moral action: A theoretical perspective. *Developmental Review, 3,* 178–210.

Blasi, A. (1984). Moral identity: Its role in moral functioning. In W. M. Kurtines & J. L. Gewirtz (Eds.), *Morality, moral behavior, and moral development* (pp. 128–139). New York: Wiley.

Blasi, A. (1990). How should psychologists define morality? Or, the negative side effects of philosophy's influence on psychology. In T. Wren (Ed.), *The moral domain: Essays in the ongoing discussion between philosophy and the social sciences* (pp. 38–70). Cambridge, MA: MIT Press.

Blasi, A. (1993). The development of identity: Some implications for moral functioning. In G. G. Noam & T. E. Wren (Eds.), *The moral self* (pp. 99–122). Cambridge, MA: MIT Press.

Blasi, A. (1995). Moral understanding and the moral personality: The process of moral integration. In W. M. Kurtines & J. L. Gewirtz (Eds.), *Moral development: An introduction* (pp. 229–253). Boston: Allyn & Bacon.

Blasi, A. (1999). Emotions and moral motivation. *Journal for the Theory of Social Behaviour, 29,* 1–19.

Block, J. (1995). A contrarian view of the five-factor approach to personality description. *Psychological Bulletin, 117,* 187–215.

Buchanan, T. (1992, November). *Why is the literature examining the moral cognition-moral action relationship inconsistent? A meta-analytic investigation of five moderating variables.* Paper presented at the meeting of the Association for Moral Education, Toronto.

Campbell, R. L., & Christopher, J. C. (1996). Moral development theory: A critique of its Kantian presuppositions. *Developmental Review, 16,* 1–47.

Colby, A., & Damon, W. (1992). *Some do care: Contemporary lives of moral commitment.* New York: The Free Press.

Flanagan, O. (1991). *Varieties of moral personality: Ethics and psychological realism.* Cambridge, MA: Harvard University Press.

Gilligan, C. (1982). *In a different voice: Psychological theory and women's development.* Cambridge, MA: Harvard University Press.

The Governor General of Canada. (2003). Canadian honours. Retrieved June 29, 2003, from http://www.gg.ca/honours/bravery_e.asp and from http://www.gg.ca/honours/caring_e.asp

Haidt, J. (2001). The emotional dog and its rational tail: A social intuitionist approach to moral judgment. *Psychological Review, 108,* 814–834.

Hart, D. (1998). Can prototypes inform moral developmental theory? *Developmental Psychology, 34,* 420–423.

Hart, D., & Fegley, S. (1995). Prosocial behavior and caring in adolescence: Relations to self-understanding and social judgment. *Child Development, 66,* 1346–1359.

Haste, H. (1990). Moral responsibility and moral commitment: The integration of affect and cognition. In T. Wren (Ed.), *The moral domain: Essays in the ongoing discussion between philosophy and the social sciences* (pp. 315–359). Cambridge, MA: MIT Press.

Hennig, K. H., & Walker, L. J. (2003). *Mapping the care domain: A structural and substantive analysis.* Manuscript submitted for publication. University of British Columbia.

Johnson, M. L. (1996). How moral psychology changes moral theory. In L. May, M. Friedman, & A. Clark (Eds.), *Minds and morals: Essays on cognitive science and ethics* (pp. 45–68). Cambridge, MA: MIT Press.

Kohlberg, L. (1969). Stage and sequence: The cognitive–developmental approach to socialization. In D. A. Goslin (Ed.), *Handbook of socialization theory and research* (pp. 347–480). Chicago: Rand McNally.

Kohlberg, L. (1981). *Essays on moral development: Vol. 1. The philosophy of moral development.* San Francisco: Harper & Row.

Kohlberg, L. (1984). *Essays on moral development: Vol. 2. The psychology of moral development.* San Francisco: Harper & Row.

Kohlberg, L., & Candee, D. (1984). The relationship of moral judgment to moral action. In L. Kohlberg, *Essays on moral development: Vol. 2. The psychology of moral development* (pp. 498–581). San Francisco: Harper & Row.

Kohlberg, L., & Diessner, R. (1991). A cognitive–developmental approach to moral attachment. In J. L. Gewirtz & W. M. Kurtines (Eds.), *Intersections with attachment* (pp. 229–246). Hillsdale, NJ: Lawrence Erlbaum Associates.

Matsuba, M. K., & Walker, L. J. (in press). Extraordinary moral commitment: Young adults working for social organizations. *Journal of Personality.*

McAdams, D. P. (1995). What do we know when we know a person? *Journal of Personality, 63,* 365–396.

McCrae, R. R., & John, O. P. (1992). An introduction to the five-factor model and its applications. *Journal of Personality, 60,* 175–215.

Punzo, V. A. (1996). After Kohlberg: Virtue ethics and the recovery of the moral self. *Philosophical Psychology, 9,* 7–23.

Thomas, L. (1989). *Living morally: A psychology of moral character.* Philadelphia: Temple University Press.

Walker, L. J. (2003). *In search of moral excellence: Brave and caring Canadians.* Research in progress, University of British Columbia.

Walker, L. J., & Hennig, K. H. (1997). Moral functioning in the broader context of personality. In S. Hala (Ed.), *The development of social cognition* (pp. 297–327). East Sussex, England: Psychology Press.

Walker, L. J., & Hennig, K. H. (2003). *Differing conceptions of moral exemplarity: Just, brave, and caring.* Manuscript submitted for publication.

Walker, L. J., & Moran, T. J. (1991). Moral reasoning in a communist Chinese society. *Journal of Moral Education, 20,* 139–155.

Walker, L. J., & Pitts, R. C. (1998). Naturalistic conceptions of moral maturity. *Developmental Psychology, 34,* 403–419.

Walker, L. J., Pitts, R. C., Hennig, K. H., & Matsuba, M. K. (1995). Reasoning about morality and real-life moral problems. In M. Killen & D. Hart (Eds.), *Morality in everyday life: Developmental perspectives* (pp. 371–407). Cambridge, England: Cambridge University Press.

Wiggins, J. S. (1991). Agency and communion as conceptual coordinates for the understanding and measurement of interpersonal behavior. In D. Cicchetti & W. M. Grove (Eds.), *Thinking clearly about psychology: Essays in honor of Paul E. Meehl* (Vol. 2, pp. 89–113). Minneapolis: University of Minnesota Press.

Wiggins, J. S. (1995). *Interpersonal Adjectives Scales: Professional manual.* Odessa, FL: Psychological Assessment Resources.

2

Identity as Motivation:
Toward a Theory of the Moral Self

Roger Bergman
Creighton University

Under the powerful influence first of Jean Piaget and then of Lawrence Kohlberg, developmental psychology has paid relatively less attention to issues of moral motivation than of moral cognition. For Kohlberg, motivation was practically subsumed under cognition. As Kohlberg (1970) reported in his essay "Education for Justice: A Modern Statement of the Platonic View," "as I have tried to trace the stages of development of morality and to use these stages as the basis of a moral education program, I have realized more and more that its implication was the reassertion of the Platonic faith in the power of the rational good" (p. 57). Although he qualified this philosophical perspective—"In speaking of a Platonic view, I am not discarding my basic Deweyism" (p. 59)—many psychologists (and moral philosophers) have objected to what they consider Kohlberg's excessive rationalism (for a summary of "Psychological and Philosophical Challenges to Kohlberg's Approach," see Rest, Narvaez, Bebeau, & Thomas, 1999, chap. 2). Some developmentalists have sought to shift the focus or broaden the purview of psychological research and theory beyond moral cognition to include issues not only of moral motivation but also of moral identity. This chapter approaches this literature from Piaget to the neo- or post-Kohlbergians with the belief that these theories can be illuminated by exploring how they implicitly or explicitly answer the question: Why be moral?

Although this question is clearly philosophical, it can also be understood psychologically. The focus for psychology is on moral functioning, on why one acts as one does in morally challenging situations, or even on why one commits oneself to moral responsibility and integrity over a lifetime. This chapter is concerned with the complex relations among moral reasoning, moral motivation, moral action, and moral identity. It explores how major figures in developmental psychology have understood these relations, with special attention to schematic models or conceptual maps. After considering Piaget, Kohlberg, Rest, Damon, Colby and Damon, and Blasi, I argue that Blasi provided the crucial elements of a critical synthesis, a model of how developmental psychology might answer the question: Why be moral? Finally, I respond to Nucci's several criticisms of this model.

PIAGET

As Piaget (1932/1997) noted, "But the relations between thought and action are very far from being as simple as is commonly supposed" (p. 176). In his classic study, *The Moral Judgment of the Child*, Jean Piaget initiated much of the scholarly research, discussion, and theorizing that has characterized developmental and moral psychology until today. Of particular importance to this chapter, and a fundamental element in his study of children's morality, is his understanding of the relation between thought and action. As the aforementioned quotation suggests, Piaget cannot be blamed for the common casting of the thought–action dynamic in terms of the problem of why moral action does not always follow moral judgment, of the problem *akrasia* (weakness of will), or of the failure of moral integrity or character. Philosopher Don Locke (1983) calls this "the Thought/Action problem: the problem at once philosophical and psychological, of explicating the relationship between what a person says he ought to do, or even what he thinks he ought to do, and what he actually does" (p. 160). Piaget did not seem to be particularly interested in this issue. Rather, he was interested in the reverse issue—of thought lagging behind action. Locke (1983) dubbed this "the Action/ Thought Problem ... the question is not how thought gets translated into action, but how action gets taken up into thought" (p. 161). Piaget's investigations led him to believe that children's social interaction led them (eventually) into new ways of moral understanding, and not the other way around. Specifically, unsupervised peer (symmetrical) interaction, which requires cooperation and not the simple obedience, unilateral respect, and authoritarian restraint of adult–child (asymmetrical) interaction, leads children to construct modes of thinking based on sympathy, mutuality, and recognition of reciprocal rights and duties, and of justice.

Questions of moral motivation and identity play no explicit role in *The Moral Judgment of the Child*. Children practice the ethic of constraint out of fear, respect, and affection for adults, and they learn the ethic of cooperation through their capacities for sympathy, mutuality, and role taking among their peers. In both cases, it might be said that what moves children to act is a concern to maintain (in the first case) or develop (in the second) harmonious relationships, so as to foster a stable and secure context for the self, although that context is defined differently for the two contrasting moralities. Indeed, in the latter case, as pointed out by Davidson and Youniss (1991), "for Piaget, the experience of cooperation is the key to both moral development and personality formation" (p. 107). Or, "to put it another way, the construction of identity and the construction of morality are aspects of the same construction" so that "spontaneous moral judgment, or moral intuition, is an expression of a person's identity or of one aspect of the identity" (p. 112). With the qualification that the development of identity can be seen as implicit in the same process (a theme to which we will return), Piaget's understanding of the moral dynamic may be summarized in the Law of Conscious Realization, according to which moral action precedes and leads to moral thought.

KOHLBERG

As Kohlberg and Candee (1984) noted, "following Jean Piaget, we see the development of moral judgment as a single-track process. In this view, moral judgment arises out of moral action itself, although there is no single causal direction. A new stage of moral judgment may guide new behavior, whereas a new action involving conflict and choice may lead one to construct a new stage of moral judgment" (p. 53). Because Kohlberg theorized more than two stages of moral development, there is a future for new thought (a conscious realization of the meaning of action, in Piaget's terms), but there is not one in his predecessor's theory. New possibilities in thinking create new opportunities for action. We can think our way into new forms of action just as we can act our way into new forms of thinking. "There is no single causal direction" in the single-track moral thought–action dynamic. But even this Kohlbergian proposition does a disservice to a complex psychology, because in Kohlberg's theory not only does thought arise from and also produce action, but moral thought or judgment itself is of two kinds. Drawing particularly on Frankena's classic *Ethics* (1973), Kohlberg distinguished between *deontic judgments* and *responsibility judgments*. The former "is a judgment that an act is right or obligatory," "typically derive[s] from a rule or principle," and can be called "first-order" (p. 57). By contrast, the latter judgment is "a second-order affirmation of the will to act in terms of that [first-order deontic] judgment" (p. 57). Quoting Blasi (1983, p. 198), Kohlberg affirmed that " 'the function of a responsibility judgment is to determine to what extent that which is morally good or right is also strictly necessary for the self' " (Kohlberg & Candee, 1984, p. 57). (In my discussion of Blasi, I show that this statement about the self has more extensive meaning for him than for Kohlberg.) In Kohlbergian perspective, "deontic judgments are propositional deductions from a *stage* or principle" (Kohlberg & Candee, 1984, p. 57, emphasis added); to put it another way, moral stage determines the principles available for a deontic judgment.

But this is further complicated by Kohlberg's very Piagetian discovery that some individuals act in concert with stages more advanced than their moral judgment stage. This is reminiscent of Piaget's (1997) insistence that articulate reflection lags behind action and is not necessary to it. Kohlberg (Kohlberg & Candee, 1984) addressed this phenomenon with his distinction between Type A and Type B moral orientations across the specific moral stages which correspond to Piaget's heteronomous and autonomous moral types. Like Piaget's as yet inarticulate but cooperative and autonomous moral type, Kohlberg's "type B person is someone who intuitively or in his or her 'heart' or 'conscience' perceives the central values and obligations … articulated rationally by stage 5 and uses these intuitions to generate a judgment of responsibility or necessity in a dilemma" (Kohlberg & Candee, 1984, p. 63).

Kohlberg (Kohlberg & Candee, 1984) himself identified moral stage or type and the two forms of judgment as three of the four functions that can be "formalized into a model of the relationship of moral judgment to moral action" (p. 71). Kohlberg and Candee's (1984, p. 71) is shown in Fig. 2.1.

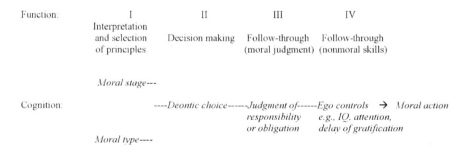

FIG. 2.1.   Kohlberg and Candee's (1984, p. 71) Schema of moral functioning. *Note.* From *Morality, Moral Behavior, and Moral Development* (p. 71), edited by W. Kurtines & J. Gewirtz, 1984, New York: John Wiley & Sons. Copyright 1984 by John Wiley & Sons. Reprinted with permission.

With Function IV, identified as nonmoral skills or ego controls, Kohlberg came as close as he ever did to acknowledging the role of the virtues or of character in moral functioning, even though he did not honor them by using a traditional name or even granting that the personal skills needed to carry out a responsibility judgment are indeed moral. Despite how necessary courage (as an ego control in the face of danger) or temperance (as in delay of gratification) might be to moral action, in Kohlberg's view only a judgment that an action is right or obligatory makes that action moral.

The important point, however, is that Kohlberg (1987) did acknowledge a psychological function necessary to the implementation of moral judgment. He also acknowledged that "situational factors are extremely important in moral action," for "in many cases peer group and institutional shared norms may be moral or nonmoral in their content" (p. 308). This explains why Kohlberg's own "approach to moral education [is] directed to making the classroom or the school a more just community" (pp. 308–309). As Kohlberg pointed out, this model of the relationship of moral judgment and moral action (Fig. 2.1) "bears considerable similarity to the one proposed by Rest" (Kohlberg & Candee, 1984, p. 72), to which we now turn.

REST

As Rest (1984) noted, "Reasoning about justice is no more the whole of morality than is empathy," p. 32). Although Kohlberg claimed similarity between his four function model and Rest's four component model, Rest himself clearly believed that Kohlberg's developmental theory of moral reasoning addresses only one (or perhaps two) of those components and that, therefore, his own model is more comprehensive. He proposed instead that we think of moral functioning as involving four inner processes or components that must perform adequately to produce moral behavior and must involve "cognitive–affective interaction" (p. 27). Rest's model is shown as in Fig. 2.2.

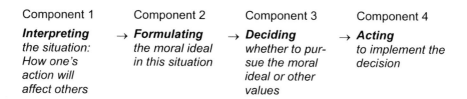

Component 1	Component 2	Component 3	Component 4
Interpreting the situation: How one's action will affect others	→ *Formulating* the moral ideal in this situation	→ *Deciding* whether to pursue the moral ideal or other values	→ *Acting* to implement the decision

FIG. 2.2. Rest's (1984) Four component model of morality.

Component or Process 1 (the terms are used interchangeably) is "to interpret the situation in terms of how one's actions affect the welfare of others" (Rest, 1984, p. 27) through processes of empathy and role taking. Component 2 is "to formulate what a moral course of action would be [and] to identify the moral ideal in a specific situation" (Rest, 1984, p. 27). Although much of his own research with the Defining Issues Test (Rest, Narvaez, Bebeau, & Thoma, 1999) has been in this area, Rest (1986) advised "that this kind of data base zeroes in on Component 2 and is ill-suited for providing information about the other components" (p. 9).

Component 3 is "to select among competing value outcomes of ideals, the one to act on," and also to decide "whether or not to try to fulfill one's moral ideal" (Rest, 1984, p. 27). Interestingly, one of Kohlberg's early papers (Kohlberg, 1969) is mentioned here, suggesting that his cognitive–developmental theory has something to say about Component 3 as well as Component 2. This would be no surprise to Kohlberg himself, of course, because he would see these two components as comparable to his deontic and responsibility judgments. The difference would seem to be that for Kohlberg the relation between these two judgments (or components) is isotonic (convergent) as one advances in moral reasoning; thus, especially at postconventional stages, which are increasingly clear about individual responsibility, deontic judgment essentially is responsibility judgment. For Rest (1986), however, the two components are distinct, because "moral values are not the only values that people have" (p. 13) and must be considered in Component 3.

Component 4 is "to execute and implement what one ought to do" (Rest, 1984, p. 27). Rest (1986) was less reluctant than Kohlberg to include success or failure here in explicitly moral and even religious context: "Perseverance, resoluteness, competence, and *character* are attributes that lead to success in Component 4. Psychologists [such as Kohlberg] sometimes refer to these processes as involving 'ego strength' or 'self-regulation.' A biblical term for failures in Component 4 is 'weakness of the flesh' "(p. 15, emphasis added). Kohlberg would be pleased to see that Rest (1986) nonetheless made the same point in this regard as he (Kohlberg) made: "Firm resolve, perseverance, iron will, strong character, and ego strength can be used for ill or for good. Ego strength comes in handy to rob a bank, prepare for a marathon, rehearse for a piano concert, or carry out genocide" (p. 15).

According to Kohlberg, because "moral stage structures *interpret* morally relevant features of a situation" (like Component 1) as well as "influence behavior through two judgments, one deontic (like Component 2) … and one responsibility (a judgment of commitment *to follow through*" (like Component 3) and take action (like Component 4; Kohlberg & Candee, 1984, p. 70, emphasis added), one can see why Kohlberg believed there is "considerable similarity" between his four function model and Rest's four component model. Nonetheless, because stage (or type) of moral reasoning is fundamentally determinative for Kohlberg through three of the four functions (or components), and as the fourth function is not properly moral at all in Kohlberg's estimation, Rest was also right to point to the difference between the two models. From his (1986) perspective, "moral behavior is an exceedingly complex phenomenon and no single variable (empathy, prosocial orientation, *stages of moral reasoning*, etc.) is sufficiently comprehensive to represent the psychology of morality" (p. 18, emphasis added).

To use the philosophical terminology of Roger Straughan (1983), Kohlberg tended toward an *extreme internalism* in the Platonic tradition, in which knowledge of the good is both necessary and sufficient to produce moral action. Rest, however, seems to be closer to Straughan's own *moderate internalism*, in which moral knowledge is necessary but sufficient only when there are not other "countervailing factors" at stake (Straughan, 1983, p. 134). Straughan (1983) pointed out that Kohlberg's own empirical evidence, as well as that reviewed in an often-cited and extensive article by Blasi (1980), reveals "only a 'modest' " (p. 132) relationship between moral judgment and moral action. That is, Kohlberg seemed to draw stronger theoretical support from the empirical evidence than it really allows. Straughan's argument is that a moderate internalism (a chastened cognitivism, but not a full-blown Platonism) can be defended both logically and empirically. That is, Kohlberg and Candee's (1984) model (Fig. 2.1) of the psychology of the moral domain is incomplete in the area of moral motivation.

In this regard, Straughan (1983) made a provocative move by drawing on a 1976 chapter by James Gilligan on shame and guilt as motivational factors in morality. Gilligan proposed, based on his analysis of Kohlberg's own data, the distinction between an "other-directed ... 'shame ethic' " and a "self-directed ... 'guilt ethic' " (Straughan, 1983, p. 136). Gilligan further claimed that development moves from the former to the latter, a pattern that Straughan interpreted to explain why Kohlberg found evidence for an isotonic relationship between advances in moral reasoning and the likelihood of action consistent with those higher levels of judgment. As Straughan (1983) put it, "other-directed sanctions are avoidable; self-directed ones are not" (p. 137).

It seems that Gilligan and Straughan are on to something crucial and heretofore neglected in the area of the development of moral motivation. That something is the role of the self, of what might be called the self's increasing ownership or personalization of, or sense of accountability for and to, its own moral reasoning and acting. With this explicit attention to the phenomena of guilt and self-regard, psychologists are on the threshold of the realm of the moral self, especially as focused in the concept of moral identity. Our prime guides to this territory are psychologists William Damon, Anne Colby (in partnership with Damon), and Augusto Blasi.

DAMON

According to Damon (1984), "A person's level of moral judgment does not determine the person's views on morality's place in one's life. To know how an individual deals with this latter issue, we must know about not only the person's moral beliefs but also the person's understanding of self in relation to these moral beliefs" (p. 110). Damon (1984) saw his approach to the study of moral development as an "alternative" to that of Kohlberg. As Damon pointed out,

> If children are presented with conflicts of authority drawn from the adult world, as in the case of Kohlberg's dilemmas, they are likely to acquiesce to the press of adult constraint and keep their moral principles to themselves. ... But, as a number of developmentalists back to Piaget have demonstrated ..., Stage 1 obedience has little to do with the lively "other morality of the child," expressed often in peer settings and based on principles of equality, cooperation, and reciprocity. (p. 113)

For Damon the "split between the two moralities of the child"— Stage 1 obedience, the morality of constraint, and "the other morality of the child," the morality of cooperation—is very real and "provides us with a clue about the nature of social knowledge during childhood" (p. 113).

Pursuing that clue, Damon recast Piaget's insistence that the morality of constraint actually reinforces childish egocentrism and that the morality of cooperation, because it requires reciprocal respect, is a developmental advance. Damon observed that in childhood, "morality and self-interest ... interact in various ways as children at different developmental levels construct their real-life decisions" (Damon, 1984, p. 118). In particular, a central finding of his two rounds of longitudinal testing with children and adolescents (Damon, 1977; Gerson & Damon, 1978) was that "only at the oldest age group (10) did we see some real consistency between hypothetical moral judgment and actual conduct" (Damon, 1984, p. 118). Furthermore, "morality does not become a dominant characteristic of self until ... middle adolescence." (Damon, 1984, p. 116). This indicates that at this developmental crux, "self-interest and morality were beginning to be integrated conceptually" (Damon, 1984, p. 118). This notion of integration is the key to Damon's alternative understanding of moral development. He considered "morality and the self as two separate conceptual systems," which are unrelated in childhood but which come together, however incompletely, "during adolescence, when changes in each system open the way for new forms of integration between the two ... which leads to the self becoming more defined in moral terms. One's moral interests and self-interests become more clearly defined and connected to each other" (p. 109). Or more simply, "during adolescence ... we see an integration of previously segregated conceptual systems: morality and the self" (p. 119). Because Damon casted moral development primarily in terms of this integration, we can chart his theory as shown in Fig. 2.3.

Four comments on this figure and the theory that it tries to represent are called for. First, moral reasoning per se is clearly not the focus, as it was in Kohlberg and Candee's (1984) theoretical schema (Fig. 2.1). Rather, cognition is subsumed under morality generally, and presumably it develops according to Kohlberg's stages. This, then, is the crucial point: Damon's approach does not so much seek to replace Kohlberg's theory as to place it in a larger context that calls attention to a personological dynamic overlooked by Kohlberg. But this shift has major ramifications, which leads to our second observation. As Damon (1984) put it, "One implication of this alternative position is that persons with the same moral beliefs may differ in their views on how important it is for them to be moral in a personal sense. Some may consider their morality to be central to their self-identities, whereas others may consider it to be peripheral" (p. 110). That is, Fig. 2.3 is meant to express a general developmental pattern toward integration of the moral self, especially during adolescence, but is not meant to suggest that this integration is always complete by adulthood or even at anytime during the adult years. Indeed, according to Colby and Damon (1992), such robust integration seems rare.

A third observation draws out the Piagetian correspondences in Damon's theory. As Davidson and Youniss (1991) reminded us, Piaget (1997) in *The*

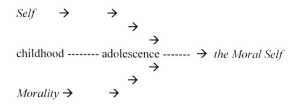

FIG. 2.3.   Damon's (1984) Theory of moral development/integration.

Moral Judgment of the Child made a crucial distinction between the egocentrism of heteronomous morality and the genuinely social and relational personality of autonomous morality. In the former, morality lies outside the self in external adult authority. In the latter, according to Piaget himself, "the self takes up its stand on the norms of reciprocity and objective discussion, and knows how to submit to these in order to make itself respected. Personality is thus the opposite of the ego. ... Cooperation being the source of personality, *rules cease to be external.* They become both the constitutive factors of personality and its fruit. ... In this way autonomy succeeds heteronomy" (quoted in Davidson & Youniss, 1991, p. 110; emphasis added). Davidson and Youniss preferred the terms *primary identity* and *autonomous identity* to Piaget's *ego* and *personality* and proposed "a conception of the two identities that is somewhat different from Piaget's" (p. 118). That conception is expressed in a hypothesis about the nature of moral development, "Moral development is the primary identity's progressive acquisition of facility in entering, or opening up to, and eventually becoming explicitly aware of, the autonomous identity ... ", and a corollary, "the autonomous standpoint would eventually become the dominant identity, superceding the previous primary identity. This conception of the normal direction of development is thus in line with Piaget's view of personality, except that we expect it to involve a number of partial constructions and also to require a more extended period of time than Piaget's writings imply" (pp. 119–120). Although the terms are different, Davidson and Youniss could almost have described Damon's theory of progressive integration of self and morality, which begins in early adolescence and extends into adulthood, but which even then may be partial and incomplete. In this process, "rules cease to be external ... [and] become both the constitutive factors of personality and its fruit" (Piaget, 1997, p. 96; quoted in Davidson & Youniss, 1991, p. 110). By *fruit* Davidson and Youniss understand Piaget to mean "spontaneous moral judgment" and behavior as an expression of personality or autonomous identity (Davidson & Youniss, 1991, p. 112). This Piagetian "link between moral judgment and moral identity" (Davidson & Youniss, 1991, p. 120) as "the normal direction of development" (Davidson & Youniss, 1991, p. 119, footnote 6) corresponds precisely with, and gives additional credibility to, Damon's theory as depicted in Fig. 2.3.

The fourth and final observation about Damon's theory is that it provides an alternative explanation to the Thought/Action Problem, the problem of weakness of will, weakness of the flesh, or akrasia. It is not so much a problem of ego controls or the influence of situational factors, as Kohlberg (Kohlberg & Candee, 1984) suggested. Rather, according to Damon (1984), although "Some may consider their morality to be central to their self-identities ... others may consider it to be peripheral. Some may even consider morality to be a force *outside of the self*, a socially imposed system of regulation that constrains or even obstructs one's pursuit of one's personal goals" (p. 110, emphasis added). In such cases, moral authority remains heteronomous, which means it is not integrated into one's own identity. People sometimes fail to act on their moral beliefs because those beliefs are not really their own. Moral "oughts" may then seem oppressive and refusal to abide by them liberating. This may help to explain the romance of the outlaw or antihero in popular culture.

COLBY AND DAMON

As Colby and Damon (1993) noted, "When there is perceived unity between self and morality, judgment and conduct are directly and predictably linked and action choices are made with great certainty" (p. 150). Happily, it is also the case that some people seem to act as if morality were the most important consideration consistently, passionately, and even heroically over a lifetime. That is the subject of Colby and Damon's (1992) book, *Some Do Care: Contemporary Lives of Moral Commitment.* Colby and Damon, with the counsel of "twenty-two moral philosophers, theologians, ethicists, historians, and social scientists" (Colby & Damon, 1992, p. 313) identified five criteria believed to characterize persons who could thereby be regarded as "moral exemplars." (See their Appendix A for a discussion of the criteria.) The same 22 consultants nominated 84 individuals as meeting all these criteria. Twenty-three of these highly diverse individuals were interviewed. (See Colby & Damon, 1992, pp. 35–36, Table 2.1 for a complete listing of the subjects' identifying characteristics.) Five of the 23 were interviewed again and are the subjects of a chapter each in *Some Do Care.*

Among several fascinating insights drawn from these interviews, Colby and Damon (1992) emphasized that what characterizes these moral exemplars most deeply is their exceptionally high degree of the uniting of self and morality: "all these men and women have vigorously pursued their individual and moral goals simultaneously, viewing them in fact as one and the same. ... Rather than denying the self, they define it with a moral center. ... *None saw their moral choices as an exercise in self-sacrifice*" (p. 300). And because of this extraordinary integration of self and morality, "Time and again we found our moral exemplars acting spontaneously, out of great certainty, with little fear, doubt, or agonized reflection. They performed their moral actions spontaneously, *as if they had no choice in the matter.* In fact, the sense that they lacked a choice is precisely what many of the exemplars reported" (p. 303, emphasis added).

When self and morality are so closely intertwined as in these moral exemplars, ego controls or situational factors are beside the point. If there is no choice, in the sense presented here, there is no Thought/Action problem. When the Self/Morality problem is resolved as successfully as in these 23 individuals, the Thought/Action problem is, one might say, dissolved. When moral beliefs are deeply and personally owned, when moral authority becomes autonomous, the will is strengthened and the usual gap between belief and action is healed by the wholeness of the personality. It is not a question of ego strength overcoming temptation, for when self and morality are so united as in these exemplars, temptation, in the normal sense of giving in to self-centered desires, simply ceases to be a factor. The self now has a moral center and its identifying desires are guided by moral goals. If there is temptation for a moral exemplar, it is not to give in to the self's fundamental desires, but to deny them. Moral exemplars seem to turn our (conventional) notions of the (post-conventional) moral life upside down.

The findings of Colby and Damon (1992) lead to a modification of Fig. 2.3, which portrays the results of Damon's (1984) research.

The difference between Fig. 2.4 and Fig. 2.3 is meant to express not only the importance of adolescence as the crucial period for the integration of self and morality (Damon, 1984) but also the insight that such development is an ongoing challenge in adulthood whose ideal or end is realized as moral exemplariness (Colby & Damon, 1992, 1993). This seems to be Colby and Damon's alternative to Kohlberg's Stage 6. It has the advantage of being grounded in actual data (interviews reflecting the lives of 23 individuals) and of making room for moral reasoning without making moral living dependent on it. Finally, I think of Fig. 2.4 and the theory it represents as a salute to the Type B moral individual whom Kohlberg acknowledged but could not explain in any depth. And, as previously noted, attention to the Morality/Self problem also corrects our vision of the Thought/Action problem raised but not persua-

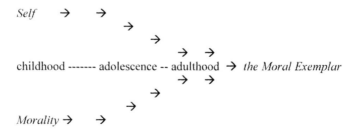

FIG. 2.4.   Colby and Damon's (1992) Theory of moral exemplariness.

sively answered by Kohlberg. Colby and Damon, I conclude, illuminated shadowy areas of Kohlberg's theory even as they offered an alternative to it.

Despite Damon's and Colby and Damon's major contributions to our understanding of the importance of the concept of self to moral development, no one has pursued this line of research and theory as consistently and with as much conceptual clarity as Augusto Blasi, to whose work we now turn.

BLASI

As Blasi (1990) noted, "We need a psychological theory to explain how and why moral understanding leads, when it does, to the desire to act morally" (p. 53). In a research project[1] on the degree of personal integration of moral responsibility and accountability among three groups of children with average ages of 6, 12, and 17, Blasi (1989) confronted each child, in an interview, "with a number of stories, each representing a typical conflict between one's wish and obedience, between one's wish and reciprocity, between obedience and altruism, and so forth" (p. 125). He concluded from an analysis of their responses that "the sense of personal obligation is largely absent among 6-year-olds, but is well understood by the large majority of 12-year-olds and is closely related by them to what they believe to be objectively right. In many 17-year-olds the sense of obligation is tied to personally held beliefs and the sense of personal integrity" (p. 126). Blasi referred to a series of studies by Nunner-Winkler and Sodian (1988), in which children between the ages of 4 and 8 were presented with and interviewed about "common situations of wrongdoing" and were asked "questions concerning the moral value of the actions and the emotions that the story character would experience" (Blasi, 1989, p. 124). Blasi reported the findings that "children of all ages understood that certain actions are unacceptable and wrong," but that "there were clearcut age differences in the responses concerning emotions" (p. 124). Younger children "don't seem to experience emotions in connection with what they understand to be wrong as such. Or, more precisely, their moral understanding does not seem to acquire the type of motivational power that is needed to counteract their present motives. In sum, moral understanding appears to be possible without it being integrated with the appropriate emotions and motives" (p. 125). In younger children, it seems that knowing right from wrong would not in itself necessarily lead to right action. Blasi concluded from these findings that "what is needed is a certain kind of integration of moral understanding in one's personality" (p. 125).

Clearly Blasi and Damon were on the same wavelength: The integration of morality and personality is key. Blasi, however, was more concerned, first, to preserve the centrality of reasoning within morality generally and, second, to enhance our understanding of the relations among moral reasoning, moral motivation, and moral identity specifically. The former of those purposes put him solidly in the Kohlbergian tradition, whereas with the latter he was clearly attempting to expand it. In pursuing these joint purposes, Blasi (1983, 1984) proposed what he called the self model that focuses on "the transition from moral cognition to moral action and on the issue of judgment–behavior consistency" (Blasi, 1983, p. 194) and that is detailed in a set of five propositions. The fifth of these is crucial: "*Proposition 5: The transition from a judgment of responsibility to action is supported dynamically by the tendency toward self-consistency, a central tendency in personality organization*" (p. 201). Why act on one's moral judgments? Because "not to act according to one's judgment should be perceived as a substantial inconsistency, as *a fracture within the very core of the self*, unless neutralizing devices are put into operation" (Blasi, 1983, p. 201, emphasis added). Daniel Lapsley (1996) succinctly captured the difference this proposition makes between Kohlberg's and Blasi's theories of moral motivation: "*For Kohlberg*, moral motivation to act comes from one's fidelity to the prescriptive nature of moral principles. ... Hence *not to act is to betray a principle. For Blasi*, in contrast, moral motivation to act is a consequence of one's moral identity, and *not to act is to betray the self*" (p. 86, emphasis added). This difference is highly significant. It seems intuitively apparent that fidelity to self—or the threat of self-betrayal, of self-*dis*-integration—has a greater motivational potential than does fidelity to an abstract principle belonging to any individual only by virtue of its belonging to every (rational) individual. Simply put, why act on a principle unless that principle is experienced as making a claim on one's very self?[2]

But this contrast of the motivational theories of Kohlberg and Blasi may be misleading if it suggests Blasi enhanced our understanding of the importance of self or identity to moral motivation and action but at the cost of downplaying the role of moral judgment. Blasi's (1984) own proposal at this point is only suggestive: "It would appear, then, that the only hope of grounding morality on the essential self without losing morality's reason is to hypothesize that the self's very identity is constructed, at least in part, under the influence of moral reasons. ... Fundamentally, ... *the direction of influence would be from moral understanding to moral identity, rather than the other way around* " (p. 138, emphasis added).

That is, "the construction of ... [a moral identity] ... is indeed a genuine moral issue, more important than altruism, honesty, or truthfulness ... morality and the good life, to use a Kantian distinction, cannot be separated" (Blasi, 1984, p. 139). In an essay published one year later than his seminal essay on moral identity (Blasi, 1984), Blasi (1985) asked "whether it makes sense to ask, not only 'What kind of person do I want to be?,' but also 'What kind of person should one, or must one, be,' " thereby suggesting that the subjective is indeed subject, in some measure, to the objective, to "the language of universal prescriptivity" (p. 438). A decade later still, Blasi (1995) elaborated this subjective–objective tension by reference to two complementary components of "the integration of moral understanding in one's motivational system. ... The first [of which] concerns the ability to bring one's moral understanding to bear on one's already existing motives" (p. 236).

In a recent article, to bring greater conceptual clarity to the empirical evidence (Blasi, 1989; Damon, 1977, 1984; Gerson & Damon, 1978; Nunner-Winkler & Sodian, 1988), Blasi (1999) drew on philosopher Harry Frankfurt's argument:

> people do not only have desires concerning objects, other people, and events (first-order desires, in [Frankfurt's] terminology); they also have reflexive desires, namely, desires about their own desires ... [and] by reflecting and taking a stance on what in us is spontaneous, we take what is natural and make it wanted; by doing so, we agentically structure our motives and desires (we structure our will, in Frankfurt's language) and begin *to establish our identity.* (p. 11, emphasis added)

Having second-order volitions seems to be the way the integration of the objective, the universally prescriptive, and the uniquely subjective take place without losing the tension between them. The objective, the morally rational, is not imposed but rather chosen by the subject in the subject's freedom of will. By such free choice, the subject shapes his or her own identity, and thereby his or her own will itself, in light of objective moral reality but not in simple obedience, internalization, or socialization.

That this choice is indeed rational and not mere submission to social pressures to conform seems to depend on acknowledgment of the "second component of the integration of moral understanding and motivation [which] concerns the investing of moral understanding with motivational force" (Blasi, 1995, p. 237). Blasi assumed—and here his Kohlbergian sympathies come to the fore—"that moral understanding eventually acquires *its own* motivational power, one, namely, that is intrinsic in the nature itself of morality" (p. 237). Blasi's difference from Kohlberg seems to lie in his insistence that moral understanding acquires motivational power through its integration into the structures of the self, into one's moral identity, and not simply because such motivational power is intrinsic to morality. To state this concretely, the intrinsic motivational power of moral understanding is not evident in research on children, for whom it remains extrinsic until early adolescence. Perhaps only in moral exemplars do we see that power fully appropriated in uniquely personal ways.

We might represent Blasi's theoretical insight and contribution to moral psychology as shown in Fig. 2.5.

According to this theory or model, moral understanding shapes personal identity even as that identitification with morality shapes one's sense of personal responsibility and unleashes moral understanding's motivational power to act in a manner consistent with what one knows and believes. In this way, the objective and the subjective, the universal and the personal, and the rational and the affective and volitional are integrated. Such integration—or integrity—is the mark of the morally mature individual.

SYNTHESIS AND APPRAISAL

There are several advantages of this model over previous models. One might say that it combines the insights of both Kohlberg and Colby and Damon. That is, it preserves the centrality of moral reasoning but does not try to explain moral psychology by reference only to reason. Or conversely, it takes individual differences, personal responsibility, and motivation seriously as independent factors in morality without succumbing to a purely subjectivist perspective. It preserves Kohlberg's two moments of moral judgment (deontic and responsibility) while distinguishing them and explaining their relation, through the innovative concept of moral identity, more substantially and clearly than Kohlberg was able to do (or interested in doing). It articulates the motivational potential of moral understanding, rather than assuming its nearly inevitable expression in action, as did Kohlberg, and thus provides a new context for thinking about the problem of akrasia, so inexplicable for a Platonist (at least in matters of motivation) like Kohlberg. And although Fig. 2.5 itself does not spell out the insights of Colby and Damon, as portrayed in

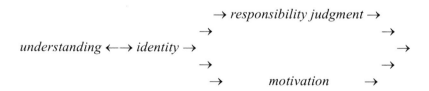

FIG. 2.5.   Blasi's (1983, 1984, 1985, 1995, 1999)Theory of moral identity and motivation.

Figs. 2.3 and 2.4, as to the importance of adolescence as a period in which identity and morality become progressively unified, it does make room for that understanding. Thus, a synthetic model in which moral identity is central can be presented (see Fig. 2.6).

Figure 2.6 should be understood as suggestive, because the two sides of the figure are not really commensurable. The developmental process outlined on the left side has a long-term temporal framework; the right side, on the contrary, is a highly schematic snapshot of how we might think about the functioning of a morally exemplary individual, one who has substantially integrated, over the long term, moral understanding into his or her sense of personal identity.

The best answer to the question, Why be moral?, may thus be, because that is who I am, or, because I can do no other and remain (or become) the person I am committed to being. Commentators on the Shoah (the genocide of the Jews during World War II) often observe that both rescuers of Jews and those who refused to take such risks on behalf of desperate and hunted strangers have explained their behavior in similar words: " 'But what else could I do?' " (Monroe, 1994, p. 201). Everything depends on how the "I" understands itself and its responsibilities.

Larry Nucci, a prominent moral psychologist and educator, however, while integrating the moral self into his own theory of moral development and moral education, also raised important philosophical questions about the model. I now turn to those concerns.

NUCCI

According to Nucci (2001), "Blasi's work is provocative in that it links Aristotelian notions of eudaimonia (self-flourishing) to the work that has been done on moral cognition" (p. 133). "But all of this work on moral self and moral identity ... comes very close to adding a 'homunculus' on the scene ... a sort of

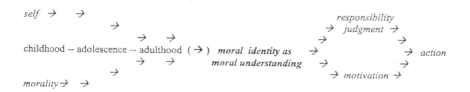

FIG. 2.6. A synthetic developmental model of exemplary moral functioning.

moral Mini-me—that actually makes the decisions after whatever other cognitive mechanisms get finished" (Nucci, 2000, p. 6).

Education in the Moral (Self) Domain

In *Education in the Moral Domain*, in a 14-page chapter on "Reconceptual-
izing Moral Character" which brings to closure his discussion of "Part One:
The Nature of Morality and the Development of Social Values," Larry Nucci
(2001) devoted 11 pages to a discussion of the moral self. Moral character is
reconceptualized not as "a constellation of personality traits or virtues but,
rather, the operation of the moral aspects of the self in relation to the self as a
whole." For Nucci, "character [is] ... defined in terms of the moral self" (p.
137). In the final chapter of Part 2, "Classroom Applications," which is also the
final chapter of the book, Nucci offered recommendations to public school
teachers for "Fostering the Moral Self." He proposed several methodologies
for "building up the linkages among children's moral affect, their moral understandings, and their construction of personal identity. The integration of these
three elements of affect, reasoning and identity form the 'moral self' " (p. 196).
As suggested by the first quotation on the linkage of eudaimonism to moral
cognition in the model of the moral self and as demonstrated by the central
place given to the moral self, Nucci's book offers a positive evaluation of the
contribution of the work of Blasi and others on moral identity to our understanding of moral development and moral education.

The only limitation Nucci identified in this model "is that it is centered
around a sophisticated form of personal identity that does not typically
emerge before adolescence or adulthood. Thus, Blasi's work does not provide us with an account of the developmental antecedents of moral identity,
nor does he provide an account of moral motivation for children prior to this
adolescent period of identity formation" (p. 133). Nucci himself, however,
made headway toward identifying "childhood antecedents of the moral self"
(Nucci, 2001, p. 133):

> The consistent picture that emerges from diverse studies of the development of
> self-undestandings is that morality and the self-system develop independently
> until middle childhood. Prior to this integration, however, children begin to
> construct modes of responding to moral situations that reflect, at least in part,
> their sense of how such actions relate back to their own goals, aims and their
> sense of what is right in relation to themselves. Gil Noam ... has captured much
> of the results of this research, as it relates to the eventual construction of the
> moral self, in his conclusion that early, secure emotional attachments, predict-
> able contexts, and a zone of trust and reciprocity are conducive to formation of
> the moral self. (p. 135)

These conclusions from Noam provide the context for Nucci's illuminating discussion of how to foster the childhood antecedents of the moral self in classroom settings. He (2001) also offered insights into "education and formation of the moral self in middle childhood and adolescence" (p. 203) by providing opportunities for encounters with "symbolic sources of self" in literature (p. 206), for "direct self-reflection" (p. 210), and for "engagement in moral action" through service-learning (p. 212).

In short, Nucci's (2001) *Education in the Moral Domain* integrates recent work on moral self and moral identity into his own domain-based theory of sociomoral development and its pedagogical applications. Furthermore, as he (2001) demonstrated, the model's limitations in explaining "moral responsibility in childhood" (p. 128) can be mitigated by reference to other research, so that the model becomes a reasonably comprehensive (and still developing) perspective on growth in morality from early childhood to adulthood. This perspective, in fact, seems to be a primary burden of Nucci's important book.

Self-Consistency as a Moral Motivation

However, Nucci's take on the moral self is decidedly less affirming. In his Presidential Address to the 30th annual meeting of the Jean Piaget Society, Nucci (2000) leveled four charges of reductionism at "all of this work on the moral self and moral identity" (p. 6). These criticisms are summarized in the first of four concerns explored in "Because It Is the Right Thing to Do," Nucci's (2002) response to my (Bergman, 2002) "Why Be Moral? A Conceptual Model From Developmental Psychology," on which this chapter is based. His basic charge of reductionism is now called *ethical egoism*. I take seriously this charge against the model I have synthesized from Piaget to Blasi, as I understand ethical egoism to be an oxymoron, an untenable contradiction. One cannot simultaneously be both ethical, which means to be concerned about others, and egoistical, which means to be concerned solely for oneself. If the charge sticks, the model is not only theoretically misconstrued but, to the extent that it has any real-world influence, potentially dangerous. It would also compel us to reevaluate Nucci's own use of the concept of the moral self in his book.

It is helpful at this point to recall Nucci's characterization of Blasi's work as combining Aristotelian eudaimonia with moral cognition and to point out that for Aristotle (as for Plato before him and Aquinas after him), "the pursuit of *good as such* and the pursuit of *my good* necessarily coincide" (MacIntyre, 1967, p. 463). As philosospher Alistair MacIntyre pointed out, "What is to my interest depends on who I am and what I want" (p. 465). This is a clear echo of a concluding sentence of the previous section of this chapter: "Everything depends on how the 'I' understands itself and its responsibilities." As MacIntyre explained,

> if I want to lead a certain kind of life, with relationships of trust, friendship, and cooperation with others, then my wanting their good and my wanting my good are not two independent, discriminable desires. It is not even that I have two separate motives, self-interest and benevolence, for doing the same action. I have one motive, a desire to live in a certain way, which cannot be characterized as a desire for my good rather than that of others. For the good that I recognize and pursue is not mine particularly, except in the sense that I recognize and pursue it. (p. 466)

It is in this sense that Plato, Aristotle, and the Stoics were egoists, as "they regard[ed] self-love not as the enemy of virtue and the larger community but as an honourable motive, *once it is developed in its proper direction*" (Kraut, 1998, p. 247). That qualification, of course, is crucial, and a prominent concern in all the moral self theorists I have described in this chapter, as well as for Nucci (2001) himself in *Education in the Moral Domain*.

Moral Centrality as an Aspect of Individual Differences

But ethical egoism is not Nucci's (2002) only challenge to the moral self- construct. He questioned a "common feature of the theories of moral-self," the assertion that "moral centrality [is] ... an aspect of individual differences" (p. 126), and doubted "that morality is somehow nearer and dearer to some people than to others" (p. 127). He asked rhetorically,

> Is it the case that the moral exemplars in Colby and Damon's [1992] research were more committed to morality than William Ayers and his wife, Bernadine Dorn, when as leaders of the Weathermen, they planned violent actions against the United States during the Vietnam war period? Or, did they read the situation they faced differently, and out of a sense of morality engage in violent actions ...? (p. 127)

Why, to state the question differently, aside from the fact that Ayers and Dorn were at the time fugitives from justice, could they not have been included among Colby and Damon's research subjects? Perhaps, Nucci seemed to suggest, given the alleged claim that moral exemplars simply care more about morality than the rest of us, Ayers and Dorn are more appropriately thought of as fugitives *for* justice. Indeed, if Nucci were correct that theorists of the moral self believe that the quality of the moral self depends solely or even mainly on the degree of single-minded passion for a moral cause—such that the nobility of their ends justify any means, no matter how objectionable in themselves; such that terrorist violence can be used and the harm done to innocent bystanders discounted as collateral damage; such that one is "beyond good and evil," in Nietzsche's (1973) titular phrase—well, then, yes, Ayers and Dorn should be thought of as exemplars of the moral self. And why not Timothy McVeigh or the 9-11 terrorists? I would simply say that Ayers and Dorn and company, when they descend to such immoral action, do not express a deep caring about morality and do not exhibit a true moral identity, a self formed and informed by universal, objective standards of justice and human welfare.[3]

Yes, some people—such as those portrayed in *Some Do Care* (Colby & Damon, 1992)—do care more about morality than others—such as Ayers and Dorn. They care so deeply about morality and about the quality of their relations with other people—or most simply and fundamentally, about other people—that it shapes who they are at a fundamental level and thereby consistently motivates them in the right direction, constrains them from exempting themselves from the claims morality makes on all of us, and compels them to ongoing moral self-reflection. Individuals like Ayers and Dorn may think they are more moral than others who are less willing to take extreme action, but that does not make it so. Or, to put the matter differently, even hardened Nazi officers were morally self-conscious and even self-righteous—"The SS [Nazi secret police or storm-troopers], despite its central role in the brutality and killings, had a conception of itself as a moral elite" (Glover, 2000, p. 358)—but that does not undermine the validity of moral identity anymore than the fact that they also had a heightened sense of duty—to do the right thing—undermines the notion of moral obligation. As Glover pointed out, "Eichmann claimed to believe in 'fulfillment of duty,' saying, 'In fact, I have taken Kant's categorical imperative as my norm' " (pp. 356–357). (For an in-depth analysis of "False Moral Identity," see Moshman, this volume—chap. 5.)

Singular Motivation and Multiple Motives

Is all moral action motivated predominately, even exclusively, and self-consciously by a determination to maintain one's own sense of moral integrity? And is this a necessary implication of the model of the moral self presented in this chapter? Nucci's (2002) final concern was that Bergman "has not fully appreciated the multifaceted aspects of moral judgments in context … nor has he sufficiently allowed for the heterogeneity that exists within a given person's self-system" (p. 129). Anne Colby (2002) raised a similar concern:

> Actual motivation in real life situations is a complex mix for most people. It would not be strange for a self-reflective person who reasons at Stage 5 to say that he does not pad his expense account because it would be morally wrong (e.g., a violation of trust with his employer), *and* because he could imagine how horrible it would be to be caught, *and* because it would be shameful, *and* because he would feel guilty even if he was not caught, *and* because it would violate his sense of integrity, and so on. (p. 133)

This is an observation of common sense, according to Colby, but it also is supported by the research of Daloz, Keen, Keen, and Parks (1996) as reported in *Common Fire: Leading Lives of Commitment in a Complex World*. The findings of Daloz et al. push the envelope even further. Not only may our motivations to act morally be multiple, they may not all be as more or less honorable as suggested by Colby's litany.

Daloz et al. interviewed 100 diverse persons selected for their sustained commitment to the common good.[4] As my undergraduate students recognize and appreciate, these individuals are more ordinary than Colby and Damon's moral exemplars, yet still praiseworthy and inspiring. One of the characteristics that makes them more like us and less like moral saints is that, in addition to having noble and admirable motivations, many also admit to what the authors called "taboo motivations": "*those motivating emotions that one is either uncomfortable with or which others regard as suspect—particularly if one aspires to work on behalf of others,*" such as "*ambition, pride, anger, need to please,* and *fear*" (pp. 177–178). For the most part, however, these dedicated activists are able to sublimate such self-acknowledged taboo motivations into their better motivations—"one aspires to work on behalf of others"—and thus they enhance and unify their moral selves.

An insight of the philosopher Thomas Wren (1991) may be helpful here. Drawing on Frankfurt's (1988) distinction between first- and second-order desires, Wren distinguished between moral motives (in the plural) and moral motivation (in the singular). The former are "relatively distinct conative dispositions, many of which bear the same names as the virtuous action patterns they generate, such as kindness, courage, fidelity, and piety" (Wren, 1991, p. 10). The latter refers to the "conative foundation" of these particular dispositions, the "*deep structure*" or "disposition to take a moral point of view, from which other action tendencies present themselves as moral motives, all charged with moral significance and overriding urgency for the agent as well as any evaluating onlookers" (p. 10). According to Wren, "moral motives are a necessary condition for any passage from moral judgment to moral action, whereas moral motivation makes possible the evaluative cognition from which moral jugments emerge" (Wren, 1991, p. 81). Wren offered the "following scheme [which] portrays this double mediation between the self and the completed action" (Wren, 1991, p. 81; see Fig. 2.7).

SELF → *Moral Motivation* → *MORAL THINKING* → *Moral Motive* → *ACTION*

FIG. 2.7.   Wren's (1991) Schema of double mediation between the self and action. *Note.* From *Caring About Morality* (p. 81), by Thomas E. Wren, 1991, Cambridge, MA: MIT Press. Copyright 1991 by Thomas E. Wren. Reprinted with permission.

Although Wren's schema unnecessarily limits the immediate antecedent of action to a single motive, it has the virtue of rooting such motives in a fundamental structure of the self where personal identity and commitment to moral living meet. That deep structure has been referred to throughout this chapter as moral identity. Wren's schema also does not attempt to indicate how that structure not only gives rise to moral thinking but is also shaped by it (see Fig. 2.6). It does not (like all of the models drawn from the theorists considered in this chapter) suggest how action is not simply the final product or expression of the self but a reflexively formative influence on the self. In Frankfurt's (1988) language, to the extent that our second-order desires can be embodied in action, our actions have both external (in the world) and internal (in the self) effects. In Aristotelian language, the desire to be just, if it leads to just action, makes me just. Wren's schema might be thought of as having a recursive as well as a linear dimension.

This distinction between moral motivation, as a deep structure of personal identity, and moral motives, as mixed and including even some motives considered taboo, suggests a response to the questions with which we began this subsection: Is all moral action motivated predominately, even exclusively, and self-consciously by a determination to maintain one's own sense of moral integrity? And is this a necessary implication of the model of the moral self presented in this chapter? Wren's distinction allows us to say that, yes, all moral action is motivated fundamentally by a determination to maintain one's own sense of moral integrity (which need not be thought of as static). But, no, that determination may not be self-consciously articulated even in adults, who may explain their action by reference to what in this context would be understood as moral motives. This would be even more the case in children, for whom a sense of moral self-consciousness may be only incipient. But we must also say that, no, moral identity cannot be exclusively the source of moral action. There must be moral motives to translate that deep structure into behavior. And those moral motives must be informed by moral understanding, even as those actions and that understanding also form and reform, reflexively, the moral self.

ACKNOWLEDGMENTS

This chapter is based on "Why Be Moral? A Conceptual Model from Developmental Psychology," *Human Development*, *45* (2002), 104–124. I am grateful to the reviewers of the original manuscript for their insightful comments, and to the editor, Barbara Rogoff, for her close reading and encouragement. Used with permission of Karger, the publisher of *Human Development*. Thanks, also, to David Moshman, for his invaluable support throughout this project.

ENDNOTES

[1]The resulting paper was published in 1984 in German but to my knowledge is not available in English. It is summarized in Blasi (1989), pp. 125–126.

[2]The significance of the difference between Blasi and Kohlberg is also philosophical. Theoretically linking moral principle with moral action through the mediation of the self and of moral identity suggests the possibility of a reconciliation between rule-based ethics (whether deontology or teleology) and virtue ethics. Exploration of that possibility is beyond the scope of this chapter.

[3]Colby and Damon (1992) pointed out that "Moral exemplars, in contrast with tyrants or fanatics, are rigorously principled about their methods as well as their objectives" (p. 30). It should be pointed out that William Ayers is now a distinguished moral educator. He was a plenary lecturer at the 2002 conference of the Association for Moral Education at the University of Illinois at Chicago, which was organized principally by his UIC colleague Larry Nucci.

[4]See the first chapter of *Common Fire* for the authors' understanding of the new commons; see chapter 1 and the appendix for a description of the selection criteria, the demographics of the sample, and explanations of the interview process and analysis of the interviews.

REFERENCES

Bergman, R. (2002). Why be moral? A conceptual model from developmental psychology. *Human Development, 45*, 104–124.

Blasi, A. (1980). Bridging moral cognition and moral action: A critical review of the literature. *Psychological Bulletin, 88*, 1–45.

Blasi, A. (1983). Moral cognition and moral action: A theoretical perspective. *Developmental Review, 3*, 178–210.

Blasi, A. (1984). Moral identity: Its role in moral functioning. In W. M. Kurtines & J. L. Gewirtz (Eds.), *Morality, moral behavior, and moral development*, pp. 128–139. New York: Wiley.

Blasi, A. (1985). The moral personality: Reflections for social science and education. In M. W. Berkowitz & F. Oser (Eds.), *Moral education: Theory and application*, pp. 433–444. Hillsdale, NJ: Lawrence Erlbaum Associates.

Blasi, A. (1989). The integration of morality in personality. In I. E. Bilbao (Ed.), *Perspectivas acerca de cambio moral posibles intervenciones educativas*, pp. 121–131. San Sebastian, Spain: Servicio Editorial Universidad Del Pais Vasco.

Blasi, A. (1990). Kohlberg's theory and moral motivation. *New Directions for Child Development, 47*, 51–57.

Blasi, A. (1995). Moral understanding and the moral personality: The process of moral integration. In W. M. Kurtines & J. L. Gewirtz (Eds.), *Moral development: An introduction*, pp. 229–253. Boston: Allyn & Bacon.

Blasi, A. (1999). Emotions and moral motivation. *Journal for the Theory of Social Behaviour, 29*, 1–19.

Colby, A. (2002). Moral understanding, motivation, and identity. *Human Development, 45*, 130–135.

Colby, A., & Damon, W. (1992). *Some do care: Contemporary lives of moral commitment.* New York: The Free Press.

Colby, A., & Damon, W. (1993). The uniting of self and morality in the development of extraordinary moral commitment. In G. G. Noam & T. E. Wren (Eds.), *The moral self,* pp. 149–174. Cambridge, MA: MIT Press.

Daloz, L., Keen, C., Keen, J., & Parks, S. (1996). *Common fire: Lives of commitment in a complex world.* Boston: Beacon Press.

Damon, W. (1977). *The social world of the child.* San Francisco: Jossey-Bass.

Damon, W. (1984). Self-understanding and moral development from childhood to adolescence. In W. M. Kurtines & J. L. Gewirtz (Eds.), *Morality, moral behavior, and moral development*, pp. 109–127. New York: Wiley.

Davidson, P., & Youniss, J. (1991). Which comes first? Morality or identity? In W. M. Kurtines & J. L. Gewirtz (Eds.), *Handbook of moral behavior development: Vol. 1. Theory*, pp. 105–121. Hillsdale, NJ: Lawrence Erlbaum Associates.

Frankena, W. (1973). *Ethics.* Second edition. Englewood Cliffs, NJ: Prentice-Hall.

Frankfurt, H. (1988). *The importance of what we care about.* Cambridge, England: Cambridge University Press.

Gerson, R., & Damon, W. (1978). Moral understanding and children's conduct. In W. Damon (Ed.), *New directions for child development* (Vol. 1), pp. 41–59. San Francisco: Jossey-Bass.

Gilligan, J. (1976). Beyond morality: Psychoanalytic reflections on shame, guilt, and love. In T. Lickona (Ed.), *Moral development and behavior: Theory, research, and social issues*, pp. 144–158. New York: Holt, Rinehart & Winston.

Glover, J. (2000). *Humanity: A moral history of the twentieth century.* New Haven, CT: Yale University Press.

Kohlberg, L. (1969). Stage and sequence: The cognitive–developmental approach to socialization. In D. Goslin (Ed.), *Handbook of socialization theory and research*, pp. 347–480. Skokie, IL: Rand McNally.

Kohlberg, L. (1970). Education for justice: A modern statement of the platonic view. In *Moral education: Five lectures*, pp. 57–83. Cambridge, MA: Harvard University Press.

Kohlberg, L. (1987). The development of moral judgment and moral action. In L. Kohlberg (Ed.), *Child psychology and childhood education: A cognitive–developmental view*, pp. 259–328. New York: Longman.

Kohlberg, L., & Candee, D. (1984). The relationship of moral judgment to moral action. In W. M. Kurtines & J. L. Gewirtz (Eds.). *Morality, moral behavior, and moral development*, pp. 52–73. New York: Wiley.

Kraut, R. (1998). Egoism and altruism. In E. Craig (Ed.), *Routledge encyclopedia of philosophy*, pp. 246–248. London: Routledge.

Lapsley, D. K. (1996). *Moral psychology.* Boulder, CO: Westview.

Locke, D. (1983). Theory and practice in thought and action. In H. Weinreich-Haste & D. Locke (Eds.), *Morality in the making: Thought, action, and the social context*, pp. 157–170. Chichester, England: Wiley.

MacIntyre, A. (1967). Egoism and altruism. In P. Edwards (Ed.), *The encyclopedia of philosophy* (Vol. 2), pp. 462–466. New York: Macmillan & The Free Press.

Monroe, K. (1994). "But what else could I do?" Choice, identity and a cognitive–perceptual theory of ethical political behavior. *Political Psychology, 15*, 201–226.

Nietzsche, F. (1973). *Beyond good and evil.* Trans. R. Hollingdale. Harmondsworth, England: Penguin.

Nucci, L. (2000, June). The promise and limitations of the moral self construct. Presidential Address presented at the meeting of the Jean Piaget Society, Montreal, Canada. Available at http://MoralEd.org

Nucci, L. (2001). *Education in the moral domain.* Cambridge, England: Cambridge University Press.

Nucci, L. (2002). Because it is the right thing to do. *Human Development, 45,* 125–129.

Nunner-Winkler, G., & Sodian, B. (1988). Children's understanding of moral emotions. *Child Development, 59,* 1323–1338.

Piaget, J. (1932/1997). *The moral judgment of the child.* New York: The Free Press.

Rest, J. R. (1984). The major components of morality. In W. M. Kurtines & J. L. Gewirtz (Eds.), *Morality, moral behavior, and moral development,* pp. 24–37. New York: Wiley.

Rest, J. R. (1986). *Moral development: Advances in research and theory.* New York: Praeger.

Rest, J. R., Narvaez, D., Bebeau, M. J., & Thoma, S. J. (1999). *Postconventional moral thinking: A neo-Kohlbergian approach.* Mahwah, NJ: Lawrence Erlbaum Associates.

Straughan, R. (1983). From moral judgment to moral action. In H. Weinreich-Haste & D. Locke (Eds.), *Morality in the making: Thought, action, and the social context.* Chichester, England: Wiley.

Wren, T. (1991). *Caring about morality: Philosophical perspectives in moral psychology.* Cambridge, MA: MIT Press.

3

The Moral Self in Community

F. Clark Power
University of Notre Dame

Oddly enough the discipline of psychology as practiced today offers few opportunities to write in the first person. We create an illusion of objectivity by writing as if there were no author, as if the data could speak for themselves. We also create an illusion of objectivity about the focus of our discipline by conceptualizing the psyche through the metaphors of the machine, organism, or computer. I am grateful for the opportunity afforded by the chapter in this volume to speak in the first person about the study of the moral self and to reflect in an autobiographical way about the path that led me from the study of moral development and the moral culture of the school to the moral self.

In this chapter, I reflect on the two principal strands of my own research that involve the self as a moral agent. The first strand comes from my work with the just community approach to moral education and addresses the self as a member of a community. The second strand focuses on one dimension of the moral self, the meaning and assessment of moral self-worth. My approach to the self in both contexts has been informed by Gus Blasi's writings although at different times and in different ways. I have only recently begun to explore the self in the community from Blasi's perspective on the self and socialization (Blasi, 1984, 1988, 1993) although Blasi's (1980) notion of moral responsibility influenced the research that I did with Lawrence Kohlberg and Ann Higgins (Power, Higgins, & Kohlberg, 1989) on the just community approach in the late 1970s. The ideas on the shared self that I offer in this chapter extend thinking in ways that will bear fruit in future research on the just community approach to moral education. Blasi influenced my approach to moral self-worth from the very beginning. Not only did he convince me to study the self, but he led me to reflect on the distinctiveness of the moral dimensions of the self and identity. Finally, Blasi's theory has led me to appreciate how these strands of my research might be woven together by studying how self-worth is mediated through the experience of belonging to a community.

MORAL JUDGMENT AND MORAL RESPONSIBILITY

Before focusing on the just community research, I briefly describe some of the concerns that I grappled with as a graduate student at Harvard in the mid- to late 1970s, concerns that led me along with Kohlberg and Higgins to consider moral responsibility as a significant variable for moral development research. Like many who became quickly immersed in Kohlberg's research on moral development, I was intrigued with the relation between moral judgment and action. In the first paper that I wrote for Kohlberg, I (Power, 1976) put forth a model, influenced by the philosopher Bernard Lonergan (1958, 1964), that attempted to describe the processes that led from moral awareness to moral action from the perspective of the moral agent. While showing some interest in my theoretical musings, Kohlberg pointed me in what appeared to be almost the opposite direction by suggesting that I write my dissertation on the just community approach and the moral atmosphere of the school. What I never would have imagined at that time was that I would, in fact, write a dissertation addressing the judgment and action issue but from a perspective that was more sociological than psychological. I focused my dissertation on the influence of group norms on individual behavior rather than on moral judgment or personality variables. I did not, however, neglect the individual altogether. Drawing principally on Blasi's (1980) thinking, Kohlberg, Higgins, and I began to describe the moral atmosphere of schools as having an influence, for better or worse, on students' sense of moral responsibility (Higgins, Power, & Kohlberg, 1984).

    While I was writing my dissertation, I was also working on the construction of the moral judgment scoring manual (Colby et al., 1987). The manual was close to completion when Gilligan's (1977) *Harvard Educational Review* article, "In a Different Voice," appeared. Much to our dismay, in her article and subsequent (Gilligan, 1982) book, Gilligan claimed that the scoring manual reflected a male moral perspective. We had, in her view, captured the rights and justice orientation to moral judgment, but we had missed the female caring and responsibility orientation. Rejecting the notion of two moralities, Kohlberg acknowledged that Gilligan had called attention to a neglected dimension of the moral life, that of moral responsibility. Kohlberg was intrigued with Gilligan's assertion that there are different experiences of moral obligation and that the experience of obligation that arises out of the context of relatedness often carries with it a distinctive sense of urgency and responsibility (Higgins et al., 1984; Kohlberg, 1984).

Kohlberg sought to integrate Gilligan's notion of responsibility, which emphasized the relational context of decision making, with Blasi's conceptualization, which focused the integrity of the moral agent. Blasi's (1980) review of the judgment–action research literature and penetrating analysis of the judgment–action question has become a classic in our field. In that article, Blasi argued that moral deliberation involves a process in which individuals must decide not only what is right but also whether they should act in a particular situation. Blasi's argument for judgments of responsibility was so powerful that, in their reanalysis of key judgment–action studies in the moral development literature, Kohlberg and Candee (1984) introduced a distinction between deontic and responsibility judgments. Higgins, Kohlberg, and I made use of that distinction in analyzing data from the assessment of the effects of the just community approach (Power, Higgins, & Kohlberg, 1989). A passage from Blasi (1980) encapsulates the insight that led to this reconceptualization of the judgment–action relationship:

> Moral judgments, before leading to action, are at times processed through a second set of rules or criteria, the criteria of responsibility. The function of a responsibility judgment is to determine to what extent that which is morally good or right is also strictly necessary for the self. ... The criteria used to arrive at responsibility judgments are related to one's self-definition or the organization of the self. The transition from judgment of responsibility to action is supported by the tendency to self-consistency. (p. 35)

Those familiar with Kohlberg's later work will note that he incorporated Blasi's idea that responsibility judgments involve a second set of rules but that he did not follow through on Blasi's more important idea that responsibility judgments relate to self-definition or the organization of the self. Although Kohlberg (1984) quoted this passage, including the reference to the self, he did not elaborate on the role of the self as the agent of responsibility. Kohlberg emphasized the cognitive side of responsibility judgments by noting that moral and responsibility judgments were related such that the higher one's stage of moral judgment, the less likely one could rationally excuse one's inaction. Blasi did not deny the role of cognition but saw self-consistency as a significant factor leading individuals to act on their moral judgments.

THE SELF IN A DEMOCRATIC COMMUNITY

Democracy and Agency

Although not directly engaging Blasi on the role of the self in his research or theory, Kohlberg (Higgins, Power, & Kohlberg, 1984) implicitly evoked the self as a source of consistency in the just community intervention. At the cornerstone of the just community approach is the process of participatory democracy in which faculty and students make and enforce school rules and policies. The experience of making and enforcing rules offers students a powerful experience of agency, an experience noticeably lacking in most schools. Generally students are expected to follow rules made by teachers and administrators. Failure to comply results in disciplinary action almost always initiated by an adult in the school. One of the most difficult challenges in establishing a just community program is to convince students that they have power, that in some sense they have ownership of what goes on in their school. Getting students to act responsibly is easy by comparison. Once students realize that the deliberative process led to meaningful outcomes, they take the process very seriously. Although some students broke the rules that they played a part in making, the inconsistency troubled them. Students felt especially bound to follow the rules that they took part in making. Moreover, the democratic enforcement of rules led students to feel accountable for their infractions. It is one thing to be answerable to a teacher for breaking a rule that the teacher had made and another thing to be answerable to one's community for a rule that one participated in making. A further feature of the just community democracy is that the deliberative process was informed by a focus on morality. The teachers asked students to reflect on problems and solutions in moral terms, which had the effect of encouraging a sense of moral responsibility.

Collective Responsibility

The most distinctive feature of the just community approach was not the use of participatory democracy but the goal of becoming a moral community. By a moral community, I mean a group that shares a an explicit commitment to a common life characterized by norms embodying high moral ideals. Through the just community approach, we hoped to accomplish more than foster a sense of personal responsibility. We encouraged students to develop a sense of collective responsibility, which meant each member of the group shared responsibility for the group as a whole. We believed that developing a sense of collective responsibility would heighten students' sense of individual responsibility although we were aware of the possibility that the opposite could oc- cur. In a highly individualistic culture responsibilities shared by everyone can become the responsibility of no one or of a very few conscientious individuals. This loss of individual responsibility is, in my opinion, brought on by a misun- derstanding of what collective responsibility entails.

I illustrate these points with examples from the first just community school, Cluster. Shortly after the establishment of Cluster, there were several incidents of stealing. The students nonchalantly accepted the thefts as part of life in school. They took responsibility for the problem insofar as they made a rule prohibiting stealing and backed the rule up with a punishment that they hoped would be severe enough to deter future theft. One year later in response to a theft that occurred in the presence of several Cluster students, the teachers at Kohlberg's instigation asked students to go further and all chip in to restitute the victim of the theft. This solution challenged students' assumption that the thief was the only person who should be held accountable for the stealing. Some of the students grasped the teachers point and strongly argued for collec- tive restitution. A student, Phyllis, in a community-wide discussion of the inci- dent put it this way, "It's everyone's fault that she don't have no money. It was stolen because people just don't care about the community. ... Everybody should care that she got her money stolen" (Power et al., 1989, p. 113).

Phyllis advocated collective responsibility for two reasons. First, she be- lieved that if the thief was not identified, members of the community should care enough for the plight of the victim to make restitution. Second, she thought that the whole community deserved some of the blame for the stealing that occurred. She did not deny that the thief was primarily responsible, but in these and other remarks, she indicated that she felt that the group as a whole had not created an environment that strongly discouraged stealing.

Almost 2 years later, Cluster students debated whether all members of the community should have to chip in to make restitution for a floating dock that had been lost because of the disobedience and carelessness of a few students. The students who had untied the lost dock did not come forward and strongly supported a motion to distribute the cost of restitution evenly among the com- munity members. Some students strongly objected to the motion because they felt that the culprits were hiding behind the motion. The objectors felt that the motion for collective responsibility was being used as a cover-up. They amended the original motion to assign a greater burden of restitution to those who untied the dock if those directly responsible would come forward (which they later did). These examples show that the notions of collective and individ- ual responsibility can become mutually supportive and that sorting the two out in particular cases is a helpful way of encouraging students to reflect on their sense of agency in a group context.

Collective Norms: The Self and Community

As is clear from this discussion of collective responsibility, the just community approach and the research that we have been doing on it bring a social dimension to Blasi's (1991) focus on the subjective self. The self does not experience a sense of obligation or responsibility to act in isolation but with others within a cultural setting. The just community approach and the research that we conducted on it provide an entryway into future explorations of how culture and conscience interact. In the section that follows, I explain the way in which we appropriated Durkheim's (1973) collectivistic theory to help us to understand the influence of moral culture and specifically group norms. After focusing on collective theory, I speculate how Blasi's (1988) identity types might shed some new light on the ways in which individuals identify with a group as moral agents.

One of the primary goals of the just community approach was to develop through community meetings and others forms of democratic deliberation group norms that would express the core ideals of the community. When Kohlberg, Higgins, and I originally developed a method for assessing these norms, we found it helpful to classify them according to what we may think of as their *subject*, *object*, and *predicate*. The subject referred to who expressed the norm—the individual as an individual, the I, or the individual as a member of the group, the we. The object referred to those bound by the norm. The predicate referred to the action content of the norm—what was expected. We focused much of our attention in our early analysis of the data on the normative content. We noted that in most instances the normative content was a value-laden type of action. For example, a norm prohibiting stealing would likely include a valuing of individual property or, in a moral community, a valuing of trust. The normative content lent itself to a stage analysis of the way in which a norm was understood and justified.

Our challenge in coding groups norms was to determine the extent these norms were shared by the members of the group. Kohlberg's (1984) moral stage analysis focused on individual moral judgment. Given our theoretical assumptions about cognitive development, we did not know whether we should even attempt to categorize the value content of a group norm in terms of moral stage. Cognitive developmental theory led us to believe that individual representations of group norms would tend to reflect the moral stage of the individuals involved because individuals would have assimilated group norms into their own stage of moral judgment. For example, individuals reasoning at Stage 2 would likely describe the norm with a Stage 2 understanding; individuals at the Stage 3 would describe the norms with a Stage 3 understanding; and so forth. Any attempt to describe group norms that went beyond the simple content of the norm would appear to dissolve into the reasoning of the individuals upholding the norm. However, as Dukheim (1925/1973) so clearly perceived, groups exert an influence as groups that cannot be reduced to the sum of the individuals who comprise them.

We thought of group norms as a feature of the culture of the school that in turn was a part of the sociomoral environment. We did this with an awareness that regarding the group as having a collective mind or of reifying the group as a collective entity apart from the individuals who composed it is mistaken. Groups are, after all, composed of individuals. However, individuals do not operate in a social vacuum. They think and act as members of a society within a culture or more accurately within a plurality of cultures. Individuals are thus as much of an abstraction as groups.

Any serious student of moral development and moral education must grapple with Durkheim's sociological approach to morality, as Piaget and Kohlberg did. In fact, Piaget's (1932/1965) seminal treatment of moral psychology, *The Moral Judgment of the Child*, may profitably be regarded as a rejoinder to Durkheim (1925/1973). A superficial reading of *The Moral Judgment of the Child* suggests that Piaget simply treated Durkheim as a foil to frame his own cognitive developmental approach. Although Piaget strongly criticized Durkheim's moral philosophy for being insufficiently Kantian, his moral psychology for being insufficiently interactive, and his moral education for being authoritarian, Piaget appropriated Durkheim's major sociological insight that a group's authority structure plays a decisive role in children's moral development. Piaget advocated a democratic authority structure as a means of moral education because he believed that such a system fostered a morality of cooperation.

Although Durkheim's (1925/1973) approach to moral education is not without problems, it provides a correction to the highly individualistic approach to psychology and education so pervasive in contemporary culture. No other moral education theorist has a deeper appreciation of and insight into the life-giving energy of the group. I use the phrase "life-giving energy" to point to the affective side of Durkheim's approach to the collectivity. Durkheim regarded society not only as the source of moral norms and values but as the ground for individual flourishing. As can most clearly be seen in Durkheim's (1951) treatment of suicide, when individuals become uprooted from their society they wither and die. Durkheim was very much concerned about how the organic solidarity present in modern social life would sustain individuals' deep needs for social connection. He believed that individuals needed to participate in voluntary associations to experience the benefits of social solidarity. In *Moral Education* (Durkheim, 1925/1973) he proposed a method for transforming the classroom into a moral community that prepared children for membership in society. Durkheim described the school as a transitional institution that would help students move from membership in the personal family to membership the impersonal society. This view of school might suggest that schools were transitory as well as transitional and that schools served the sole function of preparing students to take their place in an impersonal social world. Yet, it is clear from *Moral Education* that he envisioned schools as preparing students for participation in smaller communities, which would play a vital role in mediating their relationship to the larger society. Schools, in other words, have two sociomoral tasks. First, they must prepare students for citizenship at both the national and even global levels. Second, they must prepare students to participate in voluntary associations, which provide tangible ways of exerting collective responsibility and experiencing belonging.

The kind of preparation that Durkheim believed that schools could offer was less informational than motivational. By that I mean that in his work about moral education, Durkheim gave little attention to the content of morality. He did not stipulate the particular rules and norms of the school or to the virtues that were to be inculcated in the child. Instead, Durkheim identified three elements of morality as constituting the ends of moral education: *discipline*, *altruism*, and *autonomy*. Discipline involves the cultivation of a sense of moral duty, altruism involves a willingness to sacrifice oneself out of devotion and attachment to something greater than the self, and autonomy involves a sense of rational self-direction.

Durkheim offered us a way to think about moral education as the cultivation of the self as a moral agent. The school, in his view, should present an environment that makes moral life tangible and engrossing. Durkheim appeared in part of his book to advocate a moral education for social conformity. Had Durkheim developed a truly Kantian approach to autonomy, his collectivist educational theory may have come much closer the just community approach. Durkheim (1925/1973) unfortunately defined autonomy as desiring to act "in agreement with the nature of things" (p. 115). He elaborated that the laws of society are no different from the laws of nature. Both are facts and "individual reason can no more be the lawmaker for the moral world than that of the physical world" (p. 116).

This very brief excursion into Durkheim's theory raises the question of whether the just community approach with its Durkheimian emphasis on building a strong group culture can, nevertheless, foster the development of the self as a moral agent. I attempt to respond to this question by examining the implications of participating in the building of shared norms for the self. Our primary interest in studying shared norms was to describe the moral atmosphere or what we later called the moral culture of the school. We did not in our earlier work (Power et al., 1989) examine the psychological side of group norms—that is, what it means for an individual to identify with a community so that she or he speaks for that community. From a sociomoral development perspective, speaking for the community involves a special kind of perspective taking—that is, taking the perspective of the group as a whole or the group as having a collective consciousness. From the perspective of the self, however, speaking for the group involves a special kind of identification with the group. This identification goes beyond the recognition of the self as a member of a group or even an awareness of the feeling of belonging to a group. This identification activates one's sense of responsibility for the group as whole. A careful analysis of the ways in which individuals speak on behalf of the group reveals both a sense of self as separate from the group and a sense of self that was chosen to collaborate with others in the group. For example, Phyllis's statement quoted earlier in this chapter told us something about Phyllis as an individual and Phyllis as a spokesperson for her community. Phyllis was aware of her position vis-à-vis others in the group.

Blasi's (1988) three identity types (identity observed, identity managed, and identity constructed) may be extrapolated to open up three nested ways in which individuals identify with a group by speaking on behalf of its norms. First, individuals simply recognize that they are members of the group and are obligated to abide by the norms and rules of the group. Second, individuals become more active speakers by advocating that group members adopt a norm or exhorting group members to uphold a norm. Third, the individuals can take legislative responsibility for constructing group norms. Such responsibility involves the exercise of autonomy and engages the autonomy of the other group members. The democratic process challenges the individual members of the group to appropriate (Blasi's term) within their sense of personal identity their membership in the community. This appropriation is rational and critical and is not a passive internalization of group norms and values. Moreover, the appropriation of membership in the community is to be based on the ideals of the community. In this sense the identification with the community not only allows for but encourages a critical stance toward its practices and commitment to change it.

MORAL SELF-WORTH

One of the anecdotal findings of our just community research was that the students reported feeling respected in a way that they had not felt before in school. As members of a democratic community, they believed that they were playing an important role in serving their school. They were encouraged to speak up in meetings, and they were thrilled that by and large their teachers and peers took them seriously. They reported that others listened to them and engaged their ideas. In conventional psychological terms, it would be reasonable to surmise that the just community experience fostered students' sense of self-esteem. However, we were not prepared to investigate self-esteem as an outcome of the just community experience. The relevance of moral concerns to judgments of self-esteem has long been assumed although seldom examined. Moral development and self-esteem research has proceeded along two divergent paths, which may be expected given their distinctive theoretical foundations and methods. Moral development research has focused on moral cognition and relied on semiclinical interviews to establish the framework of the moral stages. Self-esteem research has looked at positive and negative feelings of self-regard and used Likert-scale measures to assess these feelings. Unfortunately, those studying self-esteem have paid scant empirical attention to the role of moral considerations in self-evaluation. Moreover, with the exception of Harter (1988, 1998), they have not approached self-esteem developmentally. Judgments of self-esteem involve critical self-reflection. It is impossible to interpret the meaning of affective statements of self-worth without knowing the moral criteria that individuals use to inform their self-judgments or without knowing the self that is both the subject and object of self-judgment.

I became interested in studying self-esteem from a cognitive developmental perspective in the mid-1980s while leading a workshop on moral education to a group of school teachers. I asked the teachers to list what moral education ought to be teaching and then to prioritize the items on the list. The teachers came up with a long list of virtues and values. To my surprise, they unanimously put self-esteem at the top of the list. Their reasons for prioritizing self-esteem were similar to those in the literature. High self-esteem has been thought to have a causal or at least an enabling role in promoting morally responsible behavior (e.g., Mecca, Smelser, & Vasconcellos, 1989). Low self-esteem, however, has been thought to lead to deviant behavior as, for example, is predicted by Kaplan's (1975, 1980) esteem-enhancement model. Kaplan (1975) asserted that individuals with low self-esteem deliberately engage in antisocial behavior to win approval from deviant peers.

There is little if any empirical support for a causal relation between high self-esteem and prosocial behavior (Eisenberg, 1986; Kohn, 1994; Staub, 1986) or between low self-esteem and delinquency (e.g., Dishion, Andrews, & Crosby, 1995; McCarthy & Hoge, 1984; Wells & Rankin, 1983). In their review, Scheff, Ratzinger, and Ryan (1989) noted that correlational studies of the relation between self-esteem and crime and violence yield generally weak and inconsistent results. More intriguing are the findings reported by Oyserman and Markus (1990) that the most delinquent youth report the highest self-esteem.

From a theoretical viewpoint, it is not surprising that high self-esteem is compatible with delinquency if self-esteem simply represents feelings of positive self-regard without taking into account the sources of those feelings. Such feelings may well be empowering; that is, they may encourage individuals to act on their beliefs, and the absence of such feelings may lead to resignation and passivity. Yet, if feelings of self-regard are in and of themselves morally neutral, why should they be expected to be positively related to moral behavior?

Most theorists have, however, thought of self-esteem as based (at least in part) on a moral foundation. For example, Schwalbe and Staples (1991) defined self-esteem as "a positive affective response to the self deriving from beliefs that one is competent and moral" (p. 159). Coopersmith (1967), and Harter (1983) identified moral self-approval or virtue as a basic source of self-esteem. The inclusion of moral self-approval or integrity as a dimension in theoretical self-esteem constructs has not, however, led to any systematic exploration of how moral self-approval comes about or how moral self-approval compares with other sources of self-esteem, such as achieving one's goals at school or work.

How is self-esteem related to morality? Approval from others is an important source of self-esteem. If morality is understood as embodied in the norms and values of a particular society, as the mainstream of social scientists have maintained (cf. Turiel, 1998), then the link between morality and social approval is obvious. Yet, individuals like Socrates and Martin Luther King, whom we regard as highly moral people, have incurred significant social disapproval from criticizing the conventional morality. Moreover, from the philosophical perspective that informed the moral psychological research of Piaget, Kohlberg, and Blasi, judging for oneself, that is judging autonomously, is necessary if not sufficient for being a fully developed moral person. Becoming morally autonomous entails distancing oneself from the expectations of others so that one acts according to one's own sense of what is right. Kohlberg (1984) maintained that achieving full moral autonomy requires a "prior-to-society-perspective"—that is, a perspective not based on the standards of a particular society but on the principles that ought to be at the basis of any society. My point is simply that although conforming to societal expectations does bring social approval, becoming a moral person is not the same as becoming a compliant person (even if most moral expectations are conventionally expected). If moral self-worth can be experienced even when one takes an unpopular moral stand, then we need to look further than social approval for the source of moral self-worth.

A more promising approach to understanding moral self-worth is to view moral self-worth as arising from the perception of oneself as morally competent. This approach is derived from William James' (1892/1985) classic understanding of self-esteem as the ratio of successes to one's pretensions. It has been empirically refined and tested by Harter (1988), who found it very fruitful. Harter (1986) showed that children's global estimations of their self-worth are not directly dependent on their perception of domain-specific competencies but vary in relation to the extent to which they perceive themselves to be competent in areas that they deem important. Children and adults with high self-esteem do not necessarily have to be very successful across all domains, as long as they manage to discount the importance of domains in which they are not successful. If morality may be understood as a particular area of competence, like any other area of competence, then it would appear that individuals would discount the significance that they attach to the moral domain as they would to any other domain in which they were experiencing failure.

If moral duties are unique, then discounting moral goals may pose a problem. Kant (1956/1788) claimed that moral duties are categorical imperatives that bind no matter what difficulties one may experience in upholding them. The discounting schema applies to what Kant would call hypothetical imperatives, which take the form if you want to attain Goal X, then you must do Y. Goal X may be getting all As in school or maintaining a certain scoring average on one's basketball team. These goals represent praiseworthy but not obligatory ends. Individuals can strive for other goals or adjust the goals that they are striving for to make them more attainable. Yet, most moral goals seem resistant to such adjustments by their very nature.

My colleagues and I (Makogon, Power, & Khmelkov, 2003) did a study of discounting in which we presented scenarios that involved repeated failure to meet a goal. The scenarios involved nonmoral achievement goals in school, sports, and peer relationships (popularity) and a moral goal (not teasing one's sibling). The respondents' willingness to discount and complexity of discounting strategy increased with developmental level in all of the scenarios with the exception of the one involving the moral goal. On that scenario, with few exceptions at any developmental level, the respondents simply did not discount. This finding lends empirical support to the philosophical claim that the moral domain is unique.

I believe, however, that discounting is morally permissible and even advisable with respect to certain kinds of moral goals. We may, for example, feel obligated to share our wealth with the poor but may discount the extent to what we share according to our capacity to give. Certain benevolent moral aspirations can be adjusted to suit individual circumstances without violating the strict demands of justice. We have yet to explore how individuals wrestle with the enormity of human suffering and injustice. I suspect, however, that the discounting that may take place in this moral domain operates differently than it does in the nonmoral domains. It is difficult to feel that one has done all what one can in a world with such great need.

The moral domain is unique not only because its demands are not easily set side but also because its demands seem from a philosophical view to have priority over nonmoral demands. If moral demands have preeminence in the way in which we should structure our lives, should not moral criteria weigh heavily in one's self-evaluation? Blasi (1993) maintained that, properly understood, the moral domain has a unique relationship to the self. He wrote, "The only hope of grounding morality on the essential self without losing morality's reason is to hypothesize that the self's very identity is constructed, at least in part, under the influence of moral reasons" (p. 139). Although Blasi did not develop a theory of self-esteem or address self-esteem in any systematic way, his appreciation of moral rationality and of identity development suggests some ways of pursuing self-esteem that would be at least congenial with his overall approach to the self. Blasi would be quick to point out that my emphasis on the moral dimension of self-esteem should be tempered by an acknowledgment that self-esteem can be built on other bases, that morality is but one of many human concerns. In a study of identity with adult women, Blasi (1993) found that a substantial proportion did not locate moral ideals at the core of their identity. Similarly, in a study of the adolescent self, Arnold (1993) found that individuals vary considerably in the extent to which they identify with moral values and that most see moral qualities as only moderately important. Our research on the ideal self from childhood through adolescence (Power, Khmelkov & Power, 1997) supports Blasi and Arnold's results. Individuals at all ages vary in the extent to which they make explicit reference to moral concerns in describing the selves that they aspire to become.

If moral characteristics only make up a part of the identity and for many individuals may not even be heart of their identity, we legitimately question whether should they have a special place in a psychological theory of the self. Although Blasi conceded that the self and identity may not, in fact, be influenced by moral considerations, he questioned whether the self and identity should be influenced by them. It may appear that in raising this question Blasi has left psychology for philosophy, but I do not think so. Morality, properly understood, means at the very least to serve the regulative function of steering the self away from actions that would lead to harm or injustice. Piaget noted that morality is a social logic that establishes ideals of reciprocity. It is, of course, possible to be illogical in one's relationships with others as well as in one's thinking. There is a rational press, nevertheless, both at the level of the self and of society to be moral. I suspect that individuals may be more moral than the aforementioned studies indicate.

The preceding discussion of the place of moral concerns in the constitution of the self and in the way in which we value ourselves raises the difficult question of the nature and function of self-esteem judgments. According to Blasi's approach to the self, judgments of self-esteem are judgments about the objective or the "me-self." Generally, we are not aware of our self-esteem as an object of our consciousness. We may, however, experience self-esteem as coloring or providing an emotional tone to our experience. Self-esteem is psychologically relevant because it appears to influence our sense of agency in addition to our sense of well-being. High self-esteem is presumed related to a sense of competence (e.g., Dweck & Leggett, 1988; Nicholls, 1978) and effectiveness (e.g., Bandura, 1994; Shunk, 1994) and low self-esteem the opposite.

The line of argument that I am sketching leads to a view of self-esteem that is intimately tied to a sense of agency. The consciousness of one's self-esteem may thus arise when one's sense of agency is thwarted or undermined. The ways in which individuals attempt to cope with failure offer us an opening into the ways in which individuals are conscious of their self- worth and seek to maintain it. Up to this point, I treated self-worth as earned either by winning approval from others or by meeting expectations for success in domains that one deems important. Yet, self-respect may not depend entirely on merit; it may well be grounded in an awareness of unconditional self-worth or self-acceptance (cf. Maslow, 1968; Rogers, 1961). A conscious awareness of intrinsic self-worth serves to protect the ego in times of failure—that is, when one's earned sense of self-esteem has come under assault. We use the term *intrinsic self-worth* to refer to this sense of self as having fundamental value simply because of one's humanity or personhood. Moral developmental theory (Kohlberg, 1985) suggests that an understanding of intrinsic worth of one's self develops as part of a recognition of the worth of all human beings. Within the moral judgment coding scheme (Colby et al., 1987), a valuing of human life apart from external or instrumental considerations does not appear until the third stage of moral development (Criterion Judgment No. 9, p. 20). This understanding of the inherent value of human life continues to develop through the later stages. Although a concern for intrinsic self-worth develops in the context of making decisions about the rights and welfare of others, we have yet discovered when such a concern appears in the context of self-evaluation. Some preliminary research that my colleagues and I have conducted (Power, Khmelkov, & Power, 2003) indicates that it appears no earlier than the third stage of moral judgment in early adolescence.

Although a conscious awareness of one's intrinsic self-worth may not appear until early adolescence if ever, I believe that the awareness of self-worth is implicit in all conscious action. In making this claim, I am simply extending Blasi's (1991) notion of the subjective self. The Thomistic philosopher Bernard Lonergan (1958) made the very simple but penetrating observation that all acts of human knowing and doing presuppose not only an I, the agent of knowing, but an I that underlies the unity of consciousness without which human cognition and would be impossible. Lonergan went further to note that the self is "affirmed" in such acts as a "contingent fact," which "is established not prior to our engagement in knowing and doing but simultaneously with it" (p. 332). Does the contingent fact of one's existence as a self imply that one has worth simply by virtue of one's being? Although one may answer this question in various religious and philosophical ways, the psychological experience of the self as an object does not necessarily entail a sense of the self as worthwhile. However, there is at least a tacit affirmation of self-worth in the experience of the self as subject, even when questioning one's self-worth.

I maintain that all of our conscious actions proceed from an implicit sense of meaning and worth. We act not only because we believe activities are worthwhile but because we believe our activities are worthwhile. We affirm ourselves and our worth in every conscious action. In the course of human experience, however, we experience rejection and futility. Our actions often do not bear the fruit we intend and at times undermine our very purposes. Moreover, especially in the moral domain, our actions seem so insignificant in the face of institutionalized injustice. The morally sensitive individual is perhaps the most likely of all to experience a sense of futility and lack of worth.

It is perhaps for this reason that so many of our moral leaders, such as Martin Luther King, and exemplars (Colby & Damon, 1992) have pursued their moral lives in community. Community offers a sense of belonging, which reaffirms the worth of all the members. Perhaps the greatest contribution of the just community approach was to provide adolescents with a sense that who they were and what they did together mattered. The teachers who told me to pay attention to the role of self-esteem in moral education were right. Not only children but all of us need the affirmation that ultimately comes from love. We must understand, however, that love does not confer or manufacture self-worth; it acknowledges the worth that is there. This original worth is given in our very existence; it comes with our very being. Some would say it is a gift of creative love.

REFERENCES

Arnold, M. L. (1993). *The place of morality in the adolescent self.* Unpublished doctoral dissertation, Harvard University.
Bandura, A. (1994). *Self-efficacy: The exercise of control.* New York: Freeman.

Blasi, A. (1980). Bridging moral cognition and moral action: A critical review of the literature. *Psychological Bulletin,* 88, 1–45.

Blasi, A. (1984). Moral identity: Its role in moral functioning. In W. M. Kurtines & J. L. Gewirtz (Eds.), *Morality, moral behavior, and moral development* (pp. 128–139). New York: Wiley.

Blasi, A. (1988). Identity and the development of the self. In D. K. Lapsley & F. C. Power (Eds.), *Self, ego, and identity: Integrative approaches* (pp. 226–242) New York: Springer–Verlag.

Blasi, A. (1991). The development of the sense of self in adolescence. *Journal of Personality, 59*(2), 217–242.

Blasi, A. (1993). The development of identity: Some implications for moral functioning. In G. G. Noam & T. E. Wren (Eds.), *The moral self* (pp. 99–122). Cambridge, MA: MIT Press.

Colby, A., & Damon, W. (1992). *Some do care: Contemporary lives of moral commitment.* New York: The Free Press.

Colby, A., Kohlberg, L., Speicher, B., Hewer, A., Candee, D., Gibbs, J., & Power, C. (1987). *The measurement of moral judgment: Vol. 1. Theoretical foundations and research validation.* New York: Cambridge University Press.

Coopersmith, S. (1967). *The antecedents of self-esteem.* San Francisco: Freeman.

Dishion, T. J., Andrews, D. W., & Crosby, L. (1995). Antisocial boys and their friends in early adolescence: Relationship characteristics, quality, and interactional processes. *Child Development, 66,* 139–151.

Durkheim, E. (1951). *Suicide, a study in sociology.* Glencoe, IL: The Free Press.

Durkheim, E. (1973). *Moral education: A study in the theory and application of the sociology of education.* New York: The Free Press. (Original work published 1925)

Dweck, C. S., & Leggett, E. (1988). A social–cognitive approach to motivation and personality. *Psychological Review, 95,* 256–273.

Eisenberg, N. (1986). *Altruistic emotion, cognition, and behavior.* Hillsdale, NJ: Lawrence Erlbaum Associates.

Gilligan, C. (1977). *In a different voice: Psychological theory and women's development.* Cambridge, MA: Harvard University Press.

Gilligan, C. (1977). In a different voice: Women's conceptions of the self and of morality. *Harvard Educational Review 47,* 481–517.

Harter, S. (1983). Developmental perspectives on the self-system. In M. Hetherington (Ed.), *Handbook of child psychology* (Vol. 4, pp. 275–385). New York: Wiley.

Harter, S. (1986). Processes underlying the construction, maintenance, and enhancement of the self-concept in children. In S. Suls & A. Greenwald (Eds.), *Psychological perspectives on the self* (Vol. 3, pp. 137–181). Hillsdale, NJ: Lawrence Erlbaum Associates.

Harter, S. (1988). The construction and conservation of the self: James and Cooley revisited. In D. K. Lapsley & F. C. Power (Eds.), *Self, ego, and identity: Integrated approaches.* New York: Springer-Verlag.

Harter, S. (1998). The development of self-representations. In W. Damon & N. Eisenberg (Eds.), *Handbook of child psychology, Vol. 3: Social, emotional, and personality development* (pp. 553–617). New York: Wiley.

Higgins, A., Power, C., & Kohlberg, L. (1984). The relationship of moral atmosphere to judgments of responsibility. In W. M. Kurtines & J. L. Gewirtz (Eds.), *Morality, moral behavior, and moral development* (pp. 74–108). New York: Wiley.

James, W. (1985). *Psychology: The briefer course*. Notre Dame, IN: University of Notre Dame Press. (Original work published 1892).

Kant, I. (1956). *Critique of practical reason*. Indianapolis, IN: Bobbs-Merrill. (Original work published 1788)

Kaplan, H. B. (1975). *Self attitudes and deviant behavior*. Pacific Palisades, CA: Goodyear.

Kaplan, H. B. (1980). *Deviant behavior in defense of self*. New York: Academic Press.

Kohlberg, L. (1984). *Essays on moral development: Vol. 2. The psychology of moral development*. San Francisco: Harper & Row.

Kohlberg, L. & Candee, D. (1984). The relationship of moral judgement to moral action. In W. M. Kurtines & J. L. Gewirtz (Eds.), *Morality, moral behavior, and moral development* (pp. 52–73). New York: Wiley.

Kohn, A. (1994, December). The truth about self-esteem. *Phi Delta Kappan, 76*, 272–283.

Lonergan, B. J. F. (1958). *Insight: A study of human understanding*. London: Longmans, Green.

Lonergan, B. J. F. (1964). Cognitional structure. *Continuum, 2*, 530–541.

Makogon, T., Power, F. C., & Khmelkov, V. T. (2003), *Coping with moral failure: A study of moral self-worth*. Manuscript in preparation.

Maslow, A. H. (1968). *Toward a psychology of being*. New York: Van Nostrand Reinhold.

McCarthy, G. D., & Hoge, D. R. (1984). The dynamics of self-esteem and delinquency. *American Journal of Sociology, 90*, 396–410.

Mecca, A. M., Smelser, N. J., & Vasconcellos, J. (1989). *The social importance of self-esteem*. Berkeley: University of California Press.

Nicholls, J. G. (1978). The development of the concepts of effort and ability, perceptions of academic attainment, and the understanding that difficult tasks require more ability. *Child Development, 4*, 800–814.

Nisan, M. (1985), Limited morality: A concept and its educational implications. In M. Berkowitz & F. Oser (Eds.), *Moral education: Theory and application* (pp. 219–240). Hillsdale, NJ: Lawrence Erlbaum Associates.

Nucci, L. (1982). Conceptual development in the moral and conventional domains: Implications for values education. *Review of Educational Research, 52*, 93–122.

Owens, T. J. (1994). Two dimensions of self-esteem: Reciprocal effects of positive self-worth and self-deprecation on adolescent problems. *American Sociological Review, 59*, 391–407.

Oyserman, D., & Markus, H. R. (1990). Possible selves and delinquency. *Journal of Personality and Social Psychology, 59*, 112–125.

Piaget, J. (1965). *The moral judgment of the child*. New York: The Free Press. (Original work published 1932)

Power, F. C., Khmelkov, V. T., & Power, A. M. R. (2001). The moral basis of self-esteem: A cognitive developmental approach. Unpublished manuscript, University of Notre Dame.

Power, F. C. (1976). Cognition and action in moral development. Unpublished manuscript, Harvard University.

Power, F. C., Higgins, A., & Kohlberg, L. (1989). *Lawrence Kohlberg's approach to moral education*. New York: Columbia University Press.

Rawls, J. (1971). *A theory of justice*. Cambridge, MA: Harvard University Press.

Rogers, C. (1961). On becoming a person: A therapist's view of psychotherapy. Boston, MA: Houghton Mifflin.

Rosenberg, M. (1965). *Society and the adolescent self-image.* Princeton, NJ: Princeton University Press.

Rosenberg, M. (1979). *Conceiving the self.* New York: Basic Books.

Rosenberg, M., Schooler, C., & Schoenbach, C. (1989). Self-esteem and adolescent problems: Modeling reciprocal effects. *American Sociological Review, 54,* 1004–1018.

Ruble, D. N. (1983). The development of social comparison processes and their role in achievement-related self-socialization. In E. T. Higgins, D. N. Ruble, & W. Hartup (Eds.), *Social cognition and social development: A socio-cultural perspective* (pp. 134–157). New York: Cambridge University Press.

Ruble, D. N. & Rholes, W. S. (1981). The development of children's perceptions and attributions about their social world. In J. D. Harvey, W. Ickes, & R. F. Kidd (Eds.), *New directions in attribution research* (Vol. 3, pp. 3–36). Hillsdale, NJ: Lawrence Erlbaum Associates.

Scheff, T. G., Ratzinger, S. M., Ryan, M. T. (1989). Crime, violence, and self-esteem: Review and proposals. In A. M. Mecca, N. J. Smelser, & J. Vasconcellos (Eds.), *The social importance of self-esteem.* Berkeley: University of California Press, 165–199.

Schwalbe, M. L., & Staples, C. L. (1991). Gender differences in sources of self-esteem. *Social Psychology Quarterly, 54,* 158–168.

Shunk, D. H. (1994). Self-regulation of self-efficacy during self-regulated learning. *Educational Psychologist, 26,* 207–231.

Staub, I. (1986). Altruism and aggression. In C. Zahn-Waxler, E. M. Cummings, & R. Ianotti (Eds.), *Altruism and aggression: Biological and social origins.* Cambridge, England: Cambridge University Press.

Strauman, T. J., & Higgins, T. E. (1987). Automatic activation of self-discrepancies and emotional syndromes: When cognitive structures influence affect. *Journal of Personality and Social Psychology 53*(6), 1004–1014.

Turiel, E. (1983). *The development of social knowledge, morality, and convention.* New York: Cambridge University Press.

Turiel, E. (1998). The development of morality. In W. Damon & N. Eisenberg (Eds.), *Handbook of child psychology, Fifth Edition: Vol. 3: Social, emotional, and personality development* (pp. 863–932). New York: Wiley.

Wells, L. E. & Rankin, G. H. (1983). Self-concept as a mediating factor in delinquency. *Social Psychology Quarterly, 46,* 11–22.

Wylie, R. C. (1974). *The self-concept: A review of methodological considerations and measuring instruments* (Vol. 1). Lincoln: University of Nebraska Press.

Zigler, E., Balla, D., & Watson, N. (1972). Developmental and experimental determinants of self-image disparity in institutionalized and non-institutionalized retarded and normal children. *Journal of Personality and Social Psychology, 23,* 81–87.

4

Moral Identity Development and School Attachment

Robert Atkins
Temple University

Daniel Hart
Rutgers University

Thomas M. Donnelly
Rutgers University

Schools have come under increasing scrutiny in recent years. In the United States, the focus has largely been on the perceived failings of urban schools in serving poor children. A host of remedies have been proposed, including charter schools, school reorganization, vouchers permitting children in failing public schools to attend private academies, tougher standards, and so on. The premise of much public debate is that schools develop skills that are essential for economic success. Consequently, schools that do not foster this expertise in children are failing in their responsibilities. No doubt the collection of skills valued in the workplace must be transmitted to youth, and the failure to do so cripples the financial life prospects of many youth in urban areas (see Jencks & Phillips, 1998, for a discussion).

What is often overlooked in the current debate is that schools have profound influences on social development as well as on academic achievement. Indeed, if the justification for a compulsory education system in the country is the preparation of youth for participation in a democratic society—as the decision by the U.S. Supreme Court in *Wisconsin v. Yoder* (1972) suggests—then the effects of schools on those facets of social development essential to citizenship are important to consider. In this chapter, we examine the influence of schools on the development of one of these facets, moral identity.

We have three goals. First, we review a model of moral identity that empha- sizes the importance of social resources. Second, we explore select compo- nents of our model of moral identity formation by focusing on the role of schools in fostering the development of moral identities in youth. Third, we present analyses from our ongoing work with a national data set to estimate the influences of schools on facets of moral identity development.

A MODEL OF MORAL IDENTITY FORMATION

Moral identity connotes a commitment consistent with one's sense of self to lines of action that support or protect the welfare of others. The development of moral identity has value for the community and the individual. The model in Fig. 4.1, based on our research and the research of others, represents the nature of and the process by which one constructs moral identity.

According to the model, moral identity emerges most directly from moral judgment, self-understanding, and social opportunities. In our view, enduring commitments to action on behalf of the welfare of others usually rest on the ap- praisal that the action has moral worth. Moral appraisals are often indicated in experience by their prescriptiveness (the sense that one ought to act in accor- dance with a judgment) and their perceived universality (all share a similar ob- ligation). For example, Martin Luther King Jr.'s commitment to the civil rights movement reflected his judgment that he was obligated to join the struggle (prescriptiveness), as should all Americans (universality), to ensure that Blacks receive the same opportunities as Whites. The moral judgments that undergird moral identity need not be fully elaborated ethical perspectives of the sorts found by philosophers; indeed, studies of moral commitment gener- ally suggest that judgments of exemplars are generally no more sophisticated than those of others (Colby & Damon, 1992). However, like Blasi (1999), we believe that genuinely moral action cannot derive from wholly automatic af- fective processes and must include to some degree reflective consideration of information and lines of action.

Moral identity also requires alignment of the self with moral goals. An actor must be prepared to judge the self to be successful when acting morally and to feel guilt when it is not. To play this role in self-evaluation, moral standards and moral goals must be salient in self-reflection, and constitute an ideal to-

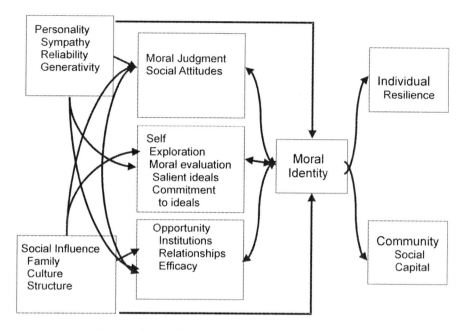

FIG. 4.1.   Model of moral identity formation.

ward which the self strives. In their study of adolescents, Hart and Fegley (1995) found that the ideal selves of morally exemplary youth were moral in content and closely linked to their views of themselves in daily life.

Finally, in our model, moral identity emerges from the opportunities offered by social relationships and institutions to observe, experiment with, and receive support for the enactment of moral action. Oftentimes those with well-developed moral identities are contrasted with members of the general public, focusing on the formers' ability to pursue moral goals that are inconsistent with the societal norms judged to orient the latters' actions. For example, we think of Ghandi's rejection of materialist values of many of his countrymen in order to pursue his goals for civil justice. While it is certainly true that moral identities can sustain moral behavior in social contexts that do not support such behavior, this does not mean that moral identities are *formed* independent of social contexts. Indeed, virtually all biographies of morally exemplary individuals document the role of particular relationships and specific institutions on moral commitment.

Moral judgment, the self, and social context, the constituents of moral identity (as already outlined), are rooted in personality and stable configurations of social influence. Decades of research (reviewed in Hart, Burock, London, & Miraglia, 2003) has demonstrated that children with positive dispositions and the capacity to regulate their emotions are better prepared to make moral judgments and to be successful in social relationships (e.g., Hart, Hoffmann, & Edelstein, 1997). However, although certain personality profiles may facilitate the development of moral identity, they are not necessary. Persons with well-developed moral identities do not share any single profile of personality dispositions (Krueger, Hicks, & McGue, 2001).

Finally, one's location in the enduring social structure characterizing a society has profound and often underappreciated effects on the development of moral identity. In the United States, for example, social class and race have enormous influence on development. In our previous work (Hart & Atkins, 2002; Hart, Atkins, & Ford, 1998) we demonstrated that poor urban children in the United States have far less access to the social opportunities that foster the development of moral identity. We return to this issue in a later section of this chapter.

THE LIFE OF NELSON MANDELA AS AN ILLUSTRATION OF MORAL IDENTITY DEVELOPMENT

Nelson Mandela's life exemplifies moral identity formation as we have just described it. Nothing in Mandela's early life in the rural areas of South African tending cattle foreshadowed his emergence as one of the 20th century's greatest statesmen. There is little to suggest that his temperament profile in childhood prepared him especially well to lead the fight against apartheid; nor did his location in the social structure of rural South Africa afford him unique opportunities to develop leadership skills.

However, the death of his father, at nine years of age, resulted in Mandela leaving the countryside to live with an influential uncle, a change in social influence that ultimately transformed his life course and the development of South Africa. Because of his uncle's prominence, Mandela received a level of education well beyond that of most Black South Africans (and most White South Africans) at the time. Mandela's (1994) autobiography makes clear that the skills learned in school prepared the way for economic success (relative to what was possible for Black South Africans of the time). More important, his experience in school prepared Mandela to make moral judgments, to explore moral action, and to experience himself as an effective agent in the pursuit of justice. In describing his experience following one conflict with his school's hierarchy, Mandela (1994) wrote, "This was one of my first battles with authority, and I felt the sense of power that comes from having right and justice on one's side" (p. 46). This sentiment is typical of the incidents occurring in schools in which he explored issues of justice, fairness, and democratic functioning, and observed the consequences of classmates' and his own actions in pursuit of justice.

Through adolescence and early adulthood, Mandela built on his experiences in school and sought out organizations in which the implications of his moral judgments for action could be tested. There seems to have been no lightening bolt of self-insight or single moral decision or social influence that created Mandela's moral identity. As Mandela noted in his autobiography, "I cannot pinpoint a moment when I became politicized, when I knew that I would spend my life in the liberation struggle. There was no particular day on which I said, 'From henceforth I will devote myself to the liberation of my people'; instead, I simply found myself doing so, and could not do otherwise" (p. 95). Yet, over time, and in the contexts of relationships and institutions that provided opportunity, Mandela's moral judgments and sense of self were forged into a powerful moral identity. This moral identity enabled Mandela to endure many hardships, including more than 20 years of imprisonment, in his campaign to free South Africa of the apartheid system.

ROLE OF SCHOOLS IN DEVELOPING MORAL IDENTITIES

Mandela's growth into a leader of courage and dignity as just described suggests that moral identity has its origins in many forms of social influence. As Fig. 4.1 suggests, families are important in the development of moral identities, partly because families determine what niche children occupy in the social structure of western societies, and partly because parents exert direct influence on the development of personality characteristics and moral judgment that also underlie moral identity (e.g. Greenberger & Goldberg, 1989; Grusec, 1991; Halberstadt, 1986).

Although the influence of families on moral development is generally recognized (indeed the general public probably accords more influence to parents on the moral development of their children than is warranted by a careful reading of the research literature), other relationships and social institutions play crucial roles in moral identity formation. In this chapter, we are particularly interested in the effects of schools on the formation of moral identity. In our sketch of Mandela, we suggested that for him school provided an opportunity to explore himself and moral judgments and to synthesize these into a moral identity. Since at least Plato's discussion in The Republic on the sculpting of moral virtue through special academies for those destined to rule, philosophers and psychologists have acknowledged the roles of schools in promoting ethical development. In terms of our model depicted in Fig. 4.1, schools are institutions that can provide crucially important opportunities for the development of moral identity. Schools can have this influence on children and youth for four reasons: time, relationships with adults, action exploration, and moral atmosphere. We describe each of these below.

Time in School

In Western societies, children spend large portions of their lives in school. In the United States, for example, children are expected to attend school for 6 or more hours per day for approximately half the days in each year, for every year from age 6 to age 18. While at school, children are fully involved in a social institution with adults and children whose complex interactions are subject to and reflective of a system of rules that is supposed to reflect ethical and moral values. Most children spend more time in school then they do interacting with their parents or attending religious instruction; it would be surprising if schools did not influence moral development given how much time children spend in the educational environment.

Interaction With Nurturing Adults

Children who have caring, concerned adults involved in their lives have better life prospects (Furstenberg, 1993; Turner, 1991). As children develop and mature, the role of nonparent adults—like coaches, scout leaders, and teachers—increases. In fact, as children become adolescents over 25% of their social support network is comprised of nonparental adults (Blyth, Hill, & Theil, 1982). For many youth, school personnel—teachers, school nurses, and guidance counselors—provide social support. Indeed, a number of studies have emphasized the role school personnel play in promoting healthy development in the lives of children. For example, in their ground-breaking study of all children born on the island of Kauai in 1955, Werner and Smith (1989) found that, "Among the most frequently encountered positive role models in the lives of [these] children, outside of the family circle, was a favorite teacher. For the resilient youngster a special teacher was not just an instructor for academic skills, but also a confidante and positive model for personal identification'"(p. 162). Adolescents may benefit especially from good relationships with teachers, because adolescents are often reluctant to discuss many issues with their parents and turn to others for emotional guidance (Hendry, Roberts, Glendinning, & Coleman, 1992).

In addition to nurturing students emotionally, there is evidence to support the proposition that school personnel, as well as other non-familial adults, affect moral identity development in at least two other ways. First, school personnel can model prosocial community standards and behavior.

Second, school personnel can assist youth in developing prosocial self-images through the provision of internal attributions (Eisenberg & Fabes, 1998). For example, a teacher who observes a student helping a peer with homework might remark to the helper, "I really appreciate having someone in the class that likes to help people like yourself." Remarks like these can assist the youth in the development of a self-image that supports prosocial behavior. As Lapsley (1996) put it, "the attributions are now part of one's self concept, and people are motivated to behave in self-consistent ways" (p. 172).

Opportunities for Enactment of Moral Behaviors

As we suggested in the discussion of Nelson Mandela, fundamentally important for the emergence of moral identity is the opportunity to explore lines of moral action. In some of our previous work (Hart, Atkins, & Ford, 1998) we demonstrated that voluntary organizations such as teams and clubs are very important in facilitating exploration of one type of moral action, community service. We found that adolescents who were involved in clubs and teams were much more likely to volunteer for community service than were adolescents without such attachments, and the effects of club or team membership on volunteering was independent of personality, academic achievement, and family demographics.

Schools can provide the same sorts of opportunities to students to explore lines of moral action that advance moral identities. Students need opportunities to take moral actions to develop an interest in future moral action. Schools can give them that first push toward acting prosocially (Eisenberg & Fabes, 1998). By identifying needs in the community (i.e., community clean up in the park) and organizing students' talents and energy to contribute to meeting those needs, the youth and the community benefit. Adolescents who contribute to their communities through voluntary service are less concerned with self-interest and more interested in the common good (Johnson, Beebe, Mortimer, & Snyder, 1998).

Moral Environment of the School

As we have suggested thus far, the importance of school in society extends well beyond simply providing training in verbal and math skills to children and youth. Like other social institutions, such as the family and church, schools contribute to the psychosocial development of children. The schools' role in fostering citizenship—one critical facet of moral identity—is an important one, and most school curriculums include content on civics and government. In addition to the elementary lessons of citizenship, schools also provide lessons in being part of a democracy (Kamens, 1988). Schools allow children to experience being a part of a community beyond their family, relating with their peers as equals and settling differences civilly (Flanagan, Bowes, Jonsson, Csapo, & Shlebanova, 1998).

In addition to the school's role in introducing youth in the civic and democratic norms of society, schools have a role in teaching justice. Lapsley (1996) described the role of schools in providing a just educational environment: "Hence, if one is going to 'teach justice,' one must also examine how authority is used, how decisions are made, how conflicts are resolved, and how responsibility is taken or shirked within the context of the school as a whole. Justice must pervade the entire context in which the teaching and learning of justice is to take place" (p. 87). As Lapsley suggested, schools have the potential to establish moral surroundings where students develop skills in perspective taking and fairness. These lessons are critical in moral identity formation.

Schools are likely to affect the development of all children, but they may have more influence on some children than on others. In recent years, a number of social scientists and social critics have suggested that the school atmosphere may be a particularly potent contributor to the failure and success for children growing up in high-poverty, urban environments (Garbarino, Dubrow, Kostelny, & Pardo, 1992). As Garmezy (1991) put it, "Given the incredible stresses in urban families and communities, for many children the inner-city school is a refuge. School serves as a protective shield to help children withstand the multiple vicissitudes that they can expect of a stressful world" (p. 427).

The possibility we consider in our analyses is that perceptions of the school atmosphere as just and compassionate may be particularly important for children living in impoverished, urban environments. Children in these environments are more likely to be a minority and are exposed to more discrimination than their minority counterparts in less urban and less impoverished communities in the United States (Hart & Atkins, 2002). The result of this discrimination is evident in poverty rates, educational achievement, infant mortality rates, household income, and so on. For these children and youth, the treatment they receive in school—the civic institutions in which they spend much of their lives—may be particularly important in shaping their judgments about whether discrimination and injustice are only one facet of American life or are instead woven into the fabric of the United States. A good school, one that exemplifies the qualities that Lapsley (1996) described in the excerpt presented earlier, can demonstrate that civic institutions can be run according to principles of justice. The hypothesis that we consider is that such an experience may be most influential for children in low-income, urban communities.

Summary

As depicted in our model of moral identity formation, moral identity arises in part from social relationships and social institutions. Children and youth spend much of their lives in one institution, the school. Schools provide opportunities for (and hazards to) moral identity development. Relationships with nonparental adults can support development; schools are contexts in which to explore moral action; and the moral atmosphere of the school can support the synthesis of moral judgment, self, and moral action.

AN EMPIRICAL EXAMPLE OF SCHOOL INFLUENCE

How much do schools affect the course of moral identity development? Framed differently, can schools make an important contribution to the moral development of the youth that they serve? In this section, we provide one illustration of the potency of school influence on moral identity development. Several caveats should be offered at this point. First, answering fully the questions with which we began this section would require an experimental study in which students were randomly assigned to a variety of different types of schools (and some youth would need to be assigned to a no-school condition!). Because this kind of study cannot ethically be done, we base estimates of school effects on a large survey study and rely on statistical controls for preexisting differences among students. Second, our index of moral identity—voluntary participation in community servicec—captures only facets of our theoretical notion. Although it is likely both that an adolescent who is volunteering for community service is doing so to benefit others, and has moral judgments and self-conceptions consistent with this action, surely there are many adolescents whose voluntary community service has other sources (e.g., to improve a college application). This means that a marker of moral identity that is a probabilistic indicator of moral identity, rather than a direct measure of it, flaws our estimates of school influence.

To provide an estimate of the influence of school on moral identity, we built on our previous work (Hart, Atkins, & Ford, 1998, 1999). In those studies, we tried to assess some of the paths of influence that are illustrated in Fig.4.1 using data from the Children of the National Longitudinal Study of Youth (Bureau of Labor Statistics, 1995). Our analyses of that data demonstrated that demographic factors (race or ethnicity, family income, and paternal educational attainment, corresponding to the lower left area of Fig. 4.1) and academic achievement were associated with voluntary community service. Of theoretical importance in one study (Hart, Atkins, & Ford, 1998) was the demonstration that involvement in clubs and teams was a powerful predictor of involvement in community service, a finding that we interpreted as demonstrating the importance of institutions and opportunities in the development of moral identity.

In our current work, described in this section of the chapter, we seek to extend our previous investigations in two ways. First, we are using a new data set, the 1999 National Household Education Survey (NHES). By using a new data set, we are able to show that our findings concerning the paths of influence in Fig. 4.1 are not an artifact of the data set we used in our previous work. Second, and most important for the goals of this chapter, we assess the role of attachment to school as a predictor of community service while controlling for the influence of the variables we studied in previous research. This strategy permits us to estimate the distinctive contribution that schools make to the development of moral identity, at least as it is reflected in community service.

Data and Analyses

The NHES Survey of Civic Development. The NHES was a random-digit telephone survey of households in the United States developed by the National Center for Education Statistics. For our analyses we utilized interview data from children in 6th through 12th grade (youth interview) and their parents (parent interview). In the youth interview children were asked questions about school and family environments, civic involvement and community service, and plans for postsecondary education. In the parent interview, parents of children interviewed in the youth interview were asked questions on a variety of topics regarding their children, such as early childhood program participation, types and frequency of family involvement in children's schooling, children's grades and behavior in school, learning activities with children outside of school, and plans for their children's postsecondary education.

The parent interview contains data from interviews completed with parents of 24,600 children—3,378 infants, 3,561 preschool children, 8,372 primary school children (Grades K–5), 4,024 middle or junior high school children (Grades 6–8), 4,980 high school children (Grades 9–12), and 285 home school children. The youth interview contains data from interviews completed with nearly 8,000 6th through 12th graders. One third of the children sampled were Black, Hispanic, Asian-Pacific, or other non-White race and ethnicity.

To represent our criterion variable, moral identity, we used questions from the NHES regarding voluntary participation in community service in school or out of school. Participants were asked whether they had done any community service or voluntary work in their school or community. Only participants who answered positively and had not done work that was court ordered, required by the school for a grade or graduation, or done for gift or payment were considered as having performed prosocial activity of the kind consistent with moral identity.

How Common is Community Service? As many commentators have noted (Putnam, 2000), American youth are volunteering are surprisingly high rates. Almost 7,000 youth between the ages of 12 and 18 answered the questions relevant for the determination of voluntary service; 32% reported that they had participated in voluntary service in the past year. This level of voluntary activity suggests substantial civic engagement on the part of youth.

Who Participates in Community Service? Table 4.1 presents the results of our logistic regression findings predicting participation in community service. The logistic regression equation was used to facilitate the comparisons relevant to our current interests in this chapter.

A number of demographic variables are used as predictors. The NHES has four categories of race or ethnicity: White, Black, Hispanic, and other. We used three orthogonal comparisons (three are needed to represent the four categories) to compare (a) Black youth against the mean of the three other groups, (b) White youth against the mean of Hispanic and other youth, and (c) to compare Hispanic youth to other youth.

There are four parenting categories in the NHES: two parent household, mother-headed household, father-headed household, and household headed by nonparental individuals (e.g., foster parents). We used dummy variables to compare the effects of each of the latter three types of households to the effect of membership in a two-parent household.

Other demographic variables are also included as predictors. These include family income (recorded in the NHES in 11 income ranges) and parental educational attainment (in 5 ranges). The neighborhood in which the family resided is represented by a 3-point scale ranging from urban (1) to rural (3). We also used a planned contrast to compare urban neighborhoods to suburban and rural.

Characteristics of the youth were also included as control variables. These include age (only those between the ages of 12 and 18 were included; the average age was 14.3 years), gender, and parent-reported grades (on a 5 point scale ranging from mostly F's [1] to mostly A's [5]). Membership in an extracurricular team or club was also included.

We noted that schools could influence the development of moral identity in many ways: changing self-appraisals of adolescents, the role modeling provided by adults, and the operation of a democratic institutions. Unfortunately,

TABLE 4.1

Logistic Regression Equation Predicting Voluntary Community Service

	B	SE	Exp(B)
Blacks contrasted with Whites, Hispanics & others	−.15	.09	.86
Whites contrasted with Hispanics & others	.29	.08	1.34***
Hispanics contrasted with others	−.04	.14	.96
Mother-headed home vs. two parent home	−.02	.08	.98
Father-headed home vs. two parent home	−.29	.15	.75*
Other-headed home vs. two parent home	−.54	.18	.58**
Member of an extracurricular team or club	.90	.07	2.46***
Parental educational attainment	.08	.03	1.09**
Household income range	.02	.01	1.02
Urbanicity (Urban = 1, Suburban = 2, Rural = 3)	.13	.03	1.14***
Age, in years	.08	.01	1.08***
Sex (Boys = 1, Girls = 2)	.22	.04	1.25***
Grades in school (parental report)	.28	.04	1.32***
School attachment	.10	.10	1.10
Interaction of Blacks contrasted with Whites, Hispanics & others and school attachment	.45	.21	1.57*
Interaction of Whites contrasted with Hispanics & others and school attachment	.23	.19	1.26
Interaction of Hispanics contrasted with others and school attachment	−.02	.35	.98

$*p < .05$; $**p < .01$; $***p < .001$.

the NHES does not have indexes corresponding to each of these potential sources of influence. However a set of ratings made by the youth of their schools is available. This set includes six items concerning (a) the respect that students and teachers have for each other, (b) student influence on the school, (c) teachers' and (d) the principal's success in maintaining discipline in the school, and the student's sense of (e) enjoyment and (f) challenge at school. Scores on these items were averaged forming a single index of what we labeled as school attachment.

The results presented in Table 4.1 are readily interpretable. As we found with the National Longitudinal Survey of Youth (Hart, Atkins, & Ford, 1998), participation in voluntary community service has multiple sources.

Previous research suggested that adolescents living in households in which parents were more able to provide them with cognitive, social, and emotional resources were more likely to become involved in voluntary service (Hart, Atkins, & Ford, 1998). Our findings in this analysis provide modest support for those earlier findings. Higher levels of parental education increased the probability that a youth would be involved in voluntary service, as did residence in a family headed by two parents (households headed by fathers and nonparental adults were less likely than households headed by two parents to have youth involved in community service).

Table 4.1 indicates that extracurricular membership in a club or a team is the strongest predictor of voluntary service. This finding supports our model of moral identity formation. As depicted in our model, moral identity arises from sustained relationships with responsible adults in community institutions. Cocurricular activities such as youth sports organizations, the Boys or Girls Club, and church or religious clubs allow youth to develop experience in working with peers and adults toward common goals (Youniss & Yates, 1997). Moreover, these types of organizations are able to structure opportunities for youth to become civically engaged through activities like community service. Finally, age, academic performance, and gender are all significant predictors of community service.

The most recent census figures indicate that rates of poverty and concentrations of minorities are higher inside central cities than in the surrounding metropolitan areas (Hart & Atkins, 2002). In our study more than 20% of Black and Hispanic youth participants lived in neighborhoods where over 20% of the population under the age of 18 lived below the poverty line. Black youth were about seven times more likely than White youth and five times more likely than youth identified as other race or ethnicity to live in high-poverty neighborhoods. Our previous study suggested that living in neighborhoods with higher concentrations of poverty diminished opportunities for community service (Hart, Atkins, & Ford, 1998). Our analysis of the NHES data indicates that living inside an urbanized area decreased the probability that a youth participated in voluntary service.

As we hypothesized, there is evidence for an interaction between race or ethnicity and school attachment in the prediction of community service. The significant interaction of the contrast variable comparing Black youth to all others with the school attachment variable suggests that school attachment is a better predictor of community service for Black youth than it is for other youth.

Because school attachment was found to be important in the prediction of community service, we used multiple regressions to identify the correlates of school attachment. Two equations were estimated. The first used the predictors used in the equation in Table 4.1 (except, of course, school attachment). The second equation added school suspension or expulsion to the set of predictors in the first equation. Because the likelihood of school suspension nearly doubles as the percentage of population under the age of 18 living below the poverty line increases from 5% or less to 20% or more (see Fig. 4.2), we hypothesized that it might effect how urban youth perceive the school environment.

The results of both equations can be found in Table 4.2. The most important points concern the influence of school suspension. First, youth who have been suspended or expelled from school are considerably less attached to school than youth who have not been suspended from school. Second, even after controlling for race, living in a central city neighborhood is a negative predictor of school attachment, though weak, with and without the suspension variable. This suggests some characteristic of the urban school or urban environment, other than school suspension, may decrease school attachment.

Our findings using the NHES both replicate and extend the findings from our previous work (Hart, Atkins & Ford, 1998, 1999). Using the NHES, we reconfirmed that demographic variables and one type of social opportunity—membership in an extracurricular team or club—predicts voluntary community service.

New to the analyses presented here are our findings demonstrating that school attachment makes a unique contribution to the prediction of community service. We found evidence suggesting that youth living in urban neighborhoods are less attached than other youth to schools. Finally, our analyses indi-

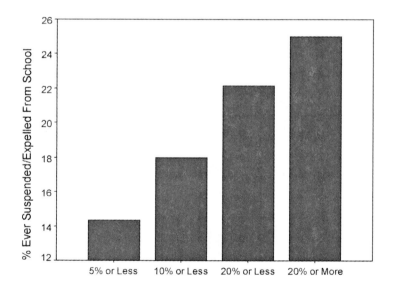

% Of Population 18 Or Younger Below In Poverty

FIG. 4.2.   Percentage of students suspended and expelled by rates of neighborhood poverty.

TABLE 4.2

Multiple Regression Equation Predicting School Attachment

	B		SE		β	
	M1	M2	M1	M2	M1	M2
Blacks contrasted with Whites, Hispanics & others	-.04	-.03	.02	.02	-.04**	-.03*
Whites contrasted with Hispanics & others	-.03	-.02	.01	.01	-.03	-.02
Hispanics contrasted with others	.00	.00	.02	.03	.00	.00
Mother-headed home vs. two parent home	-.04	-.04	.01	.01	-.04**	-.04**
Father-headed home vs. two parent home	.00	.01	.02	.03	.00	.01
Other-headed home vs. two parent home	.02	.02	.03	.03	.01	.01
Parental educational attainment	.00	.00	.00	.00	.00	-.01
Household income range	.00	-.01	.00	.00	-.03	-.03*
Urban vs. Suburban and Rural	-.02	-.01	.01	.01	-.03*	-.02*
Age, in years	-.03	-.03	.00	.00	-.14***	-.13***
Sex (Boys = 1, Girls = 2)	.00	-.01	.01	.01	.00	-.02
Grades in school (parental report)	.07	.05	.01	.01	.14***	.12***
Member of an extracurricular team or club	.09	.08	.01	.01	.09***	.09***
Suspended/expelled		-.12		.01		-.10***

$p < .05$; **$p < .01$; ***$p < .001$; M1 = without suspension/expulsion, M2 = with suspension/expulsion.

cate that low levels of school attachment among youth living in urban neighborhoods may not be a consequence of the rate at which they are suspended or expelled at school. The NHES does not follow participants longitudinally and information on why students were suspended or expelled was not collected, thus it is impossible to determine whether suspension or expulsion precedes or follows attachment to the school environment. However, it may be that youth, particularly those at urban schools, care less about being suspended or expelled from their schools because they consider schools to be fundamentally unfair institutions. Hopefully, future research on the development of moral identity in youth using different research designs will consider the role an individuals' orientation to the school environment plays in supplying opportunities to develop morally.

CONCLUSION

Moral identity is a blending of moral judgment, self-conceptions, and action that forms the foundation of personality and social opportunities. In this chapter, we illustrated the influences that schools may have on the development of moral identity in youth. Schools may affect development through the relationships youth have with teachers, through the opportunities they offer for the exploration of moral judgment and moral action, and by the operation of the system of rules and norms that govern behavior within their walls. Our empirical analyses of the NHES suggested that neighborhood may negatively affect urban adolescents perceptions of the school atmosphere. Consequently, urban adolescents are less attached to school and may not benefit from the moral lessons provided within the school environment such as community service.

That youth learn in school is a truism. They not only learn occupationally valuable literacy and computational skills, but they learn about citizenship, ethics, and the fair treatment of people. We argued that adolescent perceptions of their schools as institutions worthy of their respect influence their entry into community service. Finally, we suggested that the extraordinarily high rate of suspension and expulsion from school among students in poor urban settings undermines their judgment of school as deserving of their respect. It may not be enough for schools to succeed in their mission of promoting virtue in their students by hanging banners extolling honesty and to discuss loyalty, kindness, and other desirable characteristics in civics classes. For moral identity to flourish among all youth, schools may need to operate as institutions in ways that exemplify the virtues that youth are supposed to synthesize into their identities.

REFERENCES

Blasi, A. (1999). Emotions and moral motivation. *Journal for the Theory of Social Behaviour, 29,* 1–19.

Blyth, D., Hill, J., & Theil, K. (1982). Early adolescents' significant others: Grade and gender differences in perceived relationships with familial and nonfamilial adults as young people. *Journal of Youth and Adolescence, 2,* 425–50.

Bureau of Labor Statistics. (1995). *National Longitudinal Surveys.* Retrieved June 6, 2001 from http://stats.bls.gov/nlsmother.htm

Colby, A. & Damon, W. (1992). *Some do care: Contemporary lives of moral commitment.* New York: The Free Press.

Eisenberg, N., & Fabes, R. (1998). Prosocial development. In N. Eisenberg (Ed.), *Handbook of child psychology: Vol. 3. Social, emotional, and personality development* (pp. 701–778). New York: Wiley.

Furstenberg, F. (1993). How families manage risk and opportunity in dangerous neighborhoods. In W. J. Wilson (Ed.), *Sociology and the public agenda* (pp. 231–258). Newbury Park, CA: Sage.

Flanagan, C., Bowes, J., Jonsson, B., Csapo, B., & Shlebanova, E. (1998). Ties that bind: correlates of adolescents' civic commitments in seven countries. *Journal of Social Issues, 54,* 457–477.

Gabarino, J., Dubrow, N., Kostelny, K., & Pardo, C. (1992). *Children in danger: Coping with the consequences of community violence.* San Francisco, CA: Jossey-Bass.

Garmezy, N. (1991). Resiliency and vulnerability to adverse developmental outcomes associated with poverty. *American Behavioral Scientist, 34,* 416–430.

Greenberger, E., & Goldberg, W. A. (1989). Work, parenting, and the socialization of children. *Developmental Psychology, 25,* 22–35.

Grusec, J. E. (1991). Socializing concern for others in the home. *Developmental Psychology, 27,* 338–342.

Halberstadt, A. G. (1986). Family socialization of emotional expression and nonverbal communication styles and skills. *Journal of Personality and Social Psychology, 51,* 827–836.

Hart, D., London, B., Burock, D., & Miraglia, A. (2003). Moral development in childhood. In M. H. Bornstein, L. Davidson, C. L. M. Keyes, & K. A. Moore (Eds.), *Well-being: Positive development across the lifespan* (pp. 355–370). New York: Lawrence Erlbaum Associates.

Hart, D., & Atkins, R. (2002). Fostering citizenship in urban youth. *Applied Developmental Science, 6,* 227–237.

Hart, D., Atkins, R., & Ford, D. (1998). Urban America as a context for the development of moral identity in adolescence. *Journal of Social Issues, 54,* 513–530.

Hart, D., Atkins, R., & Ford, D. (1999). Family influences on the formation of moral identity in adolescence: Longitudinal analyses. *The Journal of Moral Education, 28,* 375–386.

Hart, D., & Fegley, S. (1995). Prosocial behavior and caring in adolescence—Relations to self-understanding and social judgment. *Child Development, 66,* 1346–1359.

Hart, D., Hofmann, V., Edelstein, W., & Keller, M. (1997). The relation of childhood personality types to adolescent behavior and development: A longitudinal study. *Developmental Psychology, 33,* 195–205.

Hendry, L., Roberts, W., Glendinning, A., & Coleman, J. (1992). Adolescents' perceptions of significant individuals in their lives. *Journal of Adolescence, 15,* 255–70.

Jencks, C., & Phillips, M. (1998). *The Black–White test score gap.* Washington, DC: Brookings Institute Press.

Johnson, M., Beebe, T., Mortimer, J., & Snyder, M. (1998). Volunteerism in adolescence: A process perspective. *Journal of Research on Adolescence, 8,* 309–332.

Kamens, D. (1988). Education and democracy: A comparative institutional analysis. *Sociology of Education, 61,* 114–127.

Krueger, R. F., Hicks, B. M., & McGue, M. (2001). Altruistic and antisocial behavior: Independent tendencies, unique personality characteristics, distinct etiologies. *Psychological Science, 12,* 397–402.

Lapsley, D. (1996). *Moral psychology.* Boulder: Westview.

Mandela, N. (1994). *The long walk to freedom: The autobiography of Nelson Mandela.* New York: Little, Brown.

National Household Education Survey 1999—Civic Involvement Surveys. (1999). [Data file]. Washington, DC: National Center for Educational Statistics.

Plato (1974). *The Republic.* Indianapolis: Hackett. Translated by G. M. A. Grube.

Putnam, R. (2000). *Bowling alone in America: The collapse and revival of American community.* New York: Simon & Schuster.

Slaughter-Defoe, D., & Carlson, K. (1996). Young African American and Latino children in high-poverty urban schools: How they perceive school climate. *Journal of Negro Education, 65,* 60–70.

Steele, C. (1992). Race and the Schooling of Black Americans. *The Atlantic Online.* Retrieved June 1, 2002 from: http://www.theatlantic.com/politics/race/steele.htm

Turner, P. J. (1991). Relations between attachment, gender, and behavior with peers in preschool. *Child Development, 62,* 1475–1488.

U.S. Supreme Court. Wisconsin V. Yoder, 406 U.S. 205 (1972) 406 U.S. 205 Wisconsin V. Yoder et al. Certiorari to the Supreme Court of Wisconsin No. 70–110. Available at: http://caselaw.lp.findlaw.com/scripts/getcase.pl?court=US&vol=406&invol=205

Werner, E., & Smith, R. (1989). *Vulnerable but invincible: A longitudinal study of resilient children and youth.* New York: Adams, Bannister, and Cox.

Youniss, J., & Yates, M. (1997). *Community Service and Social Responsibility in Youth.* Chicago, IL: The University of Chicago Press.

5

False Moral Identity: Self-Serving Denial in the Maintenance of Moral Self-Conceptions

David Moshman
University of Nebraska–Lincoln

Among developmental psychologists, identities are generally regarded as good things. We encourage and promote the formation of strong identities, especially among adolescents and young adults. Outside of the developmental realm, however, there is more caution. Social identities can, and regularly do, generate deadly violence up to and including genocide (Maalouf, 2001; Moshman, in press; Waller, 2002).

If we are to encourage identity formation, then, we need to think about how to discourage the formation of what Maalouf (2001) called "identities that kill" (p. 30). One part of the answer, it would seem, is that we should encourage the types of identities in which some sort of respect or concern for the rights or welfare of others is a central commitment. That is, we should encourage moral identities (Blasi, 1984, 1995; also see Bergman, 2002, chap. 2, this volume, for a theoretical review and synthesis; and Monroe, 2001, for a somewhat different view).

A moral identity provides an existential motivation for morality. I act morally because being moral is central to my identity—my conception of who I am as a person. If I have the sort of identity that directs me to see myself as, fundamentally, a moral agent, then to engage in immoral action is to betray myself. As a matter of self-definition, I must act morally because it would no longer be me if I were to act otherwise. To the extent that I have this sort of identity, we might say I have a moral identity.

Even if I see myself as fundamentally committed to morality, however, I may be wrong about the strength of that commitment. I may think that I am highly oriented toward perceiving moral issues, making moral judgments, and doing what I deem is right, but in fact I may be relatively oblivious to moral obligations and violations; my judgments and actions may be directed primarily by nonmoral commitments.

The central concern of this chapter is how to conceptualize this phenomenon. Starting with a conception of identity as a theory of self (Berzonsky, 1993; Moshman, 1999), I note that theories, and thus identities, can be evaluated with respect to truth and can turn out to be false. Extending this conceptualization and incorporating an objective conception of the moral domain, I propose that the phenomenon described above shows a false moral identity.

In the latter half of the chapter I present a case study of a 1981 massacre in El Salvador and the subsequent denials of what happened (Danner, 1994). We see here the danger of false moral identities and some of the cognitive mechanisms that enable us to maintain our theories of ourselves as moral agents even in the face of contrary evidence.

IDENTITIES TRUE AND FALSE

Rational Agency

Imagine a grasshopper jumping in a field. Its behavior is in part a function of its genes and current environment. A full explanation of its behavior, however, requires reference not just to a set of genes and an environment but to the grasshopper itself as an organism with a disposition to act in particular ways. The developmental interaction of genes and environment over the life of the grasshopper has created an organism that is a biological agent in its own right, a source of behavior in a way that a rock, for example, is not.

Human beings are also biological agents. As we move through infancy, it becomes increasingly difficult to explain our behavior without reference to our beliefs and values. To the extent that this is so, it might be said that even in infancy we leave grasshoppers behind as we rapidly become *rational* agents—agents who act on the basis of beliefs and values of our own.

Imagine, for example, an 18-month-old girl who chooses a candy over some alternative. To explain this, we might say she values sweetness and believes on the basis of past experience that the candy will have a sweet taste. A fuller explanation might also refer to the genetic basis of the human propensity for sweets and to the relevant reinforcement history of this particular child. Nevertheless, the girl can be said to be acting on the basis of beliefs and values that are in some sense her own. Thus, in some minimal sense, she is a rational agent.

Rationality continues to develop for many years (Flavell & Miller, 1998; Flavell, Miller, & Miller, 2002; Kuhn, 2000; Moshman, 1998, 1999). Over the course of childhood, we become increasingly conscious of our beliefs and values, increasingly systematic in coordinating them, and increasingly deliberate in applying them. We also become increasingly aware that other people act on the basis of their own beliefs and values, which may differ from ours. Our observations, reflections, and coordinations may lead us to reconsider our beliefs and values and, whether or not we choose to modify them, to take greater responsibility for them. Thus, we become increasingly rational in the sense that we increasingly act on the basis of beliefs and values that are self-constructed, or at least consciously accepted, and thus more deeply our own than the beliefs and values that earlier guided our behavior.

That is not all, however. Not only do we become increasingly rational through consciousness of specific beliefs and values, we also become increasingly conscious of ourselves—of our selves—as rational agents. We construct self-conceptions and commitments that become important motivators and directors of our behavior. In adolescence and beyond these self-conceptions and commitments may become sufficiently self-conscious and systematic that we call them identities.

Identity as a Theory of Self

"An identity is, at least in part, an explicit theory of oneself as a person" (Moshman, 1999, p. 78). To have an identity, at the very least, is to have conceptions about yourself that (a) are sufficiently organized and explanatory to be deemed a theory; (b) are construed by you as your theory; and (c) enable you to construe yourself as a person—at the very least, as a rational agent with beliefs and values of your own.

I now expand on the various aspects of this definition. Children learn things about themselves from very early ages. They learn their names, for example, and learn to identify themselves by providing those names. They learn whether they are girls or boys. They learn about their family's status or affiliation with regard to various racial, tribal, ethnic, cultural, religious, national, economic, political, ideological, or other social groupings.

An identity is not just a list of labels or self-categorizations, however. It is structured in such a way as to help you understand yourself. Its purpose is to enable you to see yourself as a person, as a rational agent with beliefs and values of your own. Because of its organization and its explanatory function, an identity can be said to be a theory.

To say a conception is only a theory if it is organized and explanatory might seem a tough standard. But children as young as age 4 show evidence that they have theories in precisely this sense, including theories of mind (Flavell & Miller, 1998; Flavell et al., 2002; Wellman & Gelman, 1998). Similarly, children's self-conceptions become sufficiently organized and explanatory to qualify as theories of self over the course of the preschool years and continue to develop long beyond that (Harter, 1999).

Even if young children are seeing the world through genuine theories, however, those structures are implicit in their conceptualizations rather than objects of consciousness. Only in adolescence and adulthood do we think about our theories as theories, as explanatory structures that are, to some degree, under our control (Kuhn, 1989, 2000). To the extent that I become conscious of my theory of self I come to see it as *my* theory. I take responsibility for my beliefs and values and feel committed to maintaining and acting in accord with them.

To qualify as an identity, however, it is not enough for a conception of self to be theoretical and explicit. I might have an explicit theory about my anatomy or physiology, for example, but this would not normally be an identity. Even an explicit theory about my personality would not by itself qualify as an identity if I saw it as nothing more than a description of or means to predict my behavior. To have an identity is to have an explicit theory whereby I construe myself as a person.

What does it mean to construe myself as a person? At the very least, it means to construe myself as a rational agent—as a being that acts on the basis of beliefs and values of my own. To see myself as a rational agent, moreover, entails a conception of myself as the same person across some set of behavioral contexts extending across time. To construe myself as a person is to see myself as a singular and continuous rational agent. That is, I see myself as an agent who acts on the basis of beliefs and values of my own and as the same agent in multiple contexts extending from the past through the present to the future. Thus, to have an identity is to have an explicit theory whereby one attributes to oneself the properties of (a) agency, (b) rationality, (c) singularity, and (d) continuity.

Beyond these basics, identities are highly variable. No two people form precisely the same identity. In trying to identify universal criteria of identity, we should not lose sight of the fact that identities, by this same definition, are highly individual.

To observe that identities are highly individual, however, is not to deny that they are also profoundly social. We conceptualize ourselves as embedded in various social relationships and as members of various groups. We theorize about our relations with other people and with various social institutions. We understand ourselves with respect to roles (e.g., teacher or parent) that could not exist without other people in complementary roles (e.g., student or child). Many of our most fundamental commitments, far from being simply theoretical, are commitments to various people and social groups.

To have an identity is to see myself as an agent with beliefs, values, and social commitments that I deem to be my own but that also embed me in networks of social relationships that entail identity-defining expectations and obligations. To the extent that I see myself in this way, I will attempt to maintain my integrity by acting in a manner consistent with what I and others expect. By personally and socially committing me to my own beliefs and values, my identity directs my behavior.

This is, at least in part, what it means to say I have an identity. Identities may be something more than this, but at the very least an identity is or includes an explicit structure of self-conceptions whereby I explain myself to myself and others by construing myself as a singular and continuous rational agent in ongoing relationship with other such agents.

The Construction of Identity

Where do identities come from? Identities, I suggest, are constructed by rational agents via processes of reflection, coordination, and social interaction (Moshman, 1999). Although these processes cannot be sharply distinguished, it is useful to consider each.

The rational agents that construct identities are something more than rocks or even grasshoppers. They are not just agents but rational agents, who act on the basis of beliefs and values of their own. They are, moreover, relatively advanced rational agents whose beliefs and values are associated with a variety of self-conceptions, including conceptions about their personal characteristics and their affiliation with various ethnic, cultural, religious, and other social groups. Identity is not generated ex nihilo but rather is constructed via reflection on a preexisting self.

The construction of identity, however, is not simply the discovery of that preexisting self. The preexisting self is a complex collection of characteristics, ideas, values, commitments, goals, and so forth. The construction of identity is in part a creative process of restructuring these aspects to form a more coherent whole that can explain and guide action. Identity formation is a process of co-ordination as well as a process of reflection.

Although reflection and coordination can take place within an individual mind, they often occur in contexts of social interaction. In the course of inter-acting with others we find that we are expected to explain and justify our be-liefs and actions, which leads us to reflect on what we believe and value. We find incentive to attend to the beliefs and values of others and perhaps to coor-dinate multiple perspectives. We find that we need to make social commit-ments and to explain these commitments to ourselves and others by linking them to our beliefs and values.

Given a conception of identity as an explicit theory of self, identity forma-tion may be construed as a process of deliberate theorizing (Berzonsky, 1993). Theorists observe patterns, formulate theories, generate predictions, seek evi-dence, make interpretations, revise theories and predictions, seek new evi-dence, and so forth. Their theories are not just copies of reality, but they are constrained by reality. In most cases the constraint is asymmetric. If my theory of the structure of DNA is mistaken, for example, it is my theory, not the struc-ture of DNA, that must change.

Theorists of self, however, face a more symmetric relation of theory and data. If I find myself behaving in a manner inconsistent with my theory of self, I not only can modify my theory to fit my behavior but can modify my behavior to fit my theory. In fact, in the case of behavior I recognize as contrary to a fun-damental principle or commitment—a principle or commitment I deem central to who I am as a person—I am more likely to change my behavior than to re-think my identity. My theory of self, then, may guide my behavior.

Thus, there is a deep sense in which my theory of self is not merely about myself but becomes myself. Not only do I theorize about who I am, but I trans-form myself, to some extent, into who I theorize myself to be (Moshman, in press).

False Identity

A fundamental characteristic of theories is that they can be true or false. If identi-ties are theories, then identities can be true or false. The truth and falsity of theo-ries and the truth and falsity of identities are not simple matters, however.

Simple hypotheses can sometimes be proved true or false. If I say there is a ball in that box, we can look in the box and determine whether my hypothesis is true or false. In marginal cases, we might argue about exactly what counts as a ball or whether the ball must be entirely in the box, but in general the concepts of truth and falsity are unproblematic in this case.

Theories, however, are complex explanatory structures that cannot be proved true in any straightforward sense. They can be supported by evidence, but it always remains possible that future evidence will disconfirm them or that a better theory will be proposed.

Can a theory be proved false? Evidence that seems to disconfirm a theory may turn out to be the unreliable result of flawed processes of inquiry. Alternatively, core premises of a seemingly falsified theory may turn out to be fully consistent with the data once minor alterations are made in some supplementary assumptions. Strictly speaking, perhaps, no theory can ever be proven false. Sometimes, however, a theory is so clearly inconsistent in such fundamental ways with so much evidence from so many credible sources that we are justified in calling it false.

In sum, although we should be cautious about labeling theories true, we properly evaluate them on the basis of truth. Sometimes we are justified in saying one theory is better supported than another, and sometimes we are justified in saying a theory is false.

If an identity is a theory of self, its truth is a matter of its objective relation to the objective self. No identity conforms exactly to some real self and is thus absolutely and entirely true. Nevertheless, some theories of self are more veridical than others, and it is possible for a theory of self to be so inconsistent with evidence about the self that we justifiably deem it false.

I suggested earlier that theorists of self can maintain their theories by adjusting their behavior. If my behavior falsifies a theory of self to which I am strongly committed, I can make the theory true by acting in accord with it, thus becoming the person I theorized myself to be. But note that I can also maintain my subjective equilibrium, without modifying either my theory or my behavior, by not attending to my behavior or by adjusting my perceptions and/or inferences to fit with my theory of myself. Thus, false identities may be maintained through self-serving manipulations of evidence about one's behavior.

MORAL IDENTITY

Moral Identity as Self-Conscious Moral Agency

To have a moral identity is to have an explicit theory of yourself as a moral agent—an agent who is committed to acting on the basis of respect and/or concern for the rights and/or welfare of others.

I explain and justify this definition by highlighting issues of subjectivity and objectivity (Moshman, 1995, 1999). As already discussed, to have an identity is to see yourself as a rational agent—that is, an agent who acts on the basis of beliefs and values of your own. Even if your beliefs and values are demonstrably wrong or evil, if you are consciously committed to acting on the basis of those beliefs and values because you see them as fundamental to who you are, then you have an identity.

To have a moral identity is to see yourself as a moral agent—that is, as an agent who acts on the basis of moral beliefs and values. Regardless of whether your moral beliefs or values are correct or justifiable, your fundamental commitment to them as central to your personhood constitutes a moral identity. If you see yourself as the sort of person who notices, reflects, and acts on moral issues, then you have a moral identity regardless of the accuracy of your perceptions, the quality of your reasoning, or the justifiability of your judgments and actions.

But what counts as a moral issue? What beliefs and values fall within the moral domain? At this point, research on morality justifies an objectivist consideration. Fully consistent with individual and cultural diversity in moral perception, reasoning, and judgment, there is substantial evidence that children and adolescents across a wide range of normal social environments, regardless of specific cultural contexts, construct some conception of a moral domain encompassing respect and/or concern for the rights and/or welfare of others (Gibbs, 2003; Moshman, 1995, 1999; Nucci, 2002; Piaget, 1932/1965; Turiel, 2002). Some conceptions of the moral domain may see respect for rights and justice as more fundamental, some may put more emphasis on care and compassion for others, and some may see these as deeply interconnected with each other and/or with related values, but there is sufficient agreement among children, adults, and theorists on the meaning of morality to justify an objective specification of the moral domain within our otherwise subjectivist definition of moral identity.

Thus, to have a moral identity is to have an explicit theory of yourself as an agent who is committed to acting on the basis of respect and/or concern for the rights and/or welfare of others. This definition does not require a theoretical commitment by the self-theorist to any particular set of moral beliefs, values, rules, or principles, and it is thus consistent with a substantial degree of moral diversity among those who have strong moral identities. It does, however, require that one's theoretical commitment be objectively moral, not in the sense of being morally correct but in the sense of falling within an objectively defined moral domain.

Having defined what it means to have a moral identity, I hasten to add that people cannot be neatly divided into those who have moral identities and those who do not. On the contrary, people can have moral identities to varying degrees. Probably almost all people, beginning in childhood, have moral self-conceptions entailing commitments to others. In cases of moderate moral identity, the commitment to others is an important aspect of a person's explicit theory of self but may be very much colored, or even compromised, by other identity commitments. In cases of strong moral identity, the commitment to others is so central as to direct and coordinate other commitments, in which case moral identity may be seen as not just an aspect of identity but as a type of identity (Colby & Damon, 1992).

The Construction of Moral Identity

Identities, as noted, are constructed by rational agents via processes of reflection, coordination, and social interaction. The construction of identity is a process of both discovery and creation, and it is best construed overall as a process of theorizing about yourself.

Children show genuine concern for the rights and welfare of others from very early ages and even preschoolers often act on the basis of such concern (Gibbs, 2003; Turiel, 2002). As early as age 4, in fact, they can see themselves as good or bad and can respond to questions about what they are like, in general, with regard to various morally relevant characteristics and dispositions (Kochanska, 2002). Thus, children have moral beliefs, values, and self-conceptions long before they have identities in the present strict sense of that term.

In some cases, the process of theorizing about yourself may include theorizing about yourself as a moral agent. You may, for example, observe that you are often helpful to people. This seems natural to you because, you realize, you are spontaneously sympathetic to others. In fact, come to think of it, you are known among your friends for your kindness, and you like being the sort of person who is viewed this way. In theorizing about who you are as a person, being the sort of person who cares for others may come to be a central commitment.

Note that this process is in part a matter of discovering that you are already a moral person, but it is not simply a process of discovery. There are many things about yourself that you can discover, but most of these never become part of your identity. Identity formation involves choosing among multiple aspects of yourself and coordinating old elements in new ways. It is thus a creative process. Constructing a moral identity is not just a matter of discovering that you are a moral person but also of deciding, at a fundamental level, that this is the sort of person you want to be. Thus, you create an identity in which moral commitment plays a central role.

Having identified yourself as a moral agent, you are more likely to discern moral issues, apply moral norms, make moral judgments, and act on the basis of moral considerations. Although your moral perception and cognition may develop as a result of this, having a moral identity does not guarantee advanced moral principles or objectively justifiable behavior. It simply makes it more likely that you will observe and think about moral issues and do what you think is moral. Having committed yourself to doing this, however, you are likely to continue doing it. Moral identity, in the sense of a continuing commitment to be moral, is likely to be relatively stable once it is achieved. Even substantial changes in your moral conceptions and evaluations may be consistent with an ongoing commitment to act on the basis of your conceptions and evaluations.

Suppose, for example, you arrive at college with an explicit theory of yourself as a nice person and then, over the next few years, you learn about injustices around the world. Your conception of morality may shift so that respect for universal rights now seems to you more fundamental than being nice to your friends, whom you increasingly see as affluent and self-centered. Do you still have a moral identity?

According to the present definition, the answer is yes. You may now be more committed to respect for rights than you are to being nice, but your identity continues to include a fundamental concern for and commitment to others and thus qualifies as moral.

Nevertheless, moral identities can wane. As you revise and elaborate on your theory of self, moral considerations may become less central. Over time, you might cease to have a moral identity.

Suppose, for example, you become affiliated with others who are fighting injustices and become deeply committed to a political ideology or organization that, you think, has convincingly identified and effectively targeted the roots of oppression. Do you still have a moral identity?

The answer depends on how you coordinate your political and moral commitments. If you see your political commitment to resisting oppression as derived from and justified by your moral commitment to human rights and welfare, then you do indeed have a moral identity. Not all political commitments, however, are fundamentally rooted in human rights and welfare. To the extent that your extramoral political commitments become central to your self-conception, your identity becomes less moral. You are committed, above all, to the pursuit of your political, not your moral, goals. You may continue to hold the same moral beliefs and values, but these will play less of a role in your behavior.

Suppose you form deep religious commitments that you come to see as central to who you are. Here too, whether you continue to have a moral identity depends on how you coordinate your religious and moral commitments. You continue to have a strong moral identity to the extent that your moral commitment to human rights and welfare guides your choice and conceptualization of religious doctrines. You continue to have at least a moderate moral identity to the extent that your moral and religious commitments are so intertwined that they cannot be meaningfully distinguished. The moral aspect of your identity may dwindle, however, to the extent that extramoral religious commitments become central to how you see yourself and gain the power to override your respect or concern for the rights or welfare of others.

Identity formation involves simultaneous and interacting consideration of multiple beliefs, values, and commitments, both actual and potential. The construction of moral identity is neither a process separate from this nor a necessary part of this. Most children construct self-conceptions that include some sense of the self as a moral agent. In the course of explicit theorizing about the self, some individuals construct theories that highlight such commitment to the rights or welfare of others; to the extent this is so, they may be said to have moral identities.

Moral identities thus differ quantitatively with regard to strength of commitment. Moral identity is, however, a fundamentally qualitative phenomenon. Each moral identity represents a unique coordination of moral commitments with political, religious, and other commitments.

False Moral Identity

If you have an explicit theory of yourself as a moral agent, then you have a moral identity. If your theory is false—if you do not really act on the basis of respect and/or concern for the rights and/or welfare of others—then you have a false moral identity. Just as false theories are still theories, false moral identities are moral identities. Thus, we must distinguish the question of whether someone has a moral identity from the question of the truth or falsity of that identity.

This leaves us, very roughly, with three categories. First, even among people who have moral self-conceptions and/or engage in good moral reasoning, there are some who lack strong identity commitments or whose strongest identity commitments do not involve the rights and/or welfare of others. Such people may be said to lack a moral identity.

Second, some people explicitly theorize themselves to be deeply committed to the rights and/or welfare of others and, for the most part, act in a manner that demonstrates the reality of this commitment. Such people may be said to have true moral identities, keeping in mind that some may be more true to their moral commitments than others.

Finally, there are people who explicitly theorize themselves to be deeply committed to the rights and/or welfare of others but whose behavior is substantially inconsistent with this theory. Such people have genuine moral identities—they really do have explicit theories whereby they conceptualize themselves at a fundamental level as moral agents—but their moral identities are false.

Our concern here is with identities of this latter sort. The concept of false moral identity may enable us to understand people who genuinely see themselves as deeply moral but do not show an objective commitment to morality. There is substantial evidence, moreover, that most people have a substantial commitment to seeing themselves as moral agents, and that few show behavior fully consistent with their moral self-conceptions (Batson, Thompson, Seuferling, Whitney, & Strongman, 1999; Bersoff, 1999). To a considerable extent, perhaps, we all have false moral identities.

THE MASSACRE AT EL MOZOTE: A CASE STUDY

La Matanza

El Mozote in 1981 was a mountain village of several hundred people in the northern part of the province of Morazan in northeastern El Salvador. (The following narratives are based on Danner, 1994, which provides the definitive account of the massacre and reprints a substantial selection of relevant documents.) Northern Morazan was widely known as the Red Zone because it was largely under the control of left-wing Salvadoran guerrillas attempting to overthrow the right-wing government of El Salvador. The guerrillas had strong support in many of the local villages but less support in El Mozote. Most of El Mozote's inhabitants, and probably most people in most of the Red Zone, tried to live their lives as best they could without antagonizing either side in the war going on around them. Thus, when they heard that the Atlacatl Battalion was conducting a sweep of northern Morazan, they debated for days whether it was riskier to leave or to stay. In the end most had stayed, and as the sounds of mortars, small arms, and aircraft drew closer, the village swelled with people from surrounding areas who thought El Mozote would be safer than where they lived.

On December 10, 1981, at twilight, after a morning of strafing and bombing by the Salvadoran Air Force, the people of El Mozote were hiding in their houses when the Atlacatl Battalion arrived. The soldiers yelled for everyone to come out and forced them all to lie face down in the street. Soon it was dark, with more than 100 children crying, and the soldiers went up and down the rows, shouting, kicking, beating, taking jewelry and crucifixes, taking names, and demanding information about guerrillas and weapons.

Later that evening, the soldiers sent everyone back to their homes. In alternating terror and relief, hoping that the worst was over, they spent the night waiting. The next morning before dawn, they were ordered out to the Plaza and required to stand, the men separate from the women and children, for hours. Finally, the men were herded into the church and the women and children into a small home nearby as a helicopter landed in the Plaza and military officers emerged. In the church, men were bound, blindfolded, and brutally interrogated, and then, after an hour, the soldiers began to decapitate them with machetes. In the nearby house, the women and children could hear them screaming, and from a small window they could see other men, their husbands, their fathers, and their sons, led in small groups, bound and blindfolded, to be killed in the forest with a shot to the head. Children became hysterical. Their mothers cried and hugged each other.

About midday, the soldiers came for the young women and the older girls, wresting them from their mothers to take them up to the hills, where their screams could be heard in the house. Then they came back for the mothers and took them in groups, one group at a time, until only the crying children remained in the house. The women were taken to another house, forced inside, and shot. The later groups, seeing the carnage through the doorway, refused to enter. But they too were forced inside, screaming and begging, and they too were shot. And when the last group of women had been killed, the house was burned.

Now the soldiers returned to the house by the church where they smashed the children's heads with the butts of their rifles, slashed them with machetes, and herded many across the street and into the tiny sacristy, into which they then shot their rifles until all of the children were dead. Then they burned the church, the sacristy, and the nearby house. The next morning, the Atlacatl Battalion moved on to continue its work in the surrounding hamlets, ultimately killing 767 individuals (listed in Danner, 1994, pp. 280–304) in what came to be known in Morazan as *la matanza*, the great killing at El Mozote.

Morality and Identity in the Atlacatl Battalion

It seems immediately obvious that what the Atlacatl Battalion did was morally wrong. Moreover, it hardly seems necessary to be at an advanced stage of moral reasoning to determine this. Indeed, for a soldier actually engaged in a massacre such as that at El Mozote, natural empathic reactions might be expected to reinforce cognitive judgments about the immorality of what one is doing (Gibbs, 2003).

How, then, can we account for the massacre? It is tempting to suggest that the men of the Atlacatl Battalion were lacking in moral identity or at least that they had alternative self-conceptions and commitments stronger than their moral self-conceptions and commitments. This explanation has a special allure, in fact, because it enables us to see the Atlacatl soldiers as fundamentally different from us; thus, we can distance ourselves from what they did.

The reality is more complex. The soldiers of the Atlacatl Battalion were a proud and dedicated group. Having received special training by U.S. Special Forces instructors, they were the elite of the Salvadoran Army. They sang together:

> We are warriors!
> Warriors all!
> We are going forth to kill
> A mountain of terrorists! (Danner, p. 50)

There is evidence that this is indeed what they thought they were doing and that they saw it as a moral mission. Chepe Mozote, one of the very few survivors of *la matanza*, accompanied soldiers of the Atlacatl as they conducted a house-to-house roundup of children whose parents had left them home on the outskirts of El Mozote. He carried his little brother on his back as they headed toward the playing field, where there were now about 30 children:

> The soldiers were putting ropes on the trees. I was seven years old, and I didn't really understand what was happening until I saw one of the soldiers take a kid he had been carrying—the kid was maybe three years old—throw him in the air, and stab him with a bayonet.

> They slit some of the kids' throats, and many they hanged from the tree. All of us were crying now, but we were their prisoners—there was nothing we could do. The soldiers kept telling us, "You are guerrillas and this is justice. This is justice." (quoted in Danner, p. 77)

How could they see this as justice? Presumably most or all members of the Atlacatl Battalion were highly committed to the government of El Salvador and the war on Communism, and they saw these political and ideological commitments as moral imperatives. They were killing those who ought to be killed, and the *ought* in their view was a moral one. From their own point of view, their most fundamental commitments were deeply moral. In fact, their moral identities might be what enabled them to do what they thought was right even when this entailed the emotionally difficult task of killing defenseless people individually in cold blood.

With regard to the children, however, there was disagreement within the Atlacatl. Survivor Rufina Amaya was hiding close enough to hear the conversation as soldiers watched the burning house of Israel Marquez, where they had just killed nearly all of the adult women of El Mozote. Now that only the children were left, one suggested that some of the kids were cute, and perhaps, rather than kill them all, they could take some along. Another scoffed at this idea, reminding him they were engaged in a scorched-earth operation "and we have to kill the kids as well, or we'll get it ourselves." "Listen," replied the first, "I don't want to kill kids." "Look," responded a third. "We have orders to finish everyone and we have to complete our orders. That's it" (Danner, p. 75).

That evening, recalled a guide to the Atlacatl, after the killing was done, soldiers talked about a particular girl who sang hymns and evangelical songs as she was repeatedly raped up in the hills and who, after the soldiers finished with her and shot her in the chest, continued to sing while they pointed her out to each other and watched in amazement, and continued to sing after they shot her again, until their wonderment turned to fear and they hacked through her neck with their machetes.

> Now [that evening] the soldiers argued about this. Some declared that the girl's strange power proved that God existed. And that brought them back to the killing of the children. "There were a lot of differences among the soldiers about whether this had been a good thing or whether they shouldn't have done it," the guide told me.
>
> As the soldiers related it now, the guide said, there had been a disagreement outside the schoolhouse, where a number of children were being held. Some of the men had hesitated, saying they didn't want to kill the children, and the others had ridiculed them.
>
> According to one account, a soldier had called the commanding officer. "Hey, Major!" he had shouted. "Someone says he won't kill children!"
>
> "Which son of a bitch says that?" the Major had shouted back angrily, striding over. The Major had not hesitated to do what an officer does in such situations: show leadership. He'd pushed into the group of children, seized a little boy, thrown him in the air, and impaled him as he fell. That had put an end to the discussion. (Danner, p. 79)

But only for the moment. The moral discussion continued that evening and the next day, as the Atlacatl Battalion moved on to Los Toriles and killed everyone there. And one can presume it was not only the guide who had empathic reactions such as this: "I saw them shoot an old woman, and they had to hold her up to shoot her. I was filled with pity. I wished we had gone out and fought guerrillas, because to see all those dead children filled me with sadness" (a guide to the Atlacatl, quoted in Danner, p. 81).

Word of soldiers' moral concerns reached Captain Walter Oswaldo Salazar, and the following morning he angrily addressed the men of the Atlacatl:

> What we did yesterday, and the day before, this is called war. This is what war is. War is hell. And, goddammit, if I order you to kill your mother, that is just what you're going to do. Now, I don't want to hear that, afterward, while you're out drinking and bullshitting among yourselves, you're whining and complaining about this, about how terrible it was. I don't want to hear that. Because what we did yesterday, what we've been doing on this operation—this is war, gentlemen. This is what war is. (Captain Salazar, as recalled by a guide, quoted in Danner, p. 82)

Although Captain Salazar provided a great deal more verbiage than the more demonstrative major, he did not provide much more in the way of moral argumentation. Instead he demanded obedience regardless of other considerations on the ground that war is a special context in which moral norms do not apply, and the major might be said to have demonstrated the same thing. In dismissing moral concerns as sentimental and irrelevant, the officers neither demonstrated nor encouraged moral identity.

Lieutenant Colonel Domingo Monterrosa Barrios, however, the charismatic commander of the Atlacatl Battalion, provided a utilitarian justification for operations such as that at El Mozote. According to *La República* correspondent Lucía Annunziata, who traveled frequently with him, Colonel Monterrosa "wanted at all costs to win the war," and believed it necessary "to turn the tide … by scaring the hell out of the enemy. It was a deliberate demonstration of cruelty to show them that the guerrillas couldn't protect them. And he understood that you do this as cruelly, as brutally as possible; you rape, impale, whatever, to show them the cost" (quoted in Danner, p. 146).

But why was Monterrosa so committed to winning the war, and how could these means be justified? The Red Zone, in his view, was a diseased part of El Salvador. Just as healthy tissue must sometimes be sacrificed to excise a cancer, some innocent people might have to be sacrificed to eliminate communism (Danner, p. 52). It seems likely, moreover, that Monterrosa saw Communism not just as a flawed political system but as an immoral one, a political ideology utterly contrary to human rights and welfare. On balance, weighing (what he saw as) the great evil of Communism against (what he saw as) the small number of innocent people in the Red Zone, he deemed the policy of massacres to be morally justified. Indeed, he may have believed that for a military officer such as himself, faced with an enemy as evil as the one he perceived, what he did was a moral obligation.

It is thus plausible that Colonel Monterrosa had a strong moral identity—that he genuinely saw himself as a person fundamentally committed to acting on the basis of respect or concern for the rights or welfare of others, including, especially, the moral right of all Salvadorans to live under a non-Communist system of government. At the same time, however, we must consider Monterrosa's utter lack of attention to the morality of his means:

> By doing what it did in El Mozote, the Army had proclaimed loudly and unmistakably to the people of Morazan, and to the peasants in surrounding areas as well, a simple message: In the end, the guerrillas can't protect you, and we, the officers and the soldiers, are willing to do absolutely anything to avoid losing this war—we are willing to do whatever it takes. (Danner, p. 141)

Thus, Monterrosa's conception of himself as fundamentally guided by respect or concern for human rights or welfare was false, but he may well have been genuinely motivated by moral commitments central to his identity. We may best understand Colonel Monterrosa by construing him as acting on the basis of a false moral identity.

Early Denials

Its mission complete, the Atlacatl left the Red Zone and the guerrillas returned. Even with the Atlacatl Battalion's history of deadly violence against civilian populations, the guerrillas were surprised and shocked by what they found at El Mozote, especially given that it was not a community they considered supportive of them or their cause. They moved quickly to publicize the massacre.

As word of the massacre at El Mozote emerged from Morazan, the government of El Salvador recognized that the actions of the Atlacatl Battalion posed a serious threat to the continuation of U.S. military aid. Under U.S. law, President Reagan was required, by January 28, 1982, to provide Congress with a formal evaluation of El Salvador's human rights record, after which Congress would decide whether to continue military aid. Rather than defend what they may have recognized as indefensible, Salvadoran officials promptly and consistently denied that any massacre had taken place. A spokesman for the armed forces dismissed reports of the massacre as "totally false," charging that they had been fabricated by "subversives" (Bonner, 1982, in Danner, p. 189). President José Napoleón Duarte likewise dismissed the massacre claims as "a guerrilla trick" intended to undermine the continuation of U.S. aid (Danner, p. 89). The Salvadoran Ambassador in Washington, D.C., emphatically rejected the very possibility that the Army of El Salvador had engaged in the killing of women and children, insisting that such behavior was "not within the armed institution's philosophy" (Guillermoprieto, 1982, in Danner, p. 183). Given what he saw, or at least claimed to see, as the moral philosophy of the armed forces, the alleged massacre could not have occurred.

As for the Atlacatl, from Monterrosa on down, they were not talking. Monterrosa was being cagey and political. His message to an American official who met with him at some length was, in effect, "I know what happened, and you know I know, but I know you don't want to hear it, so I'll be your good friend and not say it" (Danner, pp. 120–122). The silence of the soldiers, meanwhile, was literal, and struck U.S. Embassy official Todd Greentree as ominous: "I mean, you talk to a soldier who thinks he's taken part in some heroic operation—and a Latin soldier, I mean—you can't get him to shut up. But these soldiers would say nothing. There was something there" (quoted in Danner, p. 108).

Perhaps the soldiers were under orders not to speak about El Mozote, but it also seems that at least some of them were not oblivious to the immorality of at least some aspects of the massacre. To maintain a sense of themselves as moral agents, they needed to deny to others, and perhaps to themselves, what they had done.

At a public level, however, the strategy of denial was complicated by the fact that reporters Raymond Bonner and Alma Guillermoprieto and photographer Susan Meiselas were invited to El Mozote by the guerrillas now in control. An article entitled "Massacre of Hundreds Reported in Salvador Village," by Raymond Bonner, appeared on the front page of the *New York Times* on January 27, 1982. An article by Alma Guillermoprieto, appearing the same day on the front page of the *Washington Post*, was entitled "Salvadoran Peasants Describe Mass Killing; Woman Tells of Children's Death."

The *New York Times* article (p. 1) began as follows:

Mozote, El Salvador. From interviews with people who live in this small mountain village and surrounding hamlets, it is clear that a massacre of major proportions occurred here last month.

In some 20 mud brick huts here, this reporter saw the charred skulls and bones of dozens of bodies buried under burned-out roofs, beams and shattered tiles. There were more along the trail leading through the hills into the village, and at the edge of a nearby cornfield were the remains of 14 young men, women and children.

In separate interviews during a two-week period in the rebel-controlled northern part of Morazan Province, 13 peasants said that all these, their relatives and friends, had been killed by Government soldiers of the Atlacatl Battalion in a sweep in December.

The *Washington Post* article (p. 1) began as follows:

Mozote, El Salvador, Jan. 14 (Delayed). Several hundred civilians, including women and children, were taken from their homes in and around this village and killed by Salvadoran Army troops during a December offensive against leftist guerrillas, according to three survivors who say they witnessed the alleged massacres.

Reporters taken to tour the region and speak to the survivors by guerrilla soldiers, who control large areas of Morazan Province, were shown the rubble of scores of adobe houses they and the survivors said were destroyed by the troops in the now deserted village community. Dozens of decomposing bodies still were seen beneath the rubble and lying in nearby fields, despite the month that has passed since the incident.

The following day, President Ronald Reagan sent Congress his formal certification that the government of El Salvador was "making a concerted and significant effort to comply with internationally recognized human rights" (Danner, p. 102) and "is achieving substantial control over all elements of its own armed forces, so as to bring to an end the indiscriminate torture and murder of Salvadoran citizens by these forces" (Guillermoprieto, 1982, in Danner, p. 188).

"Something Happened That Should Not Have Happened"

As Congress prepared for a decision about continued funding for the Salvadoran military, the U.S. Ambassador in San Salvador, Deane Hinton, met for dinner with Salvador's Minister of Defense, General José Guillermo García. He subsequently cabled the State Department:

> Defense Minister Garcia is on his way to States to attend, among other things, a Congressional prayer breakfast. ... Warned Garcia to be ready to respond to Morazan massacre story. He was his usual cocky self, "I'll deny it and prove it fabricated." I wished him well and added he would have to explain away details provided by correspondents. It might be possible ... but he should bear in mind that something had gone wrong. (cable from Ambassador Hinton, reprinted in Danner, p. 202)

Ambassador Hinton thus seemed dubious of Defense Minister García's plan to continue the Salvadoran policy of absolutely denying reports of a massacre in El Mozote. His objection here seems pragmatic rather than moral, however. Now that reports of a massacre had reached the front pages of the two major newspapers in the United States, absolute denial no longer seemed tenable. Any credible response, in light of what was known, would have to acknowledge in some way that "something had gone wrong."

For the Reagan administration, anti-Communism was an identity-defining moral mission. To question the continuation of military aid to El Salvador, wrote Secretary of State Alexander Haig in a cable to U.S. diplomats, was to deem it "acceptable to the United States if El Salvador goes the Cuban way" (quoted in Danner, p. 92). If the Reagan administration was committed to anything, it was committed to avoiding this outcome. And this commitment could not be overridden by moral considerations of human rights because Communism was construed as the ultimate violation of human rights. As Elliott Abrams, Assistant Secretary of State for Human Rights and Humanitarian Affairs, told Danner "I used to say to people, 'I mean, I can see arguing for an FMLN [guerrilla] victory on political grounds or economic grounds—but on human-rights grounds? I mean, that's crazy' " (quoted in Danner, p. 91). Thus, Abrams echoed the utilitarian argument of Colonel Monterrosa. Whatever the moral cost of defeating Communism, it was less than the moral cost of a Communist victory.

It is unclear, however, to what extent others in the Reagan administration accepted this utilitarian calculus. Whatever the menace of Communism, to acknowledge the full extent of the massacres and other human rights violations of the government the U.S. was supporting in El Salvador would have jeopardized the administration's sense of itself as a fundamentally moral agent. The massacres, after all, were just part of the government's multifaceted program of violence against the political left:

> The most visible signs of the "dirty war" were mutilated corpses that each morning littered the streets of El Salvador's cities. Sometimes the bodies were headless, or faceless, their features having been obliterated with a shotgun blast or an application of battery acid; sometimes limbs were missing, or hands or feet chopped off, or eyes gouged out; women's genitals were torn and bloody, bespeaking repeated rape; men's were often found severed and stuffed into their mouths. And cut into the flesh of a corpse's back or chest was likely to be the signature of one or another of the "death squads" that had done the work. (Danner, pp. 25–26)

In its testimony to Congress the administration downplayed the utilitarian argument. If U.S. foreign policy was truly moral, not even the defeat of Communism could justify abuses of this nature and scope. To acknowledge the truth was an unacceptable threat to the administration's moral identity. Thus, denial was necessary to maintain an adequate level of consistency between the administration's moral self-conception and its support of the Salvadoran government and military.

Not knowing was thus crucial to the maintenance of the administration's moral identity. By not knowing the terrible things for which one does not want to be responsible, one need not lie, to others and perhaps to oneself, about one's responsibility. And so El Mozote was collaboratively denied: Salvadoran officials did not tell, and U.S. officials did not press too hard because they did not want to know what they were not being told.

Just as there are limits on what one can know, however, there are limits on what one can not know. In El Salvador, U.S. Ambassador Hinton and others knew more than they had said, and as the ambassador began to hear reports that he had denied the allegations of a massacre at El Mozote, he apparently became uncomfortable. In a February 1, 1982 cable to the State Department he clarified that for all his focus on nonconfirmation he had never explicitly denied the allegations and did not wish to be reported as having done so. Now he indicated that "additional evidence strongly suggests that something happened that should not have happened and that it is quite possible Salvadoran military did commit excesses" (cable reprinted in Danner, p. 207). In Washington, the administration did not want to know what had "happened that should not have happened," but recognized that its denial strategy would have to be more subtle than that of the Salvadoran officials.

The Epistemology of Oblivion

The task of justifying the administration's certification of El Salvador's human rights record fell to Assistant Secretary of State Thomas Enders. Testifying on February 2, 1982, before the House Subcommittee on Western Hemisphere Affairs, Enders acknowledged "that the human rights situation in El Salvador is deeply troubled" (testimony reprinted in Danner, p. 209). Rather than deny what the administration had concluded could no longer be credibly denied, he contextualized it so as to diffuse moral responsibility:

> Countless violations of human rights have arisen from partisan animosities of both left and right, personal vendettas, retaliations, provocations, intimidation, and sheer brutality. The breakdown in this society has been profound and will take years to heal. ...
>
> The most difficult of all to assess are the repeated allegations of massacres. The ambiguity lies in the fact that there are indeed incidents in which the noncombatants have suffered terribly at the hands of the guerrillas, rightist vigilantes, Government forces, or some or all of them, but at the same time the insurgency has repeatedly fabricated or inflated alleged mass murders as a means of propaganda. (Secretary Enders, in Danner, pp. 209–210)

With specific regard to the alleged massacre at El Mozote,

> It is clear ... that there has been a confrontation between the guerrillas occupying Mozote and attacking Government forces last December. There is no evidence to confirm that Government forces systematically massacred civilians in the operations zone or that the number of civilians remotely approached the 733 or 926 victims cited in the press. (Enders, in Danner, p. 211)

Overall, then, how could the human rights record of El Salvador be evaluated? Certainly, argued Enders, it would be unrealistic and unfair to apply an absolute standard unattainable in the context of El Salvador. Rather, the appropriate standard was one of progress relative to past abuses. With this in mind, he reported that the number of political murders in the last 4 months of 1980 were 800, 779, 575, and 665, respectively. The comparable figures for the last 4 months of 1981 were 171, 161, 302, and 200. These figures, he acknowledged, were at best rough approximations based on grossly inadequate information. Nevertheless, he concluded, they were the best figures available, and they justified the administration's certification and the continuation of military aid.

Enders' testimony was false on most crucial points of fact. To take just one obvious example, the figure for December 1981 immediately rises from 200 to 967 if one adds the victims of the El Mozote massacre.

We should not assume, however, that the testimony was a pack of lies, a deliberate effort to deceive. On the contrary, there is no reason to doubt that Enders and others in the administration believed most or all of what he said. They were not just trying to convince Congress to continue support for the El Salvador government; at least some, I suggest, were trying to convince themselves that the ongoing mass killings by governmental forces were really declining and that, on balance, continued support for the military was morally justified.

Ongoing support for the Salvadoran military was a commitment central to the Reagan administration's anti-Communist identity and thus essentially non-negotiable. To advocate for continuing aid while maintaining a theory of itself as a fundamentally moral agent, the administration had to maximize the evil of withdrawing aid and minimize the evil of continuing it. Simply highlighting the moral threat of Communism would not suffice to justify an ongoing moral catastrophe. Thus, it was necessary to minimize the full extent and horror of government-sponsored violence in El Salvador.

Enders employed a two-pronged strategy to achieve this—a strategy of contextualization and a strategy of not knowing. As shown, his testimony contextualized present governmental atrocities with respect to both other atrocities and its own past atrocities. Although the government and its affiliated death squads were responsible for the overwhelming proportion of killings, Enders presented a picture of atrocities perpetrated by many groups for many reasons, with governmental killings an expectable piece of a larger violent picture. Moreover, by setting the legal and moral standard as "progress," he deflected attention from the absolute level of violence by considering it in the context of history. Governmental violations of human rights were thus understandable in the moral context of El Salvador and, in any event, were declining.

Enders also minimized the extent and horror of government-sponsored atrocities through processes of not knowing, including (a) not seeking information and (b) self-serving manipulation of the standards for assessment of evidence. By not knowing, I mean processes of denial more subtle and often less conscious than withholding or lying about what one knows. If we do not know, we do not have to lie.

One way not to know is not to seek evidence. In the U.S. Embassy in San Salvador, it was well understood that reports to Washington had to be written "to have credibility among people who were far away and whose priorities were—you know, we're talking about people like Tom Enders—whose priorities were definitely not necessarily about getting at exactly what happened" (junior reporting officer Greentree, quoted in Danner, p. 116).

The United States had many leads it could have pursued and many additional steps it could have taken if finding out what happened at El Mozote had been a high priority. As we saw, Ambassador Hinton knew and said that "something happened that should not have happened." He put this as if he were glimpsing some barely discernible moral reality, but he and many others clearly knew more than they were saying. One of the original American advisors with the Atlacatl Battalion explained to Danner:

> El Mozote was in a place, in a zone, that was one hundred percent controlled by the guerrillas. You try to dry those areas up. You know you're not going to be able to work with the civilian population up there, you're never going to get a permanent base there. So you just decide to kill everybody. That'll scare everybody else out of the zone. It's done more out of frustration than anything else. (quoted in Danner, p. 52)

Not knowing can also be achieved through self-serving reasoning biases (Klaczynski, 1997, 2000; Klaczynski & Gordon, 1996; Klaczynski & Narasimham, 1998), including, in this case, self-serving manipulations of standards of knowledge. At each stage of reporting on El Mozote, from Embassy investigations through Secretary Enders' testimony to Congress, the U.S. government relied on the skeptical "assumption that in the absence of definitive proof nothing at all can really be said to be known. In effect, officials made active use of the obstacles to finding out the truth ... to avoid saying clearly and honestly what they knew and what they suspected" (Danner, p. 113).

With regard to the certification decision, however, a very different standard was put forward. Not only was any progress sufficient, but data that would be deemed worthless in any social scientific context were considered sufficient to demonstrate progress.

Representative Gerry Studds of Massachusetts was among those who were appalled by Enders' testimony:

> If there is anything left of the English language in this city …it is gone now because the President has just certified that up is down and in is out and black is white. I anticipate his telling us that war is peace at any moment. … Bodies have turned up every single day of the year, as you know, in El Salvador. What I would like to know is how long you think this administration can continue to shrug away stories of massacre, and torture, and murder of this type and how long you can downplay, as you did in your earlier remarks, killings, such as those which occurred at Mozote and the Rio Lempa before that, the murders of the churchwomen, the killing of the Archbishop, and an assassination in cold blood in November 1980 of the entire leadership of the opposition. (response from Representative Studds, reprinted in Danner, pp. 215–216)

The administration's utilitarian calculus, moreover, violated elementary moral norms of universalizability:

> You have also said to us, in your statement, if, after Nicaragua, El Salvador is captured by a violent minority, who in Central America would not live in fear?

> Mr. Secretary, you must know that El Salvador is at the moment captured by a violent minority. It has been run by a violent minority for the duration of this century, and unfortunately a violent minority supported by our own Government. (Studds, in Danner, p. 217)

Others also commented on the Orwellian nature of the certification, but Congress ultimately voted to continue and later that year to increase U.S. military aid to El Salvador. The killing raged on, and the story of El Mozote, at least outside Morazan, faded from consciousness.

Ten years later a Truth Commission was appointed, in connection with the January 1992 peace agreement, to investigate the violence of the dirty war. With regard to El Mozote, it received a detailed report of an exhumation at the sacristy by the Argentine Forensic Anthropology Team. The team, formed in Buenos Aires in 1984 in the wake of Argentina's own dirty war, found the tangled, burnt, and fragmented skeletal remains of at least 143 persons, mostly young children, and the remains of ammunition from Lake City, MO. The Truth Commission wrote: "Those small skeletons are proof not only of the existence of the cold-blooded massacre at El Mozote but also of the collusion of senior commanders of the armed forces, for they show that the evidence of the unburied bodies was there for a long time for anyone who wanted to investigate the facts" (quoted in Danner, p. 263).

CONCLUSION

To have a moral identity, I have suggested, is to have an explicit theory of yourself as a rational agent committed to acting on the basis of respect and/or concern for the rights and/or welfare of others. Our actual behavior, however, is often less based on moral considerations than we think it is, and in some cases a person's actual self is so discrepant from his or her explicit theory of self as moral agent that the theory—that is, the moral identity—is false. Even if moral identities are not universal, most people see themselves as, for the most part, moral agents, and few are highly consistent in following through on this commitment. To varying degrees, perhaps we all have false moral identities.

The concept of false moral identity reminds us that strong identities can be the basis for terrible things (Maalouf, 2001; Moshman, in press) and that this is not just the case when identities are not sufficiently moral. Even moral identities, as we have seen, can be the basis for terrible things. It matters that people act on the basis of concern for rights and welfare—it is not enough that they think they do. To whatever extent possible, we should aim to promote true moral identities.

The focus on truth highlights the epistemological dimension of advanced moral and identity development. We can maintain false theories by denying evidence, and when the theories are theories of ourselves as moral agents and when our behavior, for whatever reason, is not genuinely subject to change, the motivation to deny what we see or do may be overwhelming. Advanced development, then, must include learning to recognize and overcome our tendencies to evade disconfirming evidence, to manipulate epistemic standards in self-serving ways, and to contextualize away what we would otherwise deplore. This is no small challenge: The forces of denial, both internal and external, are ubiquitous and powerful (Batson et al., 1999; Bersoff, 1999; Chomsky, 1989; Churchill, 1997; Cohen, 2001; Klaczynski, 1997, 2000; Klaczynski & Gordon, 1996; Klaczynski & Narasimham, 1998; Moshman, 2001; Waller, 2002). Nevertheless, we can become more aware of them and can learn, to some extent, to control or compensate for them. At the very least, we can be extra careful to take note when we think we might be seeing something that should not have happened—or that should not be happening.

ACKNOWLEDGMENT

I am grateful to John Gibbs for helpful comments on an earlier draft of this chapter and to Sam Hardy for several useful references.

REFERENCES

Batson, C. D., Thompson, E. R., Seuferling, G., Whitney, H., & Strongman, J. A. (1999). Moral hypocrisy: Appearing moral to oneself without being so. *Journal of Personality and Social Psychology, 77*, 525–537.

Bergman, R. (2002). Why be moral? A conceptual model from developmental psychology. *Human Development, 45*, 104–124.

Bersoff, D. M. (1999). Why good people sometimes do bad things: Motivated reasoning and unethical behavior. *Personality and Social Psychology Bulletin, 25*, 28–39.

Berzonsky, M. D. (1993). A constructivist view of identity development: People as postpositivist self-theorists. In J. Kroger (Ed.), *Discussions on ego identity* (pp. 169–203). Hillsdale, NJ: Lawrence Erlbaum Associates

Blasi, A. (1984). Moral identity: Its role in moral functioning. In W. M. Kurtines & J. L. Gewirtz (Eds.), *Morality, moral behavior, and moral development* (pp. 128–139). New York: Wiley.

Blasi, A. (1995). Moral understanding and the moral personality: The process of moral integration. In W. M. Kurtines & J. L. Gewirtz (Eds.), *Moral development: An introduction* (pp. 229–253). Needham Heights, MA: Allyn & Bacon.

Bonner, R. (1982, January 27). Massacre of hundreds reported in Salvador village. *The New York Times*, Section A, p. 1.

Chomsky, N. (1989). *Necessary illusions: Thought control in democratic societies.* Boston: South End.

Churchill, W. (1997). *A little matter of genocide: Holocaust and denial in the Americas, 1492 to the present.* San Francisco: City Lights.

Cohen, S. (2001). *States of denial: Knowing about atrocities and suffering.* Cambridge, England: Polity.

Colby, A., & Damon, W. (1992). *Some do care: Contemporary lives of moral commitment.* New York: The Free Press.

Danner, M. (1994). *The massacre at El Mozote.* New York: Vintage.

Flavell, J. H., & Miller, P. H. (1998). Social cognition. In W. Damon (Series Ed.), D. Kuhn & R. Siegler (Vol. Eds.), *Handbook of child psychology: Vol. 2. Cognition, perception, and language* (5th ed., pp. 851–898). New York: Wiley.

Flavell, J. H., Miller, P. H., & Miller, S. A. (2002). *Cognitive development* (4th ed.). Upper Saddle River, NJ: Prentice Hall.

Gibbs, J. C. (2003). *Moral development and reality: Beyond the theories of Kohlberg and Hoffman.* Thousand Oaks, CA: Sage.

Guillermoprieto, A. (1982, January 27). Salvadoran peasants describe mass killing; woman tells of children's death. *The Washington Post*, Section A, p. 1.

Harter, S. (1999). *The construction of the self.* New York: Guilford.

Klaczynski, P. A. (1997). Bias in adolescents' everyday reasoning and its relationship with intellectual ability, personal theories, and self-serving motivation. *Developmental Psychology, 33*, 273–283.

Klaczynski, P. A. (2000). Motivated scientific reasoning biases, epistemological beliefs, and theory polarization: A two-process approach to adolescent cognition. *Child Development, 71*, 1347–1366.

Klaczynski, P. A., & Gordon, D. H. (1996). Self-serving influences on adolescents' evaluations of belief-relevant evidence. *Journal of Experimental Child Psychology, 62*, 317–339.

Klaczynski, P. A., & Narasimham, G. (1998). The development of self-serving reasoning biases: Ego-protective versus cognitive explanations. *Developmental Psychology, 34*, 175–187.

Kochanska, G. (2002). Committed compliance, moral self, and internalization: A mediational model. *Developmental Psychology, 38*, 339–351.

Kuhn, D. (1989). Children and adults as intuitive scientists. *Psychological Review, 96*, 674–689.

Kuhn, D. (2000). Theory of mind, metacognition, and reasoning: A life-span perspective. In P. Mitchell & K. J. Riggs (Eds.), *Children's reasoning about the mind* (pp. 301–326). Hove, England: Psychology Press.

Maalouf, A. (2001). *In the name of identity: Violence and the need to belong.* New York: Arcade.

Monroe, K. R. (2001). Morality and a sense of self: The importance of identity and categorization for moral action. *American Journal of Political Science, 45*, 491–507.

Moshman, D. (1995). The construction of moral rationality. *Human Development, 38*, 265–281.

Moshman, D. (1998). Cognitive development beyond childhood. In W. Damon (Series Ed.), D. Kuhn & R. Siegler (Vol. Eds.), Handbook of child psychology: Vol. 2. Cognition, perception, and language (5th ed., pp. 947–978). New York: Wiley.

Moshman, D. (1999). *Adolescent psychological development: Rationality, morality, and identity.* Mahwah, NJ: Lawrence Erlbaum Associates.

Moshman, D. (2001). Conceptual constraints on thinking about genocide. *Journal of Genocide Research, 3*, 431–450.

Moshman, D. (in press). Theories of self and theories as selves: Identity in Rwanda. In C. Lalonde, C. Lightfoot, & M. Chandler (Eds.), *Changing conceptions of psychological life.* Mahwah, NJ: Lawrence Erlbaum Associates.

Nucci, L. (2002). Because it is the right thing to do. *Human Development, 45*, 125–129.

Piaget, J. (1965). *The moral judgment of the child.* New York: The Free Press. (Original work published 1932)

Turiel, E. (2002). *The culture of morality.* Cambridge, England: Cambridge University Press.

Waller, J. (2002). *Becoming evil: How ordinary people commit genocide and mass killing.* Oxford, England: Oxford University Press.

Wellman, H. M., & Gelman, S. A. (1998). Knowledge acquisition in foundational domains. In W. Damon (Series Ed.), D. Kuhn & R. Siegler (Vol. Eds.), *Handbook of child psychology: Vol. 2. Cognition, perception, and language* (5th ed., pp. 523–573). New York: Wiley.

6

Reflections on the Moral Self Construct

Larry Nucci
University of Illinois at Chicago

Accounting for moral agency has proven to be a complex and difficult problem for moral psychology. How is it that we move from knowing right from wrong to acting in relation to that moral understanding? Are differences in the tendencies to engage in moral action a function of differences in kinds of people or differences in kinds of knowledge that people have? Can we even successfully pose such a dichotomy? What I hope to accomplish within this chapter is to examine recent attempts to resolve these questions through work that is being done on what is called the *moral self*. I explore whether the constructs of moral self and moral identity have utility or whether in fact such constructs are redundant with a structuralist moral psychology, or even reductionist and mechanistic. Unlike most chapters that one sets out to write, I did not approach this topic with a conclusion in mind. In fact, some of what I have to say is inconsistent with what I have written on this same topic in a recently published book (Nucci, 2001), and it is at odds with some of the statements included within the Presidential Adress on which this chapter draws. This inconsistency in my own writing reflects the struggle to avoid the dualism that results from the disjunction of moral motivation from moral judgment (a disjunction that dates back at least to Aristotle). As will become clear in the context of this chapter, I take issue with the notion advanced by Blasi (1993) and supported by others (Bergman, 2002) that it is the goal of maintaining self-consistency that motivates individuals to act morally.

This is not to say that there are not important connections between one's personal identity and moral conduct. These connections, however, would appear to be reciprocal, arising out of the interplay between one's moral judgments and the construction of the self within a particular lifeworld. As such, one can speculate on the relations that might exist between a person's moral understandings, their qualities as a person, and the ways in which such qualities might enter into contextualized moral actions. As the philosopher William Frankena (1963) put it, the morality of principles and the morality "of doing and being" (p. 53) are complementary aspects of the same morality such that for every principle there is a corresponding disposition or tendency to act in accordance with it. What needs to be added to Frankena's formulation is that the employment of moral principles is itself a function of contextualized decision making colored by the ways in which particular persons relate themselves to given situations. Thus, the notion of moral self cannot be easily divorced from the ways in which individuals construe themselves more generally within their particular lifeworlds. What this also implies, as argued later in this chapter, is that our theory of moral decision making must make room for such contextual factors if it is to accurately capture the ways in which individuals with particular life histories, worldviews, and personal identities weigh moral and nonmoral factors in generating particular courses of action.

The effort to define the moral self and related work on moral identity has been offered as a counterpoint to more traditional conceptions of moral agency framed in terms of personal character and moral virtue. This structuralist alternative to these traditional approaches has its roots in Kohlberg and Turiel's (1971) devastating critique of traditional character education, and their subsequent account of moral development. Therefore, we first look at the notions of moral virtue and character and the response to virtue theory offered by Kohlberg's (1984) structuralist moral theory.

ARISTOTLE AND VIRTUE

Socrates, we are told, held the view that, "nobody does wrong willingly: we choose the lesser good only as a result of ignorance" (Nussbaum, 1986, p. 240). Aristotle, in contrast, rejected this view as simply inconsistent with the phenomena (Nussbaum, 1986). On Aristotle's account, good and right action are not simply a question of epistemology, but they result from being a particular kind of person for whom virtuous conduct is part and parcel of the person's very being. Essentially all contemporary Western virtue theories are grounded in Aristotle's viewpoint. Aristotle's approach to ethics begins not with the question of what it means to act morally but with the more general question, "What does it mean to lead a good life?" Aristotle held that all things in nature are always moving toward a flourishing of their own nature. That is, all living things have a telos. Seedlings grow up to be mature trees. The business of leading a good life is to move toward the human telos and to achieve eudaimonia or a flourishing (Nussbaum, 1997). With respect to ethics, the process of flourishing entails the gradual development of virtues or personal characteristics that will support ethical conduct. In youth, this process involves the building up of habits that in time translate into ways of being that constitute virtuous conduct.

Because Aristotle wrote so long ago and because most of his surviving works are in the form of lecture notes rather than the equivalents of articles or books, his ideas have become a sort of Rorschach of the given time period (Nussbaum, 1986). Aristotle's notion of habit and his emphasis on the phenomenological have led to an assimilation of his positions to logical positivism and behaviorist theories of learning and development. His notion of human flourishing has been adopted by utilitarians who support the pursuit of happiness and an ethics based on outcomes. Modern translators of his work, such as Nussbaum (1986), have taken issue with these various assimilations. Based on Nussbaum's reading, according to Aristotle, the child is not simply a creature who is causally affected and manipulated but an active, cognitive being that responds selectively and whose actions are explained by his or her own view of things. Thus, Aristotle's approach to habit formation has more in common with such notions as the construction of cognitive schemas than it does with behaviorist notions of association. This nonbehaviorist view of habituation allowed Aristotle to propose a developmental progression in which such habits become subsumed within reasoned judgment. In terms of ethics, the core or master virtue is justice, around which the other virtues serve supporting roles.

The development of the virtuous person thus involves the cultivation of the right set of habits, ethical values, and a conception of the good human life as the harmonious pursuit of these aspects. Such a person will be "concerned about friendship, justice, courage, moderation and generosity; his desires will be formed in accordance with these concerns; and he will derive from this internalized conception of value many ongoing guidelines for action, pointers as to what to look for in a particular situation" (Nussbaum, 1986, p. 306). Because Aristotle perceived these values and commitments to be trans-situational, he took them to be what the person is in and of himself or herself.

KOHLBERG'S CRITIQUE OF VIRTUE
THEORY AND RESPONSE

Kohlberg's (Kohlberg & Turiel, 1971) critique of virtue theory was not aimed directly at Aristotle but at American traditional character education. The traditional view combined elements of Aristotle's conception of virtue with behaviorist and social learning theory conceptions of socialization. Kohlberg's critique responded to both elements of traditional character education on four main points.

First, Kohlberg established that the definition of what counts as a *virtue* varies as a function of cultural and historical setting. A humorous updating of this critique has been offered by Daniel Lapsley (1996) who compared the checklist of virtues from his own elementary school report card against the list of 23 virtues to be used as core values in character education classes, which were compiled in 1988 by The Panel on Moral Education of the American Society for Curriculum Development (ASCD). The only virtue that overlapped between the two lists was courtesy. In addition, the list compiled by the ASCD panel left out 9 of the 11 values in "The Children's Morality Code," an earlier effort to guide teachers that is similar to the ASCD list published in 1929 by W. J. Hutchins.

The second issue raised by Kohlberg was the empirical evidence provided by Hartshorne and May's (1929) research in the late 1920s and early 1930s, which challenged the assumption that there are such things as character traits. This carefully done series of studies demonstrated convincingly that whether or not a person engaged in a particular form of conduct presumed to be consistent or inconsistent with a particular character trait or virtue depended on the context. Faced with the evidence from their series of studies, Hartshorne and May were left to conclude that there was no such thing as character. For example, they concluded there were no people with the character trait of honesty. People were honest in some situations and dishonest in others. These findings were subsequently buttressed by the research conducted in the second half of the century on the related notion of personality traits (Mischel, 1973; Ross & Nisbett, 1991; Sarbin & Allen, 1968). The results of these studies led researchers to conclude that people cannot be accurately described in terms of stable and general personality traits, because they tend to exhibit different and seemingly contradictory aspects of themselves in different contexts. In place of trait theories, contemporary personality psychologists tend to view personality as something one does in particular settings, rather than as something one has independent of context (Lapsley, 1996; Mischel, 1990; Ross & Nisbett, 1991).

Kohlberg's third point builds from these conclusions about personality and virtue. The application of virtues always occurs in context, thus requiring an application of judgment not only as to which virtue is applicable but often to determine which of two or more competing virtues should hold sway. Actually, this contextual aspect of the application of virtue was anticipated by Aristotle who saw the application of virtue as entailing the use of practical wisdom. Kohlberg's insight into this issue was to recognize that moral virtue essentially reduces itself to the structures of reasoning that people employ to resolve moral situations.

Kohlberg's final point is that moral reason does not emerge spontaneously as a result of environmentally evoked hard-wired modules or Platonic forms, and the capacity for moral reasoning is not the result of the gradual building up of habits but rather the construction and reconstruction of forms of understanding that emerge through processes of cognitive equilibration, as outlined within Piaget's (1932) genetic epistemology.

Kohlberg's (1984) alternative to the morality of personal virtue is his six-stage theory of moral development. The brilliance of Kohlberg's theory is that it offers simultaneous resolution to nearly every conundrum faced by moral psychology. Kohlberg's structuralist theory accounts for the contextual variation in people's morality through the application of moral reasoning. Moral maturity is understood as the progressive development of more morally adequate forms of moral judgment. The invariance of personal virtue is replaced by the contextual invariance of cognitive structure, and the telos of eudaimonia or human flourishing is replaced by the telos of equilibration. This is not say that Kohlberg was opposed to the notion of the development of personal goals and projects as a part of self-actualization. Kohlberg did not see how one could define that aspect of personal development in any but the most individual of ways, and he felt that such aspects of personal growth were not in and of themselves aspects of morality. In essence Kohlberg agreed with the philosopher William Frankena's (1963) distinction between leading the "good life" in the Aristotelian sense of flourishing and leading a life that is good in an objectively moral sense. In what is one of the most important of his works, Kohlberg (1971) argued in his chapter, "From Is To Ought," that the process of equilibration of structures of moral thought moves inevitably toward a philosophically defensible moral ought. Kohlberg was in agreement with the notion that there is but one moral virtue—the virtue of justice. My reading of Kohlberg's (1969) early work is that he viewed the progression toward Stage 6 as culminating in structures of thought that produce decisions that are morally binding on people. Thus, his views agree with Socrates: To know the good is to do the good.

INCONSISTENCIES, CONTRADICTIONS, AND HETEROGENEITY

Unfortunately, Kohlberg's theory does not fit all of the relevant phenomena. Kohlberg (1984) acknowledged early that there were certain minor contradictions with his theory regarding the binding nature of Stage 6. He mentioned in some of his early work the well-known contradiction between the principled moral positions of Thomas Jefferson and his relationship with his slave, Sally Hemmings. Kohlberg explained this contradiction as evidence that persons knowing what is morally right may not have the will to act on that knowledge if they are under great social pressure. Kohlberg saw this as particularly the case when a person takes a moral stand at variance with generally held social convention. Kohlberg (1969) dealt with this type of contradiction by invoking the construct of ego strength—a psychological notion quite divergent from his structuralism.

The problem of social pressure arose again in the results of Milgram's (1974) studies on authority and social conformity when it was found that a portion of subjects judged to be Stage 6 moral reasoners were nonetheless willing to go along with social authority and continued to shock the supposed learner in the study to the point where the shocks caused great pain and discomfort and posed physical danger to the person supposedly receiving the shocks (Kohlberg, 1969). This study is often cited as evidence (e.g., Kohlberg, 1984) that moral development is associated with moral behavior because proportionately more postconventional reasoners resisted the authority than did subjects with lower stages of moral judgment. However, the fact that any post-conventional reasoners went along with the authority would seem to be a problem for the theory. Moreover, the fact that a considerable number of people at lower developmental stages resisted the authority suggested that personal features other than moral stage may have been involved in guiding people's behavior.

Augusto Blasi (1983) provided the first comprehensive review of the relation between moral stage and behavior that looked not simply at postconventional reasoning but at the entire developmental progression. Blasi's review concluded that there was a general trend for moral behavior to be associated with the developmental stage, and that people at higher stages of development were less likely to engage in various forms of moral misconduct than were people at lower stages. This was particularly the case if one looked at forms of behavior that had moral consequences for the welfare of others. Nonetheless, the power of the association was far less than perfect, and it suggested that other factors beyond moral judgment, as assessed by Kohlberg's stages, were involved in generating moral actions.

These results led some of Kohlberg's followers to generate multifactor models of moral reasoning (Gerson & Damon, 1978; Rest, 1983). With some variation in the number of steps, a distinction is drawn in these models between the deontic evaluation of the morally right thing to do and the evaluation of whether the moral judgment, once made, poses a responsibility for action on the person. In these formulations, Kohlberg's stage theory accounts for the judgment of moral right and wrong, whereas some other factor accounts for the actual judgment that one is personally responsible to act in a manner consistent with that deontic moral judgment.

MORAL SELF/IDENTITY

As I already mentioned, Blasi presented the first comprehensive review of the judgment–action research on Kohlberg's stage theory. Blasi also offered the first effort to fill in the perceived missing step between moral judgment and action by addressing the connection to the moral self and, more particularly, to moral identity (Blasi, 1984). Blasi's approach was built from Erikson's (1968) work on identity formation, but it is most heavily influenced by Loevinger's theory of ego development. Loevinger's (1976) theory provides a compatible bridge to Kohlberg in that it is constructivist and transformational, rather than logical positivist and behavioral. Employing Loevinger's theory as a starting point, Blasi began to look at the possibility that the link between moral judgment and action lie in the degree to which morality and moral concerns were integrated into the person's sense of self. The basic idea here is that from moral identity derives a psychological need to make one's actions consistent with one's ideals. Thus, in Blasi's (1993) words, "self-consistency is the motivational spring of moral action" (p. 99). In a similar vein, Power and Khmelkov (1998) redefined character as the specifically moral dimensions of self. Like Blasi, they stated that the motive for moral action is not simply the direct result of knowing the good, but from the desire to act in ways that are consistent with one's own sense of self as a moral being. As Power and Khmelkov put it, "Individuals may undertake a particular course of action, even at some cost, because they want to become or remain a certain kind of person" (p. 5). In contrast with the traditional character construct, and joined now by many others (as should be evident by the authors included in this volume) "does not attempt to replace moral ideas with a set of non cognitive personality characteristics: it sees personal identity as operating jointly with reason and truth in providing motives for action" (Blasi, 1993, p. 99). Thus, one's moral character is not something divorced from moral cognition and the complexity that it entails.

General Issues in the Construction of Self

Although the notion of the moral self has its roots in Blasi's work, cognitive theories of moral identity are not constrained by Loevinger's theory of ego development. If we look more broadly at cognitive accounts of the self, we see that the construction of personal identity is itself multifaceted, incorporating values and social roles from a number of contexts. Research on the development of children's conceptions of self (Damon & Hart, 1988; Harter, 1983) provides evidence that with age, children construct increasingly differentiated notions of themselves as actors within different contexts. These differentiated constructs emerge as a result of children's efforts to interpret their differential competence, their involvement in various areas of activity (academic, making friends), and a corresponding tendency with age to assign meaning to those levels of competence and commitment. Harter (1983) suggested that development of self-concepts may very well entail a reiterative process whereby a child's initial attempts to construct an integrated notion of self (e.g., in terms of characteristic behaviors) is followed by a period of differentiation (e.g., good at some things, bad at others). These differentiated general descriptions are then incorporated within a higher level of integration (e.g., general traits), which are then subsequently differentiated. This process eventuates at the most advanced levels of development in a conceptualization of the self in multidimensional and contextual terms (Broughton, 1978; Chandler, 2001; Damon & Hart, 1988).

The inherent complexity of self-definition has its counterpart in efforts at self-evaluation. Current evidence supports the proposition that we construct both a general sense of self-worth and domain-specific evaluations of our own competence (Byrne, 1984; Harter, 1985, 1986; Rosenberg, 1965). This in turn suggests that it is possible for us to have a positive view of ourselves while still having a sense that we are not very good in a particular area of performance. In other words, it may be that we can feel good about ourselves if those areas of performance in which we are not so great are not terribly important to who we are. Research examining how children apply their sense of self to academic performance provides empirical evidence that this is indeed the case. There is little evidence to suggest that students' views of themselves in terms of academic capabilities (academic self-esteem) are necessarily tied to students' general sense of self-worth (Harter, 1983; Marsh, Smith, & Barnes, 1985). For students for whom school matters, performance in school has a relation to the students' self esteem. For those for whom school matters little, their academic performance has little relation to their more general sense of self-esteem.

The question for the present discussion is whether something like this can be operating with respect to morality. If we move from the area of academics back to the issue of the moral self, one can see both parallels and differences. One significant difference is that people are not as free to discount their moral selves as they are to discount other aspects of their personal endeavors such as their performance in mathematics, or on the dance floor (Power & Khmelkov,

1998). This is because morality is inherent in human interaction, and it engages us in binding or objective ways. Perhaps, however, the objective or binding nature of morality may be overstated as a basis for presuming its centrality in the construction of personal identity. Whether one attends to the moral implications of events may be more compelling than whether one develops skill as a dancer, but it may not attain the same degree of salience or centrality for everyone. There is no prima facie reason to assume that the basic process of constructing the moral aspect of the self is fundamentally different from the construction of other aspects of personal identity. Thus, we should expect interpersonal variations in the connection between self and morality.

This assumption of interpersonal variation in moral identity has not been extensively researched. However, Blasi (1993) provided evidence that some individuals let moral notions penetrate to the essence and core of what and who they are, whereas others construct their central defining features of self in other ways. This is not to say that morality is somehow absent in many people, but rather that the moral aspects of self may be subjectively experienced in different ways. Blasi (1993) put it this way:

> Several individuals may see morality as essential to their sense of self, of who they are. For some of them, however, moral ideals and demands happen to be there, a given nature over which they feel little control. In this case moral ideals exist next to other characteristics, all equally important because they are there. Others instead relate to their moral ideals as being personally chosen over other ideals or demands, sense their fragility, and feel responsible to protect them and thus to protect their sense of self. (p. 103)

Morality and the Self

This variability in the centrality of morality within one's personal identity is of interest for the present discussion only if there is also evidence that it matters for moral action and that it serves as a bridge between moral judgment and behavior. Some interesting questions can be raised. Setting aside the small fraction of individuals who are sociopaths, people generally attend to moral social interactions and have common views of prima facie moral obligations (Turiel, 1998). Thus, it is hard to imagine how morality does not comprise an important aspect of the sense of self of most people. Of course, one can argue that people vary in their sense of what it means to be moral in a given context, and in this sense they display individual differences in how they engage the world as moral beings. But this is different from suggesting that morality is somehow nearer and dearer to some people than to others.

Let us consider some cases for sake of argument. Are people who engage in voluntarism and community service more committed to morality than William

Ayers and his wife, Bernadine Dorn, when as leaders of the Weathermen they planned violent actions against the United States during the Vietnam war period? Or, did they read the situation they faced differently and out of a sense of morality engage in violent actions (Ayers, 2001)? Are those of us who engage in research less morally committed than our colleagues who directly serve the public through their training of teachers or physicians? Was Martin Luther King's philandering indicative of his moral character, or should we assume that his moral identity is better captured by his work on civil rights? Which is the true Dr. King, or did he have dual moral identities?

The research evidence around this issue is less than compelling. What is usually presented as evidence is some association between personal definition and prosocial conduct. Hart and Fegley (1995), for example, studied the moral identities of a group of inner city adolescents who exhibited a high degree of community service voluntarism and care for others. These adolescents were identified by community leaders, teachers, and churches as youth who had done such things as organize youth groups and work in homeless shelters. They and a comparison group of adolescents from the same community were asked to generate a list of all of the important characteristics that they could think of that described themselves as they are in the present, the person they were in the past, the person they dreaded becoming, and the kind of person they would ideally like to become. What Hart and Fegley assumed was that persons whose actual selves incorporate a subset of their ideal selves will be more driven to realize the goals of the ideal self than persons whose ideal self and actual self are unrelated. What they discovered was in line with that hypothesis. Two thirds of the adolescents high on voluntarism and care and less than one third of the comparison adolescents exhibited overlap between the characteristics of their actual and ideal selves. Moreover, there was very little correlation between these adolescents' moral stage, as measured within the Kohlberg framework, and their involvement in community service.

A second, widely cited illustration of the connection between moral self and conduct is Colby and Damon's (1992) study of moral exemplars as recounted in their book *Some Do Care*. They reported a series of biographical sketches that purported to demonstrate that the decision to become active in community service or civil rights activities is linked to the ways in which these individuals constructed their own personal identities. As with Hart and Fegley's (1985) study, Colby and Damon reported that their morally exemplary people ranged widely in their Kohlbergian stage of moral development, from lower conventional stages to postconventional.

These two studies and other similar ones lead one to the conclusion that moral development seems to matter little when it comes to moral action and that what does matter are the qualities of the person. But there are several problems with such a conclusion. First, it is not clear that the actions described constitute moral conduct. If, for example, I volunteer to work in a soup kitchen because it will increase my chances of getting into my college of choice, is my voluntarism moral? If I volunteer because it will make me feel good about myself, rather than because I feel compelled to volunteer to alleviate the suffering of others, is my action moral? Without knowing why I volunteered, one cannot know to what extent I either did or did not engage in moral deliberation. This holds both for those who volunteer as well as for those who do not. After all, one third of the volunteers in Hart and Fegley's (1985) study, did not display an integration between their ideal and actual selves, and one third of the subjects who did not volunteer did display this sort of overlap between their actual and ideal self-descriptions. Finally, it is worth noting that the kinds of self-descriptions generated by adolescents in this sort of study are very general in nature. These global self-descriptions can hardly reflect an individual's goals within specific contexts.

Second, one can come to moral conclusions at any Kohlbergian stage of moral development. Colby and Damon (1992) recognized this, but they did not provide convincing evidence whether there is a linkage between the moral decisions of the people they studied, their self-definitions, and their actions.

Actually, Blasi and Glodis (1995) is the only published work that has tried to systematically explore the relationship between moral identity and motivation for moral action, and their findings and interpretations are much more nuanced than that reported in most other research. Blasi and Glodis examined whether people who define morality as a central part of their personal identity experience a sense of personal betrayal when they act in opposition to those moral values. They hypothesized that such a sense of personal betrayal would be more evident in person's whose sense of identity stemmed from their own active efforts at becoming the person they were than among persons whose identity emerged from a relatively passive, unreflective acceptance of themselves. They asked 30 women to indicate an ideal that they considered to be very important to their sense of self, one that she cared deeply about and to which she was deeply committed. Among the ideals listed were friendship, caring for others, morality and justice, self-reliance, and improving one's mind and knowledge. Six to 10 weeks later, each of the women was presented with a story in which a fictional character chooses a course of action advantageous financially and career-wise but which compromised her ideals. The compromised ideal in each case was the one listed by the subject as a central value in her earlier interview.

Blasi and Glodis (1995) found that some of their subjects tended not to see the situation as relevant to their ideals. Instead they focused on the pragmatic consequences of the decision presented in the scenario and expressed feelings of satisfaction with the protagonist's pragmatic choice. Others, on the other hand, saw the situation as entailing a serious contradiction of their ideals and expressed such feelings as shame, guilt, and depression over the protagonist's choice to violate those ideals. The feelings expressed by subjects in the study were a function of whether their own sense of identity was one for which they were actively involved. Subjects whose ideals were not experienced as passively received from outside influences but rather as central concerns to be pursued were those who reported the most distress in response to the scenario entailing a contradiction or betrayal of those ideals.

Note that in discussing their findings, Blasi and Glodis (1995) avoided claiming that it is essential for a person to have constructed a moral identity of this sort for someone to act in morally consonant ways. They recognized that morality may be viewed as important for other reasons, such as social approval, or simply out of concerns for the objective consequences of actions. The latter, of course, is a way of saying that individuals might act morally simply for moral reasons. They also suggested that such intense personal involvement may not be implicated in many day-to-day moral interactions that do not entail dilemmas that pit one's pragmatic self interests against the needs of someone else. The authors suggested that one's personal identity may only become at stake in cases requiring substantial subordination of other motives. Of course, whether one views such situations as placing the self at risk, is a function of whether morality exists as an ideal central to one's self definition. Blasi (1993) asserted that moral and other ideals are chosen as core values because they are understood to be important. As he put it, "to some extent personality is shaped by what one knows to be worthy of education and commitment" (p. 119).

Blasi's work is provocative in that it may be seen as linking Aristotelian notions of eudaimonia (self-flourishing) to the work that has been done on moral cognition. It also implies that constructivist assumptions of how one generates moral knowledge are also important to the active construction of the moral self and consequent moral responsibility and character. But all of this work on the moral self and moral identity leaves open a set of important and as yet unanswered issues:

- *Self-consistency as reductionism.* Each of the moral self theories maintain that the core motivation for moral action among adolescents and adults is the desire to maintain consistency between one's moral actions and one's moral identity. This claim is reductionist and mechanistic by reducing all complex contextualized moral judgments to the simple evaluation of whether the action is or is not consistent with one's sense of self.

- *Self-consistency as ethical egoism.* This explanation of moral action reduces questions of morality from questions about one's obligations to others through judgments of fairness and human welfare to judgments of whether or not the actor will feel right about himself or herself. There are, of course, behavioral psychologists who believe that such positive and negative consequences are at the core of all human motivation. From such a psychological premise, however, all morality is addressed through instrumentalism and ethical egoism. I doubt that was the goal of moral self theorists, particularly because their work is based on the neo-Kantian framework of Kohlberg's (1971) moral psychology. This apparent instrumentalism has not, however, been addressed in their writings.

The philosopher William Frankena (1963) avoided this problem by arguing that just because one might feel good as a result of having done something moral is not of consequence as long as one intended to do the action because it was judged to be the right thing to do. In Frankena's rendering, however, self-consistency is ruled out as a primary motive. A moral self theory can be invoked in this situation but only in a structural sense that people, being who they are, will likely read a given situation in a particular way and being who they are, act in accordance with their judgment; as a consequence; they will feel good about themselves. In this reading, however, self-consistency is the result of a concordant moral decision and subsequent action, rather than a motive for action.

One can take this recovery of theory a step further and argue that a subjective sense of moral inconsistency may be felt as a betrayal of self after the fact, and this may result in feelings of guilt and the desire to self-improve. This is similar to arguments offered by philosophers such as Rorty (1973) who suggested that reflection on and owning up to one's past is essential to the notion of moral responsibility. As Chandler, Lalonde, Sokol, and Lightfoot (2002) vividly put it, without such a backward accounting of one's self, "Judgment day would simply go out of business" (p.13). This suggests, however, that self-consistency is not a guide to moral action but rather an affective component of the process of moral equilibration and development.

- *Lack of developmental continuity from childhood to adolescence.* Perhaps the biggest gap in theory is the paucity of explanatory connection between children's morality and the period in early adolescence when the construction of moral identity is presumed to exert its influence on moral responsibility. Sources as diverse as Freud, Piaget, and the Catholic Church place the age at which children become capable of assuming moral responsibility at about 6 to 8 years at which time children's moral judgments become regulated by conceptions of just reciprocity (Turiel & Davidson, 1986). This is well before the age at which moral identity can be invoked as an explanation for moral motivation. In a recent review, Bergman (2002) offered hints at the elements of a more complete developmental model in his discussion of Damon's (1984) early work on the relations between moral development and self-understanding, but he did not make full use of the insights that were offered. This is because, Bergman, like the other theorists he reviewed, is handcuffed by his commitment to Kohlberg's stages of moral development as the account of moral growth. Thus, Bergman was quite taken with the notion of A and B moral reasoning types without recognizing that this post hoc attempt to save the Kohlberg enterprise is simply a special case better understood within theories of moral and social growth that disaggregate moral and nonmoral social judgments throughout development (Turiel, 1998). These more recent moral theories allow for the prospect that we may prioritize moral over nonmoral concerns throughout the life span and not simply at advanced stages of moral development. Children are to be seen as capable moral beings, and the construction of moral identity—the generation of moral dispositions in concert with one's moral concepts—may be viewed as more continuous than current formulations allow. Of course these newer moral theories also admit greater intraindividual contextual and interindividual cultural variation than does Kohlberg's global theory in the ways in which people interpret their social worlds and generate moral actions.

TOWARD A CONTEXTUALIST STRUCTURAL THEORY OF MORAL COGNITION

I propose that the shortcomings of present efforts to integrate some account of personal agency, and perhaps self and identity with moral judgment, can be overcome if we let go of Kohlberg's (1984) account of moral development and move toward a more contextualized structuralism and a more contextualized view of moral identity. Kohlberg's resolution of the shortcomings of classical views of character formation bound all forms of judgments of social right and wrong within a single developmental system that moved progressively to a point where morality triumphs over convention, personal interest, and pragmatics. We have come to realize that what Kohlberg treated as a single structural system was in fact several systems, or domains of social judgment, of which morality was one (Turiel, 1978, 1983, 1998). This is extensive evidence that concepts of morality center around issues of fairness and human welfare and that they emerge as distinct from conceptions of societal convention at very early ages (Smetana, 1989). Moreover, both morality and convention are distinct from a third conceptual framework concerning issue of personal prerogative and privacy (Nucci, 1996). Each of these domains—morality, societal convention, and personal—appears to undergo structural developmental changes with age. Although research on the developmental trajectories within domains is incomplete, there is evidence that each domain forms a distinct conceptual framework with an independent developmental course and sequence (Nucci, 1996; Turiel, 1983).

Within the context of this sociocognitive domain framework, Kohlberg's formulation of moral development can be understood as having captured typical age-related coordinations of moral and nonmoral concerns for children, early adolescents, and adults within modern cultures. Kohlberg did not seem to fully recognize that people's moral judgments can be employed in simple situations in the absence of recourse to other social concepts and that contextualized social judgments by people at all ages, including childhood, could be dominated by moral considerations or by nonmoral ones. In other words, understanding moral decision making requires a much richer appreciation of how moral and nonmoral social factors are evaluated in context.

An example of the utility of this approach for understanding the relations between moral reasoning and behavior is provided by Smetana's (1982) research on pregnant women's reasoning about abortion. She found that women's judgments about abortion depended on their treatment of the issue as a matter of personal choice and privacy or a moral issue involving the life of another person. Most of the women who chose to have an abortion also viewed the issue as a matter of privacy and personal choice. For these women, their reasoning about abortion was uncorrelated with their reasoning as assessed with a Kohlberg interview. Conversely, most of the women who treated abortion as a moral issue went to term with their pregnancies. Their reasoning about abortion was assessed to be the same as the level of moral judgment they displayed in a standard Kohlberg assessment of moral development. Smetana also looked at the women's religious affiliation. She found that Catholicism among her subjects was associated with the tendency to go to term with a pregnancy. However, this aspect of personal identity and religious values was mediated through the treatment of abortion as a personal or moral issue. It was the latter set of choices, not religious affiliation, that predicted the woman's decisions regarding abortion.

Thus, the interpretation of an issue as falling within in the moral domain appears to be the critical variable in predicting the force of moral judgments on moral actions. The salience of morality varies across social situations, and the assessment of salience is indeed the wild card in this formulation. To some extent, it is established by the objective situation. Usually what people mean by context is this external configuration of elements. But, context is also internal and is affected by the relative point in development the person has reached within each conceptual system, the person's informational assumptions, the person's position within the social hierarchy, his or her social role, and a series of idiosyncratic elements—the person's mood, whether he or she had a good night's sleep, if the person just had a fight with his wife, and so forth. In the case of Smetana's (1982) Catholic subjects, the context framing their reading of abortion included their identification as members of the Catholic Church. A similar mechanism may well have been at work for many of the exemplars cited by Colby and Damon (1992), who connected their moral engagement in particular situations with their own religious or spiritual commitments.

Work by Turiel (2002) and Wainryb and Turiel (1994) nicely illustrates how where one sits in the social hierarchy also affects how one reads the morality of social practices. In most of the world's cultures, men sit in positions of relative power in their relations with women. Men, for example, are accorded more decision-making authority over everyday decisions. Men tend to view these privileges as rights, and they expect obedience from their wives and daughters as a matter of duty. That is, men are inured to the apparent inequities involved and prioritize the nonmoral conventional elements of their cultural practices as more salient in the interpretation of the social situation. Women in these situations tend to see the same "objective" facts quite differently. They are more likely than men to see the inequities inherent in the social practices and to prioritize morality over social convention.

That social roles blind us to the "objectively" moral elements of the context is neither a new idea (see Sarbin & Allen, 1968, for an early discussion) nor recent phenomenon. Nicholas II, last of the Russian tsars as described by John Lawrence (1993) in his history of Russia,

> conceived it to be his duty and his fate to carry on his shoulders the whole burden of the Russian aristocracy. His duty to his family, to his country, to God were indistinguishable to him. He felt bound unconditionally to his office and by his coronation oath to preserve Russia holy and Orthodox under his absolute rule while he lived, and to hand undiminished powers to his son when he died. To limit his own powers by the acceptance of basic laws that even the tsar must not break, to accept the merest shadow of a constitution or even to appoint a prime minister would be an offense against God and against his own son even more than a political imprudence. (p. 210)

Talk about moral identity! I leave it to the reader to decide, however, whether Tsar Nicholas' integration of self, duty, and morality led to moral outcomes.

And we can take this a bit further. All of us lead lives that are multifaceted. We are parents, spouses, children, teachers, researchers, and scholars of different sorts. Some of us are community volunteers; some are not. Each of these role relationships places different demands on us that have different mixtures of moral and nonmoral elements. The self-same person, to use Michael Chandler's (2001) phrase, can appear to employ morality in inconsistent ways across these contexts. This was the very essence of Hartshorne and May's

(1928, 1929, 1930) discoveries. What are we to make of this? Does our moral identity shift with each context? Is it the case that as the self-same person it is the salience of morality that shifts with the context?

At this point, one can imagine a rising chorus of concern that a contextualist structural account of moral development and moral reasoning is relativistic. Indeed, it is in the sense that an honest moral psychology does not presume that morality is always addressed prior to nonmoral concerns. However, it is not relativist in its view of morality and in its assumptions about the directionality of individual or social practices when moral concerns are taken into account.

Consider the case of the hierarchical status of women. The moral arguments of the women reported in the research just reviewed (Turiel, 2002) were not made on the basis of consensual agreement. They were based on nonrelativist moral arguments of inequities, harm, and injustices. Those men open to hear the arguments of women would not be persuaded simply by the fact that many of the women seem to agree on a particular point but by the nonarbitrary and nonrelativist force of morality itself.

MORAL PRIORITY AND IDENTITY

The question for moral psychology is how to account for when individuals prioritize morality and when they do not. Given that morality operates independently of our other social cognitive systems (Turiel, 1983, 1998), we can expect morality to guide our actions at any point in development. This is why correlations between moral stage and behavior are often so meaningless. More recent work on moral cognition unfortunately undoes Kohlberg's (1984) unified moral stage telos. However Turiel's (2002) more recent work opens up a second possibility that moral reflection is a capacity available in different forms at all points in development and that people at all points in their social growth can evaluate social situations from a moral point of view. This does not mean that the moral reflections of a typical 4 year old are the same as those of a typical adult. The capacity to attend to and prioritize what is moral is available at all ages.

This reveals an interesting possibility for the role of self and identity in the construction of one's morality. It has to do with the very nature of moral openness. Whether we are born male or female, tsar or serf will affect our reading of the moral meaning of situations. Within those broad social categories and social roles we also operate as individuals. We are capable of independently assessing the moral meaning of practices and social events. Just as these larger external forces shape our view of things, our own individual biases, opinions, and interests alter our orientation toward the morality of social situations. Who we are as individuals and not simply "where we sit" in relation to the social system affects the way in which we read the salience of the moral elements of situations. It is this reading of the moral weighting of the situation that impacts moral action. In this way, we can argue that identity affects our moral actions. Of course, we also can and do make decisions in context that we come to regret. We may even engage in actions that shake our belief in ourselves as moral actors. But this can only come after the fact, and it does not constitute moral motivation. Blasi's (1993) work speaks directly to this point when he noted that this sort of moral identity crisis is rare.

If self and identity are a matter of connecting who we were with who we are and who we are becoming, then the possibility exists that we can construct notions of ourselves that allow us to be more or less sensitive to the moral elements of social situations but, more important, open to changes in our moral orientation—both in a developmental sense—and in terms of the ways in which we frame or attend to the moral and nonmoral elements of given situations.

The current focus on moral identity as a core aspect of moral functioning overlooks the prospect that an overly tight linkage between morality and self can actually be dysfunctional. It is possible that we can so define ourselves in terms of morality that, rather than becoming moral exemplars, we actually freeze our morality in dysfunctional ways. We have already considered the case of tsar Nicholas as an example of someone whose sense of himself so tied him to a conventional moral system that he was unable to respond to the moral contradictions inherent in his own position. But it can work the other way as well. One can become so focused on a sense of moral outrage and so identified with a moral cause as to become a one-dimensional moral zealot, such as the antiabortion extremists or the animal rights zealots who in their sense of moral purpose engage in acts of violence in the name of morality. Consider the following description of Nicoli Lenin by a former Marxist, Berdyaev:

> Lenin's revolutionary principles had a moral source; he could not endure injustice, oppression, and exploitation, but he became so obsessed with maximalist revolutionary idea, that in the end he lost the immediate sense of difference between good and evil; he lost the direct relationship to living people; he permitted fraud, deceit, violence, cruelty. He was not a vicious man, he was not even particularly ambitious or a great lover of power, but the sole obsession of a single idea led to a dreadful narrowing of thought and to a moral transformation which permitted entirely immoral methods in carrying on the conflict. (Lawrence, 1993, p. 206)

If instead of adopting a static moral identity, we remain open to the ways in which we attend to moral components of social life, then the possibility exists that we will be open to moral disequilibration. In essence, we can be more or less open to moral self-improvement—not only in the sense of development but in the ways in which we frame the moral meaning of social events or relationships. When we change those ways in which we orient toward the social world, we change a part of who we are. The direction of change will generally be toward the moral. This was at the heart of Kohlberg's (1971) bold philosophical claims in his "From Is to Ought" chapter. Moral directionality is not developmentally deterministic (as described by Kohlberg, 1984), and it is not simply a function of Western liberalism (Shweder, 1982). It results from the fact that the dialectic between moral concerns for fairness and harm to person's and nonmoral considerations such as social hierarchy are not arbitrary ones—so long as we are open to hearing the moral voice in the dialogue. When this occurs one is simultaneously altering how one thinks morally and the person in and of himself or herself. They are complementary aspects of one and the same thing. And, perhaps, this is how best to think of moral teleology and the notion of moral flourishing.

The primary contribution of Blasi's pioneering work on the moral self is that it provides a coherent basis from which to consider the interface between the development of the moral agent and the construction of moral and social understandings. This approach "does not attempt to replace moral ideas with a set of non-cognitive personality characteristics: it sees personal identity as operating jointly with reason and truth in providing motives for action" (Blasi, 1993, p. 99). Thus, such research and theory has made an important substantive contribution to public discourse at a time when notions of moral agency are being overwhelmed by the rhetoric of character formation and indoctrinative forms of socialization. If the reach of theorists following Blasi's lead has exceeded their grasp, it is because they have not fully appreciated the multifaceted aspects of moral judgments in context (Turiel, 1998) or sufficiently allowed for the heterogeneity that exists within a given person's self-system. For research on this issue to move forward and the promise of conceptual models about the moral self to be realized, research on this issue will need to go beyond biographical studies of more and less moral people or assessments of the correspondence of general ideal and actual personal values to microgenetic studies of the ways in which people's judgments and actions in context reciprocally foster the development of moral agency. As Frankena (1963) put it and as the evidence indicates, moral principles and doing and being are two sides of the same morality.

ACKNOWLEDGMENTS

This chapter is based on the Presidential Address presented at the 30th annual meeting of the Jean Piaget Society Society, Montreal, Canada, June 3, 2000, and a subsequent book chapter appearing in Lalonde, Lightfoot, and Chandler,

Changing Conceptions of Psychological Life. The current chapter appears in the present volume by agreement with Lawrence Erlbaum Associates.

REFERENCES

Ayers, W. (2001). *Fugitive days: A memoir*. New York: Beacon.

Bergman, R. (2002). Why be moral? A conceptual model from developmental psychology. *Human Development, 45*, 104–124.

Blasi, G. (1983). Moral cognition and moral action: A theoretical perspective. *Developmental Review, 3*, 178–210.

Blasi, G. (1984). Moral identity: Its role in moral functioning. In J. Gewirtz & W. Kurtines (Eds.), *Morality, moral behavior, and moral development* (pp. 128–139). New York: Wiley.

Blasi, G. (1993). The development of identity: Some implications for moral functioning. In G. Noam & T. Wren (Eds.), *The moral self* (pp. 99–122). Cambridge, MA: MIT Press.

Blasi, G., & Glodis, K. (1995). The development of identity: A critical analysis from the perspective of the self as subject. *Developmental Review, 15*, 404–433.

Broughton, J. (1978). The development of concepts of self, mind, reality, and knowledge. In W. Damon (Ed.), *Social cognition* (pp. 75–100). San Francisco: Jossey-Bass.

Byrne, B. (1984). The general/academic self-concept nomological network: A review of construct validation research. *Review of Educational Research, 54*, 427–456.

Chandler, M. (2001). The time of our lives: Self-continuity in native and non-native youth. *Advances in Child Development and Behavior, 28*, 175–221.

Chandler, M., Lalonde, C., Sokol, B., & Lightfoot, C. (2002). *Surviving time: Aboriginality, suicidality, and the persistence of identity in the face of radical developmental and cultural change*. Unpublished manuscript, University of British Columbia, Vancouver, B.C.

Colby, A., & Damon, W. (1992). *Some do care: Contemporary lives of moral commitment*. New York: The Free Press.

Damon, W. (1984). Self-understanding and moral development in childhood and adolescence. In J. Gewirtz, & W. Kurtines (Eds.), *Morality, moral behavior, and moral development* (pp. 109–127). New York: Wiley.

Damon, W., & Hart, W. (1988). *Self understanding in childhood and adolescence*. Cambridge, MA: Cambridge University Press.

Frankena, W. K. (1963). *Ethics*. Englewood Cliffs, NJ: Prentice-Hall.

Gerson, R., & Damon, W. (1978). Moral understanding and children's conduct. In W. Damon (Ed.), *Moral development* (pp. 41–60). San Francisco: Jossey-Bass.

Hart, D., & Fegley, S. (1995). Prosocial behavior and caring in adolescence: Relations to self-understanding and social judgment. *Child Development, 66*, 1346–1359.

Harter, S. (1983). Developmental perspectives on the self-system. In P. H. Mussen (Ed.), *Handbook of child psychology: Vol. IV. Socialization, personality, and social development* (pp. 275–285). New York: Wiley.

Harter, S. (1985). *The self-perception profile for children: Revision of the perceived competence scale for children*. Unpublished manuscript, University of Denver, Denver, CO.

Harter, S. (1986). *The self-perception profile for adolescents*. Unpublished manuscript. University of Denver, Denver, CO.

Hartshorne, H., & May, M. A. (1928). *Studies in the nature of character: Vol. 1. Studies in deceit*. New York: Macmillan.

Hartshorne, H., & May, M. A. (1929). *Studies in the nature of character: Vol. 2. Studies in service and self control*. New York: Macmillan.

Hartshorne, H., & May, M. A. (1930). *Studies in the nature of character. Vol. 3. Studies in organization of character*. New York: Macmillan.

Hutchins, W. J. (1929). The children's morality code. *Journal of the National Education Association, 13*, 292.

Kohlberg, L. (1969). Stage and sequence: The cognitive developmental approach to socialization. In D. A. Goslin (Ed.), *Handbook of socialization theory and research* (pp. 347–380). Chicago: Rand McNally.

Kohlberg, L. (1971). From is to ought: How to commit the naturalistic fallacy and get away with it in the study of moral development. In T. Michel (Ed.), *Cognitive development and epistemology* (pp. 151–235). Cambridge MA: Harvard University Press.

Kohlberg, L. (1984). *Essays on moral development: Vol 2. The psychology of moral development*. San Francisco: Harper & Row.

Kohlberg, L., & Turiel, E. (1971). Moral development and moral education. In G. Lesser (Ed.), *Psychology and educational practice* (pp. 410–465). Chicago: Scott, Foresman.

Lapsley, D. (1996). *Moral psychology*. Boulder, CO: Westview.

Lawrence, J. (1993). *A history of Russia* (7th rev. ed.). New York: Penguin.

Loevinger, J. (1976). *Ego development: Concepts and theories*. San Francisco: Jossey-Bass.

Marsh, H. W., Smith, I. D., & Barnes, J. (1985). Multidimensional self-concepts: Relation with sex and academic achievement. *Journal of Educational Psychology, 77*, 581–596.

Milgram, S. (1974). *Obedience to authority*. New York: Harper & Row.

Mischel, W. (1973). Toward a cognitive social-learning reconceptualization of personality. *Psychological Review, 80*, 250–283.

Mischel, W. (1990). Personality dispositions revisted and revised: A view after three decades. In L. A. Pervin (Ed.), *Handbook of personality theory and research* (pp. 11–134). New York: Guilford.

Nucci, L. (1996). Morality and the personal sphere of actions. In E. Reed, E. Turiel, & T. Brown (Eds.), *Values and knowledge* (pp. 41–60). Hillsdale, NJ: Lawrence Erlbaum Associates.

Nucci. L. (2001). *Education in the moral domain*. Cambridge, England: Cambridge University Press.

Nucci, L. (2002). Because it is the right thing to do. *Human Development, 45*, 125–129.

Nussbaum, M. (1986). *The fragility of goodness*. Cambridge, England: Cambridge University Press.

Nussbaum, M. & Dawson, J. (Producer). (1997). *Great philosophers: Martha Nussbaum on Aristotle* [BBC Education and Training motion picture,]. Princeton, NJ: Films for Humanities & Sciences.

Piaget, J. (1932). *The moral judgment of the child*. New York: The Free Press.

Power, C., & Khmelkov, V. T. (1998). *Character development and self-esteem: Psychological foundations and educational implications*. Unpublished manuscript, University of Notre Dame, Notre Dame, IN.

Rest, J. (1983). Morality. In P. Mussen (Ed.), J.Flavel & E. Markman, (Vol. Eds.,) *Handbook of child psychology: Vol. 3. Cognitive development* (4th ed.; pp. 556–628). New York: Wiley.

Rorty, R. (1973). The transformation of persons. *Philosophy, 48*, 261–275.

Rosenberg, M. (1965). *Society and the adolescent self-image.* Princeton, NJ: Princeton University Press.

Ross, L., & Nisbett, R. M. (1991). *The person and the situation: Perspectives on social psychology.* Philadelphia: Temple University Press.

Sarbin, T., & Allen, V. L. (1968). Role theory. In G. Lindsey & E. Aronson (Eds.), *Handbook of social psychology* (Vol. 2). Boston: Addison-Wesley.

Shweder, R. (1982). Liberalism as destiny. A review of Lawrence Kohlberg's essays on moral development, Volume I: The philosophy of moral development. *Contemporary Psychology 27*, 421–424.

Smetana, J. (1982). *Concepts of self and morality: Women's reasoning about abortion.* New York: Praeger.

Smetana, J. (1989). Toddler's social interactions in the context of moral and conventional transgressions in the home. *Developmental Psychology, 25*, 499–508.

Turiel, E. (1978). The development of concepts of social structure: social convention. In J. Glick & K. A. Clarke-Stewart (Eds.), *The development of social understanding (pp. 45–74)* New York: Gardner.

Turiel, E. (1983). *The development of social knowledge: Morality and convention.* Cambridge, England: Cambridge University Press.

Turiel, E. (1998). The development of morality. In W. Damon (Series Ed.), Handbook of child psychology, 5th ed., Vol. 3: N. Eisenberg (Vol. Ed.), *Social, emotional, and personality development* (pp. 863–932). New York: Academic Press.

Turiel, E. (2002). *The culture of morality.* Cambridge: England, Cambridge University Press.

Turiel, E. & Davidson, P. (1986). Heterogeneity, inconsistency and asynchrony in the development of cognitive structures. In I. Levin (Ed.), *Stage and structure: Reopening the debate* (pp. 106–43). Newark, NJ: Ablex.

Wainryb, C. & Turiel, E. (1994). Dominance, subordination, and concepts of personal entitlements in cultural contexts. *Child Development, 65*, 1701–1722.

7

Judgment and Choice in Moral Functioning[1]

Mordecai Nisan
The Hebrew University of Jerusalem and The Mandel School

BLASI AND MORAL IDENTITY

In his writings about moral identity, Blasi (1993) aims at strengthening and perhaps rescuing the cognitive approach to moral functioning. In contrast to the emotional–behavioral approach that dominated psychology until the 1960s, which reduced moral judgment to moral behavior, the cognitive approach (Kohlberg, 1984; Lapsley, 1996) views moral judgment as the core that defines and directs moral functioning. As Blasi (1997) repeatedly stresses in his writings, *moral behavior* is defined by a judgment, an intention, and a sense of obligation to behave in accordance with one's perception of the upright, rather than by the behavior that corresponds to this perception. Behavior in and of itself may be arbitrary, automatic, or conditioned; or it may grow out of calculations of self-interest. An intention to behave according to the upright rests on an understanding that a particular behavior is required or prohibited by a rule or principle that the individual accepts as binding. Kohlberg's cognitive–developmental theory of moral development was so enthusiastically received, I believe, because it was compatible with this perception of morality, which was pervasive not only in moral philosophy (e.g. Frankena, 1973) but also in common vernacular. People consider behavior to be moral when it stems from moral judgment and moral motivation and is undertaken consciously and intentionally. Blasi (1997) does not compromise this strict characterization of morality, even with regard to the judgment of young children.

Over the years, following Kohlberg's original extrapolation of his theory, a range of difficulties were identified and criticism began to mount regarding the cognitive approach to morality (e.g. Walker & Pitts, 1998). Looming large over this approach are the most troublesome problems of moral motivation and the transition from judgment to behavior. These issues comprised the hub of the emotional–behavioral approach to morality in all of its variations, beginning with Freud and extending through social learning theory. The central status of behavior in these theories stemmed not only from their theoretical foundations, and also not simply from the importance of behavior (as compared to judgment) in daily life, but primarily from the fact that people tend to perceive behavior as a reliable indicator of morality and even of moral judgment (while allowing for understandable deviations). It is thus surprising that the cognitive approach to morality almost ignored the subject of moral motivation and behavior. Although it met the expectation of all psychological theories of morality that the definition of morality would suitably address judgment and intention, it did not meet the equally strong expectation that it would assign appropriate weight to (and explanations for) moral motivation and behavior.

A "complete" cognitive theory of moral functioning will consider judgment and understanding not only a sort of evaluative label—a signpost pointing in a certain direction—but also the motivation for moral behavior. The concern of a psychological theory of morality, like the concern of the ordinary person, is not only in the individual's labeling of behavior as desirable or undesirable but his[1] understanding of behavior. Conceding the motivational function of moral judgment takes a significant, and perhaps deadly, bite out of the cognitive perception of the moral phenomenon. Indeed, although Kohlberg wrote little on moral motivation, it may be inferred from his writings that for him moral motivation and behavior are inherent in moral understanding and judgment. Presenting his approach as Platonic, Kohlberg (1970) evoked the Socratic view regarding the connection between judgment and behavior—knowledge of the good will lead to good behavior. The theoretical and empirical efforts that Kohlberg invested in his research on moral education through the advancement of moral judgment also reflect his belief that moral judgment per se has the force to motivate moral behavior.

However, research results (e.g. Blasi, 1980) generally support the common understanding that the connection between moral judgment and moral behavior is weak; that people commit moral infractions not necessarily out of weakness of will or irresistible temptation, but in full knowledge and understanding that these behaviors are wrong (Nisan, 1985); and that people who evidence high moral judgment (e.g., according to Kohlberg's theory) may well behave in ways that we consider morally reprehensible, whereas people with low moral judgment may demonstrate behavior that we consider morally venerable (Colby & Damon, 1992). It is reasonable to assert that the prevailing perception, based on the cumulative experience of individuals and society, tends more toward the opinion of Hume—knowledge of the good is not in itself capable of motivating a person to do good—and less toward the position of Socrates—knowledge of the good leads to good behavior. The problem of moral motivation and behavior was and continues to be a weak and troublesome aspect of the cognitive approach to morality, which the construct of moral identity was intended to address. Blasi linked moral judgment to moral behavior first with his model of the self vis-à-vis moral behavior (1983), and subsequently through his research on the development of moral identity (1993). Moral identity was proposed as a sort of intermediate variable between moral judgment and moral behavior.

According to the moral identity model, an individual's perception of morality as a constitutive element of his identity and the tendency toward consistency between the person's perception of the good and his behavior serve as the basis for moral motivation and bridge judgment and behavior. This model seemingly solves the problem of motivation in the cognitive approach to morality. An explanation of moral motivation and behavior through identity as an intermediate variable seems more convincing than the "direct" Socratic explanation that judgment, in and of itself, drives behavior. Explaining behavior in terms of identity correlates with human experience (at least in Western cultures) as expressed in literary works, for example, that we are often unwilling to act in ways that run contrary to our self-definition and perception. It also corresponds to our distinction (despite Hartshorne & May's, 1928, results) between people for whom morality is important—that is, morality is central to their self-definition and they tend to act accordingly—and those for whom morality is not important and who tend to denigrate it. This explanation receives certain empirical support (e.g. Colby & Damon, 1992), and it also correlates with the perception of identity as a motivating factor in other areas as well (e.g., Monroe, Hankin, & Van Vechten, 1990).

At the same time, Blasi's (1993) model leaves the scepter of morality in the hands of judgment, thereby remaining loyal to the definition of morality in terms of knowledge and understanding of the right. According to this model, moral judgment is not merely a signpost pointing in the right direction; indeed it is the core of morality and is also what motivates moral behavior. Moral identity—a person's perception of morality as an essential element of who he is—is not separate from, but rather develops from within moral judgment. And the tendency to keep our moral identity in line with our perception of the desirable is not a mere mechanical feature of our mental apparatus in its search to avoid dissonance but rather an integral and unavoidable part of the nature of human identity. This model of moral identity is intended to explain moral motivation without foregoing the "complete" cognitive theory of morality—a theory that views moral cognition not only as the brain but also as the heart of moral functioning.

The concept of moral identity offered an answer not only to the problem of moral motivation and behavior but also to the important criticism that the cognitive approach to morality "excises" morality from the complete personality (Blasi, 1990). According to this critique, by focusing on the rational side of the moral phenomenon and ignoring central components of personality, such as wills and feelings, the cognitive approach presents and fosters a partial and even biased picture of morality. It presents morality as a phenomenon that is limited to few functions of the person, whereas we experience morality as a phenomenon of the whole person. Blasi (1990) seems to believe that the model of moral identity addresses this criticism and returns us to morality as we experience it in our lives—as a phenomenon involving the entire self. He speaks about the gradual integration of morality and identity during the course of which morality becomes part of the core identity, while continuing to maintain its independent status. This implies that when integrated into identity, morality preserves its core characteristics, such as absolute obligation, objectivity, impartiality, as well as its primacy over other types of considerations. The basis for the integration of morality into identity is a deep understanding of morality that helps the person clarify and conceptualize his desires and plans in the context of a complete picture of his identity. The integration of morality and identity is reflected, inter alia, in the person's ability to master his behavior and to attain harmony between moral judgment and such behavior.

Blasi tries to keep the cake whole—to maintain moral judgment in its objective sense—while it is mixed with other, including some unsavory, ingredients—for example, when moral judgment blends with personal interests and projects. He considers both to be essential and compatible characteristics of morality—the autonomy of morality as a system transcending the individual's personal considerations and as an element within the holistic perception of the complete personality. He therefore must posit that morality can be integrated into a person's identity without compromising the autonomy of morality. Mature moral judgment integrated into identity is, in this schema, guided by conscious, considered, and substantiated thought, and it employs a moral rule or principle as part of a complete conceptual framework. We call this judgment *autonomous* in the sense that it is taken from the viewpoint of a third person, "behind a veil of ignorance" (Rawls, 1971), free of personal and contextual biases.

Blasi's model can be understood in the light of a conception of identity that lends critical weight to the universal qualities of the person. In this conception, rationality is a central characteristic of a person's identity that affords for the smooth integration of morality into identity in a way that does not undermine the autonomy of morality. Indeed, in his analysis of identity, Blasi (1993) emphasizes universal functions such as agency, continuity, and uniqueness, which are inherent to human nature. However, in contrast to this conception of identity, an alternate conception views identity as established principally by the particularistic features of the person. This conception focuses on a person's unique characteristics that have been formed by his history, family, community, culture, specific opportunities, and so on, in a process of reflection on the given, the possible, and the imagined (e.g., Ashmore & Jussim, 1997). In this conception of identity, particularistic factors are not considered "noise" that should be ignored, but rather they comprise part of the individual's self-definition, which he will not concede. Commitment to this kind of identity—linked to family ties, group loyalties, strong wills, and personal projects—may conflict strongly with "objective" or autonomous moral judgment.

Does Blasi's attempt to preserve the "complete" cognitive approach to morality succeed? Does this conception of integration between a person's autonomous moral judgment and universalistic identity, a combination that does not detract from the autonomy of moral judgment, actually address the critique of the cognitive approach to the moral phenomenon? Human experience as well as our controlled observations suggest that we often do not find the blend that Blasi describes. In many cases morality is blended in the person's particularistic identity; in many cases we discover that moral choice (i.e., choice based on conscious moral judgment and intention) does not meet the conditions of objectivity and impartiality that are expected of autonomous moral judgment. These are the cases from which critique of the cognitive approach springs and on which it is based. Because Blasi's conception of moral identity does not address this critique, we are required to look for a more appropriate description of the moral process. After returning briefly in the next section to two criticisms of the cognitive approach to morality that are not appropriately met by the moral identity model, in the following section I suggest a distinction between two types of judgment that take part in the process of moral decision making—judgment of evaluation and judgment of choice. I demonstrate this distinction with empirical research. In the third section I describe conspicuous differences between the two types of judgment, and in the fourth section I sketch a possible relationship between the two types of judgment and the person's identity.

PROBLEMS WITH THE COGNITIVE APPROACH

Fundamental criticism regarding the cognitive theory of morality (in its strict version, as formulated by Kohlberg) is rooted in observation of people's moral functioning in daily life. This observation raises doubts about the validity of the perception of morality as founded on conscious and formulated judgments and on inferences made on the basis of a system of principles and rules. Many descriptions of decision making in general, including moral decision making, suggest a process in which judgment is not fully conscious and is also not based on inference and justification, as one may tend to see it in retrospect. In other words, decision making often rests on processes of judgment that Hogarth (2000) described as "intuitive". Indeed, doubts are raised as to whether principles and rules are sufficient for moral decision making in real-life situations in which considerations are ambiguous, multifaceted, and lacking precise definitions and clear formulation. Very often, the main issue in moral decision making in such situations is not how one should behave according to moral standards but rather how to deal with the situation given the varied and complicated set of considerations that overwhelms a person. This criticism challenges the perception of the moral process as being mainly comprised of autonomous moral judgment, as already described. It does not deny the existence of such judgment but rather significantly limits its role in the process of moral decision making. It also draws our attention to the fact that moral decision making in real-life situations involves fine discernments (Nussbaum, 1986) that are anchored in the individual's experience and cannot be detached from his particular desires, plans, commitments, and values.

These doubts about the ability of autonomous moral judgment to guide and explain moral decisions and choices are augmented by the criticism mentioned above regarding the restriction of this judgment to the rational aspect of morality and its detachment from the complete personality. As shown, the model of moral identity seeks to integrate moral judgment within the individual's overall functioning, thereby making morality a phenomenon of the whole personality. However, as already maintained, the proposed model fails to achieve this aim. Even when integrated into the person's identity, autonomous moral judgment—as objective, absolutely obligating, and impartial, rising above the person's passions and tendencies, loves and hates, personal commitments and plans, social connections and hopes for personal development, in short, everything that makes up the person's reality—continues to be seen as abstract judgment that is detached from the individual's life. As previously noted, this type of judgment does not fit the observed and experienced process of moral choice in daily life. It is difficult to see this abstract judgment as a motivating force for behavior. Indeed, observation of moral choice and conduct in daily life suggests that, en route from identifying the problem to choosing the behavior, the person's judgment undergoes a deep transformation, from evaluation based on "objective" arguments to evaluation based on practical considerations and ultimately leading to a choice anchored in the person's individual identity. The latter type of judgment is not autonomous in the sense mentioned previously.

Do these criticisms oblige us to abandon the moral identity model? I argue that the two central elements of this model—moral judgment and identity—indeed play a role in the moral process as we experience it but in the course of which their meaning is transformed. The identity in which morality is integrated differs from the universalistic identity Blasi has in mind, and the judgment that grows out of the integration differs from the autonomous judgment implied by the model.

Without going into great depth, we may say that people tend to perceive morality—some more and some less—as a significant component of their identity and self-definition (Nisan, 1991). In operational terms, when describing certain behaviors many people say that they could not behave differently, because that would entail a denial of their selves (e.g., Colby & Damon, 1992). However, when a person makes his decision with regard to a specific real behavior, his choice is based on what I have described as his particularistic identity, his self-definition in terms of his personal characteristics. Judgment based on a person's particularistic identity, a judgment that is likely to have motivational power, necessarily differs in its nature from autonomous moral judgment. It cannot stand as a sole determinant in court—independent of external pressures and considerations, in a prime position as it were, backed by reason itself. Powerful considerations that do not belong to the realm of morality stand beside, rather than below, the purely moral considerations. These include the person's vested interests, personal plans, group and social connections, ideology, and so on. These considerations are (generally) not supposed to play a role in autonomous moral judgment; they are perceived as interfering considerations. But when a person's judgment is not pure evaluation but rather stems from his particularistic identity, when it is connected to the core of the person's self, personal considerations become germane. Indeed, they are not merely considerations; they are what constitute the person. His family ties, personal plans, ambitions, and idiosyncrasies are an essential part of him; they are what makes him who he is; and they are not merely considerations. Within the framework of a particularistic identity it is doubtful whether we can say that morality supercedes all other factors. Identity-based moral choice seeks a balance between the various factors involved in the situation rather than the right answer according to the right order of preference. A judgment emerging from a particularistic identity has horizons of time and space that are different from those of autonomous moral judgment. Accounts and debts from the past, as well as plans and expectations for the future, are an inseparable part of the moral map as it appears in the person's consciousness (but not necessarily in his awareness).

This type of judgment seems compatible with empirical descriptions of moral functioning; but does it suit the cognitive view of morality? As already discussed, a description and explanation of morality, if it is to maintain the concept's meaning in common language, cannot forfeit the centrality of judgment in moral functioning. Does identity-based moral judgment meet this requirement? I believe it does. Identity-based moral judgment seems to fulfill fundamental and apparently sufficient conditions for viewing it as moral judgment and for viewing an act stemming from it as a moral act: It is directed by an idea of the good and the right and by an intention to behave correctly and to be a good person. However, if this is the case, is there still a need to relate to autonomous judgment? In contrast to philosophical discussions of related issues (e.g., concerning virtue ethics; see Statman, 1997) that are essentially normative and ask whether autonomous judgment, based on obligatory standards, is necessary for efficient moral functioning, our question is essentially descriptive: Does autonomous moral judgment have any role in moral decision-making as we know it? I briefly note two arguments that encourage an affirmative answer to this question.

First, in addition to our experiences of "intuitive" moral decisions, apparently taken without formal judgment, people also describe situations in which they made formal moral judgments—that is, judgments justified on the basis of norms or principles. In addition to our experiences of moral decisions based on and emerging from our identity, we can also recall situations in which we exercised or sought to exercise autonomous judgment, free of personal considerations of any sort. Formal and autonomous judgments appear not only in response to hypothetical dilemmas, like those used in Kohlberg's research, but also in real life situations. Often enough we may find that people make an intentional attempt to free themselves of the constraints of their identity and to exercise "independent" judgment before they reach the decision-making stage. Research on decision making also suggests that, even in the many cases where autonomous judgment appears to be lacking, it may well be latent and thus influence the person by way of schemas acquired in the course of socialization (Hogarth, 2000; Smith, 1998).

Second, an argument originates in the centrality of moral standards and principles in a person's development, at least in our but probably in every culture. The psychologist who observes human behavior discovers that, from a very young age, we all learn that there are behavioral norms according to which we must direct our lives. Very quickly, the child not only learns these norms but also internalizes them and feels an obligation to behave according to them (Rest, 1983). In the course of development, the child also learns the principles of morality and applies them to real-life situations, both in judgments about himself and in evaluating the behavior of others. Moreover, he finds that a broad social agreement exists on these moral norms and principles, and it even comes to attribute objective universal validity to them (Turiel, 1983). The status of these moral norms and principles is strengthened, one may assume, by our society's high regard for the legal system as a prototype of autonomous moral judgment—judgment guided by obligatory laws and principles without the intrusion of personal factors. In any case, the high status of moral norms and principles in our society suggests that they play an important role in moral conduct and that there is a phase in the moral process when the individual looks for formulated norms and principles of morality (i.e., for autonomous moral judgment).

In conclusion, on the basis of observation and analysis of people's moral functioning, a complete description of moral decision making should include two types of moral judgment—the autonomous moral judgment that philosophers and cognitive–developmental psychologists studied and described and a different sort of judgment that is anchored in the particularistic identity of the person. In the next section I support this argument and clarify the nature of the two types of judgment.

TWO DISTINCT PROCESSES OF JUDGMENT

An analysis of the course of thought leading to normative behavior suggests two distinct processes of judgment—judgment of evaluation and judgment of choice. For brevity we occasionally call them evaluation and choice. The two often appear together and are difficult to separate. In the process of evaluation, the person evaluates behavior according to a certain standard. A person may, for example, evaluate whether an act is legal, rational, or ethical. Judgment can concern past behavior, planned behavior, or even hypothetical or imagined behavior. A person can judge his own behavior or the behavior of a stranger. The product of this type of judgment is an evaluation of whether the behavior is or is not compatible with a standard (and, if not, the extent of deviation from the standard).

In the process of choice, on the contrary, the person's intention is not just to evaluate a type of behavior but to decide which behavior he is actually going to adopt. Accordingly, a decisive difference between evaluation and choice is that choice has consequences for the person's life, as opposed to judgment that in and of itself is only theoretical. A decision that bears important consequences for the life of the person who makes it is a choice of the person as a whole; it involves all the considerations that are important to the person. Like judgment of evaluation, judgment of choice is also based on deliberation and evaluation. We assume that, generally, a person does not choose arbitrarily but rather after evaluating the alternatives in light of a set of standards. In contrast to judgment of evaluation, choice—in its "natural" meaning—does not apply to past behavior, to hypothetical behavior, or to behavior to which the person is unrelated; a person cannot choose to implement past behavior, imaginary behavior, or behavior of another person to whom he is not connected (although he can imagine similarly facing and making a choice). The natural result of choice is behavior unless an unexpected disturbance occurs in the transition from choice to behavior. The disturbance can be external—an obstacle placed before the person who is about to implement his choice—or internal—weakness of will or inability to implement the choice.

When a person's judgment relates to behavior that he considers adopting, we would expect judgment to correlate with choice, because—one may assume—both are based on the same standard. When a person seeks to read a suspense novel, for example, he will judge suggested books according to this standard, and he will choose to read a book that he believes has the greatest chance of being suspenseful. In the model of common sense, judgment and choice constitute two sequential phases—first comes the evaluation and then the choice. But the distinction between and the order of the two processes are not always clear and overt. The frequent consistency between evaluation and choice has the appearance of one process, and often the distinction between them is obscured. Judgment and choice often appear to be one not only to the outside observer but also to the person. Such are the cases, for example, of "intuitive" (Hogarth, 2000), quick, and subconscious judgments, in which the person remains unaware of the judgment process and of the standard on which it is based. In such instances, the phase of judgment "disappears" and the choice appears to be instantaneous. When the choice is not arbitrary, it often grows out of a tacit evaluation on the basis of internalized standards that have been fixed in a schema of which the person is unaware (Smith, 1998). If asked, the person will be able to justify his "intuitive" choice, but the justification may not in fact reflect the reason that actually engendered his choice. It may well reveal to us, however, the internalized norm at the base of the subconscious schema that influenced the choice.

There are instances, however, in which the distinction between judgment and choice is much clearer and sometimes even overt. Consider, for example, behavior that we tend to attribute to weakness of will. A person may well judge that it is desirable to refrain from smoking and nevertheless choose to smoke. This phenomenon was investigated intensively by philosophers and psychologists (e.g., Charleton, 1988), whose principal question was how to explain the gap between a person's judgment that it is worthwhile to behave in manner A and his choice to behave in manner B, even though B is judged to be less preferential or even harmful. In many cases a gap between judgment and choice cannot be attributed to weakness of will. When there is no reason to assume the existence of an uncontrollable urge, when the person fully controls his behavior and willfully chooses against his (better) judgment, the distinction between judgment and choice is quite explicit.

The processes of judgment and choice are also characteristic of the domain of morality. Our personal experience as well as literary works provide instances in which a person judges and then chooses behavior from a moral perspective when the judgment and the choice are clearly separate. Moreover, people often judge their own behavior or that of others, both past actions and future plans, fully aware that their judgment is theoretical and does not in fact entail choice and behavior. And sometimes, after reaching unequivocal judgment with regard to the desirable action in a given situation, they begin a new process of judgment, this time about how actually to behave. In these cases, the distinction between judgment and choice seems clear not only to the person who is experiencing it but also to whomever is observing it.

A gap between judgment and choice seems more plausible and is apparently more widespread in the domain of morality than in the domain of prudential behavior. If a person judges that a certain alternative is preferable to other alternatives from the perspective that he will benefit, we may assume that he will choose this alternative. Instances in which a person chooses consciously—not by chance, mistake, or lack of knowledge—against his own utilitarian judgment are cause for astonishment among observers as well as researchers (Elster, 1984). This is not so in the domain of morality. The gap between moral judgment and choice does not always surprise us; often we even expect it. This is because morality is perceived as aiming to limit the person's behavior, to bridle his tendency to achieve maximum benefit for himself. This role of morality is often described in blunt terms, like those of Hobbes and Freud on the necessity to suppress the egoistic and animalistic tendencies of man and to restrain his impulses, and sometimes in more delicate terms, among those hoping to educate the person to care for the other or to recognize the internal logic of morality. In either blunt or delicate terms, morality is perceived as one side in the basic conflict between the person's egoistic tendencies on the one hand and his moral tendencies that allow for the good of society and the rights of the other, on the other hand. There is no need to describe this conflict as an eternal struggle to recognize that it invites choice and behavior that deviate from moral judgment.

A gap between judgment and choice in the realm of morality is of great significance for the individual and society. Unlike prudential or aesthetic judgment, moral judgment not only invites choice but also entails obligation. Deviation from moral judgment comprises a moral transgression. Very often, moral deviation also has legal implications and warrants punishment. In any case, moral deviation is perceived as worthy of public condemnation and as damaging to the person's self-esteem. A gap between judgment and choice in the domain of morality is thus linked to the person's perception and definition of himself. It simultaneously reflects and affects the person's identity. Consequently, it should be expected that the distinction between evaluation and choice in the domain of morality would be prominent in the individual's consciousness; that he would not only recognize the distinction but also be able to describe and explain it.

Indeed, when asked to do this, subjects have no difficulty relating the infractions that they carried out wittingly, that is, knowing and understanding that their choice contradicts what they themselves consider to be desirable and right (Nisan, 1993). In many cases, the reasoning given by subjects for their failure to abide by their moral judgment is that, in the particular situation in which they had to make a choice, personal considerations seemed to outweigh the moral consideration. Our immediate tendency is to interpret this reasoning as a reflection of weakness of will, not unlike our explanation for behavior that does not correspond to the individual's rational–utilitarian judgment. But it is important to distinguish between deviation due to irresistible temptation (as in the case of a drug addict), a situation that is codified in law and approximates temporary insanity, and deviation that is chosen freely, in which we perceive the person and the person perceives himself as someone who possesses the psychological strength to behave in accordance with his judgment. This second type of deviation, what I (see Nisan, 1985) call "considered deviation," can often be interpreted as the person's conscious judgment that, in a given situation, he is justified in placing personal considerations above his own moral judgment. This interpretation is supported by subjects' descriptions and explanations of their deviations, and it is often suited to situations that we tend to perceive as expressions of moderate weakness of will. According to this interpretation, choice that deviates from moral evaluation is still based on a process of judgment. This judgment of choice is not limited to prudential considerations of personal gain and loss that accrue from submitting versus not submitting to the moral judgment; it also includes moral considerations to which the individual is fully committed. Thus, these behavioral deviations from one's own moral judgment do not reflect an abandonment of morality but rather an additional and different judgment, one that relies on considerations beyond those taken into account in the initial, autonomous moral judgment.

For a more acute demonstration and understanding of the distinction between judgment and choice I conducted the following study (Nisan, 1993). Subjects were asked to read several moral dilemmas and answer two separate questions, one soliciting their moral judgment regarding each dilemma (What is the right behavior in the situation described in the dilemma?) and another asking for their choice of action (How would you behave in the situation described in the dilemma?). Although the question about choice was hypothetical (removing its sting), we expected that a distinction between the subjects' judgment and choice would be expressed in a deviation of the choice from the judgment (not necessarily in all respondents) as well as in the sort of considerations taken into account. A serious criticism of this study is that the separation between the two research questions begs the point; it may artificially create the distinction. However, it is unclear why presenting two separate questions will create a distinction that does not exist. Only an examination of the answers to the two questions may substantiate whether the distinction is valid. In addition, earlier research found that the subjects did not perceive the separation between the two questions to be artificial; on the contrary, they saw it as valuable, helping them to better analyze their response to the dilemma. I now give a short description of the research and its results. I focus on the first dilemma presented to the subjects, which faithfully reflects the nature of the other dilemmas and the directions revealed in response to them.

The dilemma presented to Israeli students concerned a scientist who is unsure whether to accept a one-time and much desired offer to spend 1 year in the United States at a laboratory in which he can investigate a new theory he has been working on for years. Accepting the offer means that he, an only child, will temporarily abandon his elderly and ill parents, knowing that this will cause them suffering. The subjects were asked this question: "From a moral point of view, what is the right behavior in this situation?" They were presented with two alternative answers: (a) go to the United States and take advantage of this singular opportunity to investigate his theory, or (b) remain in Israel with his parents. Approximately 70% of the subjects believed that the correct behavior from a moral perspective was to forego this attractive offer and remain in Israel with his parents. They justified this, as expected, by the son's obligation to his parents; they even went to the trouble of explaining the source of this obligation. A second question asked the subjects: "We asked you what the correct behavior is in this situation from a moral point of view. Now we are asking how you would behave if you were facing this situation." Of those who said that, from a moral point of view, the scientist must stay in Israel to forestall his parents' suffering, approximately 30% said they would decide to go on sabbatical, that is, they would behave contrary to their moral judgment. The findings were similar when the second question (asked of another group of subjects) was phrased as follows: "What would you advise the scientist to do?" The results were also similar when the order of the questions was reversed, that is, when they were first asked how they would behave and asked afterwards about the correct behavior from a moral point of view. Subjects who revealed a gap between their judgment (of the right behavior) and their choice (how they would behave or advise the scientist to behave) justified their choice mainly in terms of self-actualization and a person's obligation to himself (alongside other arguments, e.g., that the parents have an interest in their son's development or that the respondents would ease the parents' situation in other ways). The important point for our discussion is that their choice to go on sabbatical was not the result of disregard for or denial of the moral claim. They perceived their choice to act against their moral judgment and leave the parents alone not as an act of moral weakness or weakness of will but as a justifiable decision. They perceived the dilemma as entailing a conflict between the demands of morality in its narrower sense and demands pertaining to the broader ethical domain which, in Williams' (1985) terms, includes a person's obligation to himself to develop, flourish, and find completeness.

Similar results were obtained for another dilemma presented to our subjects in a different content area. The dilemma presented a father who is unsure whether to surrender his son, who ran from the police after a traffic violation and may be liable to a prison sentence. Eighty-five percent of the subjects said that, from a moral point of view, the father has to turn in his son, but 40% of them said they would not do so. They justified their choice mainly by arguments pertaining to the special relationship between father and son and the father's concern for his son's future. Here, too, the subjects believed that, although from a moral perspective, lying to the police clearly constitutes improper behavior, the father's choice to lie could be justified by the special responsibility and relationship between a father and son.

I draw attention to three implications of these results. First, the study supports the distinction between judgment of evaluation and judgment of choice. Subjects who made the evaluation that, from a moral point of view, the son should remain in Israel with his ailing parents, concurrently made the choice that he should not miss the special opportunity and should go to the United States to conduct the research. They expressed a gap between judgment and choice (which is not identical to the more familiar gap between judgment and behavior). The gap found in this study is particularly significant because the choice was made concurrently with the evaluation and, moreover, concurrently with justifying the evaluation. The subjects were aware of the gap between their evaluation and their choice. They nevertheless chose to accept the fact of this gap, making no attempt to obfuscate the moral imperative. They clearly recognized the validity of the moral evaluation and felt a need to apologize for and justify their choice; they did not make this choice out of weakness of will, because they suggested this same choice also to another person (the scientist). In fact, in the dilemmas presented to the subjects, strength of will was needed to resist the moral imperative. As one subject said, "I hope I will be strong enough to stick to this decision, which goes against pure moral judgment." They made this choice because they believed that, all things considered, this was the right choice to make. Note that a distinction between evaluation and choice does not necessarily imply a gap between the two. A person can implement separate processes for evaluation and choice and reach an identical conclusion for both. An examination of the subjects' reasons for their evaluation and choice indeed suggests that the subjects who did not reveal a gap also processed judgment of evaluation and choice separately.

Second, the research supports the argument that moral choice is based on deliberation or judgment that takes moral considerations into account. As already mentioned, subjects who made choices contrary to their moral evaluation justified their choices with positive reasons—in the first dilemma, mainly by the person's right or obligation to develop and actualize himself, and, in the second dilemma, mainly by the father's special responsibility for and relationship with his son. These justifications appeared much less frequently in responses to the first question regarding the right behavior, which focused mainly on basic moral norms, such as the son's obligation to his parents and the prohibition against lying for personal gain. It can thus be said that, in many cases, judgment of choice is made on the basis of deliberation and not on the basis of an emotional attitude and that this judgment of choice does not ignore morality. It allows for the moral considerations that determined the first, evaluative moral judgment, but it also accounts for other considerations, including ones that may run counter to moral considerations. The status of judgment of choice as a considered judgment that stands on its own is evident in the subjects' perception of their choices as valid not only for themselves but also for a third party—they chose similarly for themselves and for the protagonists of the stories (e.g., when asked what they would suggest that the scientist would choose). Nevertheless, the choice was not perceived as obligatory. Although they saw their choice as a desirable option for others, most of the subjects recognized that in these dilemmas the choice remains that of the individual, according to his personal situation.

Third, and to further elaborate on the preceding point, the judgment of choice assigned importance to considerations that were not seen as relevant in the judgment of evaluation, and they challenged central principles of autonomous moral judgment. In their choice, the subjects took into account considerations such as personal development and expressing one's own aspirations and abilities, particular loyalties, and past behavior. They perceived these considerations not as egoistic passions or interests to be overcome but as legitimate rights and even obligations of a person to himself (Nisan, 1996). It is here that this presentation of two processes of moral judgment in judgment of evaluation and judgment of choice challenges most directly two central principles of autonomous moral judgment—the precedence of moral considerations over other types of considerations and the requirement of impartiality. The subjects' choices in the two dilemmas exemplify the deviation from these principles. In the first dilemma subjects gave precedence to considerations of self-development over what they perceived as the moral claim. And in the second dilemma their choice was determined by the particularistic consideration of the special relationship between father and son. These particularistic challenges account for the gaps between evaluation and choice in the two dilemmas. The gaps reveal that the two challenged principles are adopted decisively in judgment of evaluation, leading to a preference for the moral over the personal. At the same time, in their judgments of choice, the wheel turns and many subjects (those who evidenced a gap) preferred the person's rights and obligation to develop himself in the first case and loyalty to one's son in the second case over moral considerations. People's moral judgment thus reveals the coexistence in many subjects of opposing philosophical positions in regard to morality: the common position that the two principles are basic to moral judgment and the converse position that questions the validity of this common view (e.g., Foot, 1978; McIntyre, 1981). This study suggests that, empirically, these principles of autonomous moral judgment are taken as valid at the level of judgment of evaluation but not at the level of judgment of choice, which are two distinct levels in moral functioning.

Needless to say, the results of this research—which employed dilemmas that do not directly concern the subjects' lives and presented the questions in a way that invite the subject to distinguish between judgment and choice—cannot be generalized to all moral situations. But we probably can find in the results a sort of a model of moral functioning without shortcuts. According to this model, when a person confronts a situation in which he identifies a moral problem, he carries out two judgments—one regarding the right behavior in this situation, from a pure moral standpoint relying exclusively on moral standards, and the other an all things considered judgment that he will actually adopt. Some of our subjects could indeed recall situations of such a complete moral process, in which they were aware of the two judgments. But more frequent are situations in which one of the two judgments is implicit. For example, a student does not need to think or judge whether, from a moral perspective, he is allowed to cheat on an exam. The moral judgment of evaluation regarding this behavior is not absent but rather implicit. The same student would likely need to make a judgment of choice regarding the question of whether, in the specific situation, he can allow himself to cheat on an exam due to its decisive importance for his life plans. In other cases it is the judgment of choice that is implicit. Such is the case of the male student who related that he was unsure whether he should help his friend by working with him on a take-home quiz, but the moment he reached the judgment of evaluation that "from a moral perspective it is okay," he no longer needed an additional judgment about how to choose. His evaluative judgment gave him an answer to the second question—that of choice. Our interviews suggested that what looks like what Hogarth (2000) called "intuitive" moral judgment—characterized by a quick, unreflective response—may well be found, in a close analysis of its sources, implicitly to include both types of judgment.

DIFFERENCES BETWEEN JUDGMENT OF EVALUATION AND JUDGMENT OF CHOICE

We already pointed out important differences between the process of evaluation and the process of choice in the moral domain. This section provides a more complete description of the two sorts of judgment. For our purposes, we present each type in its pure form. Such a description brings out the distinction between evaluation and choice, sharpens the differences, and ignores their similarities; thus, it entails a certain amount of distortion. Generally, evaluation and choice prevail on a continuum of behavior in the same person, with a certain amount of overlap and commingling. Judgment of evaluation is ultimately intended to guide choice, and choice is expected to rely on evaluation. The relation between them is similar to that between a philosophical examination of the question of the good life and choosing a path and behavior in daily life, two processes that need one another and are partners with each other. However, a sharpening of their differences will help us appreciate the two processes and thus better understand their complementary relationship.

The immediate purposes of evaluation differ from those of choice; hence, they prescribe different starting points. These starting points induce significant differences between the two types of judgments. The purpose of judgment of evaluation is to determine whether behavior is desirable, permissible, forbidden, or obligatory with the moral standards, laws, and principles accepted by the individual as valid serving as the starting point. These standards are central to our culture and stand out strongly in our consciousness and education.

Whether their source is in gradual self-construction or in learning from an external source (internalization), the standards are imprinted in the person, and he cannot help but relate to them. The person attributes the standards' validity to authorities such as religion, reason, or society, which he perceives as beyond his choice. Moral standards generally have great force and are accompanied by strong emotions. From Freud onward, this force formed the core of psychologists' concern with morality. A central question for these researchers was: What is the source of the power of moral standards; what explains their durability, even when obeying them carries a heavy price?

The immediate purpose of choice, by contrast, is not to judge whether a particular behavior is desirable but rather to arrive at a choice of a behavior to implement it. The starting point of choice is consequently the individual's concrete reality, because his choice will have important ramifications in his life. The choice can bring profit or loss, praise or condemnation, a feeling of self-satisfaction or shame and self-construction or self-destruction. It is not surprising, therefore, that the most outstanding factors in the process of choice are its anticipated outcomes in the person's life. The person making the choice can take consequences of different types into account: consequences to his well-being, flourishing, moral standing, and so on. By focusing on the results for the life of the individual, as opposed to the evaluative standards, moral choice approximates prudential choice. But in moral choice, moral and value considerations are added to prudential considerations in the strictest sense.

As might be expected, the differences in purpose and starting point between the process of evaluation and the process of choice are conceptually similar to differences between morality of obligation and virtue ethics (Statman, 1997) and is also reflected in post-Kohlbergian approaches to morality (e.g., Gilligan, 1982). I now elaborate on four interrelated differences, already mentioned briefly, each of which is rich in content and carries secondary distinctions.

1. Judgment of evaluation is guided by the question of whether the judged behavior is right or wrong according to moral standards. These standards are perceived as valid for every individual; they are anchored in the rights and obligations stemming from the universal characteristics of the person. They intentionally ignore everything that is unique to the individual, his past and future, passions, wills, personal connections, commitments, and plans. The command "Thou Shalt Not Steal" is directed toward every person in every context, whatever his traits. The evaluation thus relates principally to the behavior and not to the person, to the immediate and not to the wider context of the behavior, and to the present and not to the past or future of the individual. It thus adresses the demands of universalism

and impartiality—judgment applies to everyone impartially; it is not expected to be influenced by personal and group loyalty considerations. In judgment of evaluation, the person is supposed to deliberate as would a judge in the legal system.

Judgment of choice, in contrast, is guided by the question: How am I going to behave in reality; what behavior should I adopt in the concrete dilemma or situation confronting me? The basis for the individual's choice is his status as a good person, as the person he would like to be. This judgment thus derives from the way the individual defines himself and from the unique circumstances and conditions in which he lives. In judgment of choice, the personal contacts and commitments of the individual are not just "noise" that he feels he should isolate himself from or overcome. Rather they are what constitutes him and are, therefore, an integral, unavoidable part of the considerations taken into account. Not only is the individual unable to distance himself from these features; he does not even want to because they are his own flesh and blood. Accordingly, from the outset, moral choice does not purport to be universal and impartial; it does not uphold the same standards to every individual; it leaves room for special considerations of the person making the choice, from his particular traits to the unique situation in which he finds himself. This feature of judgment of choice is not particular to choice regarding the self, but it is also present in choice regarding others. For example, the individual not only allows partiality by himself toward his own group, but of the other toward their group, hence universalizing the legitimacy he bestows on such partiality (Nisan, 2000).

2. Judgment of evaluation is determined by moral standards that are perceived as absolutely obligating and overriding any other type of consideration, including perceptions of good or values. This inflexible type of judgment leaves no room for concessions or compromise. Psychological theories have focused on this characteristic of morality—from Freudian theory, which explained it in terms of an irrational basis of the superego, to cognitive theory, which relies on Kant's strict categorical imperative and explains it in terms of logical necessity. The decisive influence that this type of judgment bestows on moral standards places the burden of responsibility for moral evaluation on the rules, thus limiting the actor's discretion to a certain extent.

In contrast, for judgment of choice, moral standards do not entail absolute obligation and do not override all other types of considerations. Accordingly, the individual's choice in this type of judgment would be less rigid and more open to negotiation and compromise in regard to moral demands than would be the case in his judgment of evaluation. Perhaps the most significant expression of this feature of judgment of choice is that moral standards are not its sole determining factor. The individual's choice is guided by his overall values, including self-expression and loyalty to that which he holds dear. Among these, the value of moral uprightness or appropriateness generally carries great weight, but it is part of a varied and (more or less) coordinated system of values (Schwartz & Bilsky, 1990). Indeed, moral claims may be overridden by nonobligatory perceptions of good as well as by personal values. When it comes to assessing the influence of a certain behavior on the person's image as a good person—a core criterion of judgment of choice—the individual will rely on judgment of evaluation (i.e., on moral standards). But this judgment will comprise only one factor within a broad system of factors and considerations related to the individual's good status, including past behavior and plans for the future. All of these factors and considerations are significant to the person's evaluation of himself as a reasonably good person.

3. Judgment of evaluation is perceived as objective and reliable. It is made on the basis of given standards that are supposed to be clear and sufficient. The person is conscious of and can articulate these standards to justify his decision. We expect that in their judgment of evaluation, different people will reach similar decisions because they all derive from the same standards. Judgment of this type, therefore, leaves little room for personal choice; the choice is imposed by the standards. This feature offers another explanation why judgment of evaluation leaves no room for compromise or negotiation—the evaluation is fully dictated by the standards. This characteristic of judgment of evaluation distances it from the reality of a person's life. It does not allow the individual the flexibility needed to take personal and situational factors into account and to adapt the judgment to reality. (Needless to say, this is an ideal description of judgment of evaluation. In practice, the standards and certainly the principles leave considerable room for individual discretion.)

Conversely, judgment of choice is subjective. It is made on the basis of appraisal and reasoning particular to a specific individual—the subject—in a specific situation. An individual's judgment of choice is unique to him; no one in the world can make it for him, not only physically but also in terms of the foundations of this judgment—his particular background and identity. Clearly, the considerations that determine judgment of choice also include objective data and principles. But the aggregate that guides the choice is profoundly personal—it is the subject's image of the person he would like to be and the composite identity he wishes to preserve. Choice is determined on the basis of beliefs, values, and interests, many of which may change from time to time, with no predetermined order of priority. In judgment of choice, consequently, there is much room for personal discretion. The wealth, variation, and flexibility of the considerations and data on which choice is based make it difficult to formulate and clarify the criteria for choice. It is no wonder, therefore, that judgment of choice seems intuitive. Another result is that judgment of choice is very often experienced not as a choice between a totally good and a totally bad course, but rather it is experienced between paths that each have positive and negative points. Judgment of choice thus presents possibilities for and even an invitation to what looks like moral compromise and concessions, but the possibilities are not experienced this way by the subject. His concessions are perceived by him as reasoned and justified but in a subjective way, in the sense that they are made on the basis of subjective but legitimate appraisal and considerations. Indeed, in many cases we would not expect different people confronting a similar moral dilemma to reach a similar choice. We would not even expect the same person facing a similar dilemma at another time to necessarily choose in a similar way. The reason for these variations is not likely to be brute relativism but rather a change in the person's circumstances. Almost all of our subjects believed that their choices could be and were justified, not arbitrary.

4. Judgment derived from moral standards is intended primarily to enable proper social functioning by establishing behavioral boundaries and limits. It is intended to protect individuals and society from harm by the "beast" within the man. This is the nature of social morality as described by Freud and many others, who defined correct behavior in a passive way—as behavior that does not injure the other or society. Judgment of evaluation does not reveal behavior that is desirable to adopt not as a default but rather for its own work. It is morality of the right and not of the good. It does not contain, or barely contains, components relating to the flourishing and betterment of the person. We can borrow Slote's (1992) criticism of the morality of obligation and apply it to judgment of evaluation: It is asymmetrical in that it relates to the rights of the other, but it is apathetic in relation to the point of view of the self.

     Judgment of choice, by contrast, is concerned with the good person. People's choices, in general, are intended to advance them along the full extent of their values. This orientation also applies to moral choice where it transforms the character of the moral consideration taking part in choice. In judgment of choice, moral considerations are perceived not (or not only) as a call for moderation but also as a guide for individual development—for fulfillment of the value of moral and personal wholeness. When he chooses his actual path, the individual accepts morality as a part of his personality and not as a demand imposed on him, as an expression of self and not as a binding restraint. Similarly, moral compromise is perceived as a step toward achieving a broader or other good and not as conceding a moral imperative. When he makes a choice, the individual of course recognizes the limitations that morality places on his personal plans but examines them and wants to address them with an orientation toward optimizing his self-realization as a whole person.

This difference between judgment of evaluation and judgment of choice has important ramifications for the problem of moral motivation. Moral judgment that forbids—that is, judgment made in accordance with the commandments of "Thou Shalt Not…"—invites negative motivation (i.e., motivation to avoid the forbidden behavior). Such is the moral motivation proposed by Freud and proponents of learning theory—motivation based on anxiety and guilt. The potency of this motivation is not in doubt, as are its disadvantages and limitations. Judgment of choice, to the contrary, opens a wide door for positive moral motivation, which is related to the perfection of the self, and to self-actualization through behavior that is consistent with the person's values (Maslow, 1954). As in every other choice in which values are involved, this motivation also operates in moral choice.

The preceding discussion of judgment of evaluation and judgment of choice highlights the facts that the distinction between them is not always sharp and that elements of one kind of judgment may penetrate judgment of the other kind. Indeed, judgment of evaluation—whether behavior corresponds to a specific standard—cannot escape the individual's personal viewpoint and his consideration of the specific conditions of the situation. And judgment of choice—whether a certain behavior corresponds to one's moral identity—cannot escape the objective viewpoint expressed in accepted standards. Despite this, as shown, the distinctiveness of the two judgments prevails in the individual's consciousness. Moral judgment occasionally arises within us, seemingly detached from our personal stance. Sometimes a person wants and tries to be "distanced" from himself, to stand behind the "veil of ignorance" and to attain "objective" judgment. Such are the responses of subjects to Kohlberg's Heinz dilemma, which is remote from the subjects' lives and presented to them with the most minimal information. In reaching choice, by contrast, the person cannot and does not want to be distanced from himself. This is his choice. In judgment of choice there is thus a level of countering judgment of evaluation. It is based on recognition of the unavoidable limitations of objective judgment.

EVALUATION, CHOICE, AND MORAL IDENTITY

Autonomous moral judgment is conventionally considered to be the only legitimate judgment regarding the uprightness of behavior. Divergence from this judgment in moral choice and behavior is considered deviation from proper moral functioning. Such deviation, as prevalent as it is, is perceived as stemming from extramoral factors, such as distraction, misunderstanding, weakness of will, or, in exceptional cases, as a rejection of morality. The argument presented above proposes a process of judgment of choice that diverges from autonomous moral judgment. Judgment of choice is accepted on the basis of what can justifiably be called moral judgment, that is, a judgment based on perception of the right and the good; but it is moral judgment of a different type. It is guided by an intention to preserve the individual's self-image as a moral person (while fulfilling his aims) rather than by an intention to obey moral standards. Indeed, moral judgment based on set standards is insufficient and unsuited to moral choice. A major reason for this, which concerns us now, is autonomous moral judgment's evasion of particularistic considerations, such as personal loyalties and projects that are very meaningful to the individual. Autonomous moral judgment leaves no room to contemplate these kinds of personal considerations. But very often the individual feels that ignoring them will harm him as a person more than disobeying an obligating moral standard; ignoring them entails a sort of self-denial, even to the point of negating himself and subverting his status as an agent. Philosophers theorize whether these considerations are "legitimate", but from the perspective of the individual, at least in our culture, they bear vital importance (see Taylor, 1992). It is not that the individual cannot withstand these considerations (from an emotional or prudential perspective) but that he accepts them as justified and of prime importance, such that he is unwilling to forego them.

The totality of considerations that determine choice also includes autonomous moral judgment. Although this judgment does not address the question of how to choose in a concrete situation, it does carry the flag of morality, indicates a moral direction, and serves as a basis for evaluating the behavior being considered. Autonomous moral judgment draws attention and sensitivity to the moral dimension, presents "objectively" valid and obligating commands, and does not allow the individual to ignore moral considerations. It restrains the individual's tendency to compromise and make concessions regarding the moral standards in judgment of choice, and it leads him to ask: "Can I perform this act and still see myself as a good person?" A question of this type, not rare in a person's experience, reveals that despite their limitations, moral principles and rules still play a key role in guiding choice. In a sense autonomous moral judgment constitutes the foundation for judgment of choice. This role of moral standards explains their centrality in the socialization of the child and in social discourse, which, as already noted, is an (empirical) reason why autonomous moral judgment must find its place in the description of moral functioning even though it does not dictate moral choice.

Due to its complex nature, the standard that prescribes judgment of choice is not clear and well-formulated. On the basis of human experience as expressed in literature, in philosophical research (e.g., in connection with virtue theory; Hursthouse, 1999) and in psychology (e.g., in connection with self-image; Baumeister, 1997), as well as on the basis of our interviews, one can say that moral choice is often guided by the individual's image of the good person he wants to (and can) be. This image, a sort of complex gestalt, is based on the individual's identity, on what he conceives as constituting himself, including ideals. As opposed to moral standards that are static and rigid, the gestalt of the good person that guides choice is dynamic and flexible. The traits, loyalties, and plans that it includes change in accordance with the situation and the individual's behavior and will. When the individual considers a certain behavior, he envisions the situation after performing this behavior and compares it to his current gestalt of the good person. He chooses according to the goodness of fit between the two. This "fit," which changes over time and throughout the situations in which the person finds himself, cannot be measured or defined. Needless to say, this process is not necessarily conscious and articulated (Hogarth, 2000).

Judgment of choice is, therefore, judgment linked to identity. The standard of "the good person that I want to be" (as distinct from "the good person" in a general sense) reflects the person's identity, values, and commitments that are important to him, without which he is not himself. Morality is an important component of this identity, but it is one among others. In his effort to preserve his conception of himself as a good person, the individual also strives to preserve his conception of himself as a moral person. The meaning of the integration between morality and identity in this description differs from that in Blasi's (1993) model of moral identity. In this model, the integration of morality in identity relates to the process whereby the individual comes to see morality as important to him. The concept of morality is integrated into identity as an abstract idea that joins other abstract ideas, like rationality or autonomy. This coordinated combination grants morality a "theoretical" status and importance in the individual's consciousness, but it hardly draws him closer to the concrete situation being judged. In the elaboration of judgment of choice, by contrast, morality is integrated within the framework of concrete considerations that play a role in the decision-making process. The concrete choice is made on the basis of the individual's identity, evaluation and options, reflecting its agency, uniqueness, and continuity—the central functions of identity. This integration links morality to life and to the whole personality, and it constitutes a basis for moral motivation.

This description of the process of moral evaluation and choice raises many questions. Of prime importance are the questions of limits to the influence of personal considerations on choice and of the factors and conditions—personal, cultural, and situational—affecting choice. These questions call for further examination of human experience as well as more controlled study of moral choice.

SUMMARY AND CONCLUSION

In a hard cognitive approach to morality such as Kohlberg's, moral judgment—the core of moral functioning—is perceived as conscious, based on reason, universal, obligating, impartial, and giving primacy to moral considerations over all others. Judgment possessing these characteristics I call autonomous moral judgment. It is based on moral standards that are expected to guide and motivate moral choice and behavior. Nonetheless, study and observation of individuals' moral functioning suggests that this description of moral judgment is inadequate. Autonomous moral judgment is detached from the individual's life. It is not enough to guide moral choice in concrete situations, and it is lacking in motivational force. Even when autonomous moral judgment clearly dictates behavior in a specific situation, the person may feel unobliged and unmotivated by it. Indeed, both study and observation suggest that moral choice relies on judgment of a different kind—what we called judgment of choice. This judgment is based on the person's evaluation of the significance of the behavior being considered for his status as a good and whole person. In this judgment, particularistic considerations such as personal projects and loyalties are taken into account, not out of weakness of will but out of a conception that the meaning and role of these considerations in the individual's life is so central that it is reasonable to consider them and sometimes even to prefer them to clear-cut moral considerations. In evaluating one's position as a whole and good person that is, in judgment of choice, great but not exclusive weight is given to autonomous moral judgment, which serves as a sort of compass or guide to choice and sets boundaries to taking personal factors into account. This explains the centrality of moral standards in education and social discourse.

There are those who reduce all of moral judgment to autonomous moral judgment. Indeed Kohlberg's (1973) musical chairs principle can incorporate personal and situational considerations. But if the judgment is all-inclusive, it forfeits its value and status as characterized for autonomous judgment. There are those, on the other hand, who reduce all moral judgment to subjective judgment, remaining within the boundaries of the individual's experience. In this case, an objective anchor that endows moral choice with validity and meaning is lacking. And there are those who distinguish between two different types of judgment and allow them to coexist. But in so doing, they leave each type of judgment with the problems noted above. As supported by research, we suggest that the two types of judgment possess different purposes and characteristics, and they cannot be reduced to one another. Judgment of choice is directed at choosing actual behavior on the basis of a weighted consideration of its results for the individual. Autonomous judgment is intended to submit valid moral standards and arguments and to set limits for extramoral considerations, including nonmoral values. Both types of judgments are required for a complete description of moral choice. In many instances the distinction between the two judgments is explicit, but in many others they cannot be differentiated, either because they are tightly combined or because one was internalized to the point that it became automatic.

This description of moral decision making presents a "softened" cognitive approach to moral functioning in which moral judgment and the intention to behave according to the desirable form the core of moral functioning. However, in it, moral standards lose their absolutely preferred and obligating status. They comprise an important component in the individual's complex and dynamic gestalt of the good person that he wishes to be, which includes extramoral considerations that the person views as central to his identity. This gestalt serves as the evaluatory standard for moral choice and, due to its nature, is difficult to articulate formally. This description is consistent with the objection of not a few philosophers—from Anscomb's (1968) very influential article to the current flowering of virtue theory (Statman, 1997)—that views moral standards as absolute and overriding.

ACKNOWLEDGMENTS

I express my appreciation and gratitude to Gus Blasi for inspiring friendship.

ENDNOTES

[1]While we will use masculine gender references for brevity's sake, they should be understood to apply equally in the feminine.

REFERENCES

Anscombe, G. E. M. (1968). Modern moral philosophy. In J. J. Thomson & G. Dworkin (Eds.), *Ethics*. New York: Harper & Row.

Ashmore, R.D. & Jussim, L. (Eds.). (1997). *Self and identity*. New York: Oxford University Press.

Baumeister, R. F. (1997). Identity, self concept and self esteem. In R. Hogan, J. Johnson, & S. Briggs (Eds.), *Handbook of personality psychology* (p. 681–710). New York: Academic Press.

Blasi, A. (1980). Bridging moral cognition and moral action: A critical review of literature. *Psychological Bulletin, 88*, 1–45.

Blasi, A. (1990). How should psychologists define morality? Or, the negative side effects of philosophy's influence on psychology. In T. Wren (Ed.), *The moral domain: Essays in the ongoing discussion between philosophy and the social sciences* (p. 38–70). Cambridge, MA: MIT Press.

Blasi, A. (1993). The development of identity: some implications for moral functioning. In G.G. Noam & T.E. Wren (Eds.), *The moral self* (p. 99–122). Cambridge, MA: MIT Press.

Blasi, A. (1997, July 27–August 1). *The nature of "early morality" in children's development: A case study of psychological disagreement*. Paper presented at the Fourth Ringberg Conference, Ringberg Schloss, Germany.

Charleton, W. E. (1988). *Weakness of the will*. Oxford, England: Blackwell.

Colby, A., & Damon, W. (1992). *Some do care: Contemporary lives of moral commitment*. New York: The Free Press.

Elster, J. (1984). *Ulysses and the Sirens: Studies in rationality and irrationality* (rev. ed.) Cambridge, England: Cambridge University Press. (Original work published 1979)

Foot, F. (1978). *Virtues and vices*. Oxford, England: Blackwell.

Frankena, W.K. (1973). *Ethics* (2nd ed.). Englewood Cliffs, NJ: Prentice-Hall.

Gilligan, C. (1982). *In a different voice: Psychological theory and women's development*. Cambridge, MA: Harvard University Press.

Hartshorne, H., & May, M.A. (1928). Studies in the nature of character. *Studies in Deceit,* (Vol. 1). New York: Macmillan.

Hogarth, R.M. (2000). *Educating intuition*. Chicago: University of Chicago Press.

Hursthouse, R. (1999). *On virtue ethics*. Oxford, England: Oxford University Press.

Kohlberg, L. (1970). Education for justice: A modern version of the Platonic view. In N. Sizer & T. Sizer (Eds.), *Moral education: Five lectures*. Cambridge, MA: Harvard University Press.

Kohlberg, L. (1973). The claims to moral adequacy of a highest stage of moral judgment. *Journal of Philosophy, 70*, 630-646.

Kohlberg, L. (1984). *Essays on moral development: Vol. 2. The psychology of moral development*. San Francisco: Harper & Row.

Lapsley, D.K. (1996). *Moral psychology*. Boulder, CO: Westview Press.

Maslow, A. (1954). *Motivation and personality*. New York: Harper.

McIntyre, A. (1981). *After virtue: A study in moral theory*. Notre-Dame, IN: University of Notre Dame Press.

Monroe, K. R., Hankin, D., & Van Vechten, R. B. (2000). The psychological foundations of identity politics. *Annual Review of Political Science, 3*, 419–447.

Nisan, M. (1985). Limited morality: A concept and its educational implications. In M.W. Berkowitz & F. Oser (Eds.), *Moral education: Theory and application.* Hillsdale, NJ: Lawrence Erlbaum Associates.

Nisan, M. (1991). The moral balance model: Theory and research extending our understanding of moral choice and deviation. In W.M. Kurtines & J. L. Gewirtz (Eds.), *Handbook of moral behavior and development*, (Vol. 3). Hillsdale, NJ: Lawrence Erlbaum Associates.

Nisan, M. (1993). Balanced identity: Morality and other identity values. In G. Noam & T. Wren (Eds.), *The moral self.* Cambridge, MA: MIT Press.

Nisan, M. (1996). Development of the distinction among the "desirable," morality and personal preference. *Social Development, 5*, 219-225.

Nisan, M. (2000). Parteilichkeit und Identitat. [Partisanship and identity]. In: W. Edelstein & G. Nunner-Winkler (Eds.), *Moral in Socialen Kontext.* Frankfurt, Germany: Suhrkamp.

Nussbaum, M. (1986). *The fragility of goodness.* Cambridge, England: Cambridge University Press.

Rawls, J. (1971). *A theory of justice.* Cambridge, MA: Harvard University Press.

Rest, J.R. (1983). Morality. In J.H. Flavell & E.M. Markman (Eds.), *Handbook of child psychology: Vol. 3. Cognitive development* (4th ed., pp. 556–629). New York: Wiley.

Schwartz, S.H., & Bilsky, W. (1990). Toward a theory of the universal content and structure of values: Extensions and cross-cultural replications. *Journal of Personality and Social Psychology, 58*, 878–891.

Slote, M. (1992). *From morality to virtue.* New York: Oxford University Press.

Smith, E.R. (1998). Mental representation and memory. In D. T. Gilbert, S. T. Fiske, & G. Lindzey (Eds.), *Handbook of social psychology* (4th ed). Vol. 1. Boston: McGraw-Hill.

Statman, D. (Ed.). (1997). *Virtue ethics.* Edinburgh, Scotland: Edinburgh University Press.

Taylor, C. (1992). *The ethics of authenticity.* Cambridge, MA: Harvard University Press.

Turiel, E. (1983). *The development of social knowledge: Morality and convention.* Cambridge, England: Cambridge University Press.

Walker, L. J., & Pitts, R. C. (1998). Naturalistic conceptions of moral maturity. *Developmental Psychology, 34*, 403–419.

Williams, B. (1985). *Ethics and the limits of philosophy.* London: Fontane.

8

Altruism and Character

Bill Puka
Rensselaer Institute

WHAT IS CHARACTER

Altruism and character bear many relations to each other. Some are instructively contrasting. For example, altruism is seen as the mark of moral exemplarism in our culture. Yet, we do not cite good character when praising this personal ideal. Mother Teresa is not characterized as a person of good character, for example. (Witness her autobiography, Muggeridge, 1977, and accompanying testimonials found in the Attenborough documentary of her life.) Jesus is not praised for his character despite his guiding role in much character education, neither is Buddha nor any other benevolent exemplar I can cite.

Certainly there are no bad characters here. But character does not seem to capture what these people are or show. Referring to it seems to belittle them. Despite our thinking that virtues make up character, we do not commonly view the virtues of loving kindness or generosity as expressing good character. The benevolence literature in moral philosophy and psychology is similarly bereft of character references.

This is puzzling. Character is represented as the be-all and end-all of moral personality. Conscience is either included or closely allied. (Notice that benevolent exemplars also are not seen merely as people of conscience.) As such, character seems a fit launching pad for any morally desirable trait. Indeed, where else can such traits abide or be launched? We would expect character to show most prominently in the most expressive virtues, of which the altruistic genre seems foremost. But character does not shine here. If anyone has a full, rich, and well-integrated moral personality, these benevolent exemplars do. Yet, in portraying moral personality character fails to capture them.

Character sometimes comes in a highly congealed form, akin to single traits like steadfastness, reliability, or integrity. This occasional narrowness could explain why character seems too small to fill exemplars. Still, integrity origi-nally referred to the proper integration or harmony of all virtues and still has great breadth and complexity as a concept. Steadfastness and reliability also readily stand for conscientiousness, which signals the effort to be moral across the full range of virtues.

In any event, the puzzlement is not that one brand of virtues (altruistic) overawes the entire profile of virtues. It is that character and altruism seem sep-arate and on a par. There are people of good character, and then there are altru-ists, although clearly benevolent traits are a subset of virtues, unlike integrity or steadfastness at their broadest. Morality seems to be of two minds on this matter, presenting multiple personalities.

Or is character's personality more two-faced than two-sided? Is it less the stuff of functioning saints than of sinners who have gotten their moral ducks in a row? Character brings organization and good order where morality had been out of sorts. Character brings it all together when matters are at loose ends. Thus, character has a very different role than altruism. Character is the man-ager and disciplinarian. Allied with conscience it is our overseer, coach, or per-sonal trainer, whipping us into shape and keeping us that way. Altruism neither gets us organized nor keeps us on the straight and narrow. Moreover, it does not seem dependent on any structure of propriety whatsoever, strict or casual. It is something more like flow, or overflow (as Plato put it)—a gushing forth of goodness. Although altruism is not out of control, it is not in control. It is differ-ent and more. Character, but not altruism, is closely associated with resistance to temptation and self-discipline, which Blasi (2002) made clear in his survey of the character research literature.

Benevolent exemplars may be so poorly represented in this research be-cause they have outgrown their struggle with the dark side. They have loosed their grip on the reins of self-interest. The piddling side of petty propriety no longer distracts them. Their issue is less about walking the straight and narrow than finding time. Having only 24 hr to help in 1 day is their moral nemesis, ex-plaining why character seems lower, earlier, and more minimal than an altruis-tic orientation.

Indeed it is at the extremes of charity (in the realm of selflessness) that character totally loses its place. As moral personality, identity, or self, it seems less to supplant the grasping ego than to be dispatched with it. What research there is on exemplarism seems to teach this lesson (Colby & Damon, 1992; Puka, 1999). When altruism prevails we move beyond self-sacrifice. The self has gotten out of the way before altruism arrived, allowing a more direct and fulsome river of giving to run through. The result is experienced as an expansive thrill of good fortune mixed with grateful appreciation, not of doing the right thing. (Of course, altruistic effort and sacrifice also have their place.)

Character's association with self-discipline reveals a second affinity, and a partisan one, for righteous or deontological ethics. This is the ethics of duty, obligation, and conformity to principle, not open-heartedness or effusive generosity. A person of character is usually upright and just, rendering to each his or her due. He or she is conscientious, determined, persistent, and staunch, showing moral fiber and backbone. Benevolence is less about such moral push and posture than the pull of feelings and aspirations, rising toward ideals. When we go with it, nothing is held back.

Martin Luther King is typically cited for his character as he himself cited the content of character in others. (He is criticized for indiscretions here as well.) King's ethos was that of justice, equal rights, and respect despite a backdrop of Christian love.

The same can be said for his mentor, Mohandas Gandhi. Whether duty or benevolence ethics is more elevated than the other, they are at least quite different. Placing character to one side of the difference calls character's status as a generally moral source or abode into question.

AMORAL–IMMORAL

Altruism and character share other divergences from morality. Especially in psychology, altruism is typically conceived amorally. It is researched that way as well. Altruism is a prosocial and other-directed orientation generally, spanning from fledgling attempts to do small favors or show consideration and sympathy to ultimate (but not necessarily admirable) self-sacrifice. Notice that even entrepreneurship and venture capitalizing are prosocial in this way as well, which is why most researchers see altruism as instrumental egoism. Psychologists of a biological turn of mind tend to favor ants and other social insects over humanity as exemplars of altruism. These seemingly dutiful creatures readily lay down their antennae and lives to save the hive. Yet, such species and tendencies are bereft of significant moral sensibilities. They are bereft of egoistic ones for that matter as well.

Altruism's typical emphasis on self-sacrifice raises moral suspicions as well, especially when the concept is defined as self-sacrificial. Even altruism's full focus on other-directedness can seem suspicious. Consider the perceived need in moral development and feminist ethics to balance the themes of concern and caring for others with comparable self-concern and self-care.

Utilitarians are as prosocial as they come, bidding all of humanity to maximize human (and animal) welfare. Doing so often requires us to trump our personal desires for the desires of others. But even Utilitarians criticize self-sacrifice for its inherent costs. It detracts from the social good as it contributes to it. Less costly means can be found to do good, which is preferred. Like all of us, Utilitarians admire the strength of will shown in overcoming selfish needs or desires. (Perhaps Christian ethics hold sacrifice so high because it flies in the face of selfishness and self-pride in this way—the roots of all sin.) But as J. S. Mill noted, not every challenging feat we can accomplish or noble gesture we can make is one we should attempt—one that is admirable beyond the willpower that went into it.

In place of self-sacrifice Utilitarians urge empathy and identification. These good habits allow us to make others' interests our own and share vicariously in their fulfillment. By so appropriating others' joys we compensate for the personal interests given up to help. Why forego any good in the pursuit of good? Why harm or deprive anyone—including oneself—to advance welfare? The sociologist Sorokin coined the term *creative altruist* to honor those so able at altruism as to find endless joy in its practice. Ironically, those supremely admired as saints for depriving themselves for others can be viewed as incompetents.

Is it not puzzling to place strict prohibitions on depriving others of their wellbeing but consider no holds barred when sacrificing our own? Selves are people too after all. They are others to others for example. And when we do good for others it is to advance their interests. Altruism and kindness are a kind of complicity in self-interest in this sense. If it is so admirable to abet another's self-interest, it is puzzling how aiding our own can be anathema. Indeed, self-benefit should be prescribed and held high (not merely permitted or tolerated) so long as its objective is to benefit a person, not merely serve an impulse.

Compared to altruism, character's morally dubious tendencies seem tepid. But they grow on you. Character typically takes a controlling stance toward our interests, not a spirited or free-wheeling one. It hems us in, keeping our volatility in check, and helping us toe the line. In these two roles of resistance to temptation and self-discipline, character appears comparatively straight laced and puristic. Socially, it tends toward conformism. Thus, overrigidity in character may merely extend natural rigidity found in character's very constitution.

This would help explain why character became such a close companion of Victorianism and its moralism.

A good way to fully recognize this natural tendency is to personify character. Hold its personal embodiment in mind and ask: Does character have fun or show a sense of playfulness in its moral pursuits? Does it tend toward the creative and unconventional in the way that eccentrics and other characters do? Is character known for its good cheer and sense of humor, its lusty adventurism and penchant for improvisation? Does it open its heart to joy and radiate it infectiously to others as the kindly and benevolent typically do?

These are not likely our associations with character—with any side of character. We hardly imagine it as lusty, bawdy, or otherwise expansive as it strides through the moral realm. Character is more one-sided by nature: serious and sober. It respects the respectable along with the truly respect worthy. In only giving credit where credit is due, it shows little personability or warmth.

In addition to its moralistic tendencies, however, character can reveal moral backbone or viscera in its grounding motivations and traits. Without impulse control, delay of gratification, self-discipline, focus, and resoluteness, we could not be consistently honest, reliable or courageous when necessary. We could not be fair-minded and tolerant. We would instead fold when the going got tough or become lured away by distractions. These grounding traits infuse the virtues, forming part of them. And we experience their working vividly—the self-discipline in honesty and the resoluteness in courage—when exercising these virtues. Notice, however, that this horsepower on which the virtues ride is not itself moral. Some of the virtues are not fueled by it. In fact, some show quite immoral tendencies. Honesty, for example, is often brutal and personally devastating to others—it would be more so if we were cruel enough to be honest. This was acknowledged from the start in virtues ethics but insufficiently. Brutality is not just a drawback or shortfall in a virtue, after all, but its moral antithesis. And character as the abode of virtue abides it.

As many feminists have noted, courage is the perennial champion of violence, whether on offense or defense. It is an endangerment to many who would do the right thing thereby risking the ultimate sacrifice in battle. This courageous risk-taking behavior typically has devastating consequences on dependents and loved ones waiting at home. Courage is what keeps people facing difficulty that would better be avoided, such as a courageous mother who endures an abusive husband or raises several children on her own without taking charity from the government. Courage is what keeps people fighting for lost causes and abstract principles despite the untold and futile suffering that results. Principle often shows similar results.

Most virtues can go either way: toward right or wrong, good or evil. This is why ethics moved away from virtues as a field and why mainstream ethics remains wary of their recent revival. They can also take many nonmoral roads, such as material acquisitiveness or careerism. This was recognized only in small part soon after the start of virtue ethics. (Aristotle saw vice as a shortfall or excess of the same motivations and abilities that produced virtue when moderated.) Something not at all realized, however, was that morally inherent virtues like justice and respectfulness themselves show a very dark side. (This is one of the most important contribution of critical and feminist theory.) Their administration can be callous and impersonal, calculative and inflexible, and in fact highly punitive (Gilligan 1982; Noddings, 1984). They can render to people merely what they earn when it is what they need and feel that is key, with our ability to respond compassionately to them.

This means that no virtue escapes its fate of being immoral as well as amoral and moral. Moral virtue is only part moral. Moral virtue, as traditionally conceived, is part vice. This means that character itself can go either way insofar as it is led or constituted by its component virtues. Indeed, we should expect good character to go wrong regularly by virtue of its self-consistency, its fealty to principle, and its strong fibre and backbone. These otherwise noble features are what prevent character from bending accommodatingly, from cutting slack and letting things pass—as would a generous and nonfinicky heart. Character simply cannot show the ultimate altruism of besmirching itself—willingly sacrificing its most sacred principle, its sense of identity and reputation—for a needing friend. An altruist need not even face this grave conflict.

THE BLASI FACTOR

A great deal of research has gone into determining whether genuine altruism exists at all. This is a very logical possibility that has been questioned by philosophers (Nagel, 1979). Its empirical demonstrability has been questioned by psychological egoists in the research community, including behaviorists, social learning theorists, neo-Freudians, and evolutionary psychologists. In a similar fashion, the existence of character as a distinguishable phenomenon can be put in question. Although it seems likely that personality exists, with its stable traits and dispositions, it is not clear that character exists as a subsystem of personality or as a psychological system apart from it. We should expect that modern empirical research did not find actual phenomena corresponding to age-old conceptual categories. Many of the virtues may fall here, as may virtue itself as a general category. Certain morally identifiable actions and intentions may not show an identifiable trait of this sort that gives rise to them. Their morality may instead result from the interplay of wide-ranging attitudes and actions themselves, which may be quite amoral.

Given Augusto Blasi's long track record of research in moral identity, it is not surprising that he has joined the search for moral character. We reflect on his most recent treatise in this area in the following section. But his focus on altruism may surprise many. Indeed, its fruits have yet to appear in print. Several years ago, walking and talking with Gus around a rainy Berlin, I learned of his lively interest in Batson's research on egoism and altruism. Eventually, I extracted a long manuscript (Blasi & Nunner-Winkler, 1999–2003) that he had worked up on the topic in consultation with Gertrude Nunner-Winkler. Although the monograph remains under construction, he has kindly allowed me to summarize and reflect on some of its main tenets here, along with his character essay. The second part of our discussion starts here.

THE TROUBLE WITH BATSON

For those not familiar with Batson's work, Blasi's initial depiction more or less sums it up: "Batson's goal—one that he pursues with a single-mindedness reminiscent of missionary zeal—has been to demonstrate, beyond a reasonable empirical doubt, that genuine altruism does indeed exist." Those familiar with the perennial egoism–altruism debate in ethics and action theory cannot help but be tickled by Batson's designs. The game is played (in these theoretical areas) as follows. One author poses a case of obvious altruism, perhaps dramatic altruism. The opponent then poses a self-interested or egoistic motivation (no matter how far-fetched) to explain the altruism. Sample egoist explanations for our helping others include trying to avoid the guilt we would feel if we did not help, avoid being haunted by the suffering we might have allayed had we helped but did not, gain the approval of others, avoid the censure of others, feel good about the sort of person we are, avoid feeling bad about the person we would be if we passed by, get in good with the recipient (in hopes of reciprocal benefit), experience the joy of their being benefited vicariously, and enhance our reputation among peers.

Instead of entering the fray with a pet volley against egoism or parry for altruism, the Batson group empirically operationalized the main undermining contentions from the egoist camp and designed an ingenious way to test them. (All references to positions advanced in the overall Batson research program: Batson 1987, 1989, 1990; Batson & Coke, 1981, 1983; Batson, Batson, Griffitt, Barrientes, Brandt, Sprengelmeyer, & Baly, 1989; Batson, Cowles, & Coke, 1979; Batson, Duncan, Ackerman, Buckley, & Birch, 1981; Batson, Duck, Brandt, Batson, Powell, McMaster, & Griffitt, 1988; Batson, Fultz, &

Schoenrade, 1987; Batson, Fultz, Schoenrade, & Paduano, 1987; Batson, O'Quin, Fultz, Vanderplas & Isen, 1983). Fourteen such experimental demonstrations had already been attempted when Blasi wrote this monograph almost a decade ago. To dispatch all egoist pretenders, each design rules out the foreseeable plusses and minuses of a contemplated action that could pique a would-be altruist's self-interest. In addition each design keys in on the likely role of empathy as altruism's motivational benefactor.

Blasi's main bone of contention is with Batson's claim to have demonstrated a direct and uncomplicated relation between emotional empathy and altruistic action. Blasi and Nunner-Winkler offered an alternative to Batson's empathy-altruism hypothesis that rejects emotional empathy as a key source of motivation. They noted that altruistic dispositions themselves are sufficient to produce altruistic behavior without the intervention of emotional arousal. Blasi casted this alternative in moral terms, suggesting that "only one very small step" need be added to turn social psychology's neutral conception of altruism into a moral ideal. This is the observation that "those motivated ... to act altruistically also perceive and intend that behavior as morally good."

Blasi's critique of Batson's program teaches three cognitivist lessons. The first concerns the importance of extensive conceptual analysis when formulating research hypotheses and when designing research conditions that will test for them. The second concerns how to interpret empirical findings appropriately relative to prior conceptual analysis and research design. And the third, relating to the specific case at hand, concerns how to model complex relations between complex phenomena such as empathy and altruism. I offer a summary interpretation of Blasi's critical case, indicating with an asterisk where I am padding his account.

Batson conceived empathy as a purely situational emotion, evoked by the perceived need or suffering of others. When we perceive another's distress, we feel distress ourselves. Then we either move to decrease our distress directly or to ease theirs. The first option can appear altruistic when we mitigate their distress to ease our own. But this is an instrumental form of egoism. Only the latter alternative of helping others out of felt concern for their welfare represents genuine altruism.

Reflecting a dogma of social psychology, Batson understood empathy independently of personality factors. We do not feel empathy because we value concern for others or because we have a helping disposition or altruistic nature. We just feel it spontaneously as a direct effect of the social stimulus conditions that arouse it. The empathy–altruism connection is understood in the same way. Empathy does not move altruism because we value others or hold kindness as an ideal. It is not motivated by a desire to be consistent with our beliefs or sense of ourselves as giving persons. Even social norms and obligations are not key to it. Either they do not exert significant motivational influence or they function as forms of instrumental egoism. We follow social norms and duties to avoid censure and win approval. We follow empathy, by contrast, because it moves us emotionally. Moral emotions like guilt, shame, and pride move us self-interestedly—to avoid their punishment or reap their reward. Empathy, by contrast, is a form of concern for others.

Batson restricted genuine empathy, by definition, to motivations that are not dependent on the foregoing egoistic factors. We can only infer genuine altruism, he held, where someone (a) helps another when it is easy to escape the negative consequences of not helping or (b) finds it difficult to anticipate any special reward for helping. The assumption is that because helping involves costs to oneself, we should not do it unless we truly care about the welfare of others.

Ironically, this is an egoist assumption on Batson's part.* It is of a piece with the cost–benefit perspective Batson took on altruism, predicting that subjects will act altruistically when they calculate that helping will work and that its gains are worth its costs. Blasi noted that, among other things, this perspective ignores psychological findings in moral judgment. Here research subjects often categorically refuse to do something because they regard it as unthinkable. The benefits of it are ignored. Alternatively, they feel required to do it because it is right, ignoring the costs.

Batson attempted to purify altruism in his findings, but this exclusion of personality and social norm factors is conceptually misguided. For Blasi, such factors are not inherently egoistic. We cannot assume that they are typically or predominantly egoistic. Often they are key to other-directed behavior of a moral or prosocial sort. Only in children do social obligations and norms function only as social reinforcement mechanisms. Adults typically use them to guide behavior toward other-directed and ideal ends. Altruism is governed and assessed by social norms—for example, norms of altruism, kindness, generosity, and the like. The relevant social norms and conventions actually determine for us how to act in a contextually appropriate manner for any particular situation. Without them we would not know how to act without serious deliberation.

When acting altruistically one can foresee feelings of pride. But in experience, as opposed to conceptualization, this is a rather remote and mediated goal for performing one's actions.* In adults, pride is mainly a sign of acting admirably. One welcomes it as confirmation for one's intention to act well. It is in line with the positive norms that make altruism and other forms of benevolence socially desirable. And it typically takes a compound form, closely allied with its motivational source: That is, we do not merely feel pride but pride in acting altruistically.* We take pride in feeling appropriately empathetic. To feel apathetic and unfeeling, by contrast, might make us feel guilty or ashamed—

which is guilt in apathy. Thus, aspiring toward pride or toward avoiding guilty and shame need not at all be self-interested. Research in moral development shows clearly that only young children address these matters in egoistic ways. From adolescence on, however, our motivations are mixed, taking on other-directed, social, and inherent moral rationales.

Batson's misconceptions about these mediating factors directly affect his research design and interpretation of findings. His experiments do not control for self-concept, moral emotions, or social norms. He did not monitor for their possible influence. Yet, his approach cannot rule them out. And without doing so, his findings are difficult to credit. After all, there is a wealth of research demonstrating the motivational influence of personality and moral factors. These include moral identity and self-consistency foremost.

How serious are these omissions? When these excluded factors exert influence, what Batson identified as empathy in his varied experimental conditions can be different phenomena in each case. In one, empathy might be a form of physiological arousal; in another, it might be psychological arousal. In yet another, empathy might arise in the form of memories or ideas about when empathy is socially expected. Empathy also might be the expression of personal commitments. Further, reacting to perceived need through certain self-concepts would cause emotions like empathy to be suppressed rather than expressed, perhaps through the need to be self-consistent. ("Poverty is a structural problem that should not be deal with through personal sympathy and disempowering aid."[*] "Giving to homeless people begging for spare change only keeps them on the street while abetting alcoholics and encouraging scam artists to boot."[*]) To ignore variables that can actually change the primary phenomenon one is measuring is a most serious problem.

Batson's approach also cuts altruism off from agency and personal self-expression. On his account, altruism is dependent on the immediacy of an emotional response. In a misguided attempt to protect the empathy–altruism connection from egoistic mediation, Batson deprived altruism of intention and purpose. He prevented altruism from being an action or activity, much less a self-expressive one meriting credit. Instead it mimics a kind of complex reflex. Empathy becomes a mental state popping up as a consequence of perceived situational stimuli. Altruism becomes a kind of automatic behavior, propelled by empathic arousal toward a prosocial movement of body parts.

REASONING TOGETHER

Blasi's critique is still in progress. Thus, we can explore with it the various directions it takes, might take, or might have taken so far. In this way we also can explore the many important issues it raises for our own research directions. We begin with Blasi's conceptual critique of Batson's egoism-altruism distinction.

Benefit of the Doubt

What would make Batson's attempt to eliminate any hint of egoism in the motivational source of altruism sensible? One answer seems clear. Batson was explicitly arguing to the skeptic. He was arguing to those who see self-interest hidden beneath or engineering every apparently generous or helping behavior. Within psychology he was likely arguing to the majority of researchers, all of whom are psychological egoists, who identify motivation with self-interest.

Questions: Why do people act? To get something they desire? What do they desire? Answer: A positively reinforcing experience. They wish to attain sources of pleasure and satisfaction in certain objects. Why would people act to serve the interests if it was not to serve themselves in return? If there was no reward in those efforts it would be like investing in nothing—with no hope of return. Why would they act for the inherent sake of something such as some impersonal good or ideal except to experience the pleasure accordant with it or to feel ennobled by its pursuit?

Given this wide and long field of skepticism, Batson first needs to show that some behaviors are indubitably altruistic no matter how few or how circumscribed. Only the purist strain of altruism will satisfy such skeptics, a strain for which none of the remote causes typically rallied to explain it can credibly show their face. The simpler and more unmediated cause of altruism, the more difficult it is to explain it from that direction. Empathy seems like such a cause, and it is especially so if it is a spontaneous emotion. Imagine instead that it is an emotion expressing a personal value or sense of obligation. Imagine that it is felt and acted on altruistically to achieve a kind of personal consistency. These motivations are easier to interpret egoistically. For example, we may take a personal interest in the poor or in helping the poor, and so we experience feelings that serve that self-interest when facing the poor. We have internalized or appropriated a sense of obligation to serve, so we serve our self-identified interest in doing so by helping.

But how do we view felt empathy as self-interest when evoked by the situational perception of someone in need? The only plausible way is to assume other factors: hidden interest, preference, value, and personal identification with a concern for the needy and suffering. And this is other-interest or altruism. Once some altruistic behaviors are explained in this pure way, research into mediated and mixed-motive altruism can take place. If it could be assumed that Batson had only gotten to the first step of this mission to document egoism, this additional research is yet to come, and Blasi's criticism of his egoism–altruism distinction is a bit harsh.

But Batson and colleagues devoted many years and experiments to this research program. Somewhere along the line trying to get one's foot in the door must stop and getting more realistic and subtle must start. Why Batson's approach does not broaden and qualify the concept of altruism then becomes a mystery and a problem, as Blasi pointed out.

Reiterating Blasi

Blasi's critique of Batson's altruism can go farther, questioning whether Batson himself is not primarily a psychological egoist. Batson's failure to parse tendencies toward instrumental egoism from the empathic and altruistic pulls of social norms or from moral emotions and personality factors is backwards not just biased. Blasi's (1988) long-term research on the judgment–action gap reveals that identifying ourselves as moral selves most determines whether we will practice what we preach. Yet, the processes of psychological self-identifications and self-interest differ greatly. Our interest in being a moral person itself is not an egoistic one. It is not a way to add yet another notch to the holster that is our self. Although being moral brings some rewards, its costs are obviously greater. To be moral is to be indifferent to many of our pet interests for the sake of equality. It is to override self-interest for the greater good, as well as for principle and justice. And if we already are an interested self, it is unclear how it could ever be in our (perceived) interest to become a moral one instead. (Those who identify themselves morally do not merely see this as a persona or pretension designed to get social or self-approval; their changes in perception and action make this clear.) It is as a moral self, adopting morally defined interests, that morality loses its motivational sting.

As Blasi also pointed out, it is through the use of moral norms and obligations in society that we typically figure out what is legitimately expected of us, how to fulfill that expectation, and how to adapt that fulfillment to a variety of social contexts. This is how moral self-identification expresses itself. And being moral is largely an other-directed and altruistic enterprise. (For ethical egoists, any action but a purely self-interested one is termed altruistic.) Thus, what counts as primarily egoistic motivations for Batson are essentially altruistic ones. That is indeed backwards.

A Third Category

Batson's fault, however, is not only in conceding too many motivations to egoism. It is in placing relevant motivations into merely two classes—if it is not altruistic, it is egoistic. This again is typical of egoist thinking. It is unclear if Blasi opposed this disjunction in his manuscript though I assume he did in reflection. Regardless, this is an issue worth pondering for all concerned.

There is a vast range of motivations toward people that are neither "me" nor "them." They are personally disinterested interests. Many of these target a plethora of impersonal objects—states of affairs, natural wonders, wild animals, and pets. For example, we may desire that certain knowledge be acquired, or certain art produced. We may desire that the sky stay blue and clear of pollution or that the Rocky Mountains never be turned into gravel pits. But we need not be personally invested in such ends. We may seek no satisfaction or pleasure in their being produced or hope that anyone else will. Often we may feel the opposite, as when a religious scientist pursues research likely to debunk central religious tenets. Here the scientist's self has an interest, but the interest is not in his or her self or its personal benefit. This is what phrases like "truth for its own sake" mean.

For the egoist and mainstream psychologist perhaps, such motives are at the heart of philosophy. They assume that reasons, logic, or knowledge carry their own motivational force. And this lacks empirical support. But, as Blasi pointed out, empirical research does not clearly show that any sort of physiological or emotional arousal is necessary for action. Cognitions also do seem capable of exerting motivational force generally, as witnessed in the broad scope of so-called "competence motivations" that ground cognitive psychology.

Note also that our desires need not be self-reflexive. They need not be directed at their own satisfaction or that of their author. When I desire something I do not typically desire only the impact on me of acquiring it. It is not typically only an instrument, with myself being the only true object of all desire. At most, the pleasure I draw from it is one of the contributing goals of my action, not a sufficient cause of it. (Witness especially our purchase of insurance, our long-term investments, and drawing up of wills to provide for our families after death.) It is a perennial mistake that philosophers uncovered long ago to confuse the object of desire with its source.

Batson may have had good reason initially not to count some of the mediating motivations Blasi cited as altruistic. But that should never have put these mediators into the egoist camp. We can want *that* we do our social part without wanting to do it. This is what makes hypocrisy, and there is hardly a more universal human tendency. The *that* of our wanting is enough to keep our desires in conformance with social norms. We can want to be praiseworthy and free of guilt as a person without acting for the sake of these rewards. At least the possibility of having such neutral interests should be tested and controlled for in research.

If we accept this third category of interest, we also must caution Blasi against emphasizing the connection between altruistic moral norms and altruistic motivation. Moral norms can be followed interestedly, self-interestedly, and disinterested, with the first and third options accounting for most of the empirical variance. One could want that the moral or altruistic thing be done whether one personally wants to do it or not. We can want this even while flouting morality ourselves. This would mark our being in conflict or being inconsistent and irrational, which, like hypocrisy, we seem to be very good at. Many of us apparently put ourselves at risk of failure or detection when doing wrong for this reason.

Likewise, I can personally value something yet not desire it. I can wish that the human race achieves ultimate knowledge, but wish to stay quite in the dark personally, smitten with "the mystery of life." In fact, many testify to feeling this way. Human achievement is what is valued here, not our participation in it—not even human satisfaction resulting from the achievement. This value–desire distinction provides one way of interpreting Mark Twain's comment on Wagner's music, "It's better than it sounds." It is quite common to appreciate, but not like or want to experience. (With moral values the distinction plays out like this: I want that society be just; it should be, and its members should participate loyally. But personally I like being a renegade or bad boy.)

The most plausible picture of altruism or egoism will see both orientations as motivated by a range of different motives—altruistic, egoistic, moral, nonmoral, and other. Even each contributing motivation is probably mixed—conformity to social norms to get approval, avoidance of censure, a need to feel normal by conforming, a desire to follow a habitual routine, not having to think about something, and so forth.

Morality and Amorality

Many of us share Blasi's moral view of altruism. But in so doing we still should credit the amoralistic assumptions of Batson and of social psychology generally. It is not unsatisfactory that empathy pop up as an emotion out of the blue from this perspective. It is not unsatisfactory that empathy express itself as altruism in a somewhat reflexive fashion, not intentionally or purposively. If ants can do altruism with less motivation—with virtually no psychological motivations at all—then certainly humans can do it with far more. We do not need agency or intent to do it, just behavior of a certain sort, which is caused by prosociality. If the source contains a lean or tendency toward helping, much like a situational disposition, that is a plus.

SUBJECTIVISM: PRO AND CON

Blasi's comment on the "small step" that transforms amoral altruism into moral altruism raises key questions for psychology. The Piagetian approach has been criticized roundly for transporting philosophical definitions of moral relevance and adequacy into psychological research and theory without even a nod to what research subjects feel or believe. The psychological sense of morality should at least be investigated and credited initially in psychological research. Subjectivity is the bread and butter of psychology after all, even if it is said to spawn undue relativism within moral theory and belief. As stated, Blasi's "small step" seems completely subjective. To make altruism moral simply requires that the agent "perceive and intend this behavior to be morally good." Conceptual or philosophical criteria must be used to at least limit this subjective sense, distinguishing its minimum validity and coherence. Even our subjective sense of morality must show a certain objective plausibility or intersubjective legitimacy to be taken seriously.

Morality "is what it is and not another thing." The term *morality* refers to some things and not others even if it is flexible in its use, recognizing matters of degree. Nazis may very well feel that their desire to exterminate inferior races is just, but it is not. It does not even have its facts straight. If we stretch the terms of morality too far, we bifurcate its meaning. And that means falling into intolerable inconsistencies of belief, communication, and mutual expectation. We already have terms that account for the Nazi moral sense and others like it. *Prevailing ethos* is such a term, borrowed from anthropology. *Accepted social norms* is one that has currency even in moral psychology. Using *morality* as a synonym for these concepts is not only confusing but conceptually intrusive.

There is an additional way to legitimize the foregoing moral subjectivity—Blasi's implicit route I expect. As Piagetians, we would assume that some degree of natural cognitive development and moral development occurs in everyone as they interact with others. Thus, if we perceive and intend a behavior to be morally good, we inevitably express some degree of cognitive–moral competence or understanding in doing so. This in itself legitimizes our subjective sense of morality; it provides a functional or practical-reasoning justification. But, in addition, the structure of this competence correlates with (is isomorphic to) the logical structure of conceptual or philosophical criteria of moral relevance and adequacy.

Still, we should recognize that a plausible sense of morality can remain highly subjective and relativistic. We only require generalizability in ethics when responsibilities are interpersonal or social, not personal. Even here, it is possible to work out compromises without agreement on proper ground rules or on main tenets. We might find very different reasons to accept the same policies. We might trade instead—I will give you X (which I do not credit) if you give me Y (which you find groundless). And we might agree to disagree. The only limits on relativism and subjectivity for personal ethics is their incompatibility with any minimally plausible social or interpersonal one.

The Good

It also is not clear that we should focus what is moral, as Blasi did, on what is morally good. We should not identify moral do-gooding as morally good doings. Material goods and interested and pragmatic goals and benefits might serve just as well or better. Judging from her autobiography and the Attenborough documentary, Mother Teresa did not perceive or intend her actions to be morally good. Certainly many of the moral exemplars cited in the aforementioned research do not. These everyday exemplars often explicitly replace the term *do-gooder* with *good doers* when referring to themselves. They value taking effective actions and getting things done, not some hallowed quality of being morally admirable or distinctive in one's aspirations. This is morally realistic as well, challenging the notion that morality is self-referential or deferential relative to other value systems. Morality can serve other value systems and does not require one of its own.

Most of what Mother Teresa did concerned filling drinking glasses with water and handing them to a dying patient, mixing an ideal baby formula, or cleaning a hospital gurney. Those who feed the world's poor mostly stack canned food on food bank shelves or into trucks and then they drive them down long and bumpy dirt roads. What makes these practical deeds moral is their good effects and their expression of concern. This is not distinctly moral concern for the distinctly moral well-being of others' moral selves.

Consider the puzzlements of not adopting this perspective. To help someone is kind and seemingly moral. But, as noted, it usually conspires in the recipient's self-interest. Is that morally good? We likely answer no. But is doing something self-interested morally good itself because it expresses concern and helps a self—a self who happens to be you?

When we conceive morality as nondistinctive, or at least its good or valuable side, the moral designation may be unnecessary or inappropriate. And, in part, it makes sense to see good especially as morally nondistinctive. By contrast, matters of strict obligation, rights, equality, and justice seem more morally distinctive.

In making the moral connection for altruism Blasi noted that its "the very idea of altruism … implies evaluation," and that altruism "could not be understood outside of social norms." Here again caution is advised, especially if Blasi was referring to positive evaluation and norms of social approval (not disapproval) as seems to be the case. From this perspective, after all, how would we then interpret the important dispute over whether desirable altruism (morally or otherwise) should involve self-sacrifice as opposed to joy? For those in the latter camp, Batson's form of altruism may be negatively valued or simply not valued at all.

As noted, much of the social science community seems very comfortable with researching altruism in a relatively amoralist and nonevaluative stance. Altruism is other-directed motivation—for better or worse. It may arise out of concern for others' well-being or a kind of elitist disdain, providing altruism a noblesse-oblige appearance. To these researchers altruism may appear good in some ways, bad in some others, perhaps better than worse overall, or the reverse. But whether altruism shows these value-worthy qualities does not affect whether it exists and is common in behavior. And this is what concerns research.

Research Boundaries

Blasi was right to criticize social psychology for ignoring research in other relevant research specialties. But one can hardly imagine an area of psychology that would not be guilty of this practice, including moral development and moral psychology generally. Indeed, the primary criticism made of cognitivist research in these specialty areas is that it focuses on individual choice and deliberation rather than picturing moral judgment within a sociocultural context. Here interpersonal negotiation supplants the role of deliberation. Making piecemeal moral contributions within one's roles in complex organizational systems supplants personal action, as in judgment–action. Thus, Batson might plead guilty to the charge without feeling shamed before his peers. His research takes the tunnel-vision approach of social science generally.

Batson may also retort that Blasi's position on altruism does not take pains to represent the amoral or situational stimulus–response aspects of empathy and altruism. The peculiar irony of such a retort would be that Blasi is as eclectic and inclusive a psychologist as they come. But taking charge and countercharge together here suggests a way to draw from both accounts, putting each in their place. We first add Batson's social psychology contribution to Blasi's nonoverlapping moral and personality account, then deal with conflicting positions piecemeal, breaking them down into small nonconflicting bits then piecing them together. This is no easy matter of course.

Reporting Empathy

In portions of Blasi's methodological critique, Batson's self-report measure of empathy comes under fire. Blasi noted that, being asked relevant questions for this measure, research respondents recognize the implicit expectation that they are supposed to feel something. They can easily figure out what they should feel due to their piecemeal awareness of interpersonal conventions. This is indeed a key problem because respondents might not feel anything at all yet act altruistically. Or they may feel social-norm pressures and the influences of personal dispositions, which do not have a feeling or emotional quality.

Using such a self-report index is problematic on other grounds as well. If the research on emotional intelligence has shown anything it is that some people are masterful and others dim-witted at perceiving emotions and identifying them (Mayer & Slavoney, 1990). Those respondents who misidentify certain emotions as empathy, perhaps conforming to altruistic social conventions or expectations, will record as empathic for Batson.

A third consideration casts doubt on the measure. When people honestly report feeling sad or compassionate, saying that their heart goes out to someone, they may very well not feel but think something. We use *feel* and *think* interchangeably on many occasions. I investigated this issue informally with students in class. When discussing empathy in relation to care ethics, I asked how many students felt empathic in the context raised. (About 100 students were involved.) There was almost total agreement (except for abstentions) on feeling empathy, judging by hands raised. "When I stated that seeing a homeless mother and child huddling in a doorway in the cold rain makes you sad," there was talk of feeling her pain. But when I asked students to reflect on their experience based on common psychological depictions of empathy as vicarious feeling or feeling- with a sufferer, many students changed their report. In fact most of the male students not only took back what they said but doubted publicly that they had ever experienced empathy. "I'm not sure I could do that if I tried," was a common remark.

"Then what happens inside you in these instances of being sad?" I asked. They replied that an idea occurred to them; they entertained the thought that "this is sad" or "I can feel for them." No detectable feeling takes place. One noted, "Someone would have to be a monster not to consider this sad and want to help." Their thoughts also followed social expectations.

THE ALTERNATIVE MODEL

In hopes of weaving a combined Batson–Blasi account of altruism, I briefly present Blasi and Nunner-Winkler's alternative model. The arousal of empathy is preceded by having altruistic motives and concerns in the form of stable disposition. It depends on them. These are likely to have different psychological sources such as personal attachment and identification or the internalization of social norms. Such dispositions sensitize people to situations calling for compassionate and helpful responses, direct the cognitive interpretations of them, and generate appropriate emotional reactions and support helping actions. In fact, we can only legitimately call emotional arousal empathy if is originated from and reflected enduring altruistic concerns.

Still, there may be no necessary connection between empathy and physiological arousal. It is a theoretical assumption, not an empirical finding, that emotions must get aroused to motivate. Except when caught by surprise, or in the very young, empathy is not an immediate or direct result of perceiving someone in need. The situation must be cognitively structured in an appropriate way for empathy rather than annoyance or disdain to arise. Some will see the poor as getting what they deserve for past indiscretions and may feel a sense of just satisfaction at its sight.

As noted, altruistic dispositions are sufficient to cause helping behaviors. Empathic emotions and intense arousal are not required. The connection between the situation and altruistic concerns can be established on cognitive grounds by understanding that the person is suffering and that there are certain personally appropriate and socially expected things to do. A moral self-concept depicting oneself as a kindly person will bolster this connection and its call to action.

CHARACTER RESEARCH

We arrive at our final topic. Blasi's interest in character revolves around research on willpower and the nature of self-expressive desires. Blasi saw these desires as the essence of willpower and integrity. Normally, the role of willpower in character is to tame desire or suppress it entirely. Thus, Blasi's focus is unusual. Even character rhetoric praising the longing for goodness or the love of it would balk at terming its motivations desires.

Perhaps just as unusual is the apologetic way Blasi approached his topic. Three excuses pave the way. First, Blasi cited Hartshorne and May's (1928) research challenging virtue as a concept to remind us that their findings "did not totally discredit" the notion. By this I assume Blasi meant that although differences in observed behavior that should reflect virtue were found to reflect situational contexts and social reinforcements, we cannot conclude that virtuous traits do not exist. We cannot even conclude that they exert no motivational influence in the situations tested; we can conclude that whatever the influence, it is not predominant. Hartshorne and May focused narrowly on honesty in any event, and did not cover the great array of virtues and their influence.

In fact, virtues may exert other psychological influences than motivating direct action. They may affect moral perception and interpretation, contributing to overall motivation in the way cognitive schema do. As R. S. Peters (1971) argued against Kohlberg, so-called moral reasoning schema can be interpreted as virtues in themselves. And there is good evidence for the existence of such schema. Kohlberg's criticisms of simplistic, straight-laced virtues (boy scout virtues) could be totally correct and yet irrelevant to the existence and importance of complex and mature virtues. This is fine, but holding that one's topic is not totally discredited is a rather weak basis for taking it up.

Second, Blasi's excuse is that the ideas of virtue and character are entrenched in our thinking. We cannot get away from the idea or stop thinking about it. I assume that the deeper significance of Blasi's observation is that research psychology should investigate folk psychology and have some explanation for its shape and content. Research should explain why folk beliefs may be inaccurate and why they took hold and endured. Again, this is fine. Still, given how many spurious ideas are entrenched in our thinking and in folk psychology, this also is a weak basis for taking up character as a topic.

Third, Blasi pointed to empirical evidence for stable personality dispositions, prompting us to feel and behave morally. This provides partial evidence that virtue and character references capture something real. The evidence is partial, I assume, because virtues are normally described as traits embedded in a unified moral personality. Dispositions to behave in certain ways are much less than this—mere components of this system. Thus, we have yet another weak basis for focusing on character.

A question to ask at the outset is: How much of Blasi's focus on willpower and even integrity is really focused on character. In fact, how much do moral psychology, philosophy, and character education really focus on character when they say they do?

When reading in this area I notice a recurring maneuver that casts doubt on the character focus of these fields. As soon as character is targeted for discussion, all eyes turn to virtues. And they stay there. Yet, something about character clearly differs from virtues, possibly by quite a bit. Is *character* simply meant to designate the collection of virtues as a general term we use to refer to them? Or is character perhaps like a shelf that holds virtues, akin to file folders in a cabinet? There is good reason to think not.

The qualities and powers perennially attributed to character suggest a complex and unified psychological system. Character manages the interrelation of beliefs, habits, traits, commitments, dispositions, operating principles, deep feeling, and the like. As manager of the virtues themselves, character shows capacities transcending those contributed by the virtues, functioning somewhat independently of them. Showing personality is one example. Putting this personality behind moral motivation to buttress it is another.

When functioning in any particular context, the full capacity of character need not be involved. It can field a team of component virtues and functional guidelines fit for the "game" at hand. This could be seen as a makeshift lineup or selective roster of players. Other virtues remain on the bench in reserve. This particular character capacity allows great flexibility and the ability to handle multiple issues or problems at once. But still character must show unity and consistency across its endeavors. It must get its players playing as a team to achieve a "harmony of the soul."

A reason for this is obvious. Most virtues conflict or can be brought into conflict by certain situations. Most, if not all, virtues can function admirably or badly, bringing aid or doing harm. And although Aristotle's dictum of the mean may hold true—that virtue strikes a mean between two extremes of vice—there is no dictum of the mean that defines the virtue of several virtues working together. Aristotle recognized that his dictum only applied to some virtues. Moreover, he noted that most adult virtues have no name, much less an apt mean. They are too subtle and complicated to be captured by the means of conventional virtues that handle highly conventional interactions. Thus, one cannot have virtue without character—neither a particular virtue nor a virtue overall.

Perhaps there is no empirical evidence challenging the existence of character in this systemic sense—evidence that character is a mere ideal or convenient myth for grouping important morally relevant traits. The character concept helps us account for personal goodness as a holistic quality and the habitual ordering and integration of some virtues expressing this goodness. Yet, so far as I know, no one has actually researched character in this whole-system sense, independent of the virtues, which helps explain why the notion has not been disconfirmed. This also means that there is no solid empirical confirmation of character's existence, which matters greatly in the face of two powerful bases for not believing in it.

The first source of disbelief is that character and virtue are preempirical categories. They were fashioned during times of fantastical superstition, spurious observation and false wisdom. (Willpower is not much more modern in its origins—Blasi was undaunted by the prospect of rehabilitating outdated ideas.) Character and virtue were contemporaries of the four elements that composed physical reality—earth, wind, fire, and water (or stone). Character comingled with the physiological interplay of phlegm and bile, having its metal tested by an "overheating of the blood" that conjured vice. Character and virtue apparently predated phlogiston and vital as well. All these physical categories have been exploded by careful empirical research and by a greatly improved understanding of how to interpret observations. Their contemporary categories have survived in tact within ethics, however, likely due to a host of poor practices. (Among these are a failure to carefully distinguish the empirical aspects of ethical concepts, to test them rigorously, and to revise prevailing concepts to suit—as well as a tendency to shrink from challenging hallowed traditions.

The second reason for disbelief is the very evidence that confirms personality and its many traits. What we know about their functioning seemingly can explain what we call character in totally psychological terms, leaving out a moral twist. In fact, this seems especially easy if we do not distinguish these processes by moral categories of right from wrong, virtue from vice, attributing integrity to some behaviors and bald hypocrisy to others. Both types of practices follow the same predictable psychological laws of motivation—the law of effect or reinforcement, the pleasure principle, effective coping, ego-defense, cognitive competence, and the like—depending on the situation.

In addition to character and virtue generally, particular virtues and vices also may very well be myths. They may be regular concatenations of various cognitive and emotional tendencies that are noticed and interpreted piecemeal for the shape they show when they happen to cross moral categories. Taken in their own terms these combinations might better explain our tendency not only to walk the straight and narrow at times but to walk crookedly, backtrack, hide, fall short and go too far. No special excuses for weakness of the will or surrender to temptation are required.

What little research has been done on moral exemplars, as noted, did not turn up the sorts of virtues that ancient ethical categories would welcome. In fact, most exemplars showcased petty vices—feistiness, stubbornness, judgmentalism, impatience, irritability, and the paradoxical combination of dogmatic beliefs and alertness to the lessons other could teach. Their most prominent and effective features were more easily described in leadership or entrepreneurial (success-motivated) terms than moral ones.

Of course, whether character and virtue exist as we commonly think of them, there may be some researchable phenomena worthy of these titles. In addition, the associated research on willpower and integrity that Blasi analyzed are worth pondering with him on their own. I outline them briefly now.

Blasi first dealt with what he saw as broad and foundational virtues, the motivational underpinnings of particular traits. These include the determination, self-control, and independence we need to be honest and courageous in situational conflicts. For Blasi some virtues form a network around willpower; others form a network around integrity. As noted, the core of character for Blasi is desires from which willpower and integrity derive moral meaning. Integrity relates one's committed desires to the sense of self. Willpower keeps us pursuing our desires, overcoming obstacles and distractions.

Our primary association with the term *willpower* is the exertion of effort and mental force. According to Blasi, however, this prescientific orientation to this prescientific term had been debunked by 1900 thanks to the work of phenomenological psychologists. As I recall from the history of psychology, this debunking occurred when subjects who were asked to exert effort, then not to, behaved the same way under both conditions. Their sense of struggle or ease leading to the behavior observed also made no observable difference. Willpower is not a matter of strength, and self-control is not a matter of struggle. Both are a matter of interlocking cognitive abilities. This explains the high correlation between resistance to temptation and IQ. Desires are the morally neutral capacities of translating willpower into the core of character. In this case the desires are an intensity of affect toward the moral good.

Blasi borrowed from the philosopher Frankfurt (1988) the notion of second-order desires—desires about desires. Will then becomes the desire that certain desires hold sway. Will is a motivational backing of certain existing, first-order motivations. Blasi noted that second-order desires distance us from first-order desires, creating a sense of us (at a second level) controlling them down below, and outside us, like limbs. Whereas first-order desires arise spontaneously as impulses, with us standing passive before them, second-order or reflected desires rise by volition. They are self-expressive, including us as agent in them. When their affect is intense and consistently felt, these second-order desires become commitments that are appropriated or self-identified. Blasi cited Colby and Damon's (1992) research on exemplars to note the sense of certainty and identification with moral commitments these subjects showed. No additional willpower or struggle is needed here. One need only be oneself and, therefore, be true to oneself. To an exemplar the alternative is unthinkable in the way that losing oneself is to any of us.

For Blasi, integrity is self-consistency. It expresses a concern for the unity of one's subjective sense of self through the consistency of its chosen commitments. One type of self-consistency is responsibility. It is a desire about oneself, a commitment to and feeling of duty toward certain norms and relations. Another is moral identity, a psychological merging of one's moral values and commitments with one's sense of self. A third is concern with self-deception.

THE PHENOMENOLOGICAL CHALLENGE

Blasi's account is intriguing because it substitutes for will the combination of self-expressive and reflective preference, engaging cognitive capacities. And, it substitutes for willpower strength of affect, degree of commitment (self-expressive desire), and self-identification with commitment. It seems to tell a story of how we are self-deceived as well, mistaking an investment of self (accompanied by a strong feeling) for effort and struggle. But, of course, Blasi recognized the processes involved as largely unconscious. They become habituated and function unreflectively in daily life. Thus, the illusions of effort or struggle occur chiefly when the matter of which desire to get behind has come to the fore. The struggle is over settling the question, which is a matter of volition or choice, but not willpower. Willpower and self-control, by contrast, are a function of self-expressive cognitive competence after the question is settled.

As with many intriguing ideas, it is not clear how Blasi's concept can be tested and evaluated. Presumably, we would start our observations at those junctures in which our position is to be decided and it seems that we struggle. We all know this experience of indecision and quandary. And with Blasi, I'd contend that it involves decision, not willpower. At least this is so unless in the end I do not voluntarily choose but force myself to do so.

Still, there are experiences we all seem to have with a different kind of struggle in which it feels like we exert enormous effort. On the positive side of will, it involves following through. It involves sticking to one's commitments in one's activities when one's level of energy or interest seems to flag or concentrate elsewhere. What some call the virtues of determination, persistence, and even reliability seem to be made up of exertions of will. Here we call on the power of will—"willing ourselves to do it" as we often say. The second-order desire is in place here, as is the first, but its level of affect has grown weak. Our investment of self in commitments and identification are great, but they are not strong. (Apparently, they never had to be strong on Blasi's account, just large.) But to stick with it, which is an added venture, does not seem to reiterate the desires, my commitment, or my self-identification.

Phenomenologically, it feels instead like I exert energy. That energy feels quite impersonal. I push myself in the way I keep running when my legs are exhausted—in the way I push, lift, or hold up a heavy object when my arms ache. To keep going normally rests on tricks I can use not to let the exertion end. This is not typically resistance to the temptation to give in and give up. No choice (like giving in) seems needed to give up. It comes quite naturally. So does any tendency likely to mitigate the extreme pain or discomfort we feel. Willpower holds and continues to generate energy when the supply seems near exhaustion.

On the negative side, by contrast, willpower does seem to involve battling alternative impulses of comparable strength. We feel totally on one side in the battle with regard to our second-order desires, commitments, and self-identifications. The opposing desires may seem strong or weak: It is not clear introspectively that their felt degree of affect equates with their pull or that their felt pull indicates their actual strength.

Notice that sometimes when the opposition seems so weak as to be barely noticeable, it suddenly wins. Consider what it is sometimes like when we are fighting to stay awake behind the wheel during a long late-night drive. We push away fatigue and drowsiness and an apparent desire to sleep. We push up the wakeful energy like a thermostat bringing up the heat. Then we may find ourselves waking up with a start. In stealth, sleep just snuck up and took us as if we had put our guard down or given up, which we did not.

This process might be viewed as an example of how the struggle and exertion of conflicting powers are not at work here. But surely conflicting beliefs and second-order desires also are not at work. And, phenomenologically, it does feel like a first-order struggle. The same holds with stopping while running or eating while dieting. We fight an enemy that seems to resist. It can win by overpowering us with its superior force or without overpowering us at all. In fact, it can seem to slip right through the front lines of our defense unseen, suddenly invisible. For instance, we will say, "I stopped, right after deciding I did not have to: isn't that odd?" "I don't believe I ate the whole thing."

Consider the character of St. Francis. He was able to deprive himself of all the material comfort he knew all his life as an offering to his Lord and Savior. He was able to tolerate betrayals of his ideals by trusted members of his own order. But while dying and being praised for his virtue, he replied that so long as there is breath left in him he yet may commit the sin of fornication. His willpower was so overmatched by the force of lust that he had to bolster his character by throwing himself into sticker bushes—the Franciscan version of a cold shower.

The issue of willpower or strength of will only comes up when the power is running out—when it is being overwhelmed or being snuck past. And that is the time we feel we have to exert it. We will exertion. We feel ourselves exerting power by will or volition. But as far as I can tell, none of the components mentioned by Blasi is participating here. Thus, we must ask: What is this phenomenon and why is it not willpower? Introspectively, it seems an apt match to our most common experience and understanding of that phenomenon. If it is willpower, what needs to be added to Blasi's account to cover this phenomenon?

If this phenomenon is not willpower, it may be of even greater interest to the topic. What roles does it play regarding true willpower? Does it aid or does it seriously impede will *powers*? Perhaps it is a kind of natural neurosis, a form of angst by which we make our mental life more arduous or tortured than we need to. Is it an introspective drama, directed by the brain to keep us distracted—to keep our reflective processes occupied—while apt volition takes place at an unconscious, well-habituated level? These are interesting questions.

In the case of character, as with altruism, I believe Blasi contributed something important and ingenious to our understanding. I am not sure why Blasi felt that his account of the cognitive aspects of will are the core of character in this case. We can approach Blasi's account asking how to integrate it with the best components of alternative accounts.

The same can be said for Blasi's account of integrity, which is filled with good ideas. Originally, as noted, this term was closely associated with the moral personality system and its unity. It stood for the inclusive and harmonious integration of the virtues and all their components. This is quite different from self-consistency, personal honesty or authenticity in the sense of being true to oneself and one's commitments. The modern sense of honesty, which Blasi aptly depicted, is close to honor. These days this latter virtue is rarely mentioned outside a military context (including Klingon context). Here Blasi's second-order desire model seems especially fit. Integrity rests on a desire that our morally targeted desires prevail—we do the right thing, we always deal with people fairly, showing them the respect and concern they deserve, and so forth. We are never to act in a sleazy or duplicitous way, undeserving of trust. Blasi's focus on a unity of moral personality in commitment and action is particularly apt. We normally think of consistency as something that ties beliefs together or beliefs with actions. But our concern for integrity is self-directed. It is a desire toward oneself, as Blasi noted, and a desire that we be unified in the main moral ways we are—in our beliefs, dispositions, commitments, values, speech, actions, interactions, and relationships.

Blasi's focus on the juncture of moral self, consistency, and integrity raises an intriguing prospect for future research. This prospect would harken back to an ancient focus on consistency within the integral components of character themselves—the components that constitute simply being a certain way, not expressing it in behavior. These involve having a certain quality pattern of attitudes, beliefs, and values in one's head and certain feelings or implicit predispositions in one's heart that express themselves close to home in the moral posture one holds and the moral presence one exudes.

REFERENCES

Batson, C. D. (1990). How social an animal: The human capacity for caring. *American Psychologist, 45*, 336–346.

Batson, C.D. (1989). Personal values, moral principles, and a three-path model of pro-social motivation. In N. Eisenberg, J. Reykowski, & E. Staub (Eds.), *Social and moral values* (pp. 2123–228). Hillsdale, NJ: Lawrence Erlbaum Associates.

Batson, C. D., Batson, J. G., Griffin, C. A., Barrientos, S., Brandt, J.R., Sprengelmeyer, P., & Bayly, J. J. (1989). Negative-state relief and the empathy-altruism hypothesis. *Journal of Personality and Social Psychology, 56*, 922–933).

Batson, C.D., Dyck, J. L., Brandt, J. R., Batson, J. G., Powell, A. L., McMaster, M. R., & Griffitt, C. (1988). Five studies testing two new egoistic alternatives to the empathy-altruism hypothesis. *Journal of Personality and Social Psychology, 55*, 52–77.

Batson, C. D., Fultz, J. Schoenrade, P. A., & Paduano, A. (1987). Critical self-reflection and self-perceived altruism: When self-reward fails. *Journal of Personality and Social Psychology, 53*, 594–602.

Batson, C. D., Fultz, J., & Schoenrade, P. A. (1987). Distress and empathy: Two qualitatively distinct vicarious emotions with different motivational consequences. *Journal of Personality, 55*, 19–39.

Batson, C. D. (1987). Prosocial motivation: Is it ever truly altruistic? In L. Berkowitz (Ed.), *Advances in experimental social psychology* (Vol. 20, pp. 65–122). New York: Academic Press.

Batson, C. D., & Coke, J. S. (1983). Empathic motivation of helping behavior. In J. T. Cacioppo & R. E. Petty (Eds.), *Social psychophysiology: A sourcebook* (pp. 417–433). New York: Guilford.

Batson, C. D., Coke, J. S., & Pych, V. (1983). Limits on the two-state model of empatheic mediation of helping: A reply to Archer, Diaz-Loving, Gollwitzer, Davis, & Foushee, *Journal of Personality and Social Psychology, 45*, 895–898.

Batson, C. D., Duncan, B. D., Ackerman, P., Buckley, T., & Birch, K. (1981). Is empathic emotion a source of altruistic motivation? *Journal of Personality and Social Psychology, 40*, 290–302.

Batson, C. D., O'Quin, K., Fultz, J., Vanderplats, M., & Isen, A. M. (1983). Influence of self-reported distress and empathy on egoistic versus altruistic motivation to help. *Journal of Personality and Social Psychology, 45*, 706–718).

Batson, C. D., & Coke, J. S. (1981). Empathy: A source of altruistic motivation for helping? In J. P. Rushton & R. M. Sorrento (Eds.), *Altruistic and helping behavior: Social, personality, and developmental perspectives* (pp. 167–211). Hillsdale, NJ: Lawrence Erlbaum Associates.

Batson, C. D., Cowles, C. & Coke, J. S. (1979). Empathic mediation of the response to a lady in distress: Egoistic or altruistic? (Unpublished manuscript, University of Kansas).

Blasi, A. (1980). Bridging moral cognition and moral action: A critical review of the literature. *Psychological Bulletin, 88*, 1–45

Blasi, A. (2002). Moral character: A psychological approach. In D. K. Lapsley & F. C. Power (Eds.), *Character psychology and character education. Notre Dame, IN: University of Notre Dame Press.*

Colby, A. Damon, W. (1992). *Some do care.* New York: The Free Press.

Frankfurt, H. (1988). *The importance of what we care about.* New York: Cambridge University Press.

Gilligan, C. (1982). *In a difference voice.* Cambridge, MA: Harvard University Press.

Hartshorne, H., & May, M. A. (1928). *Studies in the nature of character: Studies in self-control.* New York: Macmillan.

Mayer, J.D., & Slavoney, P. (1990). Emotional intelligence. *Imagination, Cognition and Personality, 9*, 185–211.

Muggeridge, M. (1977). *Something beautiful for god.* Garden City, NY: Image Books.

Nagel, T. (1979) *The possibility of altruism.* Princeton, NJ: Princeton University Press.

Noddings, N. (1984) *Caring: A feminine approach to ethics.* Los Angeles: University of California at Los Angeles Press.

Peters, R.S. (1971). Moral development: A plea for pluralism. In T. Mischel (Ed.), *Cognitive development and epistemology.* New York: Academic Press.

Puka, B. (1999). Moral education and the young child. In W. vanHaaften, T. Wren, & A. Tellings, (Eds.), *Moral sensibilities and education.* Amsterdam: Concorde.

9

A Social–Cognitive Approach to the Moral Personality

Daniel K. Lapsley
Ball State University

Darcia Narvaez
University of Notre Dame

In the last decade there has been a remarkable resurgence of interest in studying moral rationality within the broad context of personality, selfhood, and identity. Although a concern with the moral self was never entirely absent from the cognitive developmental approach to moral reasoning (e.g., Blasi, 1983, 1984), it is fair to say that sustained preoccupation with the ontogenesis of justice reasoning did not leave much room for reflection on how moral cognition intersects with personological processes. There were both paradigmatic and strategic reasons for this.

The paradigmatic reason can be traced to the Piagetian roots of moral developmental theory. Piaget's understanding of intelligence was profoundly influenced by his training as a biologist, his work as a naturalist, and his interest in the differential classification of species (especially mollusks) on the basis of morphological variation. Just as the classification of various biological species into zoological categories is based on formal structural characteristics, so too are certain structural characteristics critical to the differential classification of children's thinking. The young Piaget who had, as a naturalist, collected and classified specimens of mollusks is continuous with the older Piaget who, as a genetic epistemologist, collected and classified specimen's of children's thinking (Chapman, 1988; Lapsley, 1996). From this perspective, Piagetian stages are best considered descriptive taxonomic categories that classify formal "morphological" properties of children's thinking on an epistemic level. Stages describe species of knowledge, varieties, and kinds of mental operations, not different kinds of persons.

When Kohlberg appropriated the Piagetian paradigm to frame moral development he well understood the taxonomic implications of the stage concept. He understood that moral stages described kinds of sociomoral operations or different "species" of moral reasoning. The moral stage sequence was a taxonomy identified by a "morphological" analysis of formal structural characteristics of sociomoral reflection. Moral stages classify variations of sociomoral structures, not individual differences among persons. As a result, Colby, Kohlberg, Gibbs, and Liebermann (1983) wrote that moral "stages are not boxes for classifying and evaluating persons" (p.11). Consequently moral stages cannot be the basis for aretaic judgments about the moral worthiness of persons. The stage sequence cannot be used as a yardstick to grade one's moral competence. It makes no evaluative claims about character, says nothing about virtues, and is silent about the moral features of personality and selfhood. Indeed, as Kohlberg (1971) put it, "We ... do not think a stage 6 normative ethic can justifiably generate a theory of the good or of virtue, or rules for praise, blame and punishment" and hence principles of justice "do not directly obligate us to blame and to punish" (p. 217). Instead, the moral developmental stages, like Piaget's stages, describe forms of thought organization of an ideal rational moral agent, an epistemic subject, and therefore cannot be "reflections upon the self" (Kohlberg, Levine, & Hewer, 1983, p. 36). There can be no reason to wonder, given these paradigm commitments, just how personological issues or notions of selfhood and identity could matter to an epistemic subject or to a rational moral agent.

Yet, the moral development tradition had strategic reasons, too, for its minimalist account of selfhood, character, and personality. For example, Kohlberg was specifically interested in charting the development of justice reasoning, as opposed to other possible topics of investigation, just because this aspect of morality seemed most amenable to stage typing. Moreover, the possibility of stage typing gave Kohlberg what he most desired of a moral theory—a way to defeat ethical relativism on psychological grounds. Kohlberg saw that justice reasoning at the highest stages made possible a set of procedures that could generate consensus about a hard case moral quandary. This was the heart of his project. Consequently, those aspects of moral psychology that could not be stage typed or that could not be used in the struggle against ethical relativism were not the object of study in the cognitive developmental tradition. This included, of course, the Aristotelian concern with virtues and moral character.

Kohlberg's objection to a virtue-centered approach to moral character was based on at least two additional considerations. The first was that there was no sensible way to talk about virtues if they are conceptualized as personality traits. The Hartshorne and May (1928–1932) studies, for example, along with Mischel's (1968, 1990, 1999) theoretical analysis, seemed to cast doubt on a widely assumed fundamental requirement that personality traits show dispositional consistency across even widely disparate situations. This cross-situational consistency of traits was surprisingly hard to document. Consequently, the ostensible failure of traits in the study of personality made recourse to virtues an unappealing option in moral psychology. But Kohlberg's second objection to virtues was perhaps more to the point. For Kohlberg any compilation of desirable traits is a completely arbitrary affair. It entails sampling from a bag of virtues until a suitable list is produced that has something for everyone. In addition, and even worse, given Kohlberg's project, the meaning of virtue trait words is relative to particular communities. As Kohlberg and Mayer (1972) famously put it:

> Labeling a set of behaviors displayed by a child with positive or negative trait terms does not signify that they are of adaptive significance or ethical importance. It represents an appeal to particular community conventions, since one person's "*integrity*" is another person's "*stubbornness*," [one persons's] "*honesty* in expressing your true feelings" is another person's "*insensitivity* to the feelings of others." (p. 479)

Clearly, the language of virtue and moral character does not work if the point of moral development theory is to provide the psychological resources to defeat ethical relativism.

Although the cognitive developmental approach to moral reasoning is of singular importance, and it continues to generate productive lines of research, it is also true that an adequate moral psychology could not neglect issues of selfhood, identity, and personality for very long. Indeed, Augusto Blasi (1983; Walker, this volume—chap. 1) recognized many years ago that any credible account of moral action requires a robust model of the self. Moreover, its neglect of virtues and its silence on questions of character meant that the cognitive developmental tradition has had little to say to parents who are fundamentally concerned to raise children of a particular kind. Raising children of good moral character is an important goal of most parents. When one asks parents about the moral formation of their children we doubt very many will mention the need to resolve hard case dilemmas in a way that secures consensus. We doubt that many are vexed by ethical relativism and want to defeat it. Instead, many parents want their children to grow up to be in possession of certain virtues. Most parents would be pleased if their children exhibited certain traits of character, and are honest, kind, respectful, and more. As one of us (Lapsley, 1996) put it, "Although the cognitive developmental approach may be reluctant to make aretaic judgments about the moral status of persons, the language of moral evaluation comes more easily to most everyone else" (p. 196). Fortunately, there are several promising research programs that are exploring the connection between personological variables and moral functioning.

One approach is to define the role of moral commitments in the construction of identity. According to Blasi (1984; also see Bergman, this volume—chap. 2) one has a moral identity to the extent that moral notions, such as being fair, just, and good, are central, important, and essential to one's self-understanding. Moral identity is possible, according to Blasi, when the self is constructed or defined by reference to moral categories. One has a moral identity when one is committed to living out the implications of whole-hearted moral commitment. Recently Blasi (in press) attempted to provide a psychological account of moral character that builds on his understanding of moral identity Moral character, in his view, has three components: willpower, moral desires, and integrity. "All three sets of virtues," he wrote, "are necessary for moral character, but in different ways; willpower is necessary to deal with internal and external obstacles in pursuing one's long-term objectives; integrity relates one's commitments to the sense of self; moral desires guide willpower and integrity and provide them with their moral significance" (p. 5).

Recent studies of individuals who display extraordinary moral commitment seem to vindicate Blasi's understanding of moral identity and the importance of identifying the self with moral desires. For example, in their seminal analysis of moral exemplars Colby and Damon (1992, 1995) found that exemplars integrate personal and moral goals, and they identify the self with moral commitments. Similarly Daniel Hart and his colleagues (Atkins & Hart, this volume—chap. 4; Hart & Fegley, 1995; Hart, Yates, Fegley, & Wilson, 1995) report that adolescents who display uncommon caring and altruism often identify the ideal self with moral commitments and otherwise align the self with moral goals.

Blasi's work on moral identity and the moral exemplar studies clearly are important and productive contributions to moral psychology. Other lines of research, such as neo-Kohlbergian accounts of postconventional reasoning (Rest, Narvaez, Bebeau, & Thoma, 1999), the four-component model of moral functioning (Narvaez & Rest, 1995; Rest, 1983), and naturalistic studies of moral character (Walker & Pitts, 1998), are additional evidence that personological variables, including selfhood, identity, and character, will continue to figure prominently in contemporary moral psychological research. Indeed, we have argued that the next phase of research in the "post-Kohlbergian" era would profit from a broader consideration of psychological theory, constructs, and methods if our aim is to develop powerful models of moral personality, selfhood, and identity (Lapsley & Narvaez, in press; Narvaez & Lapsley, in press).

In this chapter we explore the resources of social–cognitive theory to conceptualize moral personality. In our view social–cognitive theory is an important source of insights for understanding moral functioning, although it is rarely invoked for this purpose. Indeed, the introduction of social–cognitive theory to the moral domain has at least three integrative possibilities (Lapsley & Narvaez, in press). First, it opens moral psychology to the theories, constructs, and methodological tactics of social–personality research, with its potential for yielding powerful accounts of character, identity, and personality. Second, it opens a broader array of options for conceptualizing moral rationality, including the possibility that much of our moral functioning is tact, implicit, and automatic (Narvaez & Lapsley, in press). Third, it locates the study of moral functioning within a mainstream of psychological research on cognition, memory, social cognition, and modern information–processing.

In the next section we outline the features of a social–cognitive approach to personality with two aims in mind. First, we show that social–cognition theory has considerable advantages over trait models in our understanding of personality; second, we present the resources that social–cognitive approaches have for purposes of understanding moral personality in particular. We then consider the cognitive expertise and schema accessibility literatures for insights about individual differences in moral personality functioning. We review promising empirical evidence for this perspective and conclude with a reflection on the developmental sources of the social–cognitive bases of moral functioning.

SOCIAL–COGNITIVE APPROACHES: HAVING AND DOING

We noted that a virtues approach to moral character has not had much traction in moral psychology largely because of its apparent affinity with trait models of personality. If there are doubts about traits, then virtues as traits is not an attractive option. Hence, if we are to talk sensibly about moral personality then we require an alternative way of conceptualizing the dispositional features of human behavior. In recent years a social–cognitive approach to personality has emerged to challenge the more traditional trait approach that emphasizes the structural basis of individual differences. According to Cantor (1990), the trait approach illustrates the *having* side of personality theory (as opposed to the *doing* side, which is represented by social–cognitive models of personality). That is, personality is understood to be the sum of traits that one has, and there are individual differences in the distribution of these traits. Presumably, a person of good moral character is one who is in possession of certain traits that are deemed virtues, whereas a person of poor moral character is in possession of other kinds of traits that are not considered virtues. Moreover, the traits that one has are assumed to be adhesive in the sense that they are constitutional aspects of one's personality, on display across disparate contextual settings.

The nomothetic trait approach has not, however, fared well in contemporary personality research for at least two reasons. First, it is now commonplace to note that personality dispositions do not display the cross-situational consistency desired by trait models (Mischel, 1990). Indeed, trait models generally have little to say about how dispositions are affected by situational variability. Instead, trait models assume that dispositions adhere to individuals across settings and across time, quite irrespective of environmental demands. Dispositional traits, in other words, are assumed to trump the contextual hand one is dealt. Yet, this is rarely the case. As Mischel (1968) put it, "individuals show far less cross-situational consistency in their behavior than has been assumed by trait–state theories. The more dissimilar the evoking situations, the less likely they are to produce similar or consistent responses from the same individual" (p. 177).

But the reality of situational variability in personality functioning and the apparent lack of cross-situational stability or consistency does not mean that personality fails to cohere in lawful ways. Personality is coherent, but coherence should not be reduced to mere stability of behavior across time and setting (Cervone & Shoda, 1999). Coherence is evident in the dynamic, reciprocal interaction among the dispositions, interests, capacities, and potentialities of the agent and the changing contexts of learning, socialization and development. Persons and contexts are not static, orthogonal effects, but they are instead dynamically interacting. Changes on one side of the interaction invariably induce a cascade of consequences on the other side. Both are mutually implicative in accounting for behavior. This inextricable union of person and context is the lesson of developmental contextualism (Lerner, 1991, 1995; Lerner & Busch-Rossnagel, 1981), and it is here, at the point of transaction between person and context, that one looks for intraindividual stability and personality coherence.

Hence, the second drawback of trait models is that it overlooks this complex pattern of coherence that individuals do display in response to changing contextual circumstances (Cervone & Shoda, 1999). It overlooks lawful patterns of situational variability. Mischel (1990) argued, for example, that behavioral consistency is more likely to be found in localized, contextually specified conditions. A coherent behavioral signature is evident when the display of dispositional tendencies is conceptualized in terms of if–then situation–behavior contingencies (Mischel, 1999; Shoda, 1999). Moreover, the reality of cross-situational variability is not a failure of a dispositional approach to personality. Rather, it is a failure to sufficiently analyze local features of situations. It is a failure to notice how these features dynamically interact with social–cognitive person variables, the social–cognitive units of analysis (schemas, scripts, prototypes, episodes, competencies, etc.) that give us the discriminative facility to alter our behavioral responses given the particularity of changing social contexts. Consequently, dispositional consistency is conditional on evoking contextual factors and the ability of our social–cognitive processes to discriminate them. But again it is here, at the intersection of person and context, where personality coherence is revealed.

If the trait approach illustrates the *having* side of personality, the introduction of social–cognitive person variables into the discussion of personality coherence illustrates the *doing* side of personality (Cantor, 1990). The cognitive approach to personality emphasizes what people do when they construe their social landscape and how they transform and interpret it in accordance with social–cognitive mechanisms. According to Cantor (1990), the cognitive substrate of personality consists of three elements: schemas, tasks, and strategies. Schemas are organized knowledge structures that channel and filter social perceptions and memory. They are the "cognitive carriers of dispositions" (p. 737) that guide our appraisal of social situations, our memory for events, and our affective reactions. They are organized around particular aspects of our life experience. Tasks are the culturally prescribed demands of social life that we transform or construe as personal goals. "Life tasks, like schemas, not only provide a cognitive representation for dispositional strivings but also serve to selectively maintain and foster dispositionally relevant behavior" (Cantor, 1990, p. 740). Strategies, in turn, are utilized to bring life tasks to fruition. As such they are "an intricate organization of feelings, thoughts, effort-arousal and actions" forming a "collection of goal-directed behavior unfolding over time in relation to a self-construed task" (p. 743).

PERSONALITY COHERENCE

These elements are also implicated in a recent social–cognitive account of personality coherence advocated by Cervone and Shoda (1999). They argued that a model of personality coherence must address three interrelated phenomena. First, it must account for the fact that there is an organization to personality functioning. That is, personality processes do not function independently but are instead organized into coherent, integrated systems that impose constraints on the range of possible configurations. This implies that personality is a unified cognitive–affective system and that it is illegitimate, therefore, to segregate cognition and affect into separate domains of influence. Second, it must account for the coherence evident between behavior and social–contextual expectations. What we do across different settings and over time is often interconnected and consistent. As Cervone and Shoda (1999) put it, individuals "create stable patterns of personal experience by selecting and shaping the circumstances that make up their day-to-day lives. This phenotypic coherence is key to both psychologists' and layperson's inferences about personality" (p. 17). Third, it must account for the phenomenological sense of self-coherence that orders our goals, preferences, and values, and it gives meaning to personal striving and motivated behavior.

The dynamic interaction among these features of personality coherence is grounded by social information processing. That is, the cross-situational coherence and variability of personality, the dynamic interaction among organized knowledge structures, affect, and social context, is understood not by appealing to broadband traits but to the analysis of the causal mechanisms, structures, and processes of social information processing (Cervone, 1997). Moreover, the model assumes that the activation of mental representations is a critical feature of coherent personality functioning. These representations "include knowledge of social situations, representations of self, others and prospective events, personal goals, beliefs and expectations, and knowledge of behavioral alternatives and task strategies" (Cervone & Shoda, 1999, p. 18), and they are variously conceptualized as schemas, scripts, prototypes, episodes, competencies, and similar constructs (Hastie, 1983; Mischel, 1990). It is the distinctive organization of these social–cognitive units and their mutual influence and dynamic interaction that give rise to various configurations of personality, although the range of possible configurations is not infinite, given the "system of mutual constraint" that one part of the system imposes on other parts (Cervone & Shoda, 1999, p. 19). Still, patterns of individual differences arise because people have stable goal systems (e.g., Cantor's, 1990, life tasks) that structure the organization of the cognitive–affective system and influence the perception, selection, and interpretation of various contextual settings. Moreover, people have different interpersonal and social expectations that foster "distinctive, contextualized patterns of response "(Cervone & Shoda, 1999, p. 20) and different recurring experiences that provide the "affordances" that give rise to stable configurations of the cognitive–affective system (Brandtstadter, 1999). More generally, the interrelationship among these elements of the social–cognitive personality system "yield cognitive–affective configurations that 'make sense,' cohere and thus are more stable. These stable configurations form the basis of an individual's unique personality. They contribute to the individual's recurrent style of planning, interpreting and responding to events" (Cervone & Shoda, 1999, p. 20).

SIX CRITICAL RESOURCES

There are a number of resources on the social–cognitive approach to personality that are critical for new models of moral personality. First, the social–cognitive approach retains the central importance of cognition, but cognition is viewed as a broader set of mental representations, processes, and mechanisms than was postulated by the moral development tradition. Schemas and the conditions of schema activation underwrite our discriminative facility in noticing key features of our moral environment. Schemas are fundamental to our very ability to notice dilemmas as we appraise the moral landscape (Narvaez & Bock, 2002). Moreover, as noted later, the social–cognitive approach does not assume that all relevant cognitive processing is controlled, deliberate, and explicit. There is now mounting evidence that much of our lives is governed by cognitive processes that are tacit, implicit, and automatic, but this is an issue that is new to the moral domain (Narvaez & Lapsley, in press). Still, the intersection of the morality of everyday life and the automaticity of everyday life must be large and extensive, and social–cognitive theory provides resources for coming to grips with it in ways that the cognitive developmental tradition cannot (Lapsley & Narvaez, in press).

Second, the social–cognitive approach emphasizes the central importance of self-processes, personal goals, and life tasks that give meaning to one's motivated behavior and purposive striving. Hence, it is compatible with the apparent consensus within the Kohlberg tradition that an adequate theory of moral reasoning and moral behavior requires greater attention to the motivational properties of selfhood and identity.

Third, the social–cognitive approach emphasizes the affective elements of personality. Personality is considered a cognitive–affective system that is organized, integrated, coherent, and stable. Emotional states are a regulatory factor within the information-processing system. As Bugental and Goodnow (1998) put it, "emotional states influence what is perceived and how it is processed, and the interpretations made of ongoing events subsequently influence emotional reactions and perceptual biases. Affect and cognition are appropriately conceptualized as interwoven processes" (p. 416). Affect guides selective memory retrieval, influences perceptual vigilance, and constrains the attentional resources available for rational or reflective appraisal and response selection (Bugental & Goodnow, 1998). Understanding personality as a cognitive–affective system is in contrast to some approaches in moral psychology that tend to segregate moral cognition and moral emotions.

Fourth, the social–cognitive approach is compatible with the best insights of developmental science in its insistence that the cognitive–affective system is in reciprocal interaction with changing social contexts. There is no implication that these processes operate in a passive, linear way, or as a crude input–output mechanism, which has been a traditional source of resistance by Kohlbergian researchers to information-processing models of cognition.

Fifth, the social–cognitive approach provides a way to deal with the coherence of personality in a way that acknowledges lawful situational variability. A dispositional signature can be found at the intersection of person and context, as a result of the available and accessible social cognitive schemas, the discriminative facility that it provides, and the eliciting and activating aspects of situations and contexts. This addresses one of the traditional objections of Kohlbergian researchers to the study of character or of virtue traits, namely, that the observance of moral traits (honesty) seem to hinge on numerous situational factors or that traits fail to demonstrate the cross-situational consistency one ordinarily expects of dispositions.

Sixth, the units of analysis are conceptualized in a way that is open to integration with other literatures. Indeed, the organizational features of personality and the mutual constraint evident among elements of the social cognitive–affective system make the study of other domains of psychological functioning (e.g., memory, motivation, self-regulative processes) completely relevant to the study of moral personality.

In the next section we attempt to illustrate the social–cognitive bases of the moral personality. We argue that the chronic accessibility of social–cognitive schemas is the source of individual differences in moral functioning and that this model accounts for a range of phenomena that has resisted explanation by the structural–developmental tradition. We also review preliminary data that speak to the promise of the model and reflect on its developmental and educational implications.

EXPERTISE AND SCHEMA ACCESSIBILITY

In Cantor's (1990; Cantor & Kihlstrom, 1987) model self-schemas, prototypes, scripts, and episodes are the basic cognitive units of personality—the "cognitive carriers of dispositions." Schemas "demarcate regions of social life and domains of personal experience to which the person is especially tuned, and about which he or she is likely to become a virtual 'expert' " (Cantor, 1990, p. 738). Indeed, Cantor (1990) appealed to the notion of expertise to illustrate how schemas can maintain patterns of individual differences. She pointed to three critical functions of schemas. First, if schemas are chronically accessible, then they direct our attention to certain features of our experience at the expense of others. The schematic nature of information processing disposes experts to notice key features of domain-relevant activity that novices miss. Hence, environmental scanning is more richly informative for experts than it is for novices. Chess, dinosaur, and teaching experts "see" more of an event than do novices in these domains (Chi, Glaser, & Farr, 1988). In the social domain a shy schematic or an aggressive person is more likely to notice (or remember) instances that require social reticence or aggressive conduct, respectively, than are individuals who are "social novices" in these domains (i.e., not shy or not aggressive).

Second, if schemas are chronically salient in memory, then compatible or schema-relevant life tasks, goals, or settings are more likely to be selected or sought, which, in turn, also serve to canalize and maintain dispositional tendencies. A shy schematic is likely to choose, over time, a risk-avoidance strategy when it comes to social goals, thereby reinforcing a particular pattern of social interactions. Experts in other domains similarly choose settings, set goals, or engage in activities that support or reinforce schema-relevant interests. This also illustrates the reciprocal relationship between person and context. Third, we tend to develop highly practiced behavioral routines in those areas of our experience demarcated by chronically accessible schemas, which provide "a ready, sometimes automatically available plan of action in such life contexts" (Cantor, 1990, p. 738). Experts, then, possess procedural knowledge that has a high degree of automaticity.

Schema accessibility and conditions of activation are critical for understanding how patterns of individual differences are channeled and maintained. In some ways the "shy person" or the "aggressive person" and, by extension, the "moral person" possess social cognitive mechanisms whose functioning is similar to that afforded by high levels of expertise. In the moral domain these notions have been implicated in an "expertise model" of moral character (Narvaez, in press; Narvaez & Lapsley, in press) and a social–cognitive approach to the moral personality (Lapsley, 1999; Lapsley & Narvaez, in press). Both approaches trade on the notion of knowledge activation and knowledge accessibility, and these concepts must be considered central to any account of moral character, personality, or identity.

CHRONIC ACCESSIBILITY AND INDIVIDUAL DIFFERENCES

According to Higgins (1999), one of the general principles of knowledge activation is *accessibility*. Accessibility can be defined as the activation potential of available knowledge. The more frequently a construct is activated or the more recently it is primed, the more accessible it should be for processing social information. In addition, frequently activated constructs should be, over time, chronically accessible for purposes of social information processing. And, because the social experiences of individuals vary widely, it is likely that there should also be differences in the accessibility, even in the availability of cognitive constructs.

Thus, accessibility is a person variable and a dimension of individual differences. That is, there are individual differences in the availability and accessibility of these knowledge structures (Higgins, 1996), and they are properly regarded as personality variables (Higgins, 1999). Three additional points are relevant. First, chronically accessible constructs are at a higher state of activation than are inaccessible constructs (Bargh & Pratto, 1986), and they are produced so efficiently as to approach automaticity (Bargh, 1989). Indeed, as Zelli and Dodge (1999) put it, "salient social experiences foster knowledge structures that may become so highly accessible as to pervasively influence one's social thinking" (p. 119). Second, constructs can be made accessible by contextual (situational) priming as well as by chronicity, and these two sources of influence combine in an additive fashion to influence social information processing (Bargh, Bond, Lombardi, & Tota, 1986). Third, the accessibility of a construct is assumed to emerge from a developmental history of frequent and consistent experience with a specific domain of social behavior; thus, it becomes more likely than other constructs to be evoked for the interpretation of interpersonal experience. Consequently, individual differences in construct accessibility emerge because of each person's unique social developmental history (Bargh, Lombardi, & Higgins, 1988).

CHRONIC ACCESSIBILITY AND THE MORAL PERSONALITY

We appeal to this theoretical approach to conceptualize the moral personality. We argue that the moral personality is better understood in terms of the chronic accessibility of moral schemas for construing social events. Therefore, a moral person, or a person who has a moral identity or character, would be one for whom moral constructs are chronically accessible and easily activated for social information processing. In addition, we claim that moral chronicity is a dimension of individual differences. Blasi (1984) argued that one has a moral identity just when moral categories are essential, central, and important to one's self-understanding. One has a moral personality when the self is constructed around moral commitments. But here we add that moral categories (schemas, episodes, scripts, prototypes) that are essential, central, and important for one's self-identity would also be ones that are chronically accessible for interpreting the social landscape. Such categories would be constantly on line, or at least readily primed and easily activated, for discerning the meaning of events. And, once activated, these constructs would dispose the individual to interpret these events in light of his or her moral commitments.

Indeed, moral character or what it means to be virtuous (or vicious) is better conceptualized not in terms of the *having* side of personality, not in terms of trait possession, but in terms of the *doing* side—that is, in terms of the social–cognitive schemas, the knowledge structures, and cognitive–affective mechanisms that are chronically accessible for social information processing, which underwrite the discriminative facility in our selection of situationally appropriate behavior.

INITIAL EMPIRICAL WORK

The general claim is that chronically accessible moral schemas greatly influences social information processing. Recent studies by Narvaez and her colleagues (Narvaez, 1998, 2001, 2002; Narvaez, Bentley, Gleason, & Samuels, 1998; Narvaez, Mitchell, Gleason & Bentley, 1999) attest to the plausibility of this hypothesis. She showed, for example, that individuals' prior moral knowledge greatly influences their comprehension of moral narratives, a finding that should undermine the confidence of "virtuecrats," such as William Bennett (1998), who argued that merely reading the treasury of moral stories is somehow self-instructing in the virtues. Similarly, Lapsley and Lasky (1999) showed that conceptions of good character are organized as a cognitive prototype and that the activation of a "good character" prototype biases information processing. For example, their study participants showed considerable false recognition of novel prototype-consistent ("virtue-central") trait attributes than they did of nonprototypic ("virtue-peripheral") traits. Both findings support the general claim that accessible moral knowledge structures influence what we see in our interpersonal landscape and that at least some morally relevant information processing is implicit, tacit, and automatic.

This was tested more directly by Lapsley and Lasky (2001) using the spontaneous trait inference (STI) paradigm. The STI paradigm assumes that the meaning of social events is constructed routinely, habitually, and unintentionally (Newman & Uleman, 1989). Moreover, an STI is said to occur when attending to another's behavior produces a trait inference without an explicit intention to infer traits or to form an impression (Uleman, Hon, Roman, & Moskowitz, 1996; Uleman, Newman, & Moskowitz, 1996). This is typically demonstrated using a cued-recall procedure that includes both a spontaneous and deliberate processing condition. In the spontaneous processing condition participants are instructed to memorize a list of sentences (e.g., "The lawyer strongly disagrees with the economist"). Note that this memory instruction does not ask participants to form an impression of the actors or to draw any inference about their character, motivation, or reasons for acting. Hence, it is assumed that any inference drawn about the dispositional qualities of the actors is spontaneous. In contrast, participants in a deliberate processing condition are asked to memorize the sentences after first focusing on the reasons for the actor's behavior. Consequently, inferences drawn about actors are said to be deliberate given the explicit instruction to form an impression. Two types of cues are then used at recall. Some cues are dispositional ("argumentative"), whereas others are semantic ("courtroom"). If STIs were formed at encoding, then trait-dispositional cues should elicit more recall of target sentences.

Research has shown that people not only make STIs without explicit intention of doing so but also without awareness that they have made them (Uleman et al., 1996). Is the production of STIs influenced by personality? There is indeed evidence that STIs vary along common dimensions of individual differences. For example, Zelli, Huesmann, and Cervone (1995) showed that individuals who differed in levels of aggressiveness performed quite differently on a cued-recall spontaneous trait inference task. In this study aggressive and nonaggressive participants read sentences (e.g., "The policeman pushes Dave out of the way") that included actors whose behavior could be interpreted as hostile or nonhostile. Spontaneous and deliberate processing conditions were used. During recall participants were given both semantic and dispositional cues. The dispositional cues were terms that represented hostile inferences that could be made about the behavior of the sentence actors. The results of the spontaneous processing condition showed that hostile dispositional cues prompted significantly more recall than did semantic cues for aggressive participants, whereas semantic cues prompted twice as much recall among nonaggressive participants. These differences were not apparent in the deliberate processing condition.

Similarly, Uleman, Winborne, Winter, and Schechter (1986) also demonstrated the influence of a personality variable on the production of STIs. They presented sentences that had different trait implications for individuals who were high and low on authoritarianism. For example, the sentence "The architect loved the excitement of military parades" implied the trait attribution—patriotic—for authoritarian participants, but nonauthoritarian participants were unable to reach consensus about what trait the sentence implied.

Lapsley and Lasky (2001) attempted to show that moral chronicity, much like aggressiveness and authoritarianism, is an individual differences variable that influences the production of STIs. A primacy-of-output procedure was used to determine participants' chronically accessible constructs (Higgins, King, & Mavin, 1982). Participants were asked to record the traits of someone they like, someone they dislike, someone they seek out, and someone they avoid. They were also asked to record the traits of someone they frequently encounter. Individuals were considered "moral chronics" if three of the six traits rated first for each question were traits that are highly prototypic of good moral character, as determined by Lapsley and Lasky (1999). Participants who did not name any trait adjective prototypic of good moral character were considered to be "nonchronic." The moral chronic and nonchronic groups then participated in the standard cued-recall STI manipulations. Participants were instructed either to memorize the target sentences (spontaneous processing) or to both memorize and infer motives for action (deliberate processing). Sentence recall was cued either by dispositional or semantic cues. The results showed, as expected, that moral chronics made more STIs with dispositional cues than with semantic cues, whereas nonchronics showed more recall with semantic cues. Recall that those in the deliberate processing condition were unaffected by moral chronicity.

Moral chronics, then, when instructed to memorize target sentences, appeared to form STIs of characters featured in the sentences. Hence, when participants are given no instruction about how to encode information and are simply left to their own devices, they tend to make dispositional inferences congruent with their most accessible schemas. This suggests that moral chronicity (along with authoritarianism and aggressiveness) is an individual differences dimension that influences social information processing. Moreover, this study contributes to the growing evidence regarding the tacit, implicit, and automatic nature of higher mental processes (Bargh & Ferguson, 2000). Automatic activation has been demonstrated for attitudes (Bargh, 1989), self-concepts (Bargh, 1982; Higgins, 1987), stereotypes (Pratto & Bargh, 1991), and social behaviors (Bargh, Chen, & Burrows, 1996). Indeed, quite strong claims are made for "the automaticity of everyday life" (Bargh, 1997). For example, there is evidence that nonconscious mental systems direct self-regulation (Bargh & Chartrand, 1999) and that evaluations, social perceptions, judgment, social interactions, and internal goal structures are similarly operative without conscious intention or acts of will (Bargh & Ferguson, 2000). Indeed, Bargh and Chartrand (1999) argued that we are not normally engaged in active planning, selecting, choosing, or interpreting when processing information. Moreover, "the ability to exercise such conscious, intentional control is actually quite limited" (p. 462). It is a mistake, therefore, to equate cognition with conscious cognition. As Bargh (1997) put it, "conscious processing can no longer be viewed as necessary for behavior and judgments and evaluations to be made in a given situation," and that the "black box of 'conscious choice' will grow ever smaller" (p. 52) with advances in social–cognitive research.

The notion that there is a certain automaticity in our cognitive functioning is a commonplace in the social–cognitive and intellectual development literatures—yet, curiously, it is a notion that is likely to be resisted in the moral development literature, for two reasons. The notion of automaticity is resisted because, as noted earlier, it is contrary to the "assumption of phenomenalism" (Lapsley & Narvaez, in press). It is alien to our usual working model of moral rationality, which involves deliberation, decision making, appealing to principles, balancing of perspectives, conscious weighing of factors, and imaginative thought experiments. Moral rationality is considered to be controlled processing. It is the making of explicit choices for considered reasons. It is declarative knowledge. It is knowing why. The notion of automaticity is resisted, too, because it is alien to our working model of moral education, which is something that takes place in schools as a formalized curriculum or intervention.

Yet, if the social–cognitive literature is any guide, many of our moral performances take place without explicit awareness. Many of our responses are unreflective, highly automatized, and not the result of deliberate decision-making procedures. If this is true, then the present model also suggests that moral functioning has a procedural component as well as a declarative one. There is a kind of moral knowledge that is implicit, procedural, scripted, and automatic. There is a kind of moral knowledge that is knowing how. There is a kind of moral behavior that is coherent, organized, and rule-governed without being based on explicit rules (Emde, Biringen, Clyman, & Oppenheim, 1991) or without being the result of an agonizing, deliberate decision-making calculus.

To say that moral rationality has both a procedural and a declarative component helps clarify the ongoing debate between proponents of character and virtue on the one hand and cognitive developmentalism on the other. Effective habits, scripted behavioral sequences, self-regulation, chronic accessibility of knowledge structures, and moral perception might constitute the procedural aspect of moral functioning, and they fall under the heading of character—of knowing how. It is this aspect of moral functioning that is routinized, automatic, spontaneous, and unreflective. But being conscious of moral rule systems and being able to articulate and reason about them are declarative aspects of moral reasoning. These aspects of moral functioning are more at home in the cognitive–developmental tradition.

DEVELOPMENTAL SOURCES

We argued that the dispositional features of moral character are better conceptualized in terms of the social–cognitive approach to personality. But a social–cognitive approach to moral character will share a deficiency that plagues all social–cognitive theories. These theories invariably address the mechanisms and consequences of social cognition from the perspective of adult functioning, but they rarely attempt to plot the developmental trajectory that makes adult forms of social cognition possible (Lapsley & Quintana, 1985). Yet, charting developmental features is crucial to our understanding of moral character. If, for example, the moral personality is defined in terms of chronic accessibility of moral schemas, how is chronicity made possible during the course of development? What sort of developmental experiences lead to chronically accessible cognitive–affective moral schemas? What socialization practices encourage this kind of moral expertise? What is the developmental mechanism that underlies automatic, tacit, and implicit social information–processing?

These are novel questions for developmental psychologists, which we addressed elsewhere (Narvaez, in press). Here we make suggestions about how a social–cognitive approach to moral personality development might look. There are important clues to possible developmental sources of moral chronicity. Ross Thompson (1998), for example, drew attention to the emergence and elaboration of prototypical knowledge structures in the early toddler years in his account of early sociopersonality development. These scripted knowledge structures take the form of generalized event representations that initially encode the prosaic routines and rituals of family life but become progressively elaborated into broader knowledge structures as the child develops. These representations serve as working models of what to expect of early social experience, and they allow the child to both anticipate and recall events. Indeed, event representations also support the emergence of early episodic memory, and they have been called the "basic building blocks of cognitive development" (Nelson & Gruendel, 1981, p. 131).

Nelson (1989, 1993a, 1993b) argued that event representations become more elaborated and better organized as a result of shared dialogue with caregivers. In these early conversations parents help children review, structure, and consolidate memories in script-like fashion (Fivush, Kuebli, & Chubb, 1992). Parents who do this in an elaborative way, that is, those who embed events in a rich contextual background rather than simply asking direct questions, tend to have children who have more sophisticated representations of their past (Reese & Fivush, 1993; Reese, Halden, & Fivush, 1993). It is our view that the capacity for event representation is not only the building blocks of cognitive development, as Nelson and Gruendel (1981) put it, but also the building blocks of the moral personality. It is the social–cognitive foundation of character. The foundation of the moral personality is laid down in the early construction of generalized event representations, prototypic knowledge structures, behavioral scripts, and episodic memory.

But the key characterological turn of significance for moral psychology is how these early social–cognitive units are transformed into autobiographical memory. In other words, at some point specific episodic memories must become integrated into a narrative form that references a self whose story it is. Autobiographical memories, too, like event representations, are constructed with the aid of social dialogue. Autobiographical memory is a social construction. It is coached within the web of interlocution. Parents teach children how to construct narratives by the questions that they ask of past events ("Where did we go yesterday?" "What did we see?" "Was Uncle Leon there?" "What did we do next?"). In this way parents help children identify the key features that are to be remembered, their sequence, causal significance, and timing (Schneider & Bjorklund, 1998).

It is true the extant research on early event representation, episodic, and autobiographical memory has tended to focus on relatively simple events (mealtime), routines (bedtime rituals), and scripts (going to McDonalds). As Thompson (1998) noted, "little is known about children's representation of prototypical experiences of greater emotional and relational complexity" (p. 68). Yet, there is little reason to doubt, in our view, that the representation of morally relevant events should be consolidated in young children's autobiographical memory in a directly analogous way. Parental interrogatories ("What happened when you pushed your brother?" "Why did he cry?" "What should you do next?") help children organize events into personally relevant autobiographical memories, which provide, in the process, part of the self-narrative, action-guiding scripts ("I share with him" and "I say I'm sorry") that become over-learned, frequently practiced, routine, habitual, and automatic. In these shared dialogues the child learns important lessons about "emotions, relationships and morality" (Thompson, 1998, p.70). Indeed, as Thompson (1998) put it, "the child's earliest self-representations are likely to incorporate the parent's moral evaluations, emotional inferences, dispositional attributions to the child (e.g., rambunctious, emotionally labile, cautious or impulsive, etc.), and other features of the adult's interpretation of the situations being recounted" (p. 70). We add that such interrogatories might also include moral character attributions as well, so that the ideal or ought self becomes part of one's self-understanding and part of one's autobiographical narrative. In this way parents help children identify morally relevant features of their experience and encourage the formation of social–cognitive schemas (scripts, prototypes) that are easily primed, easily activated, and chronically accessible.

CONCLUSION

In this chapter we illustrated the virtues of psychologizing the study of moral functioning by invoking such notions as schema theory and principles of knowledge activation. We showed that meaningful integrations are possible between moral psychology and the rich empirical content, research tactics, and theoretical frameworks of social–cognitive science. Indeed, social–cognitive theory provides at least six critical resources when pressed into the service of moral psychology. Moreover, the application of social-cognitive theory to moral psychology makes it possible to anticipate novel facts about moral personological and moral cognitive functioning. It touts schema accessibility as a general principle of moral knowledge activation. It draws our attention to individual differences in moral chronicity and insists that the tacit, implicit, and automatic features of social cognition find a place in the explanation of moral functioning. Finally, we made a case for a possible developmental grounding of the moral personality by invoking the literatures of early generalized event representation and autobiographical memory, among others.

We are, of course, aware of the challenges that face a social–cognitive account of moral personality (Blasi, this volume, chap. 14). But we are making a strategic bet that a moral psychology richly informed by the theoretical and empirical literatures of allied, but heretofore ignored, domains of psychology will yield a robust, productive, and progressive research program. And we take no small comfort in an assertion by Imre Lakatos (1978), that *"all theories are born refuted and die refuted"* (p. 5). Research programs, much like character itself, are often riddled with blindspots, anomaly, contradiction, and error. Yet, the true measure of a research program, in Lakatos' view, is not so much the blindspots, the contradictions, or the errors, it is not the "ocean of anomalies" that one must contend with, but rather its capacity for growth, extension, and progress. This is much like the true measure of the moral personality itself.

REFERENCES

Bargh, J. A. (1982). Attention and automaticity in the processing of self-relevant information. *Journal of Personality and Social Psychology, 43*, 425–436.

Bargh, J. A. (1989). Conditional automaticity: Varieties of automatic influence in social perception and cognition. In J. S. Uleman & J. A. Bargh (Eds.), *Unintended thought* (pp. 3–51). New York: Guilford.

Bargh, J. A. (1997). The automaticity of everyday life. In R. S. Wyer, Jr. (Ed.), *The automaticity of everyday life: Advances in social cognition* (Vol. 10, pp. 1–61). Mahwah, NJ: Lawrence Erlbaum Associates.

Bargh, J. A., Bond, R. N., Lombardi, W. J., & Tota, M. E. (1986). The additive nature of chronic and temporary sources of construct accessibility. *Journal of Personality and Social Psychology, 50*, 869–878.

Bargh, J. A., & Chartrand, T. L. (1999). The unbearable automaticity of being. *American Psychologist, 54*, 462–479.

Bargh, J. A., Chen, M., & Burrows, L. (1996). Automaticity of social behavior: Direct effects of trait construct and stereotype activation on action. *Journal of Personality and Social Psychology, 71*, 230–244.

Bargh, J. A., & Ferguson, M. J. (2000). Beyond behaviorism: On the automaticity of higher mental processes. *Psychological Bulletin, 126*, 925–945.

Bargh, J. A., Lombardi, W., & Higgins, E. T. (1988). Automaticity of chronically accessible constructs in Person Situation effects on person perception: It's just a matter of time. *Journal of Personality and Social Psychology, 55*, 599–605.

Bargh, J. A., & Pratto, F. (1986). Individual construct accessibility and perception selection. *Journal of Experimental Social Psychology, 22*, 293–311.

Blasi, A. (1983). Moral cognition and moral action: A theoretical perspective. *Developmental Review, 3*, 178–210.

Bennett, W. (1993). *The book of virtues.* New York: Simon & Schuster.

Blasi, A. (1984). Moral identity: Its role in moral functioning. In W. M. Kurtines & J. J. Gewirtz (Eds.), *Morality, moral behavior and moral development* (pp. 128–139). New York: Wiley.

Blasi, A. (in press). Moral character: A psychological approach. In D. K. Lapsley & F. C. Power (Eds.), *Character psychology and character education.* Notre Dame, IN: University of Notre Dame Press.

Brandtstadter, J. (1999). The self in action and development: Cultural, biosocial and ontogenetic bases of intentional self-development. In J. Brandtstadter & R. M. Lerner (Eds.), *Action and self-development: Theory and research through the life span* (pp. 37–65). Thousand Oaks, CA: Sage.

Bugental, D. B., & Goodnow, J. J. (1998). In W. Damon & N . Eisenberg (Eds.), *Handbook of child psychology: Vol. 3. Social, emotional and personality development* (pp. 389–462). New York: Wiley.

Cantor, N. (1990). From thought to behavior: "Having" and "doing" in the study of personality and cognition. *American Psychologist, 45*, 735–750.

Cantor, N., & Kihlstrom, J. (1987). *Personality and social intelligence.* Englewood Cliffs, NJ: Prentice-Hall.

Cervone, D. (1997). Social–cognitive mechanisms and personality coherence: Self-knowledge, situational beliefs, and cross-situational coherence in perceived self efficacy. *Psychological Science, 8*, 43–50.

Cervone, D., & Shoda, Y. (1999). Social–cognitive theories and the coherence of personality. In D. Cervone & Y. Shoda (Eds.), *The coherence of personality: Social–cognitive bases of consistency, variability and organization* (pp. 3–36). New York: Guilford.

Chapman, M. (1988). *Constructive evolution: Origin and development of Piaget's thought.* Cambridge, England: Cambridge University Press.

Chi, M. T. H., Glaser, R., & Farr, M. J. (1988). *The nature of expertise.* Hillsdale, NJ: Lawrence Erlbaum Associates.

Colby, A., & Damon, W. (1992). *Some do care: Contemporary lives of moral commitment.* New York: The Free Press.

Colby, A., & Damon, W. (1995). The development of extraordinary moral commitment. In M. Killen & D. Hart (Eds.), *Morality in everyday life* (pp. 342–370). New York: Cambridge University Press.

Colby, A., Kohlberg, L., Gibbs, J., & Lieberman, M. (1983). A longitudinal study of moral judgment. *Monographs of the Society for Research in Child Development: Vol. 48(1-sup-2)124.* Chicago: University of Chicago Press.

Emde, R., Biringen, Z., Clyman, R. B., & Oppenheim, D. (1991). The moral self of infancy: Affective core and procedural knowledge. *Developmental Review, 11,* 251–2 70.

Fivush, R., Kuebli, J., & Chubb, P. A. (1992). The structure of event representations: A developmental analysis. *Child Development, 63,* 188–201.

Hart, D., & Fegley, S. (1995). Prosocial behavior and caring in adolescence: Relations to self-understanding and social judgment: *Child Development, 66,* 1346–1359.

Hart, D., Yates, M., Fegley, S., & Wilson, G. (1995). Moral commitment in inner-city adolescents. In M. Killen & D. Hart (Eds.), *Morality in everyday life* (pp. 317–341). New York: Cambridge University Press.

Hartshorne, H., & May, M. (1928–1932). *Studies in the nature of character.* New York: Macmillan.

Hastie, R. (1983). Social inferences. *Annual Review of Psychology, 34,* 511–542.

Higgins, E. T. (1987). Self-discrepancy theory: A theory relating self and affect. *Psychological Review, 94,* 319–340.

Higgins, E. T. (1996). Knowledge activation: Accessibility, applicability and salience. In E. T. Higgins & A. W. Kruglanski (Eds.), *Social psychology: Handbook of basic principles* (pp. 133–168). New York: Guilford.

Higgins, E. T. (1999). Persons and situations: Unique explanatory principles or variability in general principles? In D. Cervone and Y. Shoda (Eds.), *The coherence of personality: Social-cognitive bases of consistency, variability and organization* (pp.61–93). New York: Guilford Press.

Higgins, E. T., King, G. A., & Mavin, G. H. (1982). Individual construct accessibility and subjective impressions and recall. *Journal of Personality and Social Psychology, 43,* 35–47.

Kohlberg, L. (1971). From is to ought: How to commit the naturalistic fallacy and get away with it in the study of moral development. In T. Mischel (Ed.), *Cognitive development and epistemology* (pp. 151–235). New York: Academic Press.

Kohlberg, L., Levine, C., & Hewer, A. (1983). Moral stages: A current formulation and a response to critics. In J. A. Meacham (Ed.), *Contributions to human development* (Vol. 10). Basel, Switzerland: Karger.

Kohlberg, L., & Mayer, R. (1972). Development as the arm of education. *Harvard Educational Review, 42,* 449–496.

Lakatos, I. (1978). Introduction: Science and pseudoscience. In J. Worrall & G. Currie (Eds)., *The methodology of scientific research programs: Imre Lakatos philosophical papers* (Vol. 2, pp. 128–210). Cambridge, England: Cambridge University Press.

Lapsley, D. K. (1996). *Moral psychology*. Boulder, CO: Westview.

Lapsley, D. K. (1999). An outline of a social-cognitive theory of moral character. *Journal of Research in Education, 8*, 25–32.

Lapsley, D. K., & Lasky, B. (1999). Prototypic moral character. *Identity, 1*, 345–363.

Lapsley, D. K., & Lasky, B. (April, 2001). *Chronic accessibility of virtue-trait inferences: A social–cognitive approach to the moral personality*. Paper presented at the biennial meeting of the Society for Research in Child Development, Minneapolis.

Lapsley, D. K., & Narvaez, D. (in press). Moral psychology at the crossroads. In D. K. Lapsley & F. C. Power (Eds.), *Character psychology and character education*. Notre Dame, IN: University of Notre Dame Press.

Lapsley, D., & Quintana, S. (1985). Integrative themes in social and developmental theories of the self. In J. Pryor & J. Day (Eds.), *The development of social cognition* (pp. 153–178). New York: Springer-Verlag.

Lerner, R. (1991). Changing organism-context relations as the basic process of development: A developmental–contextual perspective. *Developmental Psychology, 27*, 27–32.

Lerner, R. (1995). *America's youth in crisis: Challenges and opportunities for programs and policies*. Thousand Oaks, CA: Sage.

Lerner, R., & Busch-Rossnagel, N. A. (Eds.). (1981). *Individuals as producers of their own development: A lifespan perspective*. New York: Academic Press.

Mischel, W. (1968). *Personality and assessment*. New York: Wiley.

Mischel, W. (1990). Personality dispositions revisited and revised: A view after three decades. In L. A. Pervin (Ed.), *Handbook of personality: Theory and research* (pp. 111–134). New York: Guilford.

Mischel, W. (1999). Personality coherence and dispositions in a cognitive–affective personality system (CAPS) approach. In D. Cervone & Y. Shoda (Eds.), *The coherence of personality: Social cognitive bases of consistency, variability and organization* (pp. 37–60). New York: Guilford.

Narvaez, D. (1998). The influence of moral schemas on the reconstruction of moral narratives in eighth-graders and college students. *Journal of Educational Psychology, 90*, 13–24.

Narvaez, D. (2001). Moral text comprehension: Implications for education and research. *Journal of Moral Education, 30*, 43–54.

Narvaez, D. (2002). Does reading moral stories build character? *Educational Psychology Review 14*, 155–171.

Narvaez, D. (in press). The neo-Kohlbergian tradition and beyond: Schemas, expertise, and character. In C. Pope-Edwards & G. Carlo (Eds.), *Nebraska Symposium Conference Papers*, Vol. 51. Lincoln, NE: University of Nebraska Press.

Narvaez, D., Bentley, J., Gleason, T., & Samuels, J. (1998). Moral theme comprehension in third grade, fifth grade and college students. *Reading Psychology, 19*, 217–241.

Narvaez, D., & Bock, T. (2002). Moral schemas and tacit judgment or how the Defining Issues Test is supported by cognitive science. *Journal of Moral Education, 31*, 297–314.

Narvaez, D., Gleason, T., Mitchell, C., & Bentley, J. (1999). Moral theme comprehension in children. *Journal of Educational Psychology, 91*(3), 477–487.

Narvaez, D., & Lapsley, D. K. (in press). The psychological foundation of moral expertise. In D. K. Lapsley & F. C. Power (Eds.), *Character psychology and character education.* Notre Dame, IN: University of Notre Dame Press.

Narvaez, D., & Rest, J. (1995). The four components of acting morally. In W. Kurtines & J. Gewirtz (Eds.), *Moral behavior and moral development: An introduction* (pp. 385–400). New York: McGraw-Hill.

Nelson, K. (Ed.). (1989). *Narratives from the crib.* Cambridge, MA: Harvard University Press.

Nelson, K. (1993a). Events, narratives, memory: What develops? In C. A. Nelson (Ed.), *Memory and affect in development: Minnesota Symposia on Child Psychology* (Vol. 26, pp. 1–24). Hillsdale, NJ: Lawrence Erlbaum Associates.

Nelson, K. (1993b). The psychological and social origins of autobiographical memory. *Psychological Science, 4,* 7–14.

Nelson, K., & Gruendel, J. (1981). Generalized event representations: Basic building blocks of cognitive development. In M. Lamb & A. Brown (Eds.), *Advances in developmental psychology* (pp. 131–158). Hillsdale, NJ: Lawrence Erlbaum Associates.

Reese, E., & Fivush, R. (1993). Parental styles of talking about the past. *Developmental Psychology, 29,* 596–606.

Reese, E., Halden, C. A., & Fivush, R. (1993). Mother–child conversations about the past: Relationships of style and memory over time. *Cognitive Development, 8,* 403–430.

Rest, J. (1983). Morality. In P. Mussen (Ed.), *Handbook of child psychology: Vol. 3. Cognitive Development* (4th ed.: J Flavell & E. Markman, Vol. Eds., pp. 556–628). New York: Wiley.

Rest, J., Narvaez, D., Bebeau, M. J., & Thoma, S.J. (1999). *Postconventional moral thinking: A neo-Kohlbergian approach.* Mahwah, NJ: Lawrence Erlbaum Associates.

Schneider, W., & Bjorklund, D. J. (1998). Memory. In W. Damon (Ed.) *Handbook of child psychology* (5th ed., pp. 467–521). New York: Wiley.

Thompson, R. A. (1998). Early sociopersonality development. In W. Damon & N. Eisenberg (Eds.) *Handbook of child psychology: Vol. 3. Social, emotional and personality development* (pp. 25–104). New York: Wiley.

Uleman, J. S. (1989). Spontaneous trait inference. In J. S. Uleman & J. A. Bargh (Eds.), *Unintended thought* (pp. 155–188). New York: Guilford.

Uleman, J. S., Hon, A., Roman, R., & Moskowitz, G. B. (1996). On-line evidence for spontaneous trait inferences at encoding. *Personality and Social Psychology Bulletin, 22,* 377–394.

Uleman, J. S., Newman, L. S., & Moskowitz, G. B. (1996). People as flexible interpreters: Evidence and issues from spontaneous trait inference. In M. P. Zanna (Ed.), *Advances in experimental social psychology* (Vol. 28, pp. 211–280). San Diego: Academic Press.

Uleman, J. S., Winborne, W. C., Winter, L., & Schechter, D. (1986). Personality differences in spontaneous trait inferences at encoding. *Journal of Personality and Social Psychology, 51,* 396–404

Walker, L. J., & Pitts, R. C. (1998). Naturalistic conceptions of moral maturity. *Developmental Psychology, 34,* 403–419).

Zelli, A., & Dodge, K. A. (1999). Personality development from the bottom up. In D. Cerbone & Y. Shoda (Eds.), The coherence of personality: Social–cognitive bases of consistency, variability, and organization (pp. 91–126). New York: Guilford Press.

Zelli, A., Huesmann, L. R., & Cervone, D. (1995). Social inference and individual differences in aggression: Evidence for spontaneous judgements of hostility. *Aggressive Behavior, 21*, 405–417.

10

Many Are Called, But Few Are Chosen: Moving Beyond the Modal Levels in Normal Development

Wolfgang Edelstein
Max Planck Institute for Human Development, Berlin

Tobias Krettenauer
Humboldt University, Berlin

A troublesome and unresolved paradox has long beset developmental theories of the cognitive structural type: The claim for universality of the processes and sequences of development contradicts the failure of most developing individuals to reach the topmost levels or stages of developmental progress. Thus, only about one third of adolescents or young adults reach the stage of full formal operations (Neimark, 1985; Piaget, 1970, 1972; Shayer, Demetriou, & Pervez, 1988). Only a small number of Kohlberg's respondents reached the postconventional stages (Colby, Kohlberg, Gibbs, & Lieberman, 1983; Snarey & Keljo, 1991), and only a minority achieved Loevinger's (1979) integrated level of ego functioning.

How can this paradox be resolved? The question is of considerable interest for developmental theorizing. If complete developmental progression is to count as a general or even universal attribute of the species, not as a mere regulatory idea (as was all but conceded in view of the rare individual using postconventional reasoning at Stage 5 or beyond; Kohlberg, Levine, & Hewer, 1983), it appears essential for the theory to either specify those conditions that enable individuals to reach the final, most advanced and equilibrated, best adapted, and encompassing stage of the developmental trajectory or to identify functional equivalences of that stage in view of optimal psychological functioning in solving life's problems at an advanced level of adequacy.

There are various alternative paths toward the resolution of the paradox. One, of course, is the biological hypothesis: Genetic variation may produce randomly better-than-average adapted individuals with higher performance capabilities. But as the distribution of the characteristic in question makes this hypothesis less attractive and as, in particular, we have no way to control it, we leave this possibility aside for the present discussion.

A perspective more in line with Piaget's (1985) theorizing specifies development as structural transformation. Internal conditions of development take precursor states or antecedent conditions internal to the organism to their completion by dint of the internal dynamics of the developmental process itself. From this perspective a disjunction between the structural characteristics that dominate development at levels below the advanced stage and those governing it near the end of what is taken to be the developmental continuum is possible. In consequence the upper and the lower stage systems divide into two distinct processes—one universal, the other contingent.

Besides these more or less "internalist" explanations there is the "interactionist" variety, attributing the shape of the developmental trajectory to the interactions of the organism with features or forces of the environment. At least two variants emerge: (a) Features of the environment interact with characteristics of development generally, with the effect of general enhancement or deprivation, acceleration, or delay and horizontal or longitudinal enrichment or impoverishment. (b) Features of the environment interact with specific aspects of development to produce, as a specific effect, the development of a specialized competence that tops development under certain highly selective circumstances.

Finally, a set of further modes of advanced functioning have been proposed: *Postformal operations* (Commons, Richards, & Armon, 1984) represent highly adaptive logical structures beyond the formal logic expressed in formal operational reasoning. A functionally differentiated use of preultimate levels serves the imperative of adaptiveness and thus practical reversibility beyond the highest formal level of reasoning (Edelstein & Noam, 1982). Selective use of specific types of arguments within the earlier stages represent the specific quality of reasoning that characterizes the highest stages. Colby and Kohlberg (1987) described such arguments as Type B reasoning. Type B reasoning evidences characteristics of moral autonomy that are essential for the definition of postconventional stages and can be considered precursors of the highest stage moral reasoning (Krettenauer & Edelstein, 1999).

A combination of one or the other of the alternatives just outlined is conceivable. Thus, sequential structural transformations through the entire system of stages may proceed hand in hand with a functional differentiation of preultimate stages or levels to achieve either postformal and postconventional perfection or high-level adequacy. Such combinations give rise to potentially different conceptualizations of the developmental dynamic driving progression and, possibly, of the nature of development itself. We now consider the alternative of continuous and discontinuous development in greater detail.

THE DISJUNCTION BETWEEN LOWER
AND HIGHER STAGES

According to the generally accepted, normative view of universal development there are continuous internal process mechanisms that operate across the sequence of levels and stages, leading to the highest stage in the sequence. Although this is the canonical account in structural developmental theories, it fails to account for the differential achievement of the highest stage(s) and most frequently ignores it. Piaget (1985), in his account of the progression through the stages and the transitions between them, described the mechanisms of stage transition in terms of the internal progressive operation of assimilation, accommodation, and equilibration leading to a more inclusive, stable, and perturbation-free functioning of more encompassing structures universally. In a relatively late paper, however, Piaget (1970/1972) introduced a different account of the emergence of formal operations. He highlighted different mechanisms involved in the earlier and later phases of the progression in cognitive development: The earlier phases are taken to represent a universal trajectory from preoperations into mature concrete operations. The universality of this trajectory (and the concrete operations achieved by children worldwide) is traced to the experience of universal aspects of the real world, reflected by a process of empirical abstraction, whereas the transition to formal operations is brought about by the reflective abstraction contained in mental operations on operations (Piaget, 1985). These higher order operations are based on nongeneral, more specialized experiences that presuppose a world of physical, social, or scientific abstractions and relationships involving varieties of experimental or quasiexperimental settings or functions. These call for hypothetical reasoning in terms of possibilities rather than concrete relations (Inhelder & Piaget, 1955/1958). Thus, Piaget made the internal mechanisms of assimilation, accommodation, and equilibration responsible for the continuous processes driving development, whereas different classes of experience abstracted through different modalities of abstraction from different types of interaction with the world are responsible for the emergence of a different type of cognitive operations—the formal operations of mature adolescence and adulthood—if and when these emerge at all. Whereas cross-cultural studies have borne out the universality of concrete operations (Berry & Dasen, 1974; Dasen, 1977), formal operations appear to be restricted to cultures involving levels of abstraction and technological practices that presuppose an advanced system of division of labor (Piaget, 1970/1972; for notions concerning the cultural evolution of operatory thought see Edelstein, 1983, 1996; Radding, 1985). Thus, Piaget adopted a combination of internally driven development and an interactionist model of experientially driven developmental progress.

Despite many similarities, there are important differences between the ways in which Piaget and Kohlberg conceptualized developmental structures that have been overlooked. Colby and Kohlberg (1987) postulated a rough correspondence between Piagetian logical operations and moral judgment processes (which they called "justice operations"), or between Piagetian stages and moral stages, and assumed that the achievement of concrete operations is a necessary but insufficient prerequisite condition for conventional moral reasoning (Haan, Weiss, & Johnson, 1982; Kohlberg, 1976; Walker, 1980). From the postulated correspondence it can be inferred that formal reasoning counts as a prerequisite condition of postconventional moral judgment. However, the formal structures of the various levels and sublevels of moral worldviews do not simply map onto the stages of operatory reasoning, even if the internal process mechanisms of cognitive development were to remain valid for both. The progressive sequence of moral worldviews is taken to resolve contradictions that are aroused by the imperfections and restrictions that any given stage of moral judgment imposes on the adjudication of fair and inclusive solutions to conflicts at various and variously different levels of action, actor relationships, and action contexts. Justice operations thus appear much more complex and less amenable to logical relationships than the experientially based reasoning about world objects described by Piaget's theory.

The question is bound to arise whether it is the very complexity of social experience—social relations and social conflict—that drives progressive development beyond the reductive structures of logic to transitions from relatively simple and concrete constructions to ever more abstract accommodations to the complex sociomoral worldviews that are being constructed in that very same process. This formula plainly refers to the interactionist model, but the higher stage here refers to higher complexity of the reality relations organized by the higher levels of the system of moral cognition. Presupposing the validity of the interactionist model, Charles Radding (1985) reconstructed the simpler structures of social reality and relations in the early Middle Ages to demonstrate how, to accommodate increasing complexity, the evolving social and legal structures both brought about changes in the cognitive and moral reasoning structures and shaped the institutional and interpersonal contexts to which these applied. Radding addressed a wealth of evidence supporting continuous increase in the level of sociomoral reasoning to match a more or less continuous growth of the complexity of the historical social world itself. In consequence, the case for discontinuity between conventional and postconventional stages of moral reasoning is not as easily made as that for discontinuity between concrete and formal logical reasoning. Perhaps the complexity of highly developed societies represents a cultural condition for the emergence of postconventional reasoning about some social problems in several situations and contexts only by some individuals (see Nisan & Kohlberg, 1982; Snarey, 1985), whereas less developed modes of reasoning and judgment persist as functional modalities of response to less exacting situations.

However, there is certainly evidence for formal and postconventional reasoning among thinkers in premodern societies. Not unexpectedly, critics of Kohlberg's stage system have claimed that his postconventional level represents not stages of moral reasoning but education-dependent moral ideologies or mere philosophical arguments that are characteristic of a professional class of specialized intellectuals independent of the laborious historical and ontogenetic progression of moral reasoning through the system of moral stages (Gibbs, 1979; Sullivan, 1977). This critique does away with the stage of postconventional moral judgment altogether, reducing it to specialized cognitive content. The plausibility of this position, however, is not as convincing as it may first appear. Various authors have attempted to improve on the definitions of postconventional reasoning both philosophically and psychologically (Habermas, 1983, 1990; Puka, 1990). Despite various incisive critiques of postconventional moral judgment as defined by Kohlberg (Haan, Aerts, & Cooper, 1985; Shweder & Haidt, 1993; Shweder, Mahapatra, & Miller, 1990), the overall architecture of his system including postconventional reasoning now appears to possess a sufficient number of constructive features to warrant acceptance of its existence.

There is, of course, no reason to restrict the relation between the complexity of social transactions and the operations of the mind to the Middle Ages. Other things being equal, increasing complexity of social transactions and regulations will call for higher levels of moral discourse (i.e., systemic generalizations replacing the simple reciprocity of revenge that is characteristic of the resolution of conflict in the early Middle Ages) as described by Radding (1985) and borne out, for example, by the description of social conflicts in Icelandic sagas. There is no easily visible reason why, with increasing complexity of societal organization, role relationships, and conflict in need of fair regulation, this process should not transcend the limits of conventional reasoning in the same way it transcended the limits of premoral discourse and the corresponding regulations. For those convinced of the stage-like property of postconventional morality, it may represent, rather than a generalized mode of operation, a specialized function of experience in intellectually demanding professions, such as judges in a courtroom practice or doctors facing ethical dilemmas in the exercise of contradictory duties in analogy to Piaget's (1970/1972) view of formal operations. Postconventional moral judgment thus would be the rare product as well as the prerequisite for exceptional practice, whereas conventional judgment is the outflow of everyday transactions within a taxonomy of actions regulated by conventional rules and practices. In this view, endorsed by Piaget (1970/1972), mature formal operations and postconventional moral reasoning represent segmented performance failing to generalize across the domains of a circumscribed experience and beyond the exigencies of a specialized craft (see Lempert, 1988). Hence, the segmentation of the highest competence levels represents both a functional condition and a risk for the exercise of reason and moral judgment in the democratic process.

THE ROLE OF EDUCATION IN TRANSITION
TO HIGHER STAGES

As mentioned earlier, Charles Radding (1985) made the growing complexity of religious and moral transactions accountable for the increasingly sophisticated rules governing the religious life and legal practice in the later centuries of the first millennium. Functional practices and cognitive structures drive their mutual progress in an ongoing process of reciprocal differentiation. The functional history of cognitive and sociomoral development remains to be written, but clearly the impact of education plays a major role in collectively moving reasoning, moral judgment, and the structure of arguments concerning a reasoned life beyond the early concrete levels (Edelstein, 1983, 1999). Today the growing access to comparatively advanced levels of education appears to be the central social mechanism for the achievement of advanced levels of cognitive and moral operations in a large section of the citizenry. Education provides for vicarious experience of social contexts and conflicts, hypothetical and experimental reasoning, and exposure to knowledge and ways of interpreting texts that narrate how people determine their forms of life. Education thus represents a cognitive and sociomoral ecology that provides "enabling conditions" ("entgegen kommende Lebensformen," Habermas, 1991, p. 20), that is, an opportunity structure for developmental learning. Education is probably the decisive factor organizing collective cognitive experience today, thereby affecting both individual and collective developmental advances. If this is true, it is educational experience that pushes increasing numbers of educationally sensitized individuals toward structures of reasoning and judgment extending beyond the conventions and conformities of the majority.

COMPLEX DEVELOPMENTAL ENTITIES

To this point, the dynamic of ontogenetic growth in singular dimensions has been discussed: the development of cognitive operations and moral judgment. But there is development along more complex, multidimensional entities that encompass an internal relation between components, each capable of growth along its own line. In such cases an equilibration between components is the hallmark of a developmental level or stage, whereas an equilibrium at a high or even the highest level of development is taken to be the hallmark of maturity.

Ego development is the case in point. The growth of ego development represents progression from lower to higher levels of a complex and multifaceted whole that includes interpersonal and cognitive style, self-control, and conscious preoccupations as its components (Loevinger, 1987; Loevinger & Wessler, 1970). These components of the whole, however, cannot be defined in isolation of each other. On the surface, the structure of ego development does not appear basically different from the structure of moral reasoning, which represents a more narrowly defined, singular, and unidimensional developmental system (Kohlberg, 1976). A closer look reveals that the conceptual structure of ego development encompasses a plurality of elements of a universe of forms of life that together constitute "a good form of life", whereas the elements of moral judgment combine facets that are necessary to the unity of moral judgment. A high level of ego development thus carries with it the notion of general maturity of the person, whereas high-stage moral judgment does not necessarily reach beyond moral principledness.

Finally, a different type of whole was defined by Blasi (1983, 1984, 1995) to explain the operative characteristics linking moral judgment and moral action. The operatory completeness of moral functioning relies on the linkage of moral judgment, the affirmation of responsibility, and a sense of obligation rooted in the self. Although each of these elements develops and can be measured for itself, an operative structure of moral obligation as readiness to act must be assessed in terms of the conjunction of these elements. The multifaceted structure involved in shaping the prerequisites of the competence for moral action has obvious implications for the conceptualization of its development. It is, it seems, the conjunction of different and independently developing elements in a structured whole that generates the emergent capacity for moral action. The unity of this capacity is the result of the conjunction of separate developmental trajectories; this conjunction is a necessary condition for the emergence of the capacity. Thus, maturity in this sense is based on the achievement of unity through the conjunction of a plurality of elements. What does this tell us about possible modalities of growth or failure and of enhancement conditions or inhibition of development?

PROCESS STRUCTURES OF GROWTH

At this point it appears appropriate to turn to the implications of interactionist models of organism–environment transactions in human growth. In structural developmental theories such transaction should not be viewed as a causal environmental agency impacting on development. Piaget (1985) formulated an elaborate internal process structure of invariant functions regulating the inner reconstruction of the subject's experience with world objects, but most important, of the subject's logical-mathematical experience of the systems of relations in which world objects are situated. The richness of these experiential environments and the density of the networks derived from the relations interiorized by the subject constitute the enhancement conditions (or, conversely, the conditions of impoverishment and delay) of human growth—a system of complex causal–systemic interactions that cannot be captured by a construction of linear dependencies. Interactionism thus implies a system of double transactions: the internal self-energizing operation of the functional invariants in the process of disequilibration and equilibration and the interaction between the internal system and the external world that supplies the experiential resources that aliment the internal construction activity. A further level of complexity of this process is reached when the experience interiorized is rooted in the interaction between social actors, rather than the physical objects and relations that mostly populate Piaget's theory.

Thus, in Piaget's theory (which, although adopted more or less wholesale by Kohlberg, is left largely undiscussed by him) an elaborate dynamic system is hidden behind the rather trivial phrase of organism–environment transaction that is responsible for development and, incidentally, for the individual differences in development, which Piaget neglected (see Inhelder & Piaget, 1971, for a discussion of and apology for this neglect). Both Piaget's and Kohlberg's theories are professedly interactionist, attributing cognitive and sociomoral progress to constructive transactions with the environment or, rather, to the experience thereof (Chapman, 1988; Edelstein, 2001; Piaget, 1971). The chosen few, in this view, have been exposed to exceptionally advantageous experiences of enrichment or conflict—in Piaget's (1970/1972) terms, to special scientific or technological challenges. If the argument is extended to Kohlberg's system, in certain cases, individuals will be exposed to highly exacting conflictual situations that call for high-level solutions. It would be an interesting task to analyze systematically the environmental conditions and the socialization experiences of formal operatory or postconventional reasoners in search of the conditions of transition to higher stages of development.

Certainly, the immediate and the vicarious experiences provided by education play a major role in the process. Both Piaget and Kohlberg paid close attention to the role of education in development toward higher levels of cognitive functioning. Both wrote extensively about developmental effects of the experience of education and the design of educational experiences for developmental progress (see Kohlberg & Higgins, 1987; Kohlberg & Mayer, 1972; Piaget, 1998). For the more complex system derived from Piaget's and Kohlberg's theories efforts at designing interventions for development are not known. However, broadly speaking, the same Dewey-type (1944, 1963) interventions through self-government and just community experiences ought to enhance individual growth generally beyond the condition introduced into history by the collective experience of education.

CONDITIONS OF GROWTH: PREDICTORS OF DEVELOPMENTAL SUCCESS

The long developmental trajectory toward completion, the delayed emergence of a highest stage or level, has been the object of theorizing in the context of evolutionary psychology under the label of *neoteny* (see Bjorklund, 1997; Bjorklund & Green, 1992, for reviews). The principle of neoteny serves to explain the late emergence of complete organismic functioning or late transition to a highest stage as an opportunity for learning and adaptation contrived by evolution. In more normal appraisals of development, the long trajectories provide opportunities for maladaptive transitions (e.g., in the context of adolescent adjustment problems; Noam, Chandler, & Lalonde, 1995) or, conversely, differential probabilities for developmental success.

Physical or social deprivation, constrained opportunity structures and restrictions of experience with world objects and social interactions (e.g., in deprived families) are likely to delay or interfere with the course of development itself. From a constructivist perspective individuals remain, to an extent, makers of their self-constructed development. Their trajectories, however, are constrained by the opportunity structures that either enhance development or put the individual at a developmental disadvantage. This formulation, however, refers not only to the conditions that give rise to the emergence of the happy few and chosen but to the entire course of development and to the variations and the intraindividual and interindividual differences found in its progression. If environmental and intrinsic conditions are not specific to the elaboration of a highest stage, they are likely to affect the course of development more or less similarly throughout. Transitions to the highest stage will then most likely be found among those who have benefited, in earlier phases of their development, from propitious conditions as reflected by developmental advance or horizontal equilibration (Berkowitz & Keller, 1994; Snyder & Feldman, 1977). Such patterns can be identified as precursors of later transition to the highest stage. However unlikely that transition would be, it would still be most likely among those individuals who evidence earlier advancement toward higher stages. It is those individuals who benefit from propitious conditions enabling earlier transitions who, in the biblical metaphor, tend to constitute the group of those called and from whom the chosen few are selected. These may be identified empirically once the conditions that benefit growth are amenable to measurement.

But there still remains the alternative condition of achieving the highest level of development identified by Piaget in his 1970/1972 contribution to Human Development, what we called the *disjunction model of growth*. The disjunction model of growth may involve differential enhancement (or deprivation) conditions for the different levels of (lower tier vs. upper tier) development that are represented by different predictors. We have seen that different educational and professional experiences explained the performance of concrete versus formal thought. Similarly, different types of experience may predict the achievement of conformist versus postconformist levels of ego development.

EMPIRICAL STUDY

At this point we turn to an empirical study to complement the theoretical considerations offered so far. We investigate whether the continuity hypothesis or the disjunction hypothesis is more adequate to the empirical conditions of growth as assessed in the context of Loevinger's (1976) theory of ego development. In the first case, the developmental conditions and, possibly, the developmental processes leading to the highest levels of ego development are the same as those leading to average performance or middle-level development. In the alternative case, the developmental conditions or processes leading to the highest stages differ from those leading to an intermediate stage. It was argued earlier that ego development as operationalized by Loevinger (1987; Loevinger & Wessler, 1970) is a fair representation of the family of structural–developmental constructs. There are striking parallels in the stage descriptions between Loevinger's and Kohlberg's models, there is the same dearth of developmental subjects reaching the highest levels, and there are strong correlations between moral stage and ego level (Kohlberg, 1976; Lee & Snarey, 1988; Manners & Durkin, 2000). Moreover, ego development and moral development evidence similar growth curves, with a growth spurt in adolescence leveling off in early adulthood (Cohn, 1998). All of these factors support the family resemblance and the structural kinship between Kohlberg's and Loevinger's models. Therefore, findings about patterns of ego development can shed some light on the development of other such constructs.

The study reported next is based on a longitudinal study carried out in Iceland from 1976 to 1992. Project Individual Development and Social Structure was designed to investigate individual differences in cognitive, sociomoral, behavioral, and emotional development as a function of macro- as well as microsocial context variations (for an overview, see Edelstein, Keller, & Schröder, 1990). Children who participated in the study were drawn from different socialization contexts. They came from different social classes and grew up in either urban or rural environments. At the onset of the study, subjects were 7 years old and had just entered the first grade of elementary school. At that time, children were tested with a battery of Piagetian tasks assessing cognitive development. Children's social cognitive development was assessed using a variety of measures, in particular perspective taking, moral judgment, and an interview about a friendship dilemma. The procedure was repeated at ages 9, 12, 15, and (partly) 17. In addition, from age 9 to age 15 children's classroom behaviors and social orientations were rated by their main classroom teacher. Grades were collected every year. At ages 9, 12, and 15 locus of control, anxiety, and self-esteem data were collected. Overall, a wealth of data was assembled to represent various dimensions of individual development. Many of these dimensions have been demonstrated by previous research to be linked to ego development. This is the case, notably, for cognitive, social–cognitive, and moral development and for behavioral problems and locus of control (cf. Adams & Fitch, 1983; Dubow, Huesmann, & Eron, 1987; Hauser, 1976, 1993; Lee & Snarey, 1988; Loevinger, 1979; Noam et al., 1984).

Level of ego development was assessed once in the project at age 22. The measure was defined as a developmental outcome at the onset of adulthood. Previous research has borne out that ego growth levels off and often stops once teenagers grow into adulthood (Manners & Durkin, 2000). The assessment of participants' ego level at age 22 can thus be considered a fair estimate of the level of ego attainment. Later, this developmental achievement is analyzed as a function of individuals' socialization context as well as of earlier cognitive, behavioral, and emotional development. Particular attention is granted to factors that predict the attainment of higher ego levels. If the continuity hypothesis is valid, the same variables should predict high and intermediate ego levels. If the disjunction hypothesis is valid, variables that predict higher ego-level attainment should differ from those predicting an average developmental outcome.

Sample Characteristics

Project Individual Development and Social Structure includes two samples: one drawn from an urban setting and one drawn from rural contexts. Originally, the urban sample consisted of 121 seven-year-old children from Reykjavik. Children were randomly chosen from a larger pool of 319 first graders with the provision that the final sample was balanced with regard to gender and social class as assessed by a 6-point scale of social inequality (Björnsson, Edelstein, & Kreppner, 1977, pp. 31–37). For the following analyses this scale was dichotomized so as to represent lower and higher levels of socioeconomic status (SES). Blue collar workers, skilled labor, as well as office workers and lower level public employees constituted the lower SES group, whereas teachers, technicians, managers, entrepreneurs, as well as members of the political, cultural, and business elites formed the higher SES group. The rural sample consisted of 64 seven-year-olds who constituted the entire birth cohorts of three small rural communities in southern, western and northern Iceland, respectively.

Of the 165 subjects selected at onset of the study, 103 participated in the entire longitudinal project from childhood (7 years) to early adulthood (22 years). Of these participants, 45 were boys and 58 girls, 64 were from the original urban sample and 39 from the rural sample, and 62 from the lower social class and 41 from the higher social class. At age 22, subjects had attained diverse educational levels: Some had attended preacademic high school until age 18 or 19 and were enrolled in university studies ($n = 45$). We refer to these participants as the higher education group. By contrast, others had either no postsecondary education beyond the mandatory level (Grade 10 around age

16) or had only received vocational training ($n = 58$). These participants are referred to as the lower education group.

Measures

Ego-Level in Early Adulthood. In general, ego development, as described by Loevinger (1976) and assessed by the Washington University Sentence Completion Test (WUSCT; Hy & Loevinger, 1996), moves through a sequence of eight levels with the lowest levels labeled as *impulsive* and *self-protective* (Levels E2 and E3), the intermediate levels as *conformist* and *self-aware* (Levels E4 and E5), and the highest ones as *conscientious, individualistic, autonomous,* and *integrated* (Levels E6 through E9).[1] The modal level in adulthood is Level E4 (Holt, 1980). John, Pals, and Westenberg (1998) demonstrated empirically that these eight ego levels can be combined into three groups that represent different achievements with regard to ego development: The impulsive and self-protective levels (E2 and E3) represent the preconformist groups; the conformist and self-aware levels (E4 and E5) represent the conformist group, and the conscientious, individualistic, autonomous, and integrated levels (E6, E7, E8, and E9) define the postconformist group of ego levels.

In the present study, protocols of the WUSCT (Form 11–68) were scored according to the procedure detailed by Loevinger and Wessler (1970). The majority of the participants (53.8%) were assigned to Level E5 (i.e., the modal level in adulthood). Nonetheless, a broad range from Level E2 through Level E8 was represented in the sample (see Table 10.1). The overall mean of ego levels was slightly below the self-aware Level E5 ($M = 4.82$, $SD = 1.23$). Considering the spread of developmental attainments, 16 participants had not developed beyond the preconformist Levels E2 and E3, 64 belonged to the conformist group, and 22 had attained one of the higher, postconformist levels.

TABLE 10.1

Distribution of Ego Levels and Illustration of Dummy-Contrast Variables

Variable		Ego Levels						
		E2	E3	E4	E5	E6	E7	E8
	$n =$	1	15	9	56	17	3	2
Dummy-contrast A	$n =$	[——16——]		[——————————87——————————]				
Dummy-contrast B	$n =$	[——————81——————]				[——————22——————]		

Thus, the majority of the subjects had attained an average ego level; only few had moved beyond the average.

Cognitive Development. Cognitive development was measured by a battery of Piagetian tasks that assess concrete operational and formal operational thinking. For concrete operations conservation, class inclusion, verbal classification, and logical multiplication were assessed. For the assessement of formal operations, multiple compensation (invariance of volume), syllogistic reasoning, isolation of variables, and the pendulum task were used. Participants' performances on all of these tasks were aggregated. This procedure yielded a total score that reflect participants' overall cognitive development. In the sample, considerable cognitive developmental growth between the ages of 7 and 12 years and a leveling off in early adolescence was found (for details, see Schröder, 1989)

Social–Cognitive Development. At each measurement point social–cognitive development was assessed by an interview about a friendship dilemma. The dilemma describes a (male or female) protagonist who has given a promise to visit his or her best friend on their usual meeting day. Later the protagonist receives an attractive invitation from a third age-matched actor who has just moved into the neighborhood. Various psychological details make the situation more complex (e.g., the old friend does not like the new child). The interview deals with various issues involving social–cognitive development. It contains general as well as situation-specific questions, for example, about the meaning of friendship and promise keeping, the feelings of those affected by the protagonist's decision, and so on. Responses are coded for the child's level of perspective taking as defined by Selman (1980; for details, see Keller & Edelstein, 1991).

Locus of Control. At ages 9, 12 and 15 students completed the Nowicki and Strickland (1973) Locus of Control Scale, assessing children's locus of control as a bipolar construct (external vs. internal). The scale contains items such as "Do you feel that when someone doesn't like you there's little you can do about it?" and is keyed so that high scores indicate external locus of control.

Internalizing and Externalizing Problems. At ages 9, 12, and 15 behavioral problems were rated by the participants' main classroom teachers using a questionnaire assessing classroom behavior. Overall, the questionnaire contained 78 items sampled from three standard instruments that were available when the study was designed (Kohn & Rosman, 1972; Quay, 1977; Schaefer & Aaronson, 1966). Factor and scale analyses of the questionnaire yielded the two well-known broadband factors of externalizing and internalizing behavior problems (e.g., Achenbach, 1995). The scale for the assessment of externalizing problems comprises 17 items that indicate lack of impulse control and aggressive and disruptive behavior in the school setting (e.g., "student is hot tempered,"., "is impatient, if s/he does not get what s/he wants," "disturbs," "pushes, teases, bullies others"). The scale for assessing internalizing problems consists of 18 items that indicate social withdrawal and anxiousness, and depressive mood (e.g., "student withdraws," "is sad," "cries often," "feels inferior").

RESULTS

To explore whether the different socialization conditions as represented by the sample characteristics and the various dimensions of individual development are related to ego-level attainment in early adulthood, first, a multiple analysis of variance (MANOVA) was conducted with the three ego-level groups (preconformists, conformists, postconformists) defined as between-subjects factor, whereas gender, context of socialization, social class, educational attainment, cognitive development, social cognitive development, locus of control, and externalizing and internalizing problems were the dependent variables. Subsequently, two planned comparisons between (a) preconformists and conformists and (b) conformists and postconformists were conducted to identify variables that could potentially be related to the attainment of postconformist levels. For all analyses the repeated measures of cognitive and social–cognitive development, locus of control, and behavioral problems were averaged over the assessments at ages 9, 12, and 15.

The MANOVA yielded a significant multivariate F value. Thus, the sampling factors and the various dimensions of individual development were shown to relate to the three ego-level groups, $F(18, 184) = 2.49, p < .01$. The subsequent unique F tests provide a more detailed view of the nature of this multivariate effect. Overall, participants' level of education, their cognitive and social-cognitive development, locus of control, and externalizing and internalizing behavioral problems relate to differences between the three ego-level groups (see Table 10.2). By contrast, gender, urban versus rural origin, socialization context, and social class were unrelated to ego-level attainment. In sum, person variables relate to ego-level differences, whereas social structure variables do not.

The planned comparisons (a priori contrasts, $p < .05$) between, on the one hand, preconformists and conformists and between conformists and postconformists, on the other, call for a differentiation of this general picture.

TABLE 10.2

Ego-Level Attainment in Early Adulthood, Socialization Conditions, and Individual Development From Age 9 to 15: Statistical Differences Among Ego-Level Groups

	Overall	Apriori Contrasts Between Groups:	
		E2–E3 vs. E4–E5	E4–E5 vs. E6–E7
	$F(2,100)$	$t(100)$	$t(100)$
Context of socialization[a]	1.02	.85	.93
Social class[b]	2.25	.31	1.95
Level of education[b]	8.43**	1.52	3.38**
gender[c]	2.80	1.99*	.81
Cognitive development[d]	4.89**	1.94	1.95
Social–cognitive development[d]	5.59**	2.46*	1.66
Locus of control[d]	4.47*	−2.25*	−1.47
Externalizing problems[d]	5.02**	−2.18*	−1.75
Internalizing problems[d]	9.19**	−1.38	−3.65**

[a]0 = rural; 1 = urban. [b]0 = low; 1 = high. [c]0 = male; 1 = female. [d]Averaged over ages 9, 12, and 15.
*$p < .05$, **$p < .01$.

They indicate that the sample characteristics and the developmental measures are differentially related to the transition from the preconformist to the conformist level and to the transition from the conformist to the postconformist level. None of the variables under scrutiny was significantly related to both developmental transitions. In view of the transition to the conformist levels, social–cognitive development, locus of control, and externalizing behavioral problems were particularly relevant: Conformists were more advanced in social cognition than preconformists; they developed an internal locus of control earlier, and they had fewer externalizing behavioral problems (see Table 10.3). In addition, a gender difference was found, with females participants more often assigned to conformist than to preconformist levels.

A different pattern of findings emerged with regard to the transition from the conformist to the postconformist level. Conformists and postconformists did not differ significantly with regard to social–cognitive development, locus of control, externalizing behavior, and gender. Instead, they differed with regard to level of education and internalizing behavioral problems, with higher educated participants who had fewer internalizing problems achieving postconformist levels more often.

TABLE 10.3

Ego-Level Attainment in Early Adulthood, Socialization Conditions, and Individual Development From Age 9 to 15: Means of Different Ego-Level Groups

	Preconformists (E2–E3)	Conformists (E4–E5)	Postconformists (E6–E8)
Context of socialization[a]	.50	.62	.73
Social class[b]	.31	.35	.59
Level of education[b]	.19	**.38**	**.77**
gender[c]	**.31**	**.58**	.68
Cognitive development[d]	−.54	−.02	.45
Social–cognitive development[d]	**−.64**	**.02**	.41
Locus of control[d]	**.59**	**−.02**	−.37
Externalizing problems[d]	**.58**	**.00**	−.42
Internalizing problems[d]	.48	**.12**	**−.71**

[a] 0 = rural; 1 = urban. [b] 0 = low; 1 = high. [c] 0 = male; 1 = female. [d] Averaged over ages 9, 12, and 15 and z-standardized.
Note. Cells in the same row with bold-type entries indicate significant mean differences between adjacent groups (apriori contrast, $p < .05$).

The analyses conducted so far demonstrate that the variables under study are differentially related to ego-level attainment. The findings refute the continuity hypothesis, but are compatible with the disjunction hypothesis. However, they are not sufficient to demonstrate that these variables actually predict ego-level attainment differentially. To address this question, in a second step of the data analysis, we conducted a set of regression analyses with two different groups of variables as predictors and two different dummy contrast variables as dependent variables. The contrast variables represented different ego-development attainments. They were created by recoding the ego-level scores at two different cutoff points (for an illustration, see Table 10.1). Dummy-contrast A uses Level E4 as cutoff point and compares individuals scoring lower than E4 with individuals scoring at least E4, thus representing an ego-level attainment of conformity or beyond. Dummy-contrast B represents the attainment of postconformist ego levels. It uses E6 as cutoff point and contrasts participants with scores lower than E6 with respondents scoring at least E6. Each of these contrast variables was regressed on those variables that had been found to be significantly related to ego-level attainment in the MANOVA procedure already reported. Table 10.4 summarizes the results of the regression analyses.

Ego-level attainment of conformity (dummy-contrast A) was predicted significantly by the persons' social–cognitive development, locus of control, externalizing problems, and gender, with a multiple correlation of $R = .42$, $F(4, 98) = 5.18$, $p < .01$. This effect, however, cannot be attributed uniquely to a particular developmental measure. Only gender as predictor of ego-level attainment above preconformity reached the level of significance, with girls scoring higher than boys. The regression of dummy-contrast B (attainment of postconformist levels) on the same set of predictor variables yielded a multiple correlation of $R = .32$, $F(4, 98) = 2.73$, $p < .05$. Therefore, despite the fact that social–cognitive development, locus of control, externalizing problems, and gender predicted the transition beyond the preconformist level (i.e., the attainment of conformist as well as postconformist levels), the predictive effect of these variables was stronger with regard to the transition from preconformity to conformity. The reverse pattern of findings was obtained with the second set of predictor variables: level of education and internalizing problems. Although ego-level attainment below conformity (dummy-contrast A) was significantly associated with level of educational attainment and internalizing problems, R

TABLE 10.4

Summary of Regression Analyses Predicting Attainment of Conformist and Postconformist Ego Levels

Predictor Variables	Dependent Variables			
	Dummy-Contrast A		Dummy-Contrast B	
	β	t	β	t
Set I				
Gender[a]	.21	2.12*	.10	1.01
Social–cognitive development[b]	.16	1.48	.13	1.13
Locus of control[b,c]	−.18	−1.58	−.12	−1.03
Externalizing problems[b]	−.16	−1.63	−.16	−1.61
Multiple R	.42**		.32**	
Set II				
Level of education[d]	.16	1.51	.24	2.48*
Internalizing problems[b]	−.14	−1.37	−.28	−2.82**
Multiple R	.25**		.44**	

[a]0 = male; 1 = female. [b]Averaged over ages 9, 12, and 15. [c]Internal = low; external = high.
[d]0 = low; 1 = high.
*$p < .05$, **$p < .01$.

$= .32$, $F(2, 100) = 3.43$, $p < .05$, the regression with dummy-contrast B (attainment of postconformist levels) as a dependent variable yielded a much stronger correlation, $R = .44$, $F(2, 100) = 11.67$, $p < .01$. The difference between the two multiple correlation coefficients was significant, $t(100) = 2.05$, $p < .01$. Thus, level of educational attainment and internalizing problems predicted the transition from conformity to postconformity significantly better than the transition form preconformity to conformity. This finding appears consistent with the hypothesis that the developmental conditions leading to the highest developmental levels differ from those leading to the intermediate level.

DISCUSSION AND CONCLUSION

Different indicators of development predicted the attainment of advanced ego levels than those that predicted the modal levels. In the latter case the indicators reflect a continuity of internal processes driving development. Postconformist levels of ego development seem to depend on the availability of a specific set of growth-enhancing stimuli. Thus, the discontinuity hypothesis is supported. Similarly Piaget (1986) saw the formal operations stage emerge under the sway of specific scientific or technological experiences that led a minority of those potentially exposed to high-level operatory reasoning.

The continuous character of moral development beyond conventional reasoning has been contested by some scholars who argued that postconventional reasoning represents only the specialized thought of philosophical experts. The analogy to Piaget's (1970/1972) reasoning is striking. If the discontinuity is discarded, exposure to ever increasingly complex social conflicts impacting on morally increasingly sensitized minds remains the most probable systemic cause of transitions from lower to higher stages, including the postconventional level of principled moral judgment. Kohlberg (Kohlbert & Higgins, 1987) postulated that enabling conditions prevailing in supportive social contexts open to fairness-oriented discourse and conflict resolution practices were responsible for (continuous) progression through the system of moral judgment stages. Although Kohlberg did not much attend to the mechanisms of growth, it can be inferred that he took Piaget's stance of internal construction of cognitive advance as his model. Both authors, however, viewed the external experiential conditions of developmental progression as enabling (or, conversely, constraining factors instigating or delaying cognitive growth), and both proposed educational methods, didactic procedures, and organizational measures to provide children and adolescents with growth-enhancing environments.

Although ego development (and, in a somewhat different vein, moral responsibility) represents more complex constructs than do operational and moral judgment according to Piaget's and Kohlberg's theories, the question of continuity versus discontinuity of the growth trajectories and the factors that enhance growth arise in similar ways. Besides its theoretical relevance the question of continuity has practical implications because we may either rely on similar conditions or have to resort to different measures to foster development at different points of the trajectory, depending on the appropriateness of the continuity or the disjunction hypothesis. Having established that ego development is a member and an appropriate representative of the family of structural developmental constructs, the empirical investigation was conducted using ego development as testing ground for these hypotheses. The result favored the disjunction hypothesis. Factors that influence the attainment of an intermediate level of ego development were gender (with boys remaining stuck at the preconformist level more frequently than girls), externalizing problems (predicting arrest on the preconformist level), and social–cognitive development (predicting the attainment of the conformist level). Interestingly, these factors represent person rather than context variables. This gives added credence to the notion that internal mechanisms are decisive in driving development, at least in the earlier phases, with the role of experience remaining moot.

Factors that influence the attainment of advanced levels of ego development or maturity are mainly two—(higher levels of) education and (absence of) internalizing problems—whereas the previously influential factors remain ineffective. In this case we are faced with a match of person and context: At the person level the transition from preconformist to conformist levels is marked by a passage from externalizing behavioral trouble to internalizing psychological problems, both representing impediments to further growth. Thus, freedom from psychopathology appears to be a condition enhancing the transition to postconformist levels of ego development, perhaps because it leaves the person free to process his or her experience more or less unconstrained by pathology or by psychological defenses (see Block, 1982).

At the context or experience level the effective condition enabling the transition to the postconformist stage of development is participation in preacademic or academic education. Education, of course, can mean a variety of things. At the very least, it may point toward a moratorium suspending the need to work for a livelihood and thus to submit to a variety of constraining factors. Erikson (1959, 1968, 1975) made use of a similar construct to account for the process of identity formation in adolescence—yet another type of process toward maturity. But beyond the moratorium freeing the person from external constraints to growth, education represents a positive experience in itself. As such, it may refer to the cognitive activation of logical mathematical processes, as in the case of the attainment of formal operations (Piaget, 1970/1972).

Moreover, it may refer to the activation of understanding through vicarious experience of life problems that are represented in cultural forms offered to the attention of students at higher levels of education. The implicit or explicit hermeneutic experience may be conducive to forms of maturity represented by the postconformist levels of ego development.

Thus, whereas attainment of the intermediate, modal levels of ego development seems to benefit mainly from the social–cognitive qualifications that are basic to social interactions and from the absence of constraints on interpersonal communication imposed by behavior problems (externalizing symptoms), ego maturity is positively enhanced by experiences that give rise to reflection inasmuch as the attainment of reflexivity remains unhampered by internalizing processes or pathologies that may interfere with it. Education, in this perspective, asserts its function as a device driving both ontogenetic development and social evolution (Edelstein, 1983, 1999). "By calling on individuals to assimilate and appropriate a given symbolic order—a set of cognitive symbols or operators—the challenge to decenter is institutionalized as a cultural opportunity" (p. 7). Thus, perhaps more are chosen than we might expect on the basis of the internal developmental process alone.

ENDNOTES

[1]Note at his point that previous versions of the scoring manual of the WUSCT used I-level and Delta codes and distinguished between full stages and transitional levels. The current version of the scoring manual, however, uses E-level codes and does not distinguish between full stages and transitions (Hy & Loevinger, 1996). In this chapter the updated numeration system for ego-levels is used.

REFERENCES

Achenbach, T. M. (1995). Developmental issues in assessment, taxonomy, and diagnosis of child and adolescent psychopathology. In D. Cicchetti & D. J. Cohen (Eds.), *Developmental psychopathology* (pp. 57–80). New York: Wiley.

Adams, G. R., & Fitch, S. A. (1983). Psychological environments of university departments: Effects on college students' identity status and ego stage development. *Journal of Personality and Social Psychology, 44,* 1266–1275.

Berkowitz, M., & Keller, M. (1994). Transitional processes in social cognitive development: A longitudinal study. *International Journal of Behavioral Development, 17,* 447–467.

Berry, J. W., & Dasen, P. R. (Eds.). (1974). *Culture and cognition: Readings in cross-cultural psychology.* London: Methuen.

Bjorklund, D. F. (1997). The role of immaturity in human development. *Psychological Bulletin, 122,* 153–169.

Bjorklund, D. F., & Green, B. L. (1992). The adaptive nature of cognitive immaturity. *American Psychologist, 52,* 46–54.

Björnsson, S., Edelstein, W., & Kreppner, K. (1977). Explorations in social inequality: Stratification dynamics in social and individual development in Iceland. *Studien und Berichte, 38.* Berlin Germany: Max-Planck-Institut für Bildungsforschung.

Blasi, A. (1983). Moral cognition and moral action: A theoretical perspective. *Developmental Review, 3,* 178–210.

Blasi, A. (1984). Moral identity: Its role in moral functioning. In W. M. Kurtines & J. L. Gewirtz (Eds.), *Morality, moral behavior, and moral development* (pp. 128–139). New York: Wiley.

Blasi, A. (1995). Moral understanding and the moral personality: The process of moral integration. In W. M. Kurtines & J. L. Gewirtz (Eds.), *Moral development: An introduction* (pp. 229–253). Boston: Allyn & Bacon.

Block, J. (1982). Assimilation, accommodation, and the dynamics of personality development. *Child Development, 53,* 281–295.

Chapman, M. (1988). *Constructive evolution: Origins and development of Piaget's thought.* Cambridge, England: Cambridge University Press.

Cohn, L. E. (1998). Age trends in personality development: A quantitative review. In P. M. Westenberg, A. Blasi & L. D. Cohn (Eds.), *Personality development* (pp. 133–143). Mahwah, NJ: Erlbaum.

Colby, A., & Kohlberg, L. (1987). *The measurement of moral judgment* (Vol. 1). Cambridge, England: Cambridge University Press.

Colby, A., Kohlberg, L., Gibbs, J., & Lieberman, M. (1983). A longitudinal study of moral judgment. *Monographs of the Society for Research in Child Development, 48*(1–2, Serial No. 200).

Commons, M. L., Richards, F. A., & Armon, C. (Eds.). (1984). *Beyond formal operations.* New York: Praeger.

Dewey, J. (1916/1944). *Democracy and education,* New York: The Free Press.

Dewey, J. (1938/1963). *Experience and education.* New York: Collier.

Dasen, P. (Ed.) (1977). *Piagetian psychology: Cross-cultural contributions.* New York: Gardner.

Dubow, E. F., Huesmann, L. R., & Eron, L. D. (1987). Childhood correlates of adult ego development. *Child Development, 58,* 859–869.

Edelstein, W. (1983). Cultural constraints on development and the vicissitudes of progress. In F. S. Kessel & A. W. Siegel (Eds.), *The child and other cultural inventions* (pp. 48–81). New York: Praeger.

Edelstein, W. (1996) The social construction of cognitive development. In G. Noam & K. Fischer (Eds.), *Development and vulnerability in close relationships* (pp. 91–112). Mahwah, NJ: Lawrence Erlbaum Associates.

Edelstein, W. (1999). The cognitive context of historical change: Assimilation, accommodation, and the segmentation of competence. In E. Turiel (Ed.), *Developmental and cultural change: reciprocal processes* (pp. 5–17). San Francisco: Jossey-Bass.

Edelstein, W. (2001). Kognitive Entwicklung, Sozialisation und die Entstehung individueller Differenzen [Cognitive development, socialization, and the emergence of individual differences]. In S. Hoppe-Graff & A. Rümmele (Eds.), *Entwicklung als Strukturgenese* (pp. 305–333). Hamburg, Germany: Verlag Dr. Kovac Publishers.

Edelstein, W., Keller, M., & Schröder, E. (1990). Child development and social structure: A longitudinal study of individual differences. In P. B. Baltes, D. L.

Featherman, & R. M. Lerner (Eds.), *Life-span development and behavior* (pp. 152–185). Hillsdale, NJ: Lawrence Erlbaum Associates.

Edelstein, W., & Noam, G. (1982). Regulatory structures of the self and "postformal" stages in adulthood. *Human Development, 25*, 407–422.

Erikson, E. H. (1959). Identity and the life cycle. *Psychological Issues* Vol. 1, No. 1, 1–171.

Erikson, E. H. (1968). *Identity, youth and crisis.* New York: Norton.

Erikson, E. H. (1975). *Life history and the historical moment.* New York: Norton.

Gibbs, J. C. (1979). Kohlberg's moral stage theory: A Piagetian review. *Human Development, 22*, 89–112.

Haan, N., Aerts, E., & Cooper, B. A. (1985). *On moral grounds.* New York: New York University Press.

Haan, N., Weiss, R., & Johnson, V. (1982). The role of logic in moral reasoning and development. *Developmental Psychology, 18*, 245–256.

Habermas, J. (1983). *Moralbewusstsein und kommunikatives Handeln* [Moral consciousness and communicative action]. Frankfurt am Main: Suhrkamp.

Habermas, J. (1990). Justice and solidarity: On the discussion concerning Stage 6. In T. Wren (Ed.), *The moral domain* (pp. 224–254). Cambridge, MA: The MIT Press.

Hauser, S. T. (1976). Loevinger's model of ego development: A critical review. *Psychological Bulletin, 83*, 928–955.

Hauser, S. T. (1993). Loevinger's model and measure of ego development: A critical review II. *Psychological Inquiry, 4*, 23–30.

Holt, R. R. (1980). Loevinger's measure of ego development: Reliability and national norms for male and female short forms. *Journal of Personality and Social Psychology, 39*, 909–920.

Hy, L. X., & Loevinger, J. (1996). *Measuring ego development.* Mahwah, NJ: Lawrence Erlbaum Associates.

Inhelder, B., & Piaget, J. (1958). *The growth of logical thinking from childhood to adolescence.* New York: Basic Books. (Original work published 1955)

Inhelder, B., & Piaget, J. (1971). Closing remarks. In D. R. Green, M. P. Ford, & G. B. Flamer (Eds.), *Measurement and Piaget* (pp. 210–213). New York: McGraw-Hill.

John, O. P., Pals, J. L., & Westenberg, P. M. (1998). Personality prototypes and ego development: Conceptual similarities and relations in adult women. *Journal of Personality and Social Psychology, 74*, 1093–1108.

Habermas, J. (1991). *Erläuterungen zur Diskursethik [Remarks on discourse ethics].* Frankfurt/Main: Suhrkamp.

Keller, M., & Edelstein, W. (1991). The development of socio-moral meaning making: Domains, categories, and perspective-taking. In W. M. Kurtines & J. L. Gewirtz (Eds.), *Handbook of moral behavior and development* (Vol. 2), (pp. 89–114). Hillsdale, NJ: Lawrence Erlbaum Associates.

Kohlberg, L. (1976). Moral stages and moralization: The cognitive–developmental approach. In T. Lickona (Ed.), *Moral development and behavior* (pp. 31–53). New York: Holt, Rinehart & Winston.

Kohlberg, L., & Higgins, A. (1987). School democracy and social interaction. In W. M. Kurtines & J. L. Gewirtz (Eds.), *Moral development through social interaction* (pp. 102–128). New York: Wiley.

Kohlberg, L., Levine, C., & Hewer, A. (1983). *Moral stages: A current formulation and a response to critics.* Basel, Switzerland: Karger.

Kohlberg, L., & Mayer, R. (1972). Development as the aim of education. *Harvard Educational Review, 42,* 449–496.

Kohn, M., & Rosman, B. L. (1972). A social competence scale and symptom checklist for the preschool child: Factor dimensions, their cross-instrument generality, and longitudinal persistence. *Developmental Psychology, 6,* 430–444.

Krettenauer, T., & Edelstein, W. (1999). From substages to moral types and beyond: An analysis of core criteria for morally autonomous judgments. *International Journal of Behavioral Development, 23,* 899–920.

Lee, L., & Snarey, J. (1988). The relationship between ego and moral development: A theoretical review and empirical analysis. In D. K. Lapsley & F. C. Power (Eds.), *Self, ego, and identity* (pp. 151–178). New York: Springer-Verlag.

Lempert, W. (1988). Soziobiographische Bedingungen der Entwicklung moralischer Urteilsfähigkeit [Socio-biographical conditions of the development of moral judgment]. *Kölner Zeitschrift für Soziologie und Sozialpsychologie, 40,* 62–93.

Loevinger, J. (1976). *Ego Development.* San Francisco: Jossey-Bass.

Loevinger, J. (1979). Construct validity of the Sentence Completion Test of ego development. *Applied Psychological Measurement, 3,* 281–311.

Loevinger, J. (1987). *Paradigms of personality.* New York: Freeman.

Loevinger, J., & Wessler, R. (1970). *Measuring ego development.* San Francisco: Jossey-Bass.

Manners, J., & Durkin, K. (2000). Processes involved in adult ego development: A conceptual framework. *Developmental Review 20,* 475–513.

Neimark, E. D. (1985). Moderators of competence: Challenges to the universality of Piagetian theory. In E. D. Neimark, R. De Lisi, & J. L. Newman (Eds.), *Moderators of competence* (pp. 1–14). Hillsdale, NJ: Lawrence Erlbaum Associates.

Nisan, M., & Kohlberg, L. (1982). Universality and cross-cultural variation in moral development: A longitudinal and cross-sectional study in Turkey. *Child Development, 53,* 865–876.

Noam, G. G., Chandler, M., & Lalonde, C. (1995). Clinical-developmental psychology: constructivism and social cognition in the study of psychological dysfunctions. In D. Cicchetti & D. Cohen (Eds.), *Developmental psychopathology: Vol. 1. Theory and methods* (pp. 424–464). New York: Wiley.

Noam, G. G., Hauser, S. T., Santostefano, S., Garisson, W., Jacobson, A. M., Powers, S. I., & Mead, M. (1984). Ego development and psychopathology: A study of hospitalized adolescents. *Child Development, 55,* 184–194.

Nowicki, S., & Strickland, B. R. (1973). A locus of control scale for children. *Journal of Consulting and Clinical Psychology, 40,* 148–154.

Piaget, J. (1971). *The psychology of intelligence.* London: Routledge & Kegan Paul.

Piaget, J. (1972). Intellectual evolution from adolescence to adulthood. *Human Development, 15,* 1–12. (Original work published 1970)

Piaget, J. (1975/1985). *Equilibration of cognitive structures.* Chicago: University of Chicago Press.

Piaget, J. (1985). *Equilibration of cognitive structures.* Chicago: University of Chicago Press.

Piaget, J. (1986). Essay on necessity. *Human Development, 29,* 301–314.

Piaget, J. (1998). *De la pédagogie* [On pedagogy]. Paris: Editions Odile Jacob.

Puka, B. (1990). The majesty and mystery of Kohlberg's Stage 6. In T. Wren (Ed.), *The moral domain* (pp. 182–223). Cambridge, England: Cambridge University Press.

Quay, H. C. (1977). Measuring dimension of deviant behavior: The Behavior Problem Checklist. *Journal of Abnormal Child Psychology, 5*, 227–287.

Radding, C. M. (1985). *A world made by men: Cognition and society, 400–1200.* Chapel Hill: University of North Carolina Press.

Schaefer, E. S. , & Aaronson, M. R. (1966). *Classroom Behavior Inventory: Preschool to primary.* Unpublished manuscript, University of North Carolina at Chapel Hill, School of Public Health.

Schröder, E. (1989). *Vom konkreten zum formalen Denken* [From concrete to formal reasoning]. Bern, Switzerland: Huber.

Shayer, M., Demetriou, A., & Pervez, M. (1988). The structure of scaling of concrete operational thought: Three studies in four countries. *Genetic, Social and General Psychological Monographs, 114*, 309–375.

Shweder, R. A., & Haidt, J. (1993). The future of moral psychology: Truth, intuition, and the pluralist way. *Psychological Science, 4*, 360–365.

Shweder, R. A., Mahapatra, M., & Miller, J. G. (1990). Culture and moral development. In J. W. Stigler, R. A. Shweder & G. Herdt (Eds.), *Cultural psychology* (pp. 130–204). Cambridge, England: Cambridge University Press.

Selman, R. L. (1980). *The growth of interpersonal understanding.* New York: Academic Press.

Snarey, J. (1985). Cross-cultural universality of social-moral development: A critical review of Kohlbergian research. *Psychological Bulletin, 97*, 202–232.

Snarey, J., & Keljo, K. (1991). In a Gemeinschaft voice: The cross-cultural expansion of moral development theory. In W. M. Kurtines & J. L. Gewirtz (Eds.), *Handbook of moral behavior and development* (Vol. 2, pp. 395–424). Hillsdale, NJ: Lawrence Erlbaum Associates.

Snyder, S. S., & Feldman, D. H. (1977). Internal and external influences on cognitive developmental change. *Child Development, 48*, 937–943.

Sullivan, E. V. (1977). A study of Kohlberg's structural theory of moral development: A critique of liberal social science ideology. *Human Development, 20*, 352–376.

Walker, L. J. (1980). Cognitive and perspective-taking prerequisites for moral development. *Child Development, 51*, 131–139.

11

Cultural Identity and Personal Identity: Philosophical Reflections on the Identity Discourse of Social Psychology

Thomas Wren
Loyola University Chicago

Carmen Mendoza
Trinity College, Deerfield IL

Personal identity, which was originally a purely philosophical concept and then a central theme for a wide variety of psychological subdisciplines, has now become a (if not the) major social and educational issue especially, but not exclusively, in culturally diverse societies such as the United States. Consider the following set of questions posed by two prominent critical multiculturalist theorists (Kincheloe & Steinbert, 1997):

> What is the effect of the corporate commodification of black culture? How does such commodification shape and reshape black students' identities? White students' identities? How do such corporate and media depictions reconfigure the struggle for social justice? What are the openings they create for positive resistance to oppression? How do teachers incorporate these issues into the curriculum and lived world of the classroom for positive effect? (p. 105)

In this chapter we do not directly address these problems because our concern is a second-order one of seeing how those who ask (and try to answer) such questions are using the word *identity* as a category of human experience. As the quote illustrates, there is a consensus among those who write on the subject that group identity is usually forged in a social and political context that includes—but is considerably broader than—classical anthropological notions of culture as a worldview or shared way of life. However, identity is also a matter of profound importance for the psychological development and well-being of individual agents. Identity theorists sometimes emphasize the social–cultural side of identity and sometimes the personal–psychological side, but they seldom distinguish between the two. And when they do, the distinction is often flawed, as we show by discussing certain developments in social psychology.

To set the stage for that discussion, we note that the seemingly obvious distinction between personal and group identity is much more complex than it first appears, as is the subdivision of the latter into social identity and cultural identity. Part of the complexity is the fact that each of these terms has a subjective sense as well as an objective one. For instance, anyone who looks at your passport can see, as an objective fact, that you have a certain citizenship and hence a certain official group identity. Because you are personally aware of this fact about yourself, it is reasonable to assume in the absence of contrary evidence that you are complicit in it (i.e., that you are prepared to identify yourself as a citizen of the nation mentioned on your passport). This self-identification is rooted in what some call a subjective fact—that is, your disposition to endorse, affirm, or (to use R. M. Hare's, 1951, well-known phrase) "prescribe for yourself" (p. 155–158) a specific affiliation with a certain group. Although it may seem like a chicken-and-egg sort of question to ask which of these two facts ultimately depends on the other, we share Augusto Blasi's (1991) view that the subjective one is conceptually primary. What makes specifically human groups interestingly different from biological organisms or simple aggregations, such as a pile of rocks, is the cognitive state of their members and, by extension, the recognition of that cognitive state by outsiders. In other words, a human group (qua human, of course; we do not mean psychosocially irrelevant categories such as "featherless bipeds") is constituted by the affiliative dispositions, thoughts, intentions, commitments, and so on, of its members and by the supervenient realization on the part of other persons that the group in question is so constituted. Following the model proposed by Frederick Barth (discussed below), we further suggest that the paradigm case of this sort of constitution is what he called the "boundary definition" of an ethnic group, whereby some people set themselves off from their neighbors for strategic reasons and, consequently, come to think of themselves as having a special way of life, a shared history, and other such commonalities—all of which add up to their group identity.

At this point one may wonder if two very different notions of group identity are not conflated, namely (a) the objective and public identity of the collective and (b) the subjective and relatively private awareness on the part of individuals that they are somehow affiliated with that collective. But our point is that the former sense is logically and psychologically derivative from the latter, at least when the collective in question is a socially distinctive human group. Accordingly, for the rest of this chapter we use the term *group identity* and its correlative terms *social identity* and *cultural identity* to denote the subjective fact that a person perceives himself or herself as a participating in a certain web of human relationships. Of course a person has other self-perceptions besides those having to do with groups, and we certainly do not suggest that the reference of the term *personal identity* is coextensive with the shared reference of the other three terms just mentioned. On the contrary, the main issue is the difference between the referential range of personal identity and that of group, social, and cultural identity.

Because much of what we say directly applies to multicultural education, we will often use the last of these three terms—cultural identity—to represent the first pole in the contrast of group and personal identity. But the very concept of identity has a long and rather untidy philosophical history that antedates its role in current discussions by multicultural educators, anthropologists, psychologists, and cultural studies scholars. For this reason, we begin with some general philosophical remarks about how people talk about personal identity, followed by a quick look at how this concept has been constructed in the literature of contemporary social psychology and related to concepts of cultural and other sorts of group identity. In doing so we bear in mind Blasi's recommendation to those who include philosophy in the course of doing their own psychological research, which also applies to philosophers tempted to tell psychologists how they should proceed. Calling into question the metatheoretical assumption by cognitive developmentalists such as Piaget and Kohlberg that a psychological account of the moral life could—and indeed should—be based on the deliverances of moral philosophy, Blasi (1990) argued that for psychologists the principal utility of philosophy consists in the rather indirect contribution it can make to psychology by "clarifying the meaning of ordinary language and of inspiring specific hypotheses" (p. 66). We remind readers that there are many ways to clarify meanings other than by conceptual analysis. This can be done by reflecting on etymological considerations and by tracing the way once novel philosophical ideas have eventually, for better or worse, become part of our everyday parlance. All of these approaches are especially useful when the language one is trying to clarify is discourse about selfhood and personal identity.

IDENTITY DISCOURSE

According to the antiessentialist view of personal identity—which is the prevailing view among contemporary social theorists as well as the perspective from which this chapter was written—there is no determinate, de facto "hidden self" that, like a jack-in-the-box, suddenly reveals itself when conditions are right. Identities are narratives, not things. Like other narratives, identities are fashioned in discourse and hence "in specific historical and institutional sites within specific discursive formations and practices, by specific enunciative strategies" (Hall, 1996, p. 4). However, there do seem to be general features of current identity discourse that constitute a rudimentary kind of natural logic without invoking essences that are "always already there" as fixtures of the universe. Philosophers and others interested in conceptual clarity can analyze this logic without resorting to the postmodern jargon deployed by those who, like Stuart Hall in the passage just cited, only want to critique and destabilize this discourse. For instance, when we say of a person that he or she has a certain identity, we are sometimes trying to give a psychological description (invoking the subjective facts just mentioned), but more often we are picking that person out of the general population and assigning him or her to some subpopulation such as the population of male teenagers or unemployed harpsichord players. And when we say the person has a certain cultural identity, we often mean to define the subpopulation in cultural terms, using that adjective narrowly and anthropologically (Inuits, Maori, Swedes, etc.) or broadly and sociologically (ethnic Americans, gays, the deaf, etc.). But, as already noted, sometimes we are trying to do something quite different. Instead of assigning the person to a certain population, we might be trying to say how he or she feels about the group in question. In simple terms, this sort of identification is an attempt to spell out the subjective relationship the person has with the group. What is important here is not membership per se, but endorsement, solidarity, affection, or some other mode of relational consciousness. The former sort of identification is a matter of demographics; the latter a matter of internalized affiliation.

Finally, just as groups can be identified without referring to their members, so also individuals can be identified without referring to the groups to which they happen to belong. At the simplest extreme, someone can just point at you while saying something like "That person over there" or, in direct address, "You there!" This is what some philosophers call an *indexical reference*, for the same reason that we call the digit used for pointing an *index finger*: Such expressions single things out by indicating their relation to the speaker. They are not based on generic categories that would have the same meaning no matter who uttered them. The three-word sentence "Socrates is dead" is true no matter who says it (unless it is Socrates, of course). But the truth value of those other three little words "I love you" depends utterly on who is talking (and to whom).

Indexical identifications have their place in the general discourse about individual identity but not a large place. Much more common are identifications that purport to describe how individuals are related to themselves, using terms taken from either folk psychology or more systematic theories of personality. In both cases, these psychological terms are themselves a mix of ordinary language and special theoretical categories. Accordingly, when we try to clarify their use we often find that etymological considerations have heuristic value. For instance, the word *identity* is derived from the Latin *idem* or "same." Thus, the second definition of *identity* in the *Oxford English Dictionary* is "the condition or fact of a person or thing being that specified unique person or thing." Like other dictionary definitions, this emphasizes the static, almost Parmenidean character of identity, declaring that the aforesaid condition or fact is "a continuous unchanging property." Hence, psychologists necessarily stretch the original meaning of the term *identity* when they speak of one's personal identity as developing or as something to be won, although of course semantic stretching is just the way living languages work. But although it would be priggish to accuse them of making a category mistake, there are better ways to define personal identity than Erik Erikson's (1968) famous statement that identity is the answer to the question "Who am I?" For instance, one might say that personal identity is that aspect of one's subjectivity that endures through time or at least *seems* to endure over time. Like Heraclitus' river, its permanence may well be a permanence of form rather than content, but what is important to identity theorists like Erikson as well as to ordinary people who ask the "Who am I?" question is the reassuring perception of sameness from one moment of their lived experience to the next. Similarly, people tend to think of themselves as having a cultural identity because they believe, rightly or wrongly, that certain features of their common life have remained the same over many generations.

However, not all psychologists who write about personality focus on subjectivity. Many personal identity theorists focus on objective, stable personality traits such as the disposition to use a single schema (self-concept) to think of one's supposedly essential self. In their theories neither the trait nor the schema is conceptualized as fluid or dynamic, even though these theorists al-

low that people do change their self-concepts and other self-ascribed properties, especially those markedly discrepant with the views other people have of
them. In marked contrast to trait-based theories of identity as well as to
psychodynamic models, the research of object relations theorists such as
Nancy Chodorow (1978) moved the focus of identity formation research away
from the individual's self-concept to social structures of domination that are
understood in the context of feminism, gay studies, racial consciousness, and
other multicultural issues. The discourse generated by this way theorizing
about personal identity has called into question the essentialist language that
seemed so natural in earlier theories that regarded identity as a stable and stabi-
lizing property of the self. However, this difference is due not to an alternative
definition of personal identity but rather to certain fundamental revisions in the
notion of what it means to be a self.

THE UNSUBSTANTIAL SELF (PERSON):
THE PHILOSOPHICAL STORY

Regardless of what one might think about the complex philosophical debates
over methodological individualism (e.g., whether concepts of collectives are
anything more than the sum of features found in the concepts of their individual members), it seems difficult if not impossible to discuss the concept of
identity without eventually invoking the terms self and *person*.[1] However,
identity, self and *person* are separate albeit related concepts, and they have separate albeit intertwined histories, the first of which we just considered. We now
turn to the second.

   Here again etymologies have heuristic value. As just noted, the term *identity* is derived from the Latin word for *same*. In contrast, *person* is derived from
the Latin word for something that is eminently changeable, a theatrical mask
(persona). Etymologists speculate that the latter term was coined by the
Romans because they knew that in the large amphitheaters of ancient Greece
the actors' lines were sounded through—*per + sona*—little megaphones that
were part of the outsized masks they wore as part of the dramatic spectacle.
Whether or not this explanation is historically accurate, the fact remains that a
mask is a mask, something to be put on and taken off, an impermanent thing
that derives its intelligibility from its role as representing something besides itself. Indeed, a mask need not even be a thing in the sense of a solid substance,
as can be seen in sentences such as "His courtesy was a mask for his villainous
intentions." In this usage, the word *mask* is like *dance* or *song*, which refer to
actions that can be verbalized as nouns but are not thereby converted into real
things, essences, or pieces of furniture in the universe. Unfortunately for our

discussion, we have no expression such as "He has been personing all day," although we do use *impersonating* as a verb.

The theme of nonsubstantiality is also found in the etymology of the word *self*, although here as before we must remember that such considerations are only heuristic devices, not philosophical arguments or historical evidence for drawing conclusions about the world. The origins of *self* and its various European cognates are unknown, but their earliest known uses have to do with strength and weakness, depending on the inflection. Thus, the Old English word *self* meant "strong," and *selfa* meant "weak." It was used to emphasize a pronoun, such as in "She did it herself," and a bit later to suggest the idea of something being one's "own" or, more oddly still, the idea of something being "peculiar." However, in Middle English it took on the reflexive use it still has today, which led to the modern substantival use of *self* as an inner reality or essence, roughly equivalent to the Platonic–Christian notion of an immaterial soul.

What do these etymological considerations suggest beyond the bare-bones proposition that the self is not a substance or entity? If we go back to the image of the actor's mask, we notice that the point of wearing a mask is to communicate. We also notice that masks are used to perform and that the various meanings that an actor's mask takes on in the course of a dramatic performance are all fundamentally relational. In a word, it would make no sense to wear a mask unless one were in a social situation.

In Western philosophy[2] the substantial self first appeared as a distinct theme at the beginning of the so-called modern era, when Descartes (1641/1986) uttered his famous *Cogito ergo sum.* For him, to say "I think" was to say "I am" right on the spot, because he thought that each person "is in the strict sense [*sensus stricto*] only a thing that thinks" (p. 18). In such passages Descartes was doing much more than merely emphasizing the cognitive dimension of human life: he was claiming that our life simply is our thought. To say we are thinking about things is (in Descartes' "strict sense") to define our essence. Furthermore, the thinking activity Descartes had in mind is utterly solitary. The Cartesian self—that is, the thing that thinks—is a substance that has no access to reality other than through its own mental representations (ideas), which it nonetheless hopes mirror that reality. The hope is warranted, Descartes claimed, by a line of reasoning that begins with the *Cogito* and involves his famous thought experiments of an Evil Genius, our innate idea of God, and so on. Whatever one might think of the logical quality of his much-criticized argument, it was an astonishingly bold attempt to demonstrate the existence (or better, the conceivability of such an existence) of an inherently asocial entity at the core of human consciousness.

Descartes' idea of the self as an immaterial substance set the agenda for the next 3 centuries of philosophical debate about how individuals come to have knowledge about the world and, correlatively, knowledge about themselves. Throughout this long debate the image of an isolated knower has remained intact despite spirited dissent from Descartes' original view of the self's knowability (Locke), its immateriality (Berkeley and Hume), or its logical status (Kant). As the 21st century begins, few personality theorists are willing to be characterized as having a Cartesian conception of the self, but many feel compelled to recall it to clarify their own positions. Some differentiate their views by stressing the embodied character of the self, but most of today's writers about the self stress its social character. Virtually every contributor to the contemporary literature on social or cultural identity subscribes to the view that personal identity is socially constructed.

But what does this mean? This, we note in passing, is the sort of question that Blasi (1990) had in mind when he claimed that philosophy's main contribution to psychological inquiry consists in clarifying the meaning of ordinary language and occasionally inspiring specific hypotheses. To answer it, we propose that the specific hypothesis that selves are socially constructed operates in at least three general modalities of discourse. The first modality is discourse about how our identities are shaped. Nearly everyone, scholar or person in the street, recognizes that he or she would have been a much different person if the circumstances of birth, childhood, economics, and other social conditions had been different. The assumption here is that our psychological states and structures are formed in the course of social interaction. We should note that theorists who make this assumption usually supplement it with another one to the effect that we were not totally passive in the formative process—namely, that it was indeed an interaction.

This commonsense view is at least prima facie compatible with a Cartesian conception of self, because it is logically possible that social influences on our thought and behavior are completely external to the self—for example, when long exposure to the sun's light changes the color of an old painting or even that of our own skin. But there is no such compatibility when the discourse moves to the second modality, which concerns not how we think and behave but how our very capacities to think and behave have been shaped by our social world. Examples of such discourse are certain feminist arguments to the effect that our sexual capacities are themselves socially constructed, along with the gender-specific stereotypes that have influenced the way we exercise those capacities. The philosophers David Bakhurst and Christine Sypnowich (1995) made the same point, concluding that "in all these arguments, the social serves, not to mold an antecedently present self or identity, but to bring that self into existence" (p. 6).

The third modality of discourse about the self is still further removed from the Cartesian view. Here the issue is not how the capacities of the self are shaped by social interactions but rather how the very conception of selfhood emerges from such interaction. To say "the conception of selfhood" may be a bit misleading, because this rather high-sounding phrase suggests the sort of discourse that takes place at philosophy conferences or in the faculty lounge of a university psychology department, but we have more everyday contexts in mind. However, in many (most?) cultures there is a continuity between technical and lay discourse about the self, and there usually is a mutuality between them, as ethnolinguists have shown (see Shweder, 1991; Shweder & LeVine, 1984). For instance, a Western man need not have read Freud to think of his sexuality in terms of drives, energy, pressures, and so on. And a woman from India need not have an academic degree to think of her sexuality in the way charted by the Hindu scriptures and transmitted through her culture. We speak here of culture rather than social interaction (Mead, 1934) to avoid giving the impression that basic concepts like selfhood emerge from one-on-one exchanges such as a conversation between friends or even from the more intimate relationships between children and parents. Such exchanges can be important, but they are themselves conditioned by the larger cultural reality. Furthermore, it is hard not to think of social interaction episodically, as a sequence of discrete events, whereas culturation is a continuous process.

There is much more to be said about the social construction of the self, but we cannot pursue this theme here (but see Gergen, 1999; Hacking, 1999; Harré, 1984). Before we move on, however, two philosophical qualifications are in order. The first is simply that social constructions should not be thought of as arbitrary decisions. There are many constraints, some imposed by history and economics and some by psychology and biology. For instance, cognitive psychologists say that the child's tendency to sort social reality in terms of perceptual cues (e. g., skin color) is hardwired, although functional and other sorts of categories can be made more salient by appropriate childrearing practices, especially those involving language acquisition (Hirschfeld, 1996, pp. 135–140).

The second qualification is equally general. Personality theorists who prefer the social constructivist perspective over essentialism must be careful not to oversimplify the opposition between these two philosophical alternatives to avoid making the rather embarrassing mistake of essentializing social constructivism (Fuss, 1989, showed how easy it is to make this mistake). Here as elsewhere in moral psychology we should recall another caution by Blasi (1990, p. 67), namely, that there is no single voice telling social scientists how to do their empirical research. Of the many thinkers who insist on the social character of the self, some are much closer to the essentialist view than others. If essentialism can be described as the general belief that there is a certain way that things are, then philosophers like Alasdair MacIntyre or philosophically oriented psychologists like Lev Vygotsky would have to be counted as essentialists despite their sensitivity to the social, historically conditioned, and generally elusive quality of the self. Their accounts of the social formation of the self were offered in an attempt to tell their readers how things are, which means that they tried to give readers an insight into what, thanks to centuries of Aristotelian essentialism, is now routinely called *human nature.* In contrast, other theorists called into question the very reality of the self; hence, they can hardly claim to have uncovered a human or any other sort of nature. Instead they dismissed all essentialist views, treating those about the self as conceptual artifacts of the modern age that began with Descartes—which of course is why it has become fashionable to call these theorists postmodernists. A large part of their discussion of the self and cultural identity consists in attempts to decons- truct these notions by showing that the discourse which uses these terms is his- torically conditioned in every respect and that the modernists' homespun, seemingly natural metaphysical ambition (i.e., to discover how things are) is itself a delusion. This is the central tenet of the postmodernist theories of iden- tity proposed by the social philosopher Michel Foucault, the feminist thinker Judith Butler, and others who have had such an impact on the politics of cul- tural identity. Bakhurst and Sypnowich (1995) summarized the postmodernists' position quite nicely. For such writers, "the self is a fiction of modernity, constructed by discourses such as metaphysical philosophy and psychotherapy and many of the practices of everyday life. As such, selves have no nature or essence, they are not parts of the furniture of the world; they are discursive effects, products of our forms of representation" (p. 8). So put, this is a very extreme position, but it becomes plausible if it is qualified by the nor- mative claim that some of these so-called discursive effects are better than oth- ers, not because they articulate an unchanging mysterious inner self but because they capture more of the rhythms and nuances of consciousness. This, we attempt to show in the following pages, is the sense in which our selves are "always already there."

First, a few analytical notes on the meaning of the umbrella term *cultural identity*[3] are in order. The umbrella is not only wide but elastic. In ordinary English usage, cultural identity refers equally well to a property of an individ- ual person (my cultural identity) or a property of a group (the identity of our culture). It can be used in a positive sense to indicate ethnic pride or in a nega- tive sense to denote the crudest sort of ethnocentrism. And, like the term *multi- culturalism*, it is associated with a wide variety of often-conflicting social and theoretical positions. In political contexts, it suggests identity politics and even antiliberalism or at least what political theorists now call communitarianism. In clinical and other psychological contexts, cultural identity is thought of either as a relatively high level of self-actualization or, at the other extreme, as a rather regrettable stage of conformism that is just a little better than indoctrination and brainwashing. Outside the relatively narrow subdiscipline of experimental social psychology, psychologists divide on whether cultural identity enhances or competes with personal agency, as well as whether it is something one has or something one does—in short, whether it is inside, outside, or the same as one's self. Social scientists and philosophers find still other issues connected to the concept of cultural identity, such as whether groups determine individual consciousness or vice versa and whether selves and groups are stable entities or whether they are like Heraclites' river, so fluid that one can only name them but never truly know or possess them.

However, despite this diversity there are commonalities, and even orthodoxies, in the literature of modern social psychology, especially that published in the United States. Cultural identity is nearly always discussed oppositionally: It is a figure that takes its shape when contrasted with the conceptual background and social horizon of cultural assimilation. More specifically, it is those who would resist the rhetoric and social practice of assimilation who wind up talking about cultural identity; when assimilationists speak of cultural identity they only do so to characterize their opponents' position. This tendency is also found in discourse that on the surface seems purely factual rather than persuasive, such as classical ethnography and the heavily quantitative discourse of mainstream social science in North America and Britain.

CULTURAL IDENTITY:
THE SOCIAL PSYCHOLOGY STORY

In modern social psychology, especially in personality theory, the orthodox discourse treats personal identity as an epiphenomenon of social identity and an amalgam of self-concept and self-esteem. This social scientific construction has grown out of a more general discussion in 20th century social theory concerning how individuals are related to groups.[4] The latter theme can be traced back to the grand speculations of Emile Durkheim and Max Weber and, through them, to Rousseau and Kant, but took its present direction at the end of the Depression, when what is now called social psychology began to take on the more technical, experimental character it would later exhibit on so many fronts. Over the next few years emigré scholars in the United States such as Theodor Adorno and Kurt

Lewin conducted and inspired new research on the relation between personality and society, which was subsequently gathered up in Talcott Parsons' (1951) short-lived synthesis of the social and behavioral sciences.

The most important early figure in this discussion was probably Lewin, who is often considered the father of American social psychology. In 1941 (also see Lewin, 1948) he explained what he considered Jewish self-hatred—a matter of personal identity—as the product of the way Jews constructed their social identity. That is, they identified with the more powerful people who persecuted them and, as a consequence, directed their hostility toward themselves rather than toward their oppressors. A few years later, Kenneth and Mamie Clark (1947; also see their earlier studies in K. Clark & M. Clark, 1939, 1940) used the same sort of from-social-to-personal explanation for their famous experiments with Black children who disliked dolls most like themselves, preferring instead dolls with lighter skin color and other mainstream (i.e., White) features. About the same time, a similar account was given by S. W. Fernberger (1948) of women who internalized negative gender stereotypes. This way of understanding low self-esteem continued well into the 1970s (see Brody, 1964; Herzberg, 1977; Kardiner & Ovesey, 1951; Lynne, 1959). Of course there were variations on the basic theme: As time went on many social psychologists based their theories of personality (and their research methodologies) not on Lewin's quasimathematical field theory of cognition and emotion, which by 1960 or so had fallen out of favor, but on the more cognitive looking glass theory introduced much earlier by Charles Horton Cooley (1902/1964), according to which one's self-concept is directly and entirely a reflection of images of oneself picked up from significant others and from society at large.

Such identifications and reflections are undoubtedly important factors in the construction of one's self-concept, especially its evaluative dimension (self-esteem). Furthermore, variants of the looking glass theory of the self (e.g., Goffman, 1959; G. H. Mead, 1934) provided alternatives to substantival notions of the self that had dominated formal and informal personality theory since Descartes. But these alternatives, like the classical substantival notions of the self, were static and, when applied to issues of cultural identity, had their own problems, owing to their failure to appreciate the limitations of their underlying philosophical perspectives.

PERSONAL IDENTITY VERSUS
REFERENCE GROUP ORIENTATION

The first alternative we consider, which is probably more familiar to multicultural educational theorists than to mainstream psychologists, is found in William Cross' (1985, 1991) studies of Black identity. Uneasy with the crude social constructionist epistemology assumed by theories of identity developed in Lewin's wake, Cross looked more closely at the tests and constructs that had been used to tap into the self-concepts of Black children. Since Lewin's time, most of the work carried on under this general rubric had made no significant distinction between the affective construct of *self-esteem* (roughly speaking, how one feels about oneself) and its cognitive counterpart, which for Cross was *self-concept* in the narrow sense of the term (roughly speaking, how one thinks about oneself). Furthermore, despite the presence of the word *self* in their labels, each of these two secondary constructs was used to refer to what one feels or thinks (or thinks one feels) about one's group as well as about one's self. It was for this reason that postwar psychologists such as Lewin (1948) had treated group self-hatred and individual self-hatred as though they were a single variable. Cross' sad discovery was that 50 years later such confusions still lingered on in the literature and practice of psychology and multicultural education.

After reviewing 161 studies on Black identity, he (Cross, 1985) tried to sort out this confusion by breaking the notoriously vague construct of self-concept (SC) that was generally accepted in American social psychology into two component constructs or independent variables. These were personal identity (PI) and reference group orientation (RGO). Crudely put, SC = PI + RGO. His review of the technical literature on Black identity involved the usual psychometric apparatus of American social psychology (null hypotheses, chi-squares and correlations, statistical significance, etc.), but we need not go into such matters here. It is only necessary to understand that Cross was looking at a wide variety of studies, some of which tested for self-esteem, some for self-confidence, and so on. He called these studies of personal identity. In contrast, studies that tested for racial attitudes, degree of identification with a group, and so on were gathered under the rubric of reference group orientation studies.

At this point Cross made a move similar to that found in the literature of intelligence testing. He tried to extrapolate from factor analysis and other purely statistical findings a psychological theory about what was really going on inside the heads of the people who had taken the various personality tests he reviewed. To do this he examined not the responses of the testees but rather the tests themselves. Cross concluded that the various PI studies shared the assumptions that PI is something real (in the same way that IQ was considered real), that it could be measured by instruments purporting to tap into certain universal (here read "natural") human tendencies, traits, or behaviors, and that cultural differences—understood by Cross in a broad sense that included dif-

ferences in race, ethnicity, and gender as well as in traditions and symbol systems—should therefore be excluded from the criteria used to assess PI. He also
claimed that the RGO studies shared the opposite assumption, namely, that instruments used to measure what he called group identity necessarily refer to
cultural differences (which are usually specifically racial differences) such as
the colors of the different dolls, but that group identity is just as real as PI.[5]

Cross himself apparently shared both of these assumptions, while insisting
that because of the basic difference in their modes of assessment, whatever
correlations might obtain between a person's (self-ascribed) group identity
and his or her (directly experienced) PI are purely contingent relationships. To
him these two sorts of identity were distinct modules, having no semantic or
conceptual associations, entailment relationships, or any other sort of internal
connection with each other. For this reason Cross rejected the "long held
Lewinian hypothesis" (Cross, 1985, p. 170) that RGO necessarily predicts PI.

Like Cross, we consider the Lewinian hypothesis untenable, but we regard
his reasoning as somewhat simplistic. In particular, Cross failed to appreciate
that personal and cultural identities are both shaped by the way people talk and
that as social circumstances change so does the discourse within which these
two sorts of identity are fashioned.[6] To be sure, there is no preestablished harmony between the emergence of personal and cultural identity. The hardships
of minority membership, which of course include much more than sheer economic privation, can produce strong egos as well as damaged ones. Memories,
autobiographies, and other accounts of growing up Black (or Chicano, Jewish,
or other) are full of anecdotes about warm and nurturing child-rearing practices, whose natural outcome would seem to be intact egos. Such anecdotal evidence supports Cross' own belief that Blacks can and often do have high PI,
regardless of whether they think about their reference group in positive or negative terms or indeed in any terms at all. However, although public perceptions
(by insiders or outsiders) of how members of a racial group affiliate do not necessarily reflect the individual attitudes of those members, it does not follow
that public perceptions and individual attitudes develop independently or can
be understood apart from each other. On the contrary, as Hirschfeld (1996)
noted, "the psychological processes that apply to social categories cannot be
fully understood outside the cultural frame of reference in which the categories
are embedded" (p. 26).

GOING BEYOND CROSS'S CONSTRUCTS

Over the last few years social psychology (unlike most multicultural education
theory) has finally begun to recognize the difference between personal and

group identity, although it has yet to come to grips with the possibility that both of these concepts may themselves be culture specific (see D. Hoffman, 1998). For instance, the Dutch psychologist Verkuyten (1995) wrote: "Most recent studies using well-established scales and adequate control groups have shown no relationship between ethnicity and global personal self-esteem among youth in different Western countries. ... Empirical research in general does not support the assumption that Afro-Americans have lower self-esteem" (p. 156). However, empirical research continues to operate on the assumption that these constructs (i.e., ethnicity and a global personal self-esteem), as well as the several subordinate constructs that Cross considered, are either natural categories or at least indispensable heuristic devices for uncovering relationships that are "always already there" in the social world. Consider Cross' (1985) concluding assertion that "Blacks have had, and continue to have, a multifaceted reference group orientation such that black and white anchor points may determine behavior depending upon the situation being confronted. The Black Movement probably increased the number of black anchor points in a person's world view"[7] (p. 170). This assertion may seem quite reasonable to many readers, especially those dissatisfied with the sometimes excessive claims by proponents of identity politics. After all, it is easy to agree that cultural identities and other sorts of group orientation are not monolithic, and they do not determine action in abstraction from concrete situations. There is, for instance, no one right way to be Black or White. But this way of thinking about cultural identity seems reasonable only because, like Cross and other social psychologists, most of us are all too willing to continue thinking of social groups and their psychological correlates (group identities) as entities. We only require that large conceptual monoliths be broken down into smaller ones, miniliths as it were, in rough analogy to the way capitalist governments have tried to dissolve large monopolies such as Standard Oil, AT&T, Microsoft, and other huge organizations. The point of this business analogy is that such dissolution is diversification (surface reform) not deconstruction (radical revision), because at the end we still have autonomous corporations. Similarly, Cross' multifaceted theorizing about group identity simply replaces a general RGO with several more specific orientations, which are the relations a person has to several groups simultaneously albeit not in the same respects. And each of these several specific groups is just as reified as the general one.

A simple logical point may help us appreciate why social groups should not be reified— especially those social groups variously referred to as cultures, races, and ethnics or (to speak more carefully) as cultural, racial, and ethnic groups. As the term itself indicates, a *group* is not only a plurality but a *grouped* plurality, in the sense that certain items have been singled out and designated as members of the group in question. Thus, the abstract notion of a group is not quite the same as the mathematician's notion of a set (although the two notions can coincide), because a set is not a delimited collection—at least, not by its very definition. The set of all sets would not be a group, nor would the universe (using the term in the widest possible sense). Furthermore, when a group is a distinctly human group, it is normally thought of in a special way. It not only comprises human beings the way a herd of cows contains cows but also, and much more important, the very grouping of the group is a cognitive act (some philosophers would rather say a propositional attitude) carried out by the group members themselves. That is, a city, tribe, community, and so on is a group—considered both generically and in particular (i.e., this city, this tribe, etc.)—because its members recognize themselves as such. Thus, the concept of a human group is reflexive.

To this conceptual point we add the commonsense observation that the reflexivity in question admits of degrees. A nursery of wailing newborns would be a minimally human group not because the babies are minimally human (whatever that might mean) but because their awareness of the group is utterly nonverbal even though they are rudimentarily aware of each other's existence and of their common situation. It is a well-documented fact that newborn babies cry empathically, such that a misplaced diaper pin in one baby triggers a collective empathic crying that is noticeably different from simple distress crying (see M. Hoffman, 1976). But no diaper pin has ever triggered a discussion among the babies themselves of their shared plight at the hands of clumsy nurses or led them to label themselves as, say, "we newborns." Preschoolers, another minimally reflexive group, do not abandon their solitary play to discuss their common status as children of working mothers, prospective kindergartners, and so on. Even so, it is a truism in popular as well as scholarly discussions of social groups and group identities (see Barth, 1969, 1994) that the most important part of what makes an assemblage of human beings a group is their shared perception of themselves as a collective that is numerically different from other collectives (expressed indexically as "We are not they") and also qualitatively different, at least in most cases. Note that when this last feature is absent individuals tend to construct such differences for themselves, with the eventual result that the group does in fact take on qualities that differentiate it from other groups.

IDENTITY AS A DEVELOPING PROCESS

There are many ways to think of one's own identity, just as there are many ways to theorize about the concept of PI itself. Although it would be simplistic to assert that identity theorists recapitulate their own developmental histories in the psychological models they construct for identity formulation—which would be a very implausible reformulation of the maxim that ontogeny recapitulates phylogeny—rough parallels do exist between the theoretical order and what Blasi (1988, 1993), following Jane Loevinger (1976, 1979), called "identity modes." These are increasingly adequate ways of integrating one's subjectivity or, as Blasi (1993) said, ways of establishing for oneself "a basic unity by constructing the meanings that one gives to oneself, other people, and the surrounding world" (p. 103). Much of Blasi's empirical work charts four advanced modes, the first of which supposedly begins in midadolescence:

1. Social-role identity.
2. Identity observed.
3. Management of identity.
4. Identity as authenticity.

In each case some form of sameness is at stake, which as we already noted is the etymological root of the very term *identity*.

Theories of cultural identity like Lewin's, which confound PI and RGO constructs, correspond to the first of these identity modes, in which the subject's sense of self is determined and stabilized by the way he or she is usually regarded by others (individuals or representatives of groups). Theories that stress the difference between PI and RGO, such as those developed by Cross and Verkuyten, correspond to the second identity mode, in which one's inner (true) self is contrasted with the external self that others see. In this mode, the inner self is the true one because it is always the same: unchanging, real, and given. "One discovers an inner quasi-substance" (Blasi, 1993, p. 104). Social constructionist theories of the self, such as those of Gordon Allport (1954) and Kenneth Gergen (1999), correspond to the third identity mode, in which the subject understands his or her identity as something to be worked out rather than as something to be discovered. This working out is accomplished by defining and committing oneself to an enduring set of ideals and goals—a philosophy of life—that will stay the same across often greatly different situations and regardless of pressures from external agents, including those representing the interests of one's cultural group. Finally, corresponding to the fourth identity mode are theories that deconstruct the notion of self such that *personal authenticity* is defined as the acceptance of internal conflicts, dichotomous self-images, competing group loyalties, and other sorts of fluidity and ambiguity.

Although we are reluctant to make too much of the parallel between the four ways in which identity is experienced and Blasi's four ways of theorizing about it, we are struck by the relatively incoherent nature of theories that attempt to understand the fourth identity mode. Furthermore, although we have reservations about much of the postmodernist orthdoxy according to which cultural identity is hopelessly unstable, an ever-shifting amalgam of self-identifications, interpersonal relationships, moral values, and personal styles, we wonder if this incoherence does not often reflect the difficulty all of us, even personality theorists, have in tolerating our own inner ambiguities. This incoherence is especially evident in discussions of identity issues in the lives of bicultural persons, typically the adult children of immigrant parents. For this reason, we suspect that this relatively small and seemingly atypical group may actually be a paradigm for Blasi's fourth identity mode.

Interviews of 40 such subjects conducted by one of the authors of this chapter (Mendoza, 2002) revealed that the sense of identity in these adults resulted from a process first characterized by persistent shifting between their cultural frames of reference. Long-standing frustration, particularly within the intimate domains of their lives, tended to culminate in profound inter- and intrapersonal conflict. Compelled to come to terms with a pervasive off-centeredness in their personal and relational functioning, several subjects subsequently engaged in a process of making something else of their biculturality with positive outcomes. Several critical aspects of life usually neglected in the literature on cultural identity were brought to light in this study. One significant issue has to do with the locus of cultural conflict. Another concerns the challenges of complex cultural placement for individual moral functioning that include sifting through often conflicting moral claims, arriving at moral understandings, integrating these into one's sense of self, and engaging moral responsibility and action. In the following section, we review the demands of cultural change for the task of personal sense making in these individuals. Subsequently, we return to touch on linkages of the culturally composite identity, concomitant feelings of fragmentation, and the drive toward enhanced moral functioning.

CONFLICT, IMPASSE, AND ADAPTATION

Recent work from a range of disciplines—anthropology, psychology, cognitive science, linguistics, medicine, environmental engineering, culture, and communication—exploring the organization of cultural knowledge indicates that people routinely invoke consistent cultural frames or schemas across very different life situations. Because these cultural frames play a central role in structuring how people think, feel, and behave, it is not surprising to discover that individuals are simply not prone to change them (see Holland & Quinn, 1997). Scholarship from other disciplines also challenges the postmodernist picture of a widespread, culturally composite population of highly malleable individuals. In his massive *Sources of the Self* Charles Taylor (1989) developed a thesis on the depth, pervasiveness, and inevitability of cultural frameworks that underlie our claims and give our reactions their various shapes, including their cultural shapes. These frameworks, he argued, orient, compel, and motivate us and account for our strong evaluations; accordingly, they are usually difficult to exchange, substitute, or replace.

Yet, varying degrees of cultural diversity are a fact of modern individual life. In general, the subjects in this study revealed complex cultural identities that contrast not only with postmodernist accounts of selfhood as utterly rootless but also with the essentialist views presented in much of the self-concept and personal identity literature, including that of social psychologists such as Cross. First, the length of time that the subjects required to come to terms with the composite contents of their identities is far greater—a matter of decades—than one might expect. In addition, the trajectory of their adaptive changes includes, but goes far beyond, strictly cultural features. This latter factor accounts for a split in the sample for this study. Although the subjects perceived themselves as comprising many composite characteristics, when they were faced with inter- or intrapersonal conflict most came to self-identify more decidedly according to one frame only. However, a few individuals continued even in the face of such conflict to self-identify according to a composite of attributes; they were able—but only over a long period of time—to resolve their often conflicting identities in such a way as to take their cues from, but go beyond, dual frames, oppositions, and disparities.

The accounts of cultural encounter and change that provide the basis for the observations that follow derive from this smaller group. The unifying theme in their highly personal and variable accounts is that the cultural encounter resulted in unanticipated and often overwhelming conflict, impasse, and then change. In all cases, the subjects emphasized the difficulty of their various attempts to adapt to their new cultural milieu. Their main challenges consisted of dealing with the disparate framings that they had developed in the process of reorienting themselves, because this process was marked by profound conflict (usually with close family members) that was charged with moral significance. They eventually reached a point in which the place they had arrived at was simply untenable. Consider the story of Cecy (a pseudonym) who, of all those interviewed, seems to best illustrate the fourth identity mode.

Cecy, a middle-class Hispanic woman in her late 40s, is an individual whose adolescent and adult development was marked by an overlay of traditions. As revealed in her interviews, she continues to experience profound complexity, perplexity, and conflict but in a culminating process of uneasy synthesis. Her deepened personal encounter gives rise to an alternative and inclusive identity that brings to coherence or at least equilibrium previously disturbing disjunctures. Although she has lived outside her home culture since midadolescence, in childhood she had considerable contact with other cultures. She provided two stunning narratives of conflict—one that kept her marginal in American culture for 25 years and a second that moved her into a cultural commitment and, eventually, a broadened sense of identity. Articulate in her acquired language, Cecy maintained multiple cultural–linguistic frames across several decades. She is fluid with their frames and exhibits fluid thinking patterns and affect. She does not feel unlike Americans or Hispanics but rather perceives herself to be "all that and more." She rearticulates and makes "something else" of difference; thus, her identity does not reside in the possession of cultural substance but in a mindful response to and even contestation of internally situated disjunctures of cultural forms. She is insightful about correspondences and differences and is the only subject who, without prompting, takes account of moral dissonance and its links to cultural meaning systems. She claims membership in diverse communities and finds special kinship with culturally diverse people. Whether individuals such as Cecy who develop in the nexus of cultures are singularly distinctive from other bicultural people remains a question, but her case illustrates the prospect of a highly mobile personal style and highlights the ability to create something dynamic that overcomes impasse. Cecy illustrates marked cultural changes and identification, beginning with a culture of origin, subsequent cultures, and a consequent, distinctive identity. The variables that account for that identity include cultural–linguistic elements, developmental stage, and time. In addition, we noted an axial phase of intense conflict that develops in precise and characteristic ways across time. Finally, resolution of the conflict derives from elements of the culture of origin, which seem to provide a basis or permission for radical change—that is, a reconstrual of options. Her account highlights a pattern of conflict resolution that plays out successively in various domains of life. Her ensuing identity, which takes into account the culture of origin and the subsequently acquired culture, seems to be a case of the sum being greater than the parts.

TOWARD PERSONAL COHERENCE
AND MORAL ORIENTATION

Diversity is highly valued as a public commodity and a social virtue. Yet, recent findings corroborate the respondents' uneasy sense that significant difference in values leads to diminished functioning between dialogic partners and within groups (see Jehn, Northcraft, & Neale, 1991). Research has also found that shared attitudes and other types of similarities account for the most positive effects in interpersonal and group functioning. However, dissimilarities in cultural beliefs and moral view, particularly when people perceive a threat to their deeply held convictions, incite them to doubt, reject, denigrate, and even punish the offender (see Byrne & Clore, 1970, on evaluative responses; Solomon, Greenberg, & Pyszczynski, 1991, on terror management; Byrne et al., 1971, on attitude and attraction). Although people accept cultural diversity even in intimate space, in fact, it makes sense that they are not willing to share this space with those who hold different convictions from themselves (see Haidt, Rosenberg, & Hom, 2003, on diversity acceptance in college students).

For individuals such as those in this study, cultural complexity is not a choice but rather a part of their personal history. Their complex cultural orientation entails that they feel deeply committed to frames that have points of conflict in and of themselves; in addition, differing, strong evaluations bring these individuals into conflict with intimate others who hold significantly different evaluative frames. In this case, rather than promoting their well-being, their expanded base of identifications creates an unanticipated degree of misery. Having conjectured that the private lives of culturally composite individuals would be complex and discordant, we were not prepared for the levels of difficulty, sadness, and actual damage that they tend to experience. In their interpersonal tensions, they have often been in the place of the third party—the other—whom their intimates misunderstand, mistrust, fear for, and sometimes even fear. Although these subjects anticipated and could deal with external and social injustice, the conflicts of ideal, value, and belief they experienced, particularly with parents, felt like a greater injustice. And given the high value for cultural diversity, family conflicts were not only angering but also frightening and shameful. The degrees and types of emotion that they expressed serve as evidence of their expectations and the strength of their commitment to the ideals, behaviors, beliefs, and people around whom their conflicts revolve.

Over the course of interacting with these respondents, in the process of knowing and understanding them, we learned that certain feelings and experiences were omnipresent—constants across the different accounts and cases they narrated. The degree of correspondence in their stories was striking, particularly in view of differences of national, cultural, ethnic, and linguistic background; religious affiliation; social and marital status; age; and educational attainment. Through a multiplicity of accounts they discussed their conceptions and experiences of diversity; these were sub-rosa themes, embedded in images of conflict and commitment, of incoherence and disorder, and of hidden and double selves. Contrary to new orthodoxies in the field (because people are diverse and hence nonorthodox), their accounts suggest that their images and figures should be taken literally. In ordinary life, people reserve these images to represent feelings of distance, disconnectedness, alienation, instability, uncertainty, and loss. The conceptions that they shared are variants that represent their comparable states of being. Their different allusions form a common set of themes. They feel their competencies, highlighted in the literature, are the enhanced abilities to negotiate difference and disjunctures with hopes of ameliorating their perplexities.

The incoherence of frames that they sustain implies a considerable level of disorder in their knowledge systems—a basic problem, as one subject described, of "knowing how to file all the things that are inside me." The diversity of frames also implies an incoherence of behavioral options, as another subject suggested: "I didn't know what to do with all that diversity." Likewise, in their relationships, they find themselves out of step, and they give enormous effort to improving their interactions. The research process linked them in conversation to others with similar categories of disjunctures who lived similar experiences and felt comparable emotions. They found kin. Their sense of abnormality decreased. Instead, as they developed a view of the constructive nature of their diversity-based perspectives, they felt convinced of their realities ("I didn't know this was normal") and affirmed in their struggles ("Is this why I've had such trouble?"). Despite their difficulties, no respondents wished to divest themselves of their diverse forms. They liked and felt many positive effects of their discrepancies. They simply wanted to find a way to make them complementary and to unite them into a principle that would give them more vitality. They felt the opposition, but they needed something to break the impasse and help them to proceed toward deeper self–other relationality.

Their most pressing challenge is to grapple with the continuing effects of disparate framings. For example, although cultural adaptation seems to proceed according to recognizable phases, the respondents point out its complex, recursive, and never-completed nature. On reaching certain stages of their lives or when conflicts arise that touch another domain of experience, they feel as though they are starting over again. For instance, after a particularly intense quarrel, one mother felt that she "did not practice love" for her son in a way that was recognizable or adequate to a young American teen. So, she began a new, fearful, and more intense period and domain of transition. The deeper challenge for both first- and second-generation respondents has been to bring adequate coherence to their lives. Without the benefit of modeling, these individuals must create attitudes and emotions that are congruent with the internal complexity of their worldviews, beliefs, values, and moral commitments.

This sort of coherence making, as Wolfgang Iser (1993) showed, is a highly personal and deepening process characteristic of all humans. But for individuals experiencing the contest of cultures, it is essential for new, singular, and workable resolutions that acknowledge but go beyond the boundaries of difference and disjuncture. Because of the imaginative mode of human consciousness, it is possible to take disparate, inert cultural material and replicate, revise, reconceptualize, and mobilize it in such a way that it exceeds its original determinacy. This cultural "matter" can be considered as a sign that points toward a truer, more individual reality, naturalized toward the individual's sense, needs, and purposes, and overcoming its original restrictions. Its new nature derives from the interplay of frames within individuals as they become more capable of "transgressing" original boundaries, making a new "fact" from an old one. In this way, it has been possible for some individuals to change their disparate forms in a process of self-understanding that provides the basis for deep-level sociocultural boundary crossing; this is a process that takes into account the categories, junctures, and disjunctures of one's embodied cultures, giving these more satisfying cultural intelligibility and coherent internal validity as yet another form of life—one's life.

CONCLUSION: THE MORAL OF THESE STORIES

Like personal selves, cultural groups are constructions that arise not arbitrarily or subjectively but from established discursive practices that transcend individual desires and beliefs in the sense that they shape desires and beliefs. Most important, these groups are not entities in their own right. As with cultural differences such as religion or language, so also with the features that differentiate racial or ethnic groupings: They are conventional delineations, some of which are more useful than others as we pursue the business of living together. This is hardly a new claim, but it is easily forgotten. As philosophers and as consociates, we must avoid the tendency to think of such features—including even skin color—as brute facts or primordial properties rather than as conventional templates for interpreting the social world. As we just demonstrated, this tendency, which has dominated social science since it became a separate discipline in the early 20th century, can be traced back to Descartes. However, there is an alternative philosophical tradition, whose forebear is Descartes' near contemporary, Giambattista Vico, which understands social groupings and the conceptualized differences between them as products of human agency and, because agency is generally goal directed, as products of human interests. For these thinkers, social groupings are interpretations all the way down, to borrow the slogan of Clifford Geertz's (1973) hermeneutical ethnography. Not only do these interpretations understand groups as radically historical (no essences here!) but in their better moments they also understand themselves, qua interpretation, as historical, contingent, fluid, multiperspectival, self-revising, and so on. Anthropologists know this quite well, having discarded the notion of culture as a determinate, frangible unity in favor of much more sophisticated ways of understanding the other (see, inter alia, Clifford, 1988; Kahn, 1995; Rosaldo, 1989). All this is consistent with the general hermeneutical conception of knowledge as self-adjusting. Some interpretations accent and other interpretations obscure differences and continuities within individual groupings. Some accent and others obscure influences, commonalities, and contrasts among social groupings. What Handler and Segal (1990) said of cultures is actually true of all human groups: Their parsing is "a matter of interpretation, notwithstanding that at any given moment, and even for long durations, some interpretations are enforced more than others" (p. 23).

In contrast, most social psychology studies of cultural identity, including Cross' (1991), talk the talk of social construction but lack a true appreciation of the oft-stated proposition that cultures and other sorts of reference groups are socially constructed. They are not natural entities that one discovers as when one discovers a lump under one's arm. But who constructs them? In the case of Black identity in America, one answer to this question is that in the course of maintaining its own dominance the White mainstream constructed the pre-Civil Rights conception of Black ethnicity, which was embodied in Booker T. Washington, and that emerging Black leaders constructed a later and more militant conception, which was associated with figures such as W. E. B. DuBois. Another answer is that both of these constructions were byproducts of social processes that transcended the intentions of individual agents, Black or White; this answer seems much more plausible to us although we cannot explore it in these pages. Even more plausible, however, is a third answer that includes but goes beyond the first two: The members of this reference group have constructed it themselves by accepting and passing on to their children the collective names ascribed to them, the latest of which is the term *African American*. To Cross' credit, he got it right when he said that African Americans "superimpose a black orientation" (1985, p. 170) on their own experience. In this respect they are not different from any other social group, although admittedly until recently African Americans had much less control over the way people referred to them than did other reference groups. The greatest significance of what Cross called the Black Movement is not that it put Black Americans in touch with their true or authentic selves (a fundamentally essentialist notion), but that it gave them a new set of interpersonal relationships that matched the changing political climate of the larger society. If one must use the language of discovery, then the thing to say is that Blacks discovered new solidarity, not race, which is to say that they created a new (but, of course, it was not altogether new) collectivity for themselves.

The identity struggles of Cecy and the other subjects interviewed by Mendoza (2002) are far more complex than those reported, or better reconstructed, in the large-scale black identity studies such as Cross' (1991). Would in-depth interviews with the real individuals whose subjectitivities have been scrubbed out of the latter's empirical studies reveal similar complexities? We suspect they would, at least for those individuals who retain and cherish their deep roots in their Black culture even as they successful integrate themselves into mainstream society. As DuBois (1990) showed so poignantly, double consciousness is possible but it is always an unfinished project.

ENDNOTES

[1]For convenience, we use these two terms interchangeably, but see Rom Harré's (1984) *Personal Being* for a helpful fine-grained differentiation between them.

[2]In non-Western philosophy one finds various notions corresponding to our idea of the self, but they are very hard to describe in Western terms. This discussion makes no pretense of offering such a description. Furthermore, we severely telescoped the story of the self in modern western philosophy by speaking as though Descartes himself normally used terms such as *self* or *soi* in the way described here. In fact it was his great successors—Locke, Berkeley, Hume, and Kant—who used the term self and its cognates to express Descartes' basic idea of subjectivity as a thinking thing, as well as their own misgivings about that idea.

[3]As noted, readers not used to the broad sociological sense of cultural identity now commonplace in the United States may wish to mentally substitute social identity in what follows.

[4]In the following pages most comments about psychology and other domains of social science are, regrettably, limited to what we know about the literature in the United States and Canada. Because this literature has been heavily influenced by European thinkers, it seems reasonable to hope non-American readers, at least those educated in the Western tradition, will find these remarks of some use. However, readers of all nationalities deserve our apologies for the unmistakable, although because of our own limitations unavoidable, Western bias in this essay.

[5]Unfortunately, when both sorts of instrument were used in the same study, the corresponding subordinate constructs were not distinguished. Alternatively, authors of studies that used only one type of instrument—usually RGO studies—summarized their results as though the study had actually assessed both sorts of constructs, including self-esteem or some other PI variable. As a result, the difference between disaffection for one's group and disaffection for one's own self was erased. Terms such as *self-hatred* were used to refer to both sorts of alienation, à la Lewin.

[6]For example, as Cross himself observed, the test data he considered actually suggest that, from the beginning of World War II until well into the Civil Rights Movement, many Black people were indeed more out-group oriented than whites, as evidenced by the Black children's general preference for White dolls and by Black adults' general preference for commodities, social policies, and personal behaviors associated with the

White mainstream. When Blacks of that era did prefer alternatives specifically associated with the Black community, their pro-Black preferences were normally mixed in with other preferences for White symbols. However, there was virtually no evidence collected during this time about how Black children or adults felt about themselves personally. Even so, studies carried out over the subsequent decades that were more carefully designed and did test both PI and RGO suggest that long before the Civil Rights Movement, Black people's personal self-esteem was normally not a problem—not even for those Blacks least inclined to identify themselves with their racial group. Furthermore, there seems to be no reason to expect other racial or cultural minorities to be different in this respect.

REFERENCES

Allport, G. W. (1954). *The nature of prejudice*. Reading, MA: Addison-Wesley.

Barth, F. (1969). Introduction. In F. Barth (Ed.), *Ethnic groups and boundaries: The social organization of cultural difference* (pp. 9–38). Boston: Little, Brown.

Barth, F. (1994). Enduring and emerging issues in the analysis of ethnicity. In H. Vermeulen & C. Govers (Eds.), *The anthropology of ethnicity: Beyond ethnic groups and boundaries* (pp. 11–32). Amsterdam: Het Spinhuis.

Bakhurst, D., & Sypnowich, C. (Eds.). (1995). *The social self*. London: Sage.

Blasi, A. (1988). Identity and the development of the self. In D. K. Lapsley and F. C. Power (Eds.), *Self, ego, and identity: Integrative approaches* (pp. 226–243). NY: Springer Verlag.

Blasi, A. (1990). How should psychologists define morality? Or, the negative side-effects of philosophy's influence on psychology. In T. Wren, *The moral domain: Essays in the ongoing discussion between philosophy and the social sciences* (pp. 38–79). Cambridge, MA: The MIT Press.

Blasi, A. (1991). The self as subject in the study of personality. In D. J. Ozer, J. M. Healy, Jr., and A. J. Stewart (Eds.), *Perspectives in personality: Vol. 3. Self and emotion* (pp. 19–37). London: Kingsley.

Blasi, A. (1993). The development of identity: Some implications for moral functioning. In G. Noam & T. Wren (Eds.), *The moral self* (pp. 93–122). Cambridge, MA: The MIT Press.

Brody, E. (1964). Marginality, identity and behavior in the American Negro: A functional analysis, *International Journal of Social Psychiatry 10*, 7–12.

Byrne, D., &Clore, G. I. (1970). A reinforcement model of evaluative responses. *Personality: An International Journal 1*, 103–128.

Byrne, D., Gouaux, C., Griffitt, W., Lamberth, J., Murakawa, N., Prasad, M., Prasad, A., & Ramirez, M. (1971). The ubiquitous relationship: Attitude similarity and attraction: A cross-cultural study. *Human Relations 24*, 201–207.

Chodorow, N. (1978). *Reproduction of mothering: Psychoanalysis and the sociology of gender*. Berkeley, CA: University of California Press.

Clark, K., & Clark, M. (1947). Racial identification and preference in Negro children. In T. M. Newcomb & E. L. Hartley (Eds.), *Readings in social psychology* (pp. 602–611). New York: Holt.

Clark, K., & Clark, M. (1939). The development of consciousness of self and the emergence of racial identification in Negro pre-school children. *Journal of Social Psychology, 10*, 591–599.

Clark, K., & Clark, M. (1940). Skin color as a factor in racial identification of Negro pre-school children. *Journal of Social Psychology, 11*, 159–169.

Clifford, J. (1988). *The predicament of culture: Twentieth-century ethnography, literature and art.* Cambridge, MA: Harvard University Press.

Cooley, C. H. (1964). *Human nature and the social order.* New York: Schocken. (Original work published 1902)

Cross, W. E. (1991). *Shades of Black: Diversity in African-American identity.* Philadelphia: Temple University Press.

Cross, W. E. (1985). Black identity: Rediscovering the distinction between personal identity and reference group orientation. In M. Spencer, G. Brookins, and W. Allen (Eds.), *Beginnings: The social and affective development of Black children* (pp. 155–171). Hillsdale, NJ: Lawrence Erlbaum Associates.

Descartes, R. (1986). *Meditations on first philosophy* (John Cottingham, trans.). Cambridge, England: Cambridge University Press. (Original work published 1641)

Du Bois, W. E. B. (1990). *The souls of Black folk.* New York: Vintage.

Erikson, E. (1968) *Identity, youth, and crisis.* New York: Norton.

Fernberger, S. W. (1948). Persistence of stereotypes concerning sex differences. *Journal of Abnormal and Social Psychology, 43*, 97–101.

Fuss, D. (1989). *Essentially speaking: Feminism, nature, and difference.* New York: Routledge, Chapman, and Hall.

Geertz, C. (1973). *The interpretation of cultures.* New York: Basic.

Gergen, K. (1999). *An invitation to social construction.* Thousand Oaks, CA: Sage.

Goffman, E. (1959). *The presentation of self in everyday life.* Garden City; NY: Doubleday.

Hacking, I. (1999). *The social construction of what?* Cambridge, MA: Harvard University Press.

Haidt, J., Rosenberg, E., & Hom, H. (2003). Differentiating diversities: Moral diversity is not like other kinds. *Journal of Applied Social Psychology 33*, 1–36.

Hall, S. (1996). Who needs "Identity"?, In S. Hall and P. du Gay (Eds.), *Questions of cultural identity* (pp. 1–17). London: Sage.

Handler, R., & Segal, D. (1990). *Jane Austen and the fiction of culture: An essay on the narration of social realities.* Tucson, AZ: University of Arizona Press.

Hare, R.M. (1952). *The language of morals.* Oxford: Oxford University Press.

Hare, R.M. (1963). *Freedom and reason.* Oxford: Oxford University Press.

Harré, R. (1984). *Personal being.* Cambridge, MA: Harvard University Press.

Herzberg, J. (1977). Self-excoriation by young women, *American Journal of Psychology, 134*, 320–321.

Hirschfeld, L. (1996). *Race in the making: Cognition, culture, and the child's construction of human kinds.* Cambridge, MA: The MIT Press.

Hoffman, M. (1976). Empathy, role-taking, guilt, and development of altruistic motives. In T. Lickona (Ed.), *Moral development and behavior: Theory, research and social issues* (pp. 124–143). New York: Holt, Rinehart & Winston.

Hoffman, D. (1998). A therapeutic moment? Identity, self, and culture in the anthropology of education. *Anthropology and Education Quarterly, 29*, 324–346.

Holland, D., and Quinn, N. (Eds.). (1995). *Cultural models in language and thought.* NY: Cambridge University Press.

Iser, W. (1993). *The fictive and the imaginary: Charting literary anthropology.* Baltimore, MD: Johns Hopkins University Press.

Jehn, K. A, Northcraft, G. B, & Neale, M. A. (1991). Why difference makes a difference: A field study of diversity, conflict, and performance in workgroups. *Administrative Science Quarterly 44,* 741-763.

Kahn, J. (1995). *Culture, multiculture, postculture.* London: Sage.

Kardiner, A., & Ovesey, L. (1951). *The mark of oppression.* New York: Norton.

Kincheloe, J., & Steinbert, S. (1997). *Changing multiculturalism.* Philadelphia: Open University Press.

Lewin, K. (1941). Jewish self-hatred. *Contemporary Jewish Record, 4,* 219–232.

Lewin, K. (1948) *Resolving social conflicts.* New York: Harper & Row.

Loevinger, J. (1976). *Ego development: Conceptions and theories.* San Francisco, CA: Jossey-Bass.

Loevinger, J. (1979). Theory and data in the measurement of ego development. In J. Loevinger, *Scientific ways in the study of ego development.* Worcester, MA: Clark University Press.

Lynne, D. B. (1959). A note on sex differences in the development of masculine and feminine identification. *Psychological Review, 66,* 126–135.

Mead, G. H. (1934). *Mind, self, and society.* Chicago: University of Chicago Press.

Mendoza, C. (2002). *Third culture: Movement toward moral inquiry and orientation.* Ph.D. dissertation, Loyola University, Chicago, IL.

Parsons, T. (1951). *The social system.* New York: The Free Press.

Rosaldo, R. (1989). *Culture and truth.* Boston: Beacon.

Shweder, R. (1991). *Thinking through cultures: Expeditions in cultural psychology.* Cambridge, MA: Harvard University Press.

Shweder, R., & LeVine, R. (Eds.). (1984). *Cultural Theory: Essays on mind, self and emotion.* Cambridge, England: Cambridge University Press.

Solomon, S., Greenberg, J., & Pyszczynski, T. (1991). A terror management theory of social behavior: The psychological functions of self-esteem and cultural worldviews. In M. Zanna (Ed.), *Advances in Experimental Social Psychology, 24,* 93-159, Orlando, FL, Academic.

Taylor, C. (1989). *Sources of the self: The making of the modern identity.* Cambridge, MA: Harvard University Press.

Verkuyten, M. (1995). Self-esteem, self-concept, stability, and aspects of ethnic identity among minority and majority youth in the Netherlands. *Journal of Youth and Adolescence, 24,* 155–175.

Wylie, R. C. (1979). *The self-concept: Vol. 2. Theory and research on selected topics.* Lincoln, NE: University of Nebraska Press.

12

Self in Relationship

Monika Keller
Max Planck Institute for Human Development, Berlin

in cooperation with

Fang Fuxi and Fang Ge
Academia Sinica, Bejing

Wolfgang Edelstein, Lucienne Cecora, and Ulrike Eckert
Max Planck Institute for Human Development, Berlin

DEVELOPMENTAL CHANGES IN ADOLESCENCE FROM A CROSS-CULTURAL PERSPECTIVE

Adolescence is a phase in which a sense of a psychological self as a specific person embedded in time and relationships is established. Authors from different theoretical traditions have consistently pointed out that this adolescent sense of self is deeply integrated in relationships. In particular, experiences in relationships with close friends and peers help the adolescent develop a psychological understanding of himself or herself as a specific person. Affective bonding in relationships with close friends plays a central role in the development of a moral self because in these relationships loyalty and commitment to another person are built. In adolescence the *self* is defined in terms of relationships and as Kegan (1982) aptly phrased it, the self is the relationship. Therefore, the developmental task in the transition into late adolescence and adulthood is to establish autonomy and a sense of moral self that transcends group conformity. The conception of self in relationships in middle and late adolescence is the focus of this chapter.

In the following sections we first summarize the major developmental stage characterizing the understanding of self and relationships in the period of middle adolescence as it has been outlined in different theories of development. We then discuss a theoretical conception of the development of the moral self in adolescence that Keller and Edelstein (1993; Keller, 1996) outlined some years ago. This conception was empirically based on longitudinal interview data focusing on the understanding of close friendship and moral norms in 7- and 9-year-old children and 12- and 15-year-old adolescents in a Western society (Iceland). We reflect on the theoretical assumptions of this conception in light of cross-cultural findings with Chinese children and adolescents who have been assessed cross-sectionally at the same ages with the same social–cognitive interviews. From this cross-cultural perspective it becomes clear that some central assumptions about the development of the moral self in our—as well as other Western—theories are culturally biased and have to be revised in light of the cross-cultural findings. Finally, we include data from 19-year-old participants assessed longitudinally in Iceland and cross-sectionally in China, and we compare the developmental transition from middle into late adolescence or young adulthood as it has been described in Western cognitive–developmental theories in a cross-cultural perspective.

SELF AND RELATIONSHIPS IN ADOLESCENCE: A COGNITIVE–DEVELOPMENTAL VIEW

Cognitive–developmental theories of understanding relationships, in particular, close friendships (Damon & Hart, 1982; Selman, 1980; Youniss, 1980), have maintained that adolescents emphasize intimacy and communication as central components of their close friendships. Adolescents consider it most important that they can share with a close friend their psychological concerns such as their inner feelings, problems, and views of others. They perceive it as necessary that they can trust and rely on a close friend as a partner who understands the needs and reflections of the self and thus can help solve problems of everyday life. Communication with friends helps adolescents to understand the psychological complexity of the self and the social world. In interactions with close friends the adolescent comes to understand his or her own personality, dispositions, feelings, and worldviews in which he or she is both the same and different from the close friend or others in general. Close relationships with friends are particularly important for the development of the self in adolescence. In the neopsychoanalytic tradition Sullivan (1953) was the first to describe early adolescence as a critical phase in which the development of intimate bonding and the experience of shared emotions with a close friend becomes an important source for the establishment of a sense of a unique psychological self. More recently, the experience of affective bonding in relationships has been seen as an important motivational basis for the development of moral responsibility and interpersonal sensitivity (Blum, 1980; Bukowski & Sippola, 1996; Keller, 1996; Keller & Edelstein, 1991). Responsibilities toward a close and intimate friend are particularly significant in adolescence and become a strong motivational force in regulating decision making in interpersonally and morally relevant situations. Therefore, the development of intimacy in personal relationships can be seen as closely interconnected with the development of a moral self and moral responsibility.

In Kohlberg's (1984) cognitive–developmental theory of moral judgment adolescence is described as the phase in which obligations and responsibilities of the self result from the expectations of significant others in significant role relationships. Interestingly, close friendship as a role relationship of specific developmental significance has been neglected completely in Kohlberg's theory of moral development. At Stage 3 of moral judgment, which is the prototypical stage for adolescents, a first conception of a moral self emerges as embedded in relationships. It is important to be a trustworthy, honest, and loyal person in the eyes of one's significant others or other persons in general. The self is seen to have an obligation to maintain relationships by showing concern for others, being loving and caring, and taking others' perspectives into account. As Gilligan (1982) emphasized in her theory of moral development, at Stage 3 the morality of justice, which is the central concept in Kohlberg's theory and the morality of care, converge. Care is the predominant component in the definition of the moral self at Stage 3. As we discuss next in connection with cross-cultural research the higher stages of Kohlberg's theory are not well designed to include aspects of care.

In Loevinger's (1976) theory of ego development the conformist stage is the equivalent to Stage 3 in Kohlberg's theory and is typical for adolescents. At this developmental stage the person has a strong need for belonging and perceives it as most important to be with other people, to get along with others, and to be loved by others. Relationship concerns are the most important motives. It is important that the needs, concerns, and interests of the self are in congruence with those of significant others. Similarly, in Kegan's (1982; Noam & Kegan,

1982) cognitive–developmental theory of the self, the self in adolescence is seen as intimately interconnected with significant others—in such a way that the adolescent not only has a relationship but is the relationship. Because there is no self independent of significant relationships, self-worth depends completely on others' view of the self. Therefore, interpersonal harmony with significant others is of major importance. In adolescence close friendship is the kind of relationship in which interconnectedness is particularly strong. It may even be compensatory when conflicts with parents or other authorities emerge.

In these theories of understanding self and relationships adolescence is seen as a stage of initial reflexive awareness of self and others as persons with specific enduring personality characteristics and values that determine their actions. Persons are seen as having a specific and unique self in terms of dispositions and values. Maintaining good relationships with others is the most important value in adolescence. Therefore, persons at this stage have a strong motive to avoid hurting others' feelings or not caring for others. Guilt feelings emerge as the consequence of violating relationship responsibilities. They indicate that a person is morally aware of a violation of harmony and trust. Anticipatory guilt serves as an emotion regulation to avoid the violation of relationship responsibilities. In our theoretical approach we defined guilt (Keller, 1996) and moral consistency (Keller & Edelstein, 1993) as two central indicators of a moral self that accepts responsibility for a person's actions. This conception of self begins to emerge in adolescence.

THE DEVELOPMENT OF THE MORAL SELF IN ADOLESCENCE: MORAL FEELINGS AND MORAL CONSISTENCY

The Development of Guilt Feelings

According to Kohlberg's (1984) theory guilt feelings are a rather late developmental achievement of Stage 3 moral reasoning in adolescence, in which the self is experienced as part of ongoing relationships and is strongly concerned with maintaining harmony in those relationships. Cognitively, the emergence of guilt feelings is based on the ability to evaluate the self from an impartial—or third-person—observer perspective that allows the understanding of generalized norms of reciprocity and trust (Kohlberg, 1984). In contradistinction, research with children has demonstrated that the understanding of guilt feelings occurs earlier than assumed in Kohlberg's theory yet developmentally later than the understanding of the validity of moral norms. In research on the "happy victimizer phenomenon" (Arsenio & Lover, 1995; Nunner-Winkler & Sodian, 1988), 5- and 6-year-old children evaluated moral transgressions as wrong—independent of sanctions—but attributed positive feelings to the violator because he or she had achieved a personal egoistic goal, for example. From about age 7 on children attributed negative (moral) feelings or at least mixed feelings to the moral transgressor.

One explanation for the discrepancies in these findings on the emergence of guilt may be the different methodologies of the studies. In Kohlberg's (1984) dilemma method a person must reflect on the morally right choice in a situation of conflicting moral obligations. Thus, in Heinz's dilemma property rights are in conflict with the value of life and guilt feelings are mentioned as moral justifications or evaluative criteria in reflections about the morally right choice. In contradistinction, in the "happy victimizer" research children were asked how a protagonist would feel in the situation of moral transgression and not which was the morally right feeling in this situation (see Keller, Lourenço, Malti, & Saalbach, 2003) or which was the right choice in a situation of moral temptation. We agree with Harris (1989) that the awareness of guilt feelings cognitively presupposes only Stage 2 perspective coordination (Selman, 1980) where the self can look at his or her own actions through the eyes of another person. This ability to coordinate also underlies Stage 2 of preconventional moral development in Kohlberg's theory. Ascribing guilt feelings to a transgressor presupposes that a child takes into account not only the effects of his or her actions on others but also the evaluation of the action by others. The child no longer focuses exclusively on the subjective perspective of a transgressor—which would lead to the attribution of positive feelings—but takes into account the standards of moral rightness and the negative evaluation of the violation by others, which leads to the attribution of negative or guilt feelings. In contradistinction, Kohlberg's Stage 3 conception of guilt feelings presupposes a self-evaluative process of the moral quality of the self as a person. This self-evaluative process presupposes the coordination of perspectives of self and others from a general third-person observer perspective, which is the cognitive prerequisite of both Stage 3 as defined in Selman's (1980) theory of friendship reasoning and in Kohlberg's theory of moral development. This Stage 3 perspective includes a conception of how a morally good person should (ideally) act to be a valuable person in the eyes of significant others and to maintain trust in a relationship. Moral feelings of shame or guilt as Kohlberg defined them arise if the person's acts were inconsistent with the moral self-ideal of how a morally good person (e.g., a loyal husband or a friend) ought to act. Pride and contentment as positive moral feelings arise if the person resists egoistic strivings or moral temptations. Thus, moral feelings are tied to an image of the moral self that the person wants to establish or seeks to maintain.

Moral Consistency

The second indicator of the moral self that we addressed is moral consistency. This concept has several meanings as Blasi (1983) documented in a theoretical discussion of the relationship between moral judgment and moral action. Kohlberg and Candee (1984) showed that moral consistency increases with stage development. Research with children supports this assumption. Blasi (1984) demonstrated that childrens' motivation to accept a moral norm as strictly binding lagged behind their knowledge of moral norms. 6- to 10-year-old children and 12 year olds did not experience moral obligations as strictly binding. According to Blasi, children frequently stated that a promise must always be kept. At the same time they maintained that promise keeping in the concrete situation depended on the (subjective) wishes or preferences of the person: If the person does not like to keep the promise because of other concerns, then he or she must not keep it. Gerson and Damon (1978) observed a similar inconsistency between children's hypothetical judgments of fair distribution and their concrete acts of sharing when they favored themselves. These findings are consistent with Piaget's (1932/1965) early observations that young children claimed that the rules of a marble game could never be changed but nevertheless violated the rules when playing the game.

The Moral Self and Close Friendship

In an earlier theory of the development of the moral self in close relationships (Keller, 1996; Keller & Edelstein, 1993; see the following for a detailed description) we assessed guilt feelings and moral consistency based on children's and adolescents' reasoning about a morally relevant friendship dilemma. In this research 9- and 12-year-old children attributed Stage 2 negative (guilt) feelings to a protagonist who violated a friendship—or promise—obligation to a close friend. At the same time, these children frequently revealed a pattern of moral inconsistency in a split between descriptive reasoning—how a protagonist would decide in the conflict—and prescriptive moral judgment—what is the right choice. Although nearly all children judged it as morally right for the protagonist to keep the promise to the friend, they frequently stated that the protagonist would prefer an interesting invitation from a newcomer to visiting the close friend as promised. Guilt feelings were anticipated as the consequence of the violation of an obligation, but these feelings did not determine the action choice. The 15-year-old adolescents did not evidence such inconsistency between action choice and moral judgment. They judged it as necessary for the protagonist or self to act on the basis of promise and friendship commitments. The justifications of this action choice revealed the Stage 3 reasons of a conception of the self as a trustworthy, loyal, and dependable friend or person in general. We interpreted this type of moral consistency as depending on the self-evaluative system of Stage 3 interpersonal and moral reasoning as already described. Only at this stage does the person experience the need to establish and maintain consistency between what is judged to be right and responsible and what one would do in situations of conflicting interpersonal and moral claims. Anticipated guilt feelings over the violation of relationship responsibilities in this case serve to support moral consistency. Moral consistency between a general moral judgment and a contextualized personal decision in a morally relevant friendship dilemma was established only when the person was at Stage 3 interpersonal moral reasoning.

Our findings support the assumption of cognitive–developmental theories that the need to establish consistency between action and thought is a rather late achievement that emerges in adolescence. By referring to Blasi (1984; Blasi & Oresick, 1986) we argued that the need for moral consistency is based on the development of a self that accepts responsibility for his or her actions and defines the self in morally relevant categories. Cognitively, this presupposes the Stage 3 third-person perspective that Kohlberg assumed. Facing the violation of moral standards and ideals, the self experiences anticipatory moral feelings of shame and guilt that have the function of regulating actions to maintain the self's status as a reliable and trustworthy moral actor, both in the eyes of others and in the eyes of the self. We argued that a close friendship might be the first developmentally significant relationship in which children, on the basis of empathy and care for another person, experience genuine interpersonal loyalty and a moral sense of self independent of authority and sanctions. In the following section we examine these findings and theoretical conclusions in light of a cross-cultural comparison.

SELF, RELATIONSHIPS, AND MORALITY IN CROSS-CULTURAL PERSPECTIVE

The concepts of individualism and collectivism or of independence and interdependence (Triandis, 1990) have been used as central explanations of cultural differences between Western and Asian cultures. Although the distinction of societies and persons according to these dimension has been critically discussed (Kim, Triandis, Kagitçibasi, Choi, & Yoon, 1994; Turiel, 1998), consistent differences between persons from Western and Asian cultures were observed in the understanding of self, relationships, and moral norms (Bond, 1996; Boyes & Walker, 1988; Markus & Kitayama, 1991; Miller & Bersoff, 1992; Shweder, Mahapatra, & Miller, 1987). Persons from individualistic—mostly Western—cultures emphasize autonomy, personal and emotional independence, and personal goals. Members of collectivist—mostly Asian—cultures reveal a strong communal identity and feelings of interconnectedness with others. Persons from Asian cultures are traditionally oriented and define themselves in terms of membership to groups or collectives. The interdependent self in collectivist cultures is embedded in intimate social relationships (Markus & Kitayama, 1991).

In comparison, the self in individualistic cultures has been described as independent, such that role obligations are less important than personal attributes and skills in establishing social relations. In particular, Miller and Bersoff (1992) and Shweder et al. (1987) documented differences in moral reasoning and decision making. Persons from individualistic—mostly American cultures—stress personal rights over duties and have a universalistic orientation of human rights. Persons from collectivist societies—mostly from India—strongly emphasize duties and obligations to the group and shared role expectations. For China it has been doubted whether it completely fits the criteria of a collectivist society. On one hand, using scales of collectivism–individualism China is closer to a middle point (Bond, 1996). On the other hand, in an analysis of ancient Chinese moral philosophy, Roetz (1997) documented the evidence of contractual reasoning. Despite this, the empirical research with persons from Chinese cultures have been rather consistent with the findings with persons from India (see Boyes & Walker, 1988). We will discuss later how this cultural difference relates to the differences between Stage 3 and Stage 4.

UNDERSTANDING PROMISE KEEPING AND CLOSE FRIENDSHIP: A CROSS-CULTURAL COMPARISON

The findings from our previous study in a cross-cultural comparison are discussed here. In our first study (see Edelstein, Keller, & Schröder, 1990; Keller, 1996) 180 participants from different social classes and ecologies in Iceland, about equally distributed according to sex, were interviewed longitudinally at ages 7, 9, 12, 15, and 19. In cooperation with researchers from the Chinese Academy of Sciences (see Keller, Edelstein, Schmid, Fang, & Fang, 1998) we assessed 90 participants of the corresponding ages from different social settings in Bejing (China) in a combined cross-sectional and longitudinal design. Participants were about equally distributed according to sex. Trained interviewers asked children and adolescents semistructured questions, including information about their general and situation-specific understanding of relationships and moral norms. Only the participants from the cross-sectional study are included in this analysis.

In this chapter we focus on general reasoning about close friendship and promise keeping and situation-specific reasoning about a morally relevant dilemma in which the protagonist had a choice between keeping a promise to the best friend or accepting an interesting invitation from a third child who was new in class. Among other aspects, participants were asked about their decision in the dilemma and the reasons for this choice as well as reasons for choosing the alternative option (practical judgment), the consequences of the choice from the perspective of the protagonist or self (moral emotions), and the evaluation of the choice from a moral point of view (moral judgment). We defined full and transitional stages or levels for the different issues of social and moral reasoning (see Keller, 1984, 1996; Keller & Edelstein, 1991, 1993; Keller & Reuss, 1984, for dilemma, interview, and scoring of the issues of reasoning).

The definition of Levels 1 to 3 was first derived from interviews with the Icelandic participants and later validated with interviews from other Western and Asian cultures, including China. All interviews were translated into English and were scored cooperatively by raters from within each culture as well as expert raters. Interrater reliabilities for full and transitional levels for all issues varied between 80% and 95% full agreement for all age groups within the cultures.

In the following section we focus on Stage 3 interpersonal and moral reasoning in comparing Icelandic and Chinese adolescents, differentiating between general and situation-specific reasoning about close friendship and promise-keeping. First, we provide a general description of Level 3. Second, we present examples of Level 3 reasoning that serve to exemplify the emergence of a moral self in both cultures. Letters and numbers in brackets after the examples refer to participants' culture (IC for Iceland or CH for China), participants' identification number, and age.

Understanding Promise Keeping

Moral reasoning about promise keeping was assessed according to Kohlberg's (1984) Stage 3 with the following questions: Why it is important to keep a promise? What would be the consequence of not or never keeping a promise? What is the evaluation of a person who never keeps a promise? In general, questions could be elaborated and modified slightly in probing.

Consistent with Kohlberg's (1984) definition of Stage 3 moral reasoning, the obligation to keep a promise is seen to result from a generalized conception of how one ought to treat another person under the norm of reciprocity and how one ought to act as a reliable and trustworthy person in the eyes of the other. Promising means having committed or having obliged oneself to do something. The violation of the obligation to keep a promise is interpreted as betrayal of trust. Moral feelings of guilt are interpreted in terms of consequences for the self-image: A person who does not keep promises is evaluated as an unreliable person who cannot be trusted or depended upon. The following statements from interviews exemplify the conceptual structure:

Question: Can you tell me what it means to promise something?

Answer: You really have to do it.

Question: Why?

Answer: Because it maintains the trust of the person to whom you've promised.

Question: But what happens if you don't keep a promise you have made?

Answer: Then no one trusts you.

Question: Yes, what kind of person would that be who never kept his promises?

Answer: Not very nice.

Question: Why not?

Answer: He couldn't be relied upon.

Question: Why should promises be kept?

Answer: So that the other person will have faith in you. I feel a promise is always binding (IC, 57, 12).

Question: What kind of a person would that be who never kept promises?

Answer: Irresponsible—then one can never rely on him (IC, 101, 12).

Question: Why is it necessary to keep a promise?

Answer: Because one wouldn't want to be irresponsible in anyone's eyes—stand by everthing one says—that's why one wouldn't betray anyone (IC, 114, 12).

Question: Why it is important to keep a promise?

Answer: Some things can get held up if one doesn't keep one's promise, if you keep your promise, people will think you are rather trustworthy (CH, 1801, 15).

Question: Why should a person keep a promise?

Answer: Since you promised, the other person trusts you, puts belief in you. If you give him an unsatisfactory answer, the other person will change the belief into hatred. A person should uphold one's prestige and benefit and one's status in other people's eyes (CH, 1828, 15).

Question: What do you think of a person who doesn't keep his word?

Answer: I don't have a good impression of him, he is not worth being a friend (CH, 2824, 15).

In general, the arguments of the Icelandic and Chinese adolescents were very similar. Adolescents from both cultures referred to the concepts of trust, trustworthiness, and dependability as the major defining concepts both in giving reasons why a promise should be kept, in reasoning about the consequences of promise violation, and in evaluating the moral worth of a person.

The opinion of others and the impression that others get from the self's actions are highly important concerns for the self.

Understanding Close Friendship

Reasoning was assessed according to Selman's (1980) questions about meaning of close friendship: Why it is important to have a close friend and what it means to be really close? At Level 3 close friendship is interpreted in terms of intimacy, trust, and mutual dependability. A close friend is someone whom the self knows well and who knows the self well. Close friends share not only common interests but also personal experiences and inner feelings. They understand each other and are intimately related. Close friends trust each other; they must be able to rely completely on each other and be available to each other in times of need. The following statements illustrate the structure:

Question: What does it actually mean to be best friends?

Answer: Standing by each other through this and that.

Question: What is it that makes a close friendship?

Answer: One just has something in common with one's friends—one can discuss things—then there is always a fairly firm friendship established.

Question: Can you be with your girlfriend in some way other than you can be with others?

Answer: Of course one has much more self-confidence—knows her much better—one can show other sides of oneself (IC, 53, 15).

Question: Do you think it necessary to have a good friend?

Answer: Yes, I think so. It is one of the fundamental things for being able to live.

Question: Why is this?

Answer: Because if one has a problem it's like it was described earlier—a world without trust—one might have someone who is like a part of oneself. If one got into difficulties he'd help one.

Question: What does it actualy mean to be good friends?

Answer: Mutual trust. Of course it is not like a sentence being pronounced if they do fail one another—then they lose their friendship (IC, 57, 15).

Question: What does it mean to be close friends?

Answer: It means being able to trust him completely.

Question: What ties friends together?

Answer: A best friend is the person in whom you have the greatest trust regarding your affairs, and on whom you rely and who is your right hand in every way.

Question: What qualities must a good friend have?

Answer: He has to be able to understand you. If you tell him about your problems—that he can understand you—not just saying "oh, yes, you'll just take care of that yourself," but instead bringing forth his ideas—pointing things out to you (CH, 3802, 15).

Question: Do you feel you can be different with your friends from how you are with others?

Answer: Yes, I'm able to open up much more with him (IC, 117, 15).

Question: What is a good friendship?

Answers: It means good relations, to understand each other when they have difficulties, not to hide one's mistakes (CH, 3802, 15). Good friends have mutual affinity, exchange their inner thoughts, if the friend makes a mistake, criticize him and not protect him (CH, 3817, 15). [Good friends] help each other, say what is in their heart, point out what is not correct, in this way he corrects the mistake (CH, 3826, 15). Good friends trust each other, understand each other, exchange feelings, tell the friend when one feels upset, don't keep it inside.

Question: What makes people become good friends?

Answer: They say to each other what they wouldn't say to others, they have heart-to-heart talks, understand the other's feelings (CH, 2829, 15).

Overall, the arguments exemplify the notion of intimacy and moral responsibility that are characteristic for both Icelandic and Chinese adolescents at Level 3. One aspect is exclusively brought up by the Chinese participants: They take an educational attitude toward their friends and see it as their task to develop and foster the personality of the friend. This role of the friend as a corrector was rarely mentioned by Icelandic adolescents.

Situation-Specific Reasoning About Promise Keeping in Close Friendship

Participants were asked about practical decision making (what the protagonist would do and why and why he or she might also want to choose the alternative option) and about moral judgment (whether the choice was right and why or why not). Reasons referring to friendship and promises were of major importance.

At Level 3 the wish or necessity to keep a promise to the best friend is derived from a generalized norm of reciprocity involving trust and specific emotional bonding to the friend. Friendship expectations and moral responsibilities achieve equal salience in decision making and moral judgment. Responsibilities toward the friend result from the promise given and from an understanding that one is obliged in general to keep one's promises. They also result from the relationship itself: Friends have to take each other's feelings into account and assist each other in situations of need. Therefore, the friends' wish to talk about something that is mentioned in the story acquires specific moral valence. Friendship responsibilities appear to be derived from a conception of the self as part of the relationship. The self feels closely connected with the friend and wants to be viewed as reliable. The following examples demonstrate how commitment to obligations and affective bonding in relationships determines decision making, the moral evaluation of action choices, as well as the anticipation of consequences of violating obligations and responsibilities:

Question: What will Sigga do?

Answer: Of course she'll rather go to her old girlfriend because she has depended on her and they have known each other much longer and they have firmer ties of friendship, she can always go to a movie later, or even on Saturday (IC, 70, 15).

Question: You also said that this was her best girlfriend. What difference does that make?

Answer: Just being with ones' best girlfriend and being faithful to ones' friend and so on. If she breaks the promise she might easily do that any time, and then her friend will stop trusting her and so on (IC, 95, 15).

Question: What would cause Sigga to go to her friend?

Answer: It might probably be some fairly serious matter which she was going to discuss with her, and her friend would be very depressed if she went to the movie.

Question: Why is that important?

Answers: Well, true friends should stand by one another (IC, 114,15). He intends to go to his friend because he promised he would come to him. He saves going to the movie for later. It's just important with regard to honesty. If he goes running off to the movie people will stop being able to trust him (IC, 84, 15).

Question: Might Xiao Bao also first go to the newcomer?

Answer: I wouldn't go.

Question: Why?

Answer: The affection of new friends isn't as deep as between old friends, it would be more serious if he hurt the old friend's feelings (CH, 1820, 15).

Question: Why would he decide to go to the old friend's home?

Answer: Because the new friend only wanted to play with her, nothing important. But firstly, Xiao Bei has been a friend for a long time, they are on very good terms. Secondly, Xiao Bei is disturbed in her heart, so she [protagonist] should consider to go to her to make her feel relaxed (CH, 2826, 15).

Question: To whose home would he go?

Answer: He might go to Xiao Bei's home, because Xiao Bei is his old friend, he should respect the old friend's ties of friendship, he has other opportunities for Xiao Gang's friendship (CH, 1805, 15).

Question: What would Xiao Bao do?

Answer: He should go to Xiao Bei's home, because he already promised him, if he withdraws his previous commitment he will break his promise, so he should refuse Xiao Gang's invitation politely and apologize to him (CH, 1802, 15).

Question: What is the right thing for him to do?

Answer: He should explain to his new friend Xiao Gang and then go to his old friend Xiao Bei's home.

Question: Why does Xiao Bao have to keep his word to his friend?

Answer: I feel he should.

Question: Why?

Answer: Good friends should be honest to each other, they shouldn't cheat (CH, 1806, 15)

Question: Is it the right decision to go to her friend?

Answer: Yes, in the first place she has been invited and one shouldn't go around betraying.

Question: You say betraying, what difference does a promise make?

Answer: A promise is very important. For example if one has promised something and breaks it, then the person to whom you save the promise may get a bad impression of you. It's really just ... oh, this is so very difficult to explain. I just feel a promise is very important (IC, 33, 15).

Question: Do you feel this is the right decision?

Answer: Yes

Question: Why?

Answer: Because they will continue being good friends.

Question: Why is that important?

Answer: It may not be certain that they will meet someone else whom they can confide in and so on. They have started to confide so much in each other and trust each other completely. They have been together for such a long time (IC, 101, 9).

The examples show rather striking similarities in how Chinese and Icelandic adolescents interpret the friendship dilemma. The strict obligation to keep a promise, outlined both in general moral reasoning about promise keeping and in the general understanding of close friendship, is evidenced in the reasons given for practical and moral choice. Responsibilities toward the friend and the special needs of the friend acquire primary significance in the situation. Trustworthiness and dependability represent central attributes of the self. In close friendships the obligations that we owe to everyone—such as keeping one's promises—are transformed into special responsibilities arising from the close interconnectedness of friends. Thus, in both cultures the moral self at Level 3 is defined as a relationship self.

Moral Feelings From a Cross-Cultural Perspective

Next, we compared the feelings ascribed to the protagonist as a function of the action choice. Participants were asked about the consequences related to the action choice or to the alternative option—how the protagonist would feel or would have felt if he or she was meeting the friend as promised or how he or she would feel or would have felt visiting the movie with the newcomer—and to give reasons for these feelings.

Feelings were scored at Level 3 when the participants explained the feelings of the protagonist by referring to a violation of trust and intimacy in the friendship or the trustworthiness of the person in general or altruistic obligations toward the newcomer (Keller, 1996). The following examples illustrate this:

Question: Well, let us imagine Sigga had gone to the movies. What will she then be thinking?
Answer: About her girlfriend, mostly.
Question: How does she then feel?
Answer: Just feels she has failed her girlfriend (IC, 53, 15).
Question: How would she feel at her friend's house?
Answer: Of course, if she had said no to Inga [newcomer] she would feel good.
Question: Yes, why would she then feel good?
Answer: She feels she has a clean conscience (IC, 51, 15).
Question: How would he feel at his friend's house?
Answer: He feels very good, he didn't break a promise, he's in the clear (IC, 117, 15).
Question: Let us suppose Xiao Bao went to his old friend Xiao Bei's home, how would he feel?

Answers: He feels he let Xiao Gang down. Because Xiao Gang is a newcomer, he doesn't know the other schoolmates, he only knows
these two. Now he invited one of the friends, but this friend went to
his old friend's home, so Xiao Gang feels very lonely, Xiao Bao let
him down (CH, 1823, 15). Xiao Gang might be anxiously waiting
at the cinema, or his feelings are hurt and he is disappointed, he
feels this is the first time he invites Xiao Bao, but Xiao Bao doesn't
come, 'Xiao Bao does not want to be good friends with me' (CH,
1823, 15).

The feelings reveal the same conceptual structure of Stage 3 reasoning in
both cultures. The violation of responsibilities leads to guilt feelings, which
may concern either the friend or the newcomer or both. Positive moral feelings
are experienced when the situation is interpreted such that the self has resisted
a moral temptation. As discussed next there are clear cultural differences in
patterns of decision making and moral feelings.

ACTION CHOICE, MORAL JUDGMENT, AND MORAL
FEELINGS FROM A CROSS-CULTURAL PERSPECTIVE

Moral Consistency

One of the central arguments concerning the emergence of the moral self in adolescence (Keller & Edelstein, 1993) was that adolescents experienced a necessity to establish consistency between their practical choice and moral
judgment (e.g., how will the protagonist decide in this situation, what is the
right choice?). The cross-cultural comparison reveals that this previous assumption must be modified.

Fig. 12.1 shows the relation between the actual choices in the dilemma and
the moral judgment of these choices from childhood to late adolescence, age
19 years. Nearly all Icelandic participants from the youngest age on saw it as
morally right to visit the old friend in this situation. The practical choice revealed a different pattern than the moral judgment. Especially the youngest
children argued much more frequently that the protagonist would opt to be
with the newcomer. The inconsistency between practical choice and moral
judgment decreased over time and moral consistency became the predominant
pattern. Particularly the 15 year olds and the 19 year olds established consistency between practical and moral judgment. This finding supports the assumption that the importance of close friendships increases in adolescence and
remains stable even in late adolescence.

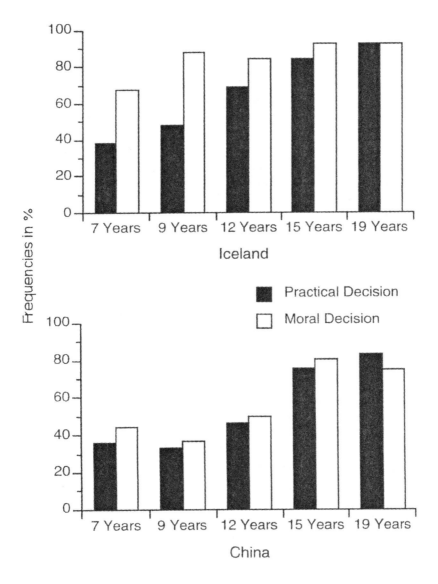

FIG. 12.1. Practical and moral decision for option "friend" in Iceland and China.

For the Chinese participants consistency is not a developmental phenomenon. In contrast to the Icelandic subjects, they showed consistency between the action choice of the protagonist or self and the moral judgment of this choice at all ages. Even the youngest Chinese subjects evidenced no split between practical and moral reasoning. Most remarkably, consistency was maintained despite the fact that the Chinese subjects changed the direction of both their practical choice and, correspondingly, their moral judgment. The younger subjects more frequently opted for the newcomer and evaluated this as the morally right choice. The older subjects and, in particular, the 15 year olds opted for the friend and judged this choice as morally right. This pattern remains for the 19 year olds.

Keller et al. (1998) analyzed the reasons given for the options of friend or newcomer and for the moral judgments until age 15. For the Icelandic participants the hedonistic quality of the newcomer's offer played an important role in the practical choice. In contrast, the Chinese participants focused on altruistic aspects: that this child was new in school or that one wants to or must help somebody who has no friends. The increasing similarities in practical choice and moral judgment in the older participants from both cultures indicated that over time close friendship became a more important value in both cultures. Reasons referring to close friendship over time gained precedence in practical and moral decision making over hedonistic or altruistic concerns.

Moral Feelings

Keller, Schuster, and Jacob (1996) compared the attribution of feelings to the protagonist in the dilemma on the basis of the practical choice (e.g., meeting the friend or the newcomer). Concerning both options—if the protagonist would be meeting with the newcomer or friend—the questions were as follows: How would you feel in this situation? Why would you feel this way? The 15-year-old adolescents from the two cultures revealed striking differences in the pattern of moral feelings (the 19 year olds had not yet been available at that time). Both Icelandic and Chinese adolescents argued that not visiting the friend as promised would lead to guilt feelings in the protagonist or self. However, their argument concerning the newcomer was very different. The Icelandic adolescents imagined that the protagonist or self most frequently felt good in the situation of visiting the friend, because he or she had done the right thing and not hurt the friend's feelings. The Chinese participants, contrarily, imagined that the protagonist or self mostly felt bad because he or she had hurt the feelings of the newcomer. Although this cultural difference was most pronounced in the adolescents, it was also visible in the younger participants. When opting for the friend, the younger Icelandic children more frequently felt ambivalent about having missed an interesting invitation. The younger Chinese children mostly were worried about having left out the newcomer. Interestingly, the 7 year olds frequently referred to an authority rule in school—that one should help somebody who is new in class. Only later the feelings of the newcomer became salient. This is a very good example of an authority-oriented empathy.

Overall, the cross-cultural comparison of the feelings of the protagonist or self revealed that the Chinese participants experienced guilt feelings independent of how they opted. They interpreted the situation as a moral dilemma of conflicting obligations to the friend and to the newcomer. The Icelandic children and adolescents tended to interpret the dilemma in terms of a conflict between obligations to the friend and an egoistic desire (Keller, 1996; Keller & Edelstein, 1993; Keller et al., 1998). Therefore, they predicted guilt feelings only when friendship responsibilities were violated or positive moral feelings only when consistency was established between action choice and perceived obligation. Thus, for the Icelandic participants friendship has emotional priority over the relationship to the newcomer, but this is not the case for the Chinese participants.

The results show that moral inconsistency is not a general phenomenon in younger children across cultures. However, the importance of close friendships in adolescence seems to be universal across the two very different cultures studied here (and for the other cultures included into our broader cross-cultural project [Keller, Kolbe, & Edelstein, 1998]). For the Icelandic participants the value of close friendships gains precedence over egoistic concerns. The Chinese adolescents change their value priorities from explicitly socialized authority rules in childhood to a more self-constructed responsibility in friendship in adolescence. Despite this change in value priority, however, the collectivist values of the culture are represented in guilt feelings that arise from the violation of normative expectations in relationships. For both Icelandic and Chinese adolescents close friendship is a particularly important relationship for the development of a moral self in adolescence. But friendship appears to be less exclusive or private among Chinese adolescents. Even at Stage 3 the self seems to be embedded in the broader system of relationships. This integration of self in relationships is maintained in the transition into the higher stages of development.

SELF AND RELATIONSHIPS IN THE TRANSITION FROM MIDDLE TO LATE ADOLESCENCE

From a cognitive–developmental perspective the developmental task of the transition into late adolescence or young adulthood has been described as the necessity to acquire reflexive distance to relationships and to establish an understanding of the self as an autonomous actor. In reasoning about close friend-ships (Selman, 1980) the late adolescent has achieved simultaneous understanding of both the psychological complexities of the human mind and other personalities and of uniqueness and individuality. Close friendships are seen as a matching of individual personalities, and respect for each other's in-dividuality is the prerequisite for establishing and maintaining closeness. Due to their psychological complexity, persons are seen to have multiple interests. Therefore, they need multiple relationships to satisfy these different concerns. Relationships may have different degrees of intimacy and serve different func-tions, such as pursuing common interests or communicating about psychologi-cally relevant matters. It is understood that persons can change in their personalities and their interests so that close friends can grow apart as a result of different developments. In late adolescence dialectic between intimate in-terconnection and individuality emerges and emotional closeness and auton-omy needs to be balanced. The self and close relationships have to be integrated into the wider social system.

In Kohlberg's (1984) theory of moral development Stage 4 contains two components. On one hand, the self is defined in terms of obligations and re-sponsibilities in the broader social system. On the other hand, an inner psycho-logical self emerges in terms of autonomy and responsibility. Responsibility is no longer exclusively rooted in stereotypically defined role obligations and conformity to significant others or groups but now finds a place in the consis-tency of the inner moral self. At Stage 4 it is no longer exclusively important how one appears in the eyes of others but also how one appears in the eyes of the self. The meaning of personal integrity is to be consistent with one's own beliefs. Violating obligations and responsibilities is not only wrong because it hurts the feelings of others but also because it indicates a moral weakness of the self and thus violates the person's self-respect.

Loevinger (1976) described the conscientious stage of ego development as characteristic of late adolescence or young adulthood. Similarly to Kohlberg's theory, at this stage the more stereotypic interpretation of the world is substituted by a more differentiated view on the self and relation-ships. The person begins to establish a sense of self-independence of group demands and sanctions. Conformity to the group is less important than con-sistency with the inner standards of the self. The person has established evaluative standards of the self in terms of goals and ideals and uses these standards to judge his or her performance in terms of the achievement of these goals and ideals. The self is understood in its psychological complexity, and the evaluation of the moral rightness of behavior does not depend exclu-sively on the opinion of others. Kegan (1982) described Stage 4 of the devel-opment of the self in terms of an "institutional balance." Compared to the previous stage, in which the self is defined in terms of relationships (i.e., the self is the relationship), the self now has its relationships. The self is seen as the actor who is in control of relationships and can coordinate multiple relationships and choose between them. At the same time, the needs, interests, and feelings of the self are no longer determined exclusively by these relationships; rather, a person can exert inner control and select between conflicting tendencies as well as set priorities according to the values the person affirms as important for the self.

Underlying the two stages that prototypically characterize reasoning about self and relationships in adolescence and late adolescence or young adulthood are the two opposing poles of connectedness and fusion with others or autonomy and individuality of the self. From the perspective of the mature adult stages that have been described in these theories, each of the two stages is characterized by an imbalance between these two poles. In the adolescent stage the inner psychological self is fused with others; it is mirrored back to the self from the eyes of significant others in relationships. Thus, the developmental task is to establish a sense of separateness and independence. To achieve this goal the person has to balance the needs for intimacy and exclusive emotional ties, such as in close friendships, with a growing awareness of diverging values, needs, and interests of the self in a network of relationships. In theories of friendship, Selman (1980) defined the Stage 4 of autonomy as the final developmental stage. In theories of morality and self, Kegan (1982) pointed out that in the phase of young adulthood individuality and control may be overemphasized and the person may be preoccupied with separateness and with establishing distance at the price of losing connectedness and intimacy. The contradiction between the two positions of fusion and separateness can only be transcended at the higher stages of development. Interestingly, the distinction between Stage 3 interconnectedness and Stage 4 individuality and separateness is inherent in the distinction between collectivism and individualism from the cross-cultural perspective, such as was previously described, distinguishing Asian and Western cultures. It is not surprising, therefore, that cross-cultural research on moral development critically discussed a Western bias.

THE TRANSITION FROM MIDDLE TO LATE ADOLESCENCE IN A CROSS-CULTURAL PERSPECTIVE

Research about Chinese moral reasoning in the framework of Kohlberg's theory of moral judgment has consistently emphasized the validity of the sequence of stages at least until Stage 4 but highlighted differences in the content of moral reasoning. Many researchers in the Kohlberg tradition have pointed out that the scoring manual for moral judgments developed on the basis of interviews with Americans did not capture various issues of interpersonal connectedness and harmony mentioned by persons from Asian cultures (Boyes & Walker, 1988; Snarey, 1985). Only at Stage 3, during which the self is defined in terms of relationships and interpersonal care is an important concern, the stage definition is consistent with the description of a collectivist orientation. Research has been mostly interested in the higher stages of moral development and criticized these as ethnocentric. As we showed the lower stages, particularly Stage 2 in Kohlberg's theory, also have to be revised to include empathic or collectivistic concerns (Keller, Eckensberger, & von Rosen, 1989; Keller & Edelstein, 1991). Ma (1988) has criticized that Stage 4, with its focus on the individual and independent self, cannot capture issues of care and interpersonal harmony adequately. He defined a Chinese Stage 4 perspective characterized not by the separation of self from others but by a growing concern about the stability and harmony of group relationships and society in general. He concluded that norms in Asian cultures are more rigid and behavior in relationships is guided by strong normative expectations. In particular, the self must subordinate personal wishes and even rights to the welfare and harmony of group and society (Shweder et al., 1987). In most cases, relationships are hierarchically structured, but conflicts have to be negotiated in a soft and harmonious way (Bond, 1996). Ma's description of Stage 4 resembles the description of Stage 3. It maintains the perspective of the interdependent self but defines characteristics of Stage 3 from a broader societal perspective.

REASONING ABOUT PROMISE KEEPING AND CLOSE FRIENDSHIPS IN LATE ADOLESCENCE

On the basis of our cross-cultural interviews with 19 year olds, we specified indicators for the transition into Stage 4 social–moral reasoning (Cecora & Eckert, 2002; Cecora, Eckert, Gummerum, & Keller, 2002). The statements confirmed the Stage 4 friendship conception in Selman's (1980) theory. Concerning self and moral development these indicators may sometimes not be fully representative of Stage 4, but they are different from the indicators of adolescent Stage 3 reasoning in our study. One should keep in mind that Ma (1988) analyzed reasoning about classical moral dilemmas in the Kohlberg tradition, in which mostly hierarchically structured relationships are involved. In contrast, we analyzed reasoning about friendship, a relationship of equality. In the Chinese culture friendship is seen as the only relationship of equality, whereas all other relationships are hierarchically structured throughout life (Bond, 1996).

The indicators of Level 4 interpersonal moral reasoning occurred far more frequently in general reasoning about moral norms and relationships than in situation-specific reasoning about the friendship dilemma, which was mostly scored at Stage 3. Overall, Stage 4 reasoning is characterized by a deeper psychological understanding of the complexity of personalities and relationships. The self is seen as a person with beliefs, values, and goals, and relationships are seen as embedded in more complex social systems. Trust is seen as the basis of relationships and responsibility, and respect is viewed as the basis of the moral person. This is exemplified in the following.

Chinese young adults define promise keeping as the basis, the criterion, or the prerequisite for being a moral person: "It is one aspect of self respect" (CH, 27, 19). "[Not keeping a promise] is not good for a person, if she has no belief or aim it will affect her behavior and she also does not feel well either" (CH, 29, 19). For the Icelandic participants promise keeping is "like trying to stand by the goals one has set for oneself" (IC, 108, 19). "Keeping a promise is just a question of honor, but perhaps you could look at it from a wider perspective—in such a perspective that it is a question of mutual responsibility" (IC, 89, 19). Not keeping a promise means "that one betrays one's inner person. I think it so important to be responsible towards other people" (IC, 82, 19). "[Never keeping a promise] that's clear, must be lacking a part called responsibility and I sometimes feel that it just shows a lack of respect" (IC, 82, 19) (IC, 65, 19). Promise keeping is closely interconnected with relationships. It is seen as "the basis for true friendship" (CH, 17, 19) and "the basis for making friends and being a person" (CH, 14, 19).

Living in society and concern with the integration and the advancement of persons in society are central aspects frequently emphasized by the Chinese 19 year olds reasoning about promise keeping: "We live in society and society is the grouping of people. A person will surely meet some difficulties which he can't solve, so he asks for others to help. A person who doesn't keep his promise will be isolated in society; nobody speaks to him; he won't exist in society very long" (CH, 16, 19). "If in society nobody keeps promises to each other, then society cannot advance, so keeping promises is of help to the development of society" (CH, 13, 19). "By not keeping a promise people won't trust you; you can't stand in society; if you just keep promises among friends, then it is among a small circle, you can't expand, but if you keep promises to everyone you will be acknowledged by everyone" (CH, 25, 19). Promise keeping also serves to maintain business transactions: "One must cooperate with others, then one can succeed in society. People who do not keep their promise can fool others for a short time, but won't get the trust of others for a long time, few people will have good relations with this kind of person, and these people cannot always succeed in trade. Connecting with society, if an enterprise does not keep its promise it will be eliminated by the market" (CH, 24, 19).

It was more typical for the Chinese than for the Icelandic young adults to emphasize that persons are interconnected with each other in society and that they must cooperate and develop each other's and society's welfare.

Concerning the importance of close friendships both Chinese and Icelandic 19 year olds see it as necessary for the development of the self. "[Without my friend] my spiritual life wouldn't be so good, she has the effect on me that I can stop and give a little thought to myself" (IC, 48, 19). Persons are described on the basis of enduring dispositions, attitudes and biographical experiences that produce unique characters and must be respected by others.

Question: What if you do not have a friendship?

Answer: If you are an introverted person you will be even more introverted, you will be eccentric and think very extremely.

Question: How would life be without friendship?

Answers: It depends on the characteristics of the person, extroverts when they suddenly lose the friend can't bear it, they will be low-spirited, whereas introverts won't feel anything (CH, 25, 19). Friends are selected according to values and principles that should match. It is important that they share basic values and have understanding for each other.

Question: What type of a person is a good friend?

Answers: It's just a person who I like, who suits me and has qualities that I value (IC, 53, 19). It is important to "choose friends according to one's principles" (CH, 20, 19), and according to the moral quality of the person: "One should believe in him, believe in his character and morals, and his friendship to you" (CH, 1, 19).

In contrast to Stage 3 this matching of personalities does not imply that friends always have the same opinion or have the same interests. Rather, they must understand each other psychologically, have a similar orientation to life, and tolerate each other's personalities.

Question: How do you know he's your good friend?

Answer: Same outlook on life, same characteristics (CH, 25, 19).

Question: What makes good friends?

Answer: Character, personality, such as extroverts like extroverts, introverts like introverts (CH, 28, 19).

Question: What qualities does a good friend need to have?

Answers: Perhaps some tolerance toward the other person and some mutual
interests and so on (IC, 19, 89). Good friends need not talk when
being together because they understand each other's heart, even
friends with different temperament can be long lasting friends
(CH, 9, 19).

Question: Do good friends quarrel?

Answers: Yes, anybody would, because people are not perfect, they make
mistakes, quarrelling won't influence friendship, one should be
tolerant to the other's mistakes (CH, 17, 19). People have the right
to their opinions, I don't want everyone to be alike, think alike and
act alike (IC, 78, 19). I don't believe friends are friends unless they
quarrel, because it shows one has independent thoughts and dares
express them and has no hesitation about doing that (IC, 107, 19).

Trust and trustworthiness are important at Stage 3, but at Stage 4 trust is
seen as the basis and the prerequisite of friendship. Icelandic participants mention this most frequently.

Question: What ties friends together?

Answers: Faith and trust, that is what friendship is based on (IC, 111, 19). I
believe friendship is greatly based on trust (IC, 107, 19). Friendship is built on trust—one has to be able to trust the person completely and if that doesn't exist the will isn't sufficient (IC, 108,
19). Mutual trust is the basis for friends (CH, 13, 19).

Friendship is seen as mutual support and as a chance for personal development.

Question: How important is friendship to you?

Answers: It's very important––especially with regard to one's
self-confidence, one always needs to have someone standing besides you if you're about to weaken in something (IC, 53, 19).
Friendship is a kind of supporting force (CH, 19, 25). Friendship
will make you have confidence in life (CH, 9, 19).

The Icelandic participants see the friend predominantly as a therapist who
through his or her empathy and understanding helps to clarify and understand
problematic life situations: "I want to be available for my friends when they
need me emotionally, but I also want them to be there for me when I need them"
(IC, 65, 19). "You are able to put yourself into his position, and you can look at
the world with his eyes. It is of course better if you can look at the world from

both sides" (IC, 90, 19). This caring attitude is specific to relationships of equality: "Parents cannot replace friends because care of another generation is different from the same generation" (CH, 1, 19).

Similar to reasoning about promise keeping, the Chinese participants emphasized that friendship is embedded in society: "Without friendship the person would be isolated and lonely and could not function as a member of society. He needs help in society, for a long time they help each other, they compensate each other, when one is frustrated one needs comfort to overcome difficulty, and obtain happiness in helping others" (CH, 17, 19). "Friendship gives convenience to oneself, one has a safe surrounding, society would be rather cold and detached without friendship. One is born with friends because a person is in society" (CH, 20, 19). "One lives in society, associates with people, so one needs the understanding and help of others" (CH, 21, 19). "Without friendship one feels lonesome, very lonely, no sustenance in life, pessimistic outlook, one drifts away from society" (CH, 11, 19). "If a person does not have friendship he stands alone in society" (CH, 14, 19). "Without friendship one will be alone in social life, after all, people live in the group, live in colonies" (CH, 15, 19). "If one is alone one can't live well in society, if there is no friendship one gets more and more eccentric" (CH, 23, 19). "A person lives in society, he can't be isolated, friendship is a kind of supporting force" (CH, 25, 19).

Overall, these qualitative examples reveal a lot of communality in the arguments of the 19 year olds from the two cultures, concerning promise keeping and close friendship. First, the growing psychological complexity of arguments is visible in both groups. Second, with regard to the Stage 3/4 or collectivist/individualistic distinction of relationship integration versus self-differentiation, the examples document that the individual self is emphasized in both groups. When arguing about promise keeping, concepts like self-respect, honor, and responsibility are mentioned frequently. This is consistent with Kohlberg's Stage 4 of moral reasoning. However, the second aspect of Kohlberg's Stage 4, the integration of the person into society, seems to be far more salient in the Chinese participants. They pointed out much more frequently that a person is a part of society and that the individual behavior serves to maintain and foster relationships in society. The Icelandic participants use this argument rarely. The arguments about the importance of close friendships are consistent with Selman's (1980) description of Stage 4 friendship reasoning. Again, in both groups the psychological complexity of persons is revealed in the statements and both intimacy and individuality are seen as necessary for close friendships. However, there also seem to be cultural differences in the use of arguments. The Icelandic participants frequently emphasized trust as the basis of relationships—a prototypical argument also in

Kohlberg's Stage 4 of moral reasoning. The intimacy aspect of Stage 3 is transformed into defining the friend as a consultant for problems and questions of life. The Chinese participants see friendship as a relationship that is functional and necessary to live in society. This aspect is not mentioned at all by the Icelandic participants who see friendship exclusively as an intimate and private relationship. Thus, the collectivist self of relationship integration is maintained in Stage 4 reasoning by the Chinese, whereas the aspect of individuality is more prominent in the Icelandic participants. Further quantitative analyses of the content of the arguments are necessary to confirm the intuitions from the qualitative examples given here.

CONCLUSIONS

This chapter serves two purposes. On one hand, we showed how the definition of self in adolescence is closely interconnected with relationships and how in the transition to late adolescence or young adulthood a conception of an individual self emerges. Close friendships remain an important value in the definition of the self in late adolescence. This is probably due to the fact that friendship is one of the most important relationships in life, besides the parent–child relationship and the love relationships beginning in adolescence. As the results show, the importance of close friendships in adolescence seems to be universal across the two different cultural contexts.

On the other hand, we showed that the culture or the society in which the person is living is an important factor in defining the meaning of the self in relationship. Cross-cultural data revealed that findings from one culture—or from similar Western cultures—cannot be universally generalized to other—in particular Asian—cultures. We discussed this with regard to the role of moral consistency and moral feelings that were defined as central components in the emergence of the moral self in adolescence. Both components have to be seen differently in light of our cross-cultural research. One difference concerned the fact that the Chinese participants nearly never showed a pattern of moral consistency, whereas consistency was a developmental phenomenon in the Icelandic participants. The other difference concerned the moral feelings that included the newcomer in China.

Some may argue that Chinese participants are authority oriented and do not dare to reveal their real thinking. This, however, does not explain why they changed their options during development—a change that clearly went against the values taught in school to integrate newcomers. These rules were mentioned by the younger children themselves (e.g., there is a rule in school or the teacher says you should help somebody who is new). Our Chinese research colleagues confirmed that there are 10 rules for pupils in elementary school among which is helping a newcomer. This rule is consistent with Berndt's (1993) analysis that highly personal close friendships were not favored in China. Despite this, the Chinese participants increasingly favored the friend over the newcomer, just as the Icelandic adolescents did. Thus, they opted against explicit and implicit cultural values. This does not diminish their high value of collectivist ideals as the altruistic concerns and the moral feelings reveal. The Chinese participants defined the situation as a moral dilemma and felt bad about their choice however they opted in contradistinction to the Icelandic participants who predominantly emphasized the obligation toward the friend. The 19-year-old Chinese participants emphasized the interconnection of self, close relationships, and society, whereas the Icelandic late adolescents emphasized the individual self and the private and exclusive status of close friendships.

Again, this raises the question how far the Chinese conceptions of self, relationships, and society are the product of explicit moral socialization and cultural ideology that is present in everyday life of Chinese children and adolescents and in explicit moral socialization. Claudia Schneider (2003) analyzed Chinese schoolbooks to get a better understanding of explicit moral socialization. Icelandic schools do not teach values in this way, and concepts about self and relationships are much more constructed by experiences than explicitly learned in school. Historically, friendship had for Icelanders a similar function as a social support system as it has for the Chinese now. This is evidenced in the medieval sagas, where close friendships are based on the exchange of blood—signalizing that they are like family bonds. However, the Icelandic type of living as isolated farmers or fishers has historically produced a strong value of individualism with strong family ties. The title of the book *Independent People* by the Icelandic Nobel Prize winner in literature—Halldor Laxness (1996)—captures this nicely. Iceland has experienced a radical modernization from a farming and fishing society after World War II (see Edelstein, 1983, 1999 for a description of growing up in premodern and modern Iceland). One of the reasons why Wolfgang Edelstein performed a longitudinal study in Iceland was to analyze the effects of this modernization process on individual development. One of the reasons why our Chinese colleague Fang Fu-Xi started the joint venture of a cooperative comparative project was the intuition that China would experience a similar radical process of modernization. History has proven him more than correct. It is a question for future research whether and how the capitalistic modernization in China, which has proceeded with increasing speed since the late 1980s when our study began, will affect sociomoral reasoning about self, relationships and society. The initial results from our Chinese longitudinal data reveal such changes (Keller, Edelstein, Gummerum, Fang, & Fang, 2003).

ACKNOWLEDGMENTS

This research was conducted in cooperation with Wolfgang Edelstein at the Max Planck Institute for Human Development, Berlin, and Fang Fu-Xi and Fang Ge at the Institute of Psychology at the Chinese Academy of Sciences. The authors gratefully acknowledge the support of the Center for Adaptive Behavior and Cognition at the Max Planck Institute for Human Development (Director: Gerd Gigerenzer). We wish to thank Michaela Gummerum and Claudia Schneider for the discussion of the examples and helpful comments on the chapter. Zu Liqi from the Institute of Psychology at the Chinese Academy of Sciences gave us further insights into Chinese reasoning about self and relationships.

REFERENCES

Arsenio, W. F., & Lover, A. (1995). Children's conceptions of sociomoral affect: Happy victimizers, mixed emotions and other expectancies. In M. Killen & D. Hart (Eds.), *Morality in everyday life: Developmental perspectives* (pp. 87–128). New York: Cambridge University Press.

Berndt, T. J. (1993, March). *The morality of friendship.* Paper presented at the 60th anniversary meeting of the Society for Research in Child Development, New Orleans, LA.

Blasi, A. (1983). Moral cognition and moral action: A theoretical perspective. *Developmental Review, 3,* 178–210.

Blasi, A. (1984). Autonomie im Gehorsam. Der Erwerb von Distanz im Sozialisationsprozeß [Autonomy in obedience: The development in process of socialization]. In W. Edelstein & J. Habermas (Eds.), *Soziale Interaktion und soziales Verstehen: Beiträge zur Entwicklung der Interaktionskompetenz* [Social interaction and social understanding: Contributions to the development of interaction competence] (pp. 300–347). Frankfurt am Main, Germany: Suhrkamp.

Blasi, A., & Oresick, R. J. (1986). Emotions and cognitions in self-inconsistency. In D. J. Bearison & H. Zimiles (Eds.), *Thought and emotion* (pp. 147–165). Hillsdale, NJ: Lawrence Erlbaum Associates.

Blum, L. A. (1980). *Friendship, altruism and morality.* London: Routledge & Kegan Paul.

Bond, M. H. (1996). *The handbook of Chinese psychology.* New York: Oxford University Press.

Boyes, M., & Walker, L. J. (1988). Implications of cultural diversity for the universality claims of Kohlberg's theory of moral reasoning. *Human Development, 31,* 44–59.

Bukowski, W. M., & Sippola, L. K. (1996). Friendship and morality: (How) are they related? In W. M. Bukowski, A. F. Newcomb & W. W. Hartup (Eds.), *The company they keep* (pp. 238–261). Cambridge, MA: Cambridge University Press.

Cecora, I., & Eckert, U. (2002). *Entwicklung soziomoralischen Verstehens im Jugendalter* [Development of sociomoral understanding in adolescence]. Unpublished diploma thesis, Free University, Berlin, Germany.

Cecora, L., Eckert, U., Gummerum, M., & Keller, M. (2002). *Manual for scoring stages of moral reasoning.* Max-Planck Institute for Human Development, Berlin: Unpublished manuscript.

Damon, W., & Hart, D. (1982). The development of self-understanding from infancy through adolescence. *Child Development, 53,* 841–864.

Edelstein, W. (1983). Cultural constraints on development and the vicissitudes of progress. In F. S. Kessel & A. W. Siegel (Eds.), *Psychology and society: The child and other cultural inventions* (pp. 48–81). New York: Praeger.

Edelstein, W. (1999). The cognitive context of historical change: Assimilation, accommodation, and the segmentation of competence. In E. Turiel (Ed.), *Developmental and cultural change: Reciprocal processes* (pp. 5–17). San Francisco: Jossey-Bass.

Edelstein, W., Keller, M. & Schröder, E. (1990). Child development and social structure: A longitudinal study of individual differences. In P. B. Baltes, D. L. Featherman, & R. M. Lerner (Eds.), *Life-span development and behavior* (Vol. 19, pp. 151–185). Hillsdale, NJ: Lawrence Erlbaum Associates.

Gerson, R. R., & Damon, W. (1978). Moral understanding and children's conduct. In W. Damon (Ed.), *Moral development* (pp. 41–61). San Francisco: Jossey-Bass.

Gilligan, C. (1982). *In a different voice: Psychological theory and women's development.* Cambridge, MA: Harvard University Press.

Harris, P. L. (1989). *Children and emotion.* Oxford, England: Basil Blackwell.

Kegan, R. (1982). *The evolving self: Problem and process in human development.* Cambridge, MA: Harvard University Press.

Keller, M. (1984). Resolving conflicts in friendship: The development of moral understanding in everyday life. In W. M. Kurtines & J. L. Gewirtz (Eds.), *Morality, moral behavior, and moral development* (pp. 140–158). New York: Wiley.

Keller, M. (1996). *Moralische Sensibilität: Entwicklung in Freundschaft und Familie* [Moral sensibility: Development in friendship and family]. Weinheim, Germany: Psychologie-Verlags Union.

Keller, M., Eckensberger, L. H., & von Rosen, K. (1989). A critical note on the conception of preconventional morality: The case of stage 2 in Kohlberg's theory. *International Journal of Behavioral Development, 12,* 57–69.

Keller, M., & Edelstein, W. (1991). The development of socio-moral meaning making: Domains, categories, and perspective-taking. In W. M. Kurtines & J. L. Gewirtz (Eds.), *Handbook of moral behavior and development: Vol. 2. Research* (pp. 89–114). Hillsdale, NJ: Lawrence Erlbaum Associates.

Keller, M., & Edelstein, W. (1993). The development of the moral self from childhood to adolescence. In G. G. Noam & T. E. Wren, in cooperation with G. Nunner-Winkler & W. Edelstein (Eds.), *The moral self* (pp. 310–336). Cambridge, MA: MIT Press.

Keller, M., Edelstein, W., Gummerum, M., Fang, F. X., & Fang, G. (2003, July). Moral reasoning, culture and change. Paper presented at the 29th annual conference of the Assoication for Moral Education. Krakow, Poland.

Keller, M., Edelstein, W., Schmid, C., Fang, F.-X., & Fang, G. (1998). Reasoning about responsibilities and obligations in close relationships: A comparison across two cultures. *Developmental Psychology, 34,* 731–741.

Keller, M., Kolbe, S., & Edelstein, W. (1998, September). *Moralische Entscherdungen und begründgen im Ku Hurvergleich* (Moral decision making in different cultures].

Paper preseneted at the 41st Congress of the German Society for Psychology, Dresden, Germany.

Keller, M., Lourenço, O., Malti, T., & Saalbach, H. (2003). The multifacetted phenomenon of happy victimizers: A cross-cultural comparison. *British Journal of Developmental Psychology, 21*, 1–18.

Keller, M., & Reuss, S. (1984). An action-theoretical reconstruction of the development of social-cognitive competence. *Human Development, 27*, 211–220.

Keller, M., Schuster, P., & Jacob, S. (1996, September). *Die Interaktion von Entwicklung und Sozialisation in der Entwicklung moralischer Gefühle.* [The interaction of development and socialization in the development of moral feelings]. Paper presented at the 40th convention of the German Psychological Association, Munich, Germany.

Kim, U., Triandis, H. C., Kagitçibasi, C., Choi, S.-C., & Yoon, G. (1994). *Individualism and collectivism.* London: Sage.

Kohlberg, L. (1984). *Essays on moral development: Vol. 2. The psychology of moral development: The nature and validity of moral stages.* San Francisco: Harper & Row.

Kohlberg, L., & Candee, D. (1984). The relationship of moral judgment to moral action. In W. M. Kurtines & J. L. Gewirtz (Eds.), *Morality, moral behavior, and moral development* (pp. 52–73). New York: Wiley.

Laxness, H. K. (1946). *Independent people: An epic.* New York: Knopf.

Loevinger, J. (1976). *Ego development: Conceptions and theories.* San Francisco: Jossey-Bass.

Ma, H. K. (1988). The Chinese perspectives on moral judgment development. *International Journal of Psychology, 23*, 201–227.

Markus, H. R., & Kitayama, S. (1991). Culture and the self: Implications for cognition, emotion, and motivation. *Psychological Review, 98*, 224–253.

Miller, J. G., & Bersoff, D. M. (1992). Culture and moral judgment: How are conflicts between justice and interpersonal responsibilities resolved? *Journal of Personality and Social Psychology, 62*, 541–554.

Noam, G. G., & Kegan, R. (1982). Soziale Kognition und Psychodynamik: Auf dem Weg zu einer klinischen Entwicklungspsychologie [Social cognition and psychodynamics: On the way to a classical developmental psychology]. In W. Edelstein & M. Keller (Eds.), *Perspektivität und Interpretation: Beiträge zur Entwicklung des sozialen Verstehens* [Perspectivity and interpretation: Contribution to the development of social understanding] (pp. 422–460). Frankfurt am Main, Germany: Suhrkamp.

Nunner-Winkler, G., & Sodian, B. (1988). Children's understanding of moral emotions. *Child Development, 59*, 1323–1338.

Piaget, J. (1965). *The moral judgment of the child.* New York: The Free Press. (Original work published 1932).

Roetz, H. (1997). Kohlberg and Chinese moral philosophy. *World Psychology, 2*(3–4), 335–363.

Schneider, C. (2003). *Moralische Wertkonzepte in chinesischen Schulbuchern* [Moral value concepts in chinese school books]. Unpublished thesis, University of Leipzig, Germany.

Selman, R. L. (1980). *The growth of interpersonal understanding: Developmental and clinical analyses.* New York: Academic.

Shweder, R. A., Mahapatra, M., & Miller, J. G. (1987). Culture and moral development. In J. Kagan & S. Lamb (Eds.), *The emergence of morality in young children* (pp. 1–83). Chicago, IL: University of Chicago Press.

Snarey, J. R. (1985). Cross-cultural universality of social-cognitive development: A critical review of Kohlbergian research. *Psychological Bulletin, 97,* 202–232.

Sullivan, H. S. (1953). *The interpersonal theory of psychiatry.* New York: Norton.

Triandis, H. C. (1990). Cross-cultural studies of individualism and collectivism. In J. J. Berman (Ed.), *Nebraska Symposium on Motivation 1989: Vol. 37. Cross-cultural perspectives* (pp. 41–133). Lincoln, NE: University of Nebraska Press.

Turiel, E. (1998). The development of morality. In W. Damon (Series Ed.) & N. Eisenberg (Vol. Ed.), *Handbook of child psychology: Vol. 3. Social, emotional, and personality developoment* (5th ed., pp. 863–932). New York: Wiley.

Youniss, J. (1980). *Parents and peers in social development: A Sullivan–Piaget perspective.* Chicago, IL: University of Chicago Press.

13

Sociohistoric Changes in the Structure of Moral Motivation

Gertrud Nunner-Winkler
Max Planck Institute for Psychological Research

Morality requires not only knowledge of moral rules but also the willingness to abide by them. People differ with respect to moral motivation. Some do not care at all about morality; others follow norms even at high personal costs (intensity of moral motivation). They also differ in the types of concerns motivating their conformity and the way these are anchored in the personality (structure of moral motivation). The study reported in this chapter deals with the question of whether there are generational differences indicating sociohistoric changes in the structure of moral motivation. In the first section I discuss theoretical assumptions. Socialization theories are briefly reviewed, learning mechanisms for social conformity are extracted, the corresponding types of concerns are classified according to ego syntony and moral affinity, and these concerns are critically related to Kohlberg's theory of moral development. The central hypothesis—that there is a sociohistoric change in the structure of social conformity toward increased ego syntony—is then derived within the theoretical framework of Norbert Elias' (Elias, 1978a, 1978b) theory of civilization. In the second section I empirically substantiate the main claim. Data on children's moral understanding are briefly recapitulated that show that an intrinsic judgment-related (ego syntonic) type of moral motivation does exist. The results of an intergenerational comparison of types of concerns motivating norm conformity, which was conducted in Germany, are presented. In the third section I argue that the changes in the structure of moral motivation correspond to changes in the cognitive understanding of morality that are first theoretically exposed and then empirically supported.

We owe much to Augusto Blasi for the issues pursued and the research strategies used. In his pioneering work he kept insisting that morality requires both reasoned judgment on the one hand and an intrinsic concern about the importance of morality on the other hand. With high theoretical acuity he analyzed the interplay of these two aspects; critiqued mistaken measurement procedures or pitfalls in interpretations of moral research results; and with inventive diligence conducted his own studies on moral judgment, moral responsibility, and their import for personal identity. Over and above having intensely profited from this insightful work, I am personally deeply indebted to Blasi. Over many years he has been a careful and critical discussant of my research and kept advising me on theoretical and methodological issues. More important still, he is and has always been a friend.

SOCIALIZATION THEORY AND NORM CONFORMITY

Socialization–Theoretical Approaches

Each generation of newborns is an invasion of barbarians (Parsons, 1964). It is by socialization that (most of) these barbarians are transformed into members well-adapted to those life conditions and expectations that are dominant in the society in which they happen to be born. Socialization theories tackle the question of just how this transformation is effected. They differ widely in many respects. They pursue different research interests: Some focus on the explanation of intraindividual differences, and others on universals in human development. They are based on different assumptions about the nature of man: Some conceptualize him as a basically asocial being who experiences norms as an externally imposed yoke and forever suffers from the "discontent of culture" (Freud, 1929/1989), others (e.g., Durkheim and Parsons) see him as a social being whose very personhood is constituted by social integration and adoption of social expectations. Some approaches (e.g., behaviorism and psychoanalytic theory) see the child as passively subjected to the power of external influences, others (e.g., Piaget and Kohlberg) see the child as actively selecting inputs and constructing his of her own perception of reality. Different motives are taken for granted: According to some theories (e.g., rational choice) man is solely interested in maximizing benefits; according to others (e.g., cognitive–development theory) man also strives for truth and pursues values for their intrinsic worth. Also, different degrees of freedom are imputed: Some approaches (e.g., sociobiology, behaviorism, and psychoanalytic theories) see him as largely determined (by his genetic endowment, his conditioning history, or his relational experiences); others (e.g., social interactionism, ethnomethodology, constructivism) see him as capable of freely choosing and actively creating the world in which he lives. Given the contradictory nature of these assumptions and the exclusive validity claimed by each of these approaches, an attempt at theoretical integration seems of little avail. Nevertheless, each of these paradigms generated valuable insights inasmuch as they described specific learning mechanisms and produced empirical evidence for their effectiveness. Thus, rather than aiming at a theoretical synthesis, it seems more promising to focus on these individual mechanisms and analyze the way they function and the conditions under which they operate.

Becoming a competent member of society involves different dimensions: By interacting with their natural surroundings, children develop initial intuitions of objects, of time and space, and of causality. By interacting with their caretakers, they develop initial conceptions of man and form internal representations of social relationships. By participating in a culture, they become acquainted with the knowledge and belief systems, the rituals and practices of everyday life, and the social institutions and regularities prevalent in their society. In the following section, I focus on how children acquire the readiness to comply with normative expectations.

Learning Mechanisms for Norm Conformity

Classical conditioning starts from an inborn (unconditioned) reaction to a specific (unconditioned) stimulus (e.g. spontaneous salivation at the sight of food). After a new (conditioned) stimulus has been presented several times in close spatiotemporal contiguity with the original stimulus (e.g. sound of a bell at feeding), it will suffice to elicit the reaction. This mechanism, first explored in animal experiments (e.g., Pavlov's dog), can easily be translated in socialization theory. If the child suffers immediate punishment every time he or she violates a rule, the very idea of transgressing will soon come to elicit the excitement and fear reactions that accompanied the experience of punishment: "Conscience is a conditioned reflex" (Eysenck, 1960, p. 13), that is "a conditioned anxiety response to certain types of situations and actions" (Eysenck, 1976, p. 109).

Operant conditioning starts from spontaneously emitted behaviors and selectively rewards those that are deemed desirable or gradually approximate the desirable ones. This way behavior is continuously shaped, and a free and easy conformity is produced. Animal training (Miller, 1948; Skinner, 1938) as well as curative effects of behavior therapies testify to the efficacy of reinforcement schedules.

Both types of conditioning assume primarily instrumentalist motives and view behavior as a result of intentionally applied educational measures. Yet, there are also decisive differences: In classical conditioning the individual is conscious of deviant impulses that he or she represses for fear of sanction, whereas in operant conditioning—being busy striving for desired rewards—the person comes to believe that he or she is doing what he or she wants to do and remains largely unaware of the external manipulations by which behavior is shaped.

Imitation. Conditioning theory, however, does not tell the whole story. Social learning theories (Bandura, 1977) show that behavior is not always guided by punishments and rewards. Without reinforcement children may imitate powerful, interesting, or same-sex models from sheer curiosity or from a competence motive (White, 1954). Thus, children's own choices matter: It is not the educator who determines what the child is to learn, rather the child himself or herself decides which behavior is deemed interesting or what kind of person he or she wants to be.

Behaviorism and social learning theory describe observable behavior. The following mechanisms deal with the genesis of generalized motives.

Superego. In the Freudian tripartite personality model the id is but "a chaos, a kettle bubbling with excitement" (Freud, 1922, p. 511). The ego is capable of rational consideration and anticipation. In controlling the satisfaction of the drives (i.e., of the id) the ego is informed by external circumstances and conditions (the reality principle) and by the normative expectations anchored in the superego. The superego is the heir of the Oedipus complex. From fear of castration the boy gives up the desire for his mother (i.e., adopts the incest taboo) and (by way of an identification with the aggressor) internalizes the prohibitions and demands set up by his father. The girl, in contrast, lacking a strong motive to exit from the oedipal constellation, will never acquire a superego that is "as strict, as impersonal and as independent of its affective origins as we require of males" (Freud, 1925, p. 265).

Need-Disposition. Parsons (1964) described socialization as a process of reciprocal role taking. From the beginning on the infant is ascribed a role: "The behavior of adults towards him is not like their behavior towards purely physical objects, but is contingent on his behavior and very soon what are interpreted to be his expectations" (p. 209). The dependent, sensitive, and plastic infant soon begins to develop affective attachments to his or her caretakers, that is, the child comes to feel dependent not merely on the caretakers fulfilling his or her physical needs but also on the attitudes underlying their behavior. As the child begins to realize that these are contingent on his or her own behavior he or she starts developing a "system of need-dispositions towards the fulfilment of role expectations" (p. 32). Thus (by way of an anaclitic identification), "to act in conformity becomes a need-disposition in the actor's own personality structure, relatively independent of any instrumentally significant consequences of that conformity" (p. 37).

The accounts given by Freud and Parsons can be read as generalized and internalized versions of the learning mechanisms described in behaviorism. They are no longer about individual responses produced by purposefully applied educational measures but rather about generalized dispositions based on individual experiences of social relationships. Behavior is no longer seen as determined by external punishments or rewards but by internalized superego controls or a deeply ingrained conformity disposition. Freud's superego model corresponds to classical conditioning inasmuch as conformity is produced by social constraints, and the individual remains conscious of deviant impulses. In contrast, the Parsonian concept of need-dispositions corresponds to operant conditioning inasmuch as unconstrained conformity happens; namely, the desire to comply with social expectations has become second nature and the individual remains unaware of deviant impulses and social constraints. Bourdieu's (1984) concept of *habitus* refers to the same phenomenon: Habitus is a way of reacting and presenting the self that is socially shaped, especially by social class membership, yet, nevertheless subjectively experienced as spontaneous and natural.

Subsequent theories within this psychoanalytic frame of reference have mitigated the determinism implied by the two classical models. Ego psychology holds that during an intense adolescence crisis the subject can retouch early affective attachments and free himself or herself from the dictates of a rigid superego (cf. Jacobson, 1964). Similarly, the theory of socializatory interaction (Oevermann et al., 1976) assumes that early imprinting resulting from interactions with caretakers can later be reflected on, and by conscious deliberation and reinterpretation subjects can neutralize its fateful power. Attachment theory (Ainsworth, Blehar, Waters, & Walls, 1978; Bowlby, 1986) from the beginning on concedes some latitude. Conformity is not enforced by fear (of castration or of love withdrawal); instead, securely bound children tend to voluntarily follow the expectations held by their sensitive mothers (in contrast to insecurely bound children who respond with retreat, protest, or resistance to demands set up by their intrusive or negligent mothers).

With his concept of postconventional moral thinking Kohlberg went beyond behavioristic and psychoanalytic explanations of norm conformity. As far as cognitive moral understanding is concerned he introduced the (philosophical) distinction between legal and legitimate norms—namely, between actually dominant social conventions and universally justifiable rules—into the discourse of empirically oriented social sciences. With respect to the motivational dimension he introduced a new type of motive: a voluntary readiness to abide by rules that are understood to be valid because they are derived from universal moral principles (e.g., equality, justice, dignity of the individual). This Kantian type of an intellectual moral motive (respect for the law) can be given more psychological power if combined with Frankfurt's (1988) concept of *second-order volition*. This term signifies a commitment to an ideal the person cares so much about that he or she cannot bring himself or herself to betray it. For example, Frankfurt quoted Luther's declaration, "Here I stand; I can do no other" (p. 86) and explained that the "impossibility to which Luther referred was a matter neither of logical nor of causal necessity. ... He had the capacity to do it. What he was unable to muster was not the power to forbear but the will" (p. 86; cf. Also Frankfurt, 1993). "His unwillingness itself is something which he is unwilling to alter. ... he cannot bring himself to overcome the constraint to which he is subject, because in other words: He does not really want to do so" (Frankfurt, 1988, p. 87).

Types of Motives for Norm Conformity

From this brief overview different types of motives for norm conformity emerge that can be classified with respect to two dimensions: proximity to volitional affirmation (ego syntony) and proximity to conformist or moral concerns (morality). The content of the intentional state defines proximity to conformity or morality; the way the action disposition is anchored in the personality determines ego syntony. An orientation solely toward external (physical or social) consequences marks the amoral pole; respect for the validity of norms or concern for consequences to third persons constitutes the moral pole. Conscious awareness of relevant considerations is typical of the ego-syntonic pole whereas the ego alien pole is characterized by quasi-automatic response habits or compulsively rigid superego controls. Using this grid the different types of conformity motives are classified as shown in Table 13.1.

The orientation toward punishment–reward (2a) is the type of motive described in behaviorism. Conscious conformity to internalized norms (3a) or ideals (e.g., power and esthetic values (4a)) and a habitualized (moral or amoral) conformity disposition (3b and 4b) are modeled in psychoanalytic theories. Point (1a) corresponds to Kant and Kohlberg's postconventional stage and Point (1b) to Frankfurt's (Frankfurt, 1988) concept of second-order volition, given that moral values are at stake.

TABLE 13.1

Types of Conformity Motives

Ego Syntony/ Morality	High	Low
High	1 (a) Respect for the moral law (b) Second-order volition bound to moral judgment	2 (a) Orientation toward punishment–reward (b) Strategic cost–benefit calculations
Low	3 (a) Superego dictates (Obligations) (b) Conformity need- disposition	4 (a) Superego ideals (Ambitions) (b) Amoral response habitus

Rational choice theory bluntly denies the existence of any moral orientation, even of premoral motives (e.g., an orientation to punishment–reward held
out by authorities). It assumes that individuals are motivated only by
self-serving concerns (2b). They follow norms solely in view of material or social costs–benefits (e.g., profits–losses or a good–bad reputation). Critics have
pointed out that some people most times, or many people sometimes, act without receiving immediate material or social gratifications (e.g., they give to
charity in private and they vote). In response, a type of internal self-reward has
been introduced—a "warm glow feeling" (Andreoni, 1990). In other words,
such seemingly unselfish actions are seen as being motivated by the desire to
feel content with oneself. This theoretical innovation serves to immunize the
core assumption from refutation—the assumption that everybody strives to
maximize his or her own interests. Even moral action can now be explained: It
simply results from the fact that the interests of some people happen to concern
not material benefits or social acceptance but an internal feeling of moral
self-satisfaction.

Kohlberg: Individual Development of Conformity Motives

Kohlberg (1981, 1984) integrated these different motives into a developmental
hierarchy. Individual moral development is described as a sequence of stages.
Each stage is a structured whole characterized by cognitive–affective parallelism—namely, a structural affinity between types of reasons justifying moral
norms and types of concerns motivating conformity. Thus, at the
preconventional level norms are taken to be valid because they are set by author-

ities and backed by sanctions, and they are followed to avoid punishment or secure concrete reciprocity. At the conventional level norms are deemed valid
because they hold in one's group or society and are obeyed to win social acceptance or to avoid superego sanctions (pangs of conscience). At the
postconventional level only social contracts or universal moral principles enjoy
validity and are respected from insight in their legitimacy. Thus, development
proceeds from a premoral orientation to punishment and concrete reciprocity
(2a) via social conformity needs and submission to superego dictates (3) toward
a Socratic willingness to do what one knows to be right (1a).

In later writings, the assumption of a strict cognitive–affective parallelism
was substituted by the claim of a developmentally increasing consistency between judgment and action (Kohlberg & Candee, 1984). Of higher theoretical import, however, was the introduction of new conceptual strategies and
research techniques that clearly differentiated and disentangled the cognitive
and the motivational dimension. Thus, Helkama (1979, cited in Kohlberg &
Candee, 1984) and Blasi (1983, 1984) supplemented Kohlberg's original
question for an action recommendation ("What should the protagonist do?")
with questions about responsibility judgments ("Is the protagonist personally responsible for doing what ought to be done?"). And Kohlberg's original
developmental sequence was expanded by distinguishing between two types
of judgments at each stage: Type A, a more pragmatic orientation (i.e., expressing low moral motivation) and Type B, a more reversible, prescriptive,
and universalistic type of judgment (i.e, expressing high commitment to morality). The latter is described as a kind of intuitive postconventionalism:
spontaneous perception (by heart or by conscience) of those core values or
obligations in a dilemma that can rationally be articulated only at the
postconventional level.

This first step toward separating cognitive moral development and moral
motivation was supported by later empirical research. Thus, Colby and Damon
(1993) showed that moral exemplars (i.e., persons who care very much about
morality and have made the realization of moral values a personal project) are
found at all stages of moral development. Nunner-Winkler (1998) found that
moral development proceeds in two learning steps: Universally children acquire an early cognitive moral understanding. Yet, it takes several years before
some of the children begin to make morality an important personal concern
(i.e., to develop moral motivation, which is discussed later).

These findings imply that cognitive moral understanding and the intensity
of moral motivation are independent dimensions. However, this still leaves
open the question as to what kind of concerns motivate conformity and how
these conformist–moral motives are anchored in the personality. According to

Colby and Damon (1995), moral "exemplars come to see morality and self as inextricably intertwined. ... [Their] moral identities become highly integrated, almost fused with their self-identities" (p. 364). Oliner and Oliner (1988) also studied a group of morally exceptional persons—rescuers of Jews during Nazi dictatorship. All of them knowingly incurred great personal risk in doing what they felt was morally correct, although they did so for different reasons. Some—like Colby and Damon's moral exemplars—saw morality as central to their sense of self. Others acted from a feeling of moral duty; still others acted due to religious persuasion or compassion. Thus, different types of motives are found among highly moral persons: Besides empathy there is ego syntonic moral commitment and submission to superego controls or to divine commands. According to Kohlberg's original stage theory these concerns form a hierarchy in which individual development proceeds from submission to (parental) authorities to a conformity with the dictates of one's conscience and, finally, to respect for moral principles. This ontogenetic developmental model, however, stands in some contradiction with the socialization–theoretical explanations of different types of conformity motives just sketched. These theories assume that early biographical experiences shape basic needs and motives that tend to remain stable over a lifetime except in intense personal crises (e.g., adolescence crisis, midlife crisis, and pension shock). In other words, socialization theory agrees better with a typological classification than an ontogenetic ordering of conformity motives.

Norbert Elias: Sociohistoric Changes in Conformity Motives

Yet, there is another theory that provides a developmental ordering of the different types of conformity concerns—albeit not on the individual but on the macrosociological level. Norbert Elias' (1978a, 1978b) theory of civilization arranges different types of conformity motives in a sociohistorical order. He claimed that there is a coevolution of societal and personality structure. Empirically he supported this theoretical assumption by an analysis of the emergence of the absolutist state in France, its implications for functional prerequisites on the part of individuals, and a description of family arrangements producing the necessary individual competences. In the beginning many small principalities competed with each other. An "integrative centre," a "higher order human web," and a "state of organization" (Elias, 1978b, p. 435) evolved gradually: It proved to be functional during the 100-year war between England and France to have a king who coordinated the military personel that was contributed by the various independent knights or princes. The king then tried to consolidate his position by institutionalizing a standing army and a right to taxation. Eventually, the centralized state claimed and put through a

monopoly on legitimate physical power. This required that individuals re-
nounce personal violence. Also, with the integration of formerly independent
units, complex administrative hierarchies evolved, reciprocal dependency increased, and chains of interdependence were alongated. These changes called
for individual presight and consideration, and the ability to coordinate.
Norbert Elias summarized these new demands on the psychological makeup of
individuals, claiming that during that period a change took place "from external constraints to self-constraint": The "coercion by immediate physical
threat," "the immediate endangering of one by the affects of the other," and
"the outside constraints" are replaced by "self-constraints," namely, "constant
self-control and a stable super-ego" (Elias, 1978b, p. 368), "a regulation of
drives and control of affects that has become automatized and turned into a natural habit" (ibid., p. 343). As this "habit equipment" consolidates, it takes on
"an ahistoric quasi 'natural' character, a subconscious quality" (ibid., p. 321).
The "social nature of prohibitions [fades] from consciousness"—the societal
standards come to appear "as commands arising from a person's interiors"
(ibid., p. 403). This way the differentiation between the "centre of drives and
the ego-centre" becomes increasingly sharper (ibid., p. 378): "Consciousness
becomes less permeable for drives and the drives become less permeable for
consciousness" (p. 378).

The socialization theoretical mechanism producing this "relatively high degree of a split of the ego or of consciousness that is characteristic of man in our
phase of civilization" (Elias, 1978a, p.262) is the segregation of the nuclear
family: "The more social life requires shaping and regulating individual drives
… the more the task of first cultivating these habits is concentrated within the
intimate circle of the nuclear family, i.e. mother and father" (ibid., p. 260). Yet,
the shaping of the child is not affected by consciously planned educational
measures, rather it results "mostly automatically and quasi by reflexes—by
way of interweaving habits of parents and children" (ibid., p.260): Parental
fears and desires for (over-) conformity are mediated to the child and begin to
channel his or her reaction dispositions long before the child is capable of reflexive distancing. Elias' socialization model is psychoanalytically inspired: It
combines Freud's idea of strict superego censureship acquired through identification with the aggressor (i.e., with an authoritarian father) with Parsons'
(Parsons, 1964) concept of need-dispositions developed through processes of
anaclitic identification with an (over-) protective mother. Elias' account postu-
lates a historical sequence of (prototypical) conformity motives starting from
an initial orientation to external sanctions and constraints (2 in Table 13.1) that
is replaced by internalized and habitualized modes of self-constraints (3) as
small decentralized political units are integrated into large, hierarchically
structured, complex political systems.

Since Norbert Elias first published his theory of civilization in 1939 far-reaching changes have taken place. These concern both the structure of society and the structure of the family. The model of a strictly hierarchically organized society, the (political, religious, moral) unity of which is unmistakenly represented by the top (i.e., the king), is making way to a horizontal network of structurally coupled autonomous subsystems (Luhmann, 1998).

Family life has changed as well. Elias described the secluded nucleus family in which a dominant father uses power (threat of castration), whereas the mother (more or less consciously) uses the technique of love withdrawal. Jointly, these parental socialization styles tend to produce strict superego controls and a prereflexive social shaping of spontaneous desires (need-disposition, habitus). Since the beginning of the 20th century in Germany the intrafamilial climate has gradually changed. Increasingly, the former educational goals of order, cleanliness, and obedience have receded to an emphasis on autonomy and independence. Also, children have increasingly been granted more of a say in family decisions (Reuband, 1988, 1997); today, they are even granted legal rights against their parents. To the extent that children are seen as equals, norms can no longer simply be authoritatively set and enforced, rather parents need to justify them and negotiate intrafamilial regulations. Thus, children today grow up in a more open democratic atmosphere in which early conditioning and power threats give way to bargaining and reasoning. As children come to understand the meaning of moral rules they may come to voluntarily follow them. At the same time children's formerly secluded and protected world has been widely opened to external influences. As children come to read the importance of success, wealth, and power from commercial advertisements and the media, they may give priority to such goals over moral rules and may do so more openly than previous generations.

If Elias' claim of a coevolution of personality makeup and sociostructural exigencies holds true, the changes in core features of the organization of modern societies and families might have consequences for the structure of conformity motives. The gradual replacement of authoritative command structures in society and family by egalitarian relations and democratic procedures of negotiation might effect a corresponding change of conformity motives: Individual submissiveness to preordained rules (produced by threat or manipulation) might fade away and be replaced by more ego syntonic types of motives (i.e., a willingly affirmed commitment to morality or candid cost–benefit calculations unrestrained by social desirability concerns or conformity needs). From these assumptions the following claim is derived.

Hypothesis. Due to sociohistorical changes in societal structure and in socialization styles there is a change from superego controls and habitualized conformity dispositions towards more ego-syntonic types of conformity motivation —that is, there is a change from (3) and (4) to (1) and (2). This change in motive structure also corresponds to a change in cognitive moral understanding.

This hypothesis is tested by way of an intergenerational comparison that was conducted in Germany. Before I report on this study, I briefly sketch children's moral understanding to provide an anchor for the analysis of cross-generational changes.

EMPIRICAL STUDIES

Children's Understanding of Moral Motivation[1]

Sample. Subjects were participants of the Munich longitudinal study on the genesis of individual competence (Weinert & Schneider, 1999) that comprises a cohort of more than 200 children who started to attend 22 different preschools in the Munich area in the fall of 1984 and whose first language was German. This is a relatively unbiased sample because the preschoolers were selected from a broad spectrum of neighborhoods and more than 90% of the parents who were asked for permission to include their child in the study gave their consent (Schneider & Nunner-Winkler, 1989). The data were obtained from 213 children (110 boys and 103 girls) with an average age of 5.59, 203 children (105 boys and 98 girls) with an average age of 7.25, and 185 children (96 boys and 89 girls) with an average age of 9.25.

Procedure. At three measurement points subjects were presented with four picture stories of moral conflicts in which a same-sex protagonist is tempted to transgress a simple moral rule (e.g., to secretly take another child's sweets, not to share his own drink with a thirsty child who asks for a sip, not to share an un-fairly won prize with the discriminated child, and not to help another child in fulfilling a task). (Although I use masculine gender references for brevity's sake, they should be understood to apply equally in the feminine.) In the temp-tation situation the children were questioned about their rule understanding (e.g., May one take the sweets or may one not? Must one share or help in the given situation or does one not have to? Why?). Then they were shown that the protagonist transgressed the rule (e.g., stole and did not share or help); with the intent to tap moral motivation, children were asked to state how they expected him to feel and justify this expectation. This operationalization is derived from a cognitivist theory of emotion (Montada, 1993; Solomon, 1976), according to which emotions are (albeit rash and global) cognitive judgments about the subjective importance attributed to given facts. Thus, by ascribing an emotion to the hypothetical wrongdoer, children can indicate which of the two simultaneously true facts they personally deem more important—the fact that the protagonist transgressed a norm and that he satisfied a desire. By justifying negative emotion ascriptions they can indicate which types of concerns they assume will motivate norm conformity.

Results and Discussion. From very early on children have a good cognitive moral understanding: They know simple moral rules (e.g., 98% of the 4- to 5-year-olds judged stealing to be wrong; by age 8, more than 80% to 90% deemed it obligatory to share or help in the situations presented). They also understand that these rules are intrinsically valid; that is, across all stories and measurement points fewer than 12% referred to positive or negative consequences ensuing for the wrongdoer (e.g., praise or punishment by adults, acceptance or rejection by other children, and concerns about concrete reciprocity) when asked to justify the rules. This finding agrees with (the more carefully probed) results of studies of children's understanding of moral, conventional, and religious rules by Turiel (1983) and Nucci and Turiel, (1993).[2]

Nevertheless, a large majority of children expect the protagonist to feel good after transgressing (e.g., almost 80% at ages 4 to 5 and still 60% at ages 6 to 7 expected the hypothetical thief to feel good after having taken the sweets). This finding is contraintuitive–older children and adults expect a wrongdoer to feel bad after having transgressed (Barden, Zelko, Duncan, & Masters, 1980). It could, however, be shown to be robust (Nunner-Winkler & Sodian, 1988) and—as the "happy victimizer phenomenon"—has been replicated (Arsenio & Kramer, 1992; Arsenio & Lover, 1995). It could also be shown that emotion ascriptions are predictive of behavior in real-life moral conflict situations—at least until ages 6 to 7[3]: children who consistently expected a wrongdoer to feel bad after transgressing cheated significantly less often in a guessing game (to win a prize) or ruthlessly pushed through their own interests (in a conflict concerning the distribution of scarce resources in a group; Asendorpf & Nunner-Winkler, 1992). These results demonstrate that the growth of moral motivation involves a second differential learning process. (In fact, data from the LOGIC (Munich Longitudinal Study on the Genesis of Individual Competencies) follow-up study show that even by age 17 quite a few subjects do not care much about morality; cf. Nunner-Winkler, 2003).

An analysis of the justification of negative emotion ascriptions showed that consequences either for the wrongdoer (fear of sanctions) or for the victim (empathy) were rarely mentioned (across stories and measurement points by 18% at most). Most children gave norm-oriented justifications. (For example, the protagonist feels bad, because what he did was wrong. He should have acted differently. He proved to be unfair.) Given that younger children expect a protagonist to feel good whenever he successfully does what he wants to do (e.g., steals the sweets he wants to have) and to feel bad, when he does not do what he wants to do (e.g., resists the temptation to take the sweets he wants to have) or does what he does not want to do (e.g., hurts another child by mistake; cf. Nunner-Winkler & Sodian, 1988), the emotion ascriptions can be taken as an indicator of intentions children experience as their own. Thus, by expecting a wrongdoer to feel bad children intimate that they experience rule following as a personal desire, an ego-syntonic wish. Some further observations support this interpretation. Thus, very few and only older children (10% at age 8 to 9) refer to superego controls (e.g., bad conscience). However, at younger ages children quite frequently (more than 20% of the 4 to 5 year olds and more than 15% of the 6 to 7 year olds) use the adjective *sad* to describe the emotion expected after wrongdoing Hascher, 1994). Given that normally the term *sad* (if applied not to events but to acts) tends to denote someone's failure to realize personal aspirations, rather than a failure to obey preordained commands, this language use indicates that children wish to follow the norms on their own account.[4] And by explaining the protagonist's regret by pointing out that he committed a wrong, they show that their desire to conform is not an unreflected need-disposition but rather tied to a cognitive judgment process.

The claim that children's moral motive is of an intrinsic nature can be backed by another more indirect argument (cf. Nunner-Winkler 1999)—the fact that its growth is structurally similar to the formation of an intrinsic achievement motive (Heckhausen, 1982, 1985). In both domains—morality and achievement behavior—first (cold) knowledge of the norms (achievement standards and moral rules) is acquired. Next, a desire to fulfill these norms is developed. In the positive case of success or conformity or the negative case of failure or transgression, joy or regret is experienced. In other words, object related emotions like joy or regret (involving two agruments only, e.g., X regrets Z) precede the cognitively more complex self-reflexive emotions like shame and guilt (involving three arguments, e.g., X is ashamed at Y [himself] because of Z). Nevertheless, the two developmental strands differ in one respect: The growth of moral motivation lags considerably behind the development of an achievement motive. Presumably this time lag is due to the different requirements posed in the two domains. Children can easily identify with achievement standards—usually they want to master given tasks themselves; with respect to morality, however, spontaneous first-order desires quite often contradict the standards.[5] Thus, the ability to distance oneself from one's first-order desires (Blasi 1984) and form a second-order desire (i.e., a second-order moral volition) is required. If moral motivation is conceived as a (second-order) desire, moral emotions assume a different meaning: They are seen as indicative of rather than as functional for morality. In Freudian theories the anticipation of guilt feelings operates as a barrier to transgression (i.e., norm conformity is motivated by the desire to avoid internal sanctions). If, however, children are motivated to follow a norm because they want to do what is right, regret or feelings of guilt are a consequence of not a cause of transgression (i.e., these emotions indicate or express moral commitment rather than motivating it).

Intergenerational Comparison[6]

Sample. The sample was comprised of 95 (49 men, 46 women) 20- to 30-year old, 95 (47 men, 48 women) 40- to 50-year-old, 100 (50 men, 50 women) 65- to 75-year-old, and 100 (50 men, 50 women) 17-year-old German subjects. The 17 year olds constitute a representative sample (based on sex and education) of the 175 LOGIC subjects who had taken part in a LOGIC-Replication Study conducted in 1998. The 20 to 30 and 40 to 50 year olds constitute a representative sample (using sex and education as the criteria) chosen from one mostly Protestant and one mostly Catholic part of West Germany and were interviewed by a staff member from a commercial research center. The 65- to 75-year-olds were randomly drawn from the 377 participants of GOLD (Genetically Oriented Lifespan study of differential Development, a study of elderly twins (Weinert & Geppert, 1996) matching the educational levels prevalent in Germany at the time, and—as far as was possible—only one twin of each pair was drawn.

Procedure. First, subjects' understanding of the concept of morality was explored ("In your opinion: What is morality? Can you give me some examples of behavior you consider to be immoral?"). Next, their moral convictions were investigated. Twenty-five vignettes depicting norms concerning gender roles and family life (e.g., homosexuality and working mother), the political system (e.g., draft resistance), the religious system (e.g., secession), ecological norms (e.g., separation of refusal), and duties against self (e.g., suicide and drugs) were presented. For each situation subjects were asked to make and justify an evaluation ("How do you feel about this situation? Why? Is this a question of morality? Why?"). For several situations the willingness to grant exceptions ("Can you imagine a situation in which you might judge differently? Why?") and the estimation of the moral attitudes of other age cohorts were also explored ("What do younger/older generations think about this situation?").

Then the structure of moral motivation was ascertained in the following way: Subjects were presented a grave transgression[7] and asked how they would feel had they themselves committed this wrong. Next they had to equally distribute 36 emotional reactions on a 6-point scale ranging from *I would feel exactly that way* (1) to *I couldn't feel that way at all* (6; Q-sort, Block, 1961). The requirement of equal distribution forces subjects to carefully compare each reaction with all the others, that is, all differences (even in the middle range of values) can meaningfully be interpreted. It also counteracts social desirability concerns because the total range of the scale has to be used. The emotional reactions presented formulated different types of concerns: fear of religious sanctions (e.g., God might punish me), fear of external sanctions (e.g., I'd be afraid to be put into prison), fear of social disdain (e.g., I'd be afraid that my friends would turn away from me), fear of superego sanctions (e.g., I'd forever be conscience stricken), a more habitualized need-disposition (e.g., This is against nature), ego-syntonic moral concerns (e.g., I'd feel very sorry; I would consider how to make up for it), and openly amoral considerations (e.g., I could imagine that I'd feel quite o.k. about it).

The emotional reactions were analyzed in two ways: Intergenerational differences in individual item ratings were computed, and a principal components analysis was performed.

Results and Discussion. A comparison of item averages across generations (see Table 13.2) shows that the openly amoral reactions are rejected by all (scale values of 3.5 and higher) but more clearly so by the two oldest cohorts (all item values of 4.0 and higher). Items expressing fear of inner worldly sanctions in no generation were highly accepted (lowest value was 2.8). Yet, there are differences with respect to religious sanctions: The older subjects somewhat dreaded them; the younger ones clearly rejected them. Significant intergenerational differences are found in items referring to superego sanctions and to a habitualized conformity disposition—with the older subjects scoring higher on both. Younger subjects, especially the 17 year olds, in contrast, prefer egosyntonic motives. The data also show that the oldest subjects judge more homogeneously: There are more items they highly accept (i.e., nine scale values lower than 2.5), whereas the ratings of younger subjects differ more widely (among the 17 year olds only four items and among the 20 to 30 year olds only three items drew such nearly unanimous acceptance). In other words, the older generation makes use of a much more standardized moral language game that attests the importance of practically all conformity related concerns. Over the generations, this language seems to differentiate, with the 40 to 50 year olds primarily emphasizing internalized self-constraints and the youngest group emphasizing ego-syntonic reactions.

TABLE 13.2
Concerns in Motivating Norm Conformity: ANOVA Results of Q-Sort Ratings

	Age									
	17[a]		20–30[b]		40–50[c]		65–75[d]		$F_{(3,396)}$ Value	p Value
	M	SD	M	SD	M	SD	M	SD		
Sanctions										
Religious										
I'd be afraid God would punish me	5.07	(1.24)	4.70	(1.61)	4.45	(1.61)	4.18	(1.71)	5.91	.00
That would be a sin	4.41	(1.46)	4.02	(1.74)	3.75	(1.71)	3.14	(1.76)	10.20	.00
If something really awful happened to me, I'd always think that God had punished me	3.77	(1.44)	4.11	(1.84)	3.68	(1.67)	3.58	(1.78)	1.76	.15
I'd fear a buffet of fate	4.77	(1.32)	4.54	(1.65)	4.04	(1.64)	3.71	(1.60)	9.49	.00
God sees and knows everything	4.48	(1.72)	4.51	(1.69)	4.30	(1.61)	4.13	(1.77)	1.10	.35
Formal										
I'd be afraid to be put into prison	4.81	(1.34)	3.96	(1.61)	4.06	(1.77)	4.48	(1.70)	5.94	.00
If that became known at my work, I'd fear consequences to my disadvantage	3.05	(1.57)	4.01	(1.66)	4.38	(1.45)	3.69	(1.35)	13.76	.00
But this is a criminal offence	2.95	(1.45)	3.39	(1.77)	2.99	(1.69)	3.74	(1.88)	4.74	.00
That could one day be used against me	3.31	(1.56)	3.34	(1.65)	3.34	(1.66)	3.44	(1.48)	0.13	.94
If that ever became known...	2.83	(1.33)	3.05	(1.61)	3.31	(1.70)	3.15	(1.49)	1.68	.17

315

TABLE 13.2 (cont.)

Concerns in Motivating Norm Conformity: ANOVA Results of Q-Sort Ratings

	17[a]		20–30[b]		40–50[c]		65–75[d]		F(3,396) Value	p Value
	M	SD	M	SD	M	SD	M	SD		
Informal										
I'd be afraid that the others got to know about it	3.01	(1.47)	2.89	(1.55)	3.52	(1.68)	3.04	(1.48)	3.11	.03
I'd be afraid that my friends would turn away from me	3.94	(1.50)	3.21	(1.59)	3.47	(1.68)	3.51	(1.38)	3.85	.01
I'd be afraid that others would despise me for it	3.61	(1.56)	2.95	(1.64)	3.35	(1.71)	3.25	(1.54)	2.88	.04
I'd have the feeling that others are talking behind my back	3.62	(1.36)	3.72	(1.53)	4.01	(1.58)	3.33	(1.42)	3.57	.01
I'd become the laughingstock of others	4.44	(1.29)	4.61	(1.30)	4.57	(1.41)	4.03	(1.49)	3.74	.01
I'd have the feeling that everybody could tell by my face	3.00	(1.44)	3.60	(1.66)	3.51	(1.67)	3.51	(1.66)	2.89	.04
Superego										
I'd forever be conscience stricken	2.77	(1.64)	2.26	(1.57)	2.24	(1.53)	1.84	(1.38)	6.19[e]	.00
I could never forgive myself	3.17	(1.46)	2.52	(1.63)	2.57	(1.57)	2.03	(1.38)	9.52	.02
I'd be desparate	3.74	(1.47)	3.40	(1.83)	3.33	(1.74)	2.86	(1.60)	4.71	.00
Even if nobody ever knew about it, I could never get over it	2.80	(1.37)	2.57	(1.54)	2.43	(1.46)	2.09	(1.19)	4.48	.00
I'd consider suidice	5.81	(0.66)	5.41	(1.05)	5.39	(0.84)	5.15	(1.14)	8.41	.00

TABLE 13.2 (cont.)

Concerns in Motivating Norm Conformity: ANOVA Results of Q-Sort Ratings

		Age							
	17[a]		20–30[b]		40–50[c]		65-75[d]		
	M	SD	M	SD	M	SD	M	SD	F(3,396) Value	p Value
Id										
I find this so wrong, I could never imagine to do something liike that	2.58	(1.38)	2.76	(1.71)	2.30	(1.56)	1.79	(1.27)	8.07	.00
The mere thought is repulsive	3.17	(1.41)	2.87	(1.71)	2.45	(1.55)	2.03	(1.26)	11.11	.00
I can only think about it with repulsion	3.14	(1.45)	3.22	(1.69)	2.92	(1.62)	2.65	(1.59)	2.63	.05
For me this is actually unthinkable	2.33	(1.48)	2.47	(1.63)	2.32	(1.60)	1.87	(1.45)	2.85	.04
This is against nature	4.33	(1.47)	4.64	(1.70)	4.03	(1.76)	3.75	(1.62)	5.53	.00
Such a thing could never happen to me	2.72	(1.37)	2.99	(1.86)	2.95	(1.75)	2.52	(1.54)	1.77	.15
Ego										
I'd feel very sorry	1.70	(0.96)	2.65	(1.68)	2.76	(1.55)	2.08	(1.22)	12.95	.00
I'd be disappointed at myself	1.87	(1.15)	2.03	(1.47)	2.16	(1.55)	1.91	(1.33)	0.90	.44
I would consider how to make up for it	2.43	(1.39)	3.14	(1.68)	2.91	(1.50)	2.40	(1.29)	6.13	.00
It would be great help if I could confess to some-body	2.54	(1.45)	3.27	(1.73)	3.52	(1.69)	3.06	(1.61)	6.64	.00

317

TABLE 13.2 (cont.)

Concerns in Motivating Norm Conformity: ANOVA Results of Q-Sort Ratings

		Age							
	17[a]		20–30[b]		40–50[c]		65-75[d]		F(3,396)	p
	M	SD	M	SD	M	SD	M	SD	Value	Value
Amoral										
I could imagine that I'd feel relieved	4.52	(1.46)	5.09	(1.41)	5.05	(1.22)	4.82	(1.31)	3.75	.01
I could imagine that I'd feel quite o.k. About it.	4.38	(1.64)	4.94	(1.52)	5.02	(1.38)	5.00	(1.21)	4.45	.00
Probably I'd get over it quite soon	3.59	(1.68)	4.39	(1.52)	4.69	(1.44)	4.71	(1.16)	12.81	.00
I'd suppose it wouldn't matter that much to me.	4.15	(1.60)	4.94	(1.26)	4.96	(1.36)	5.13	(1.08)	10.75	.00
If I had decided to do such a thing I'd feel glad once I had done with it	3.49	(1.76)	4.01	(1.87)	4.32	(1.69)	3.81	(1.66)	3.92	.01

Note. 1 = I would feel exactly that way to 6 = I wouldn't feel that way at all.
[a]n = 100. [b]n = 103. [c]n = 97. [d]n=100.
[e]For this item the F(3.395) value is reported because there is one value missing for the 65- to 75-year-old subjects.

This interpretation is confirmed by a principal components analysis followed by a Varimax rotation (see Table 13.3). Five factors emerge that explain a total of 44.8% of the variance. Factor 1 can be interpreted as amoral–low superego factor: Openly amoral reactions are affirmed and superego controls rejected. Factor 2 is an orientation to inner worldly sanctions; Factor 3 expresses a habitualized conformity disposition; Factor 4 stands for fear of religious sanctions; Factor 5 represents ego-syntonic reactions. Figure 13.1 shows the average values of each generation on these factors.[8] As shown, the 17 year olds most clearly rejected religious sanctions and superego controls, but they clearly affirmed (openly amoral as well as moral) ego-syntonic reactions. Both middle cohorts display a higher affinity to the superego language—the 20- to 30-year-old subjects, however, explicitly distanced themselves from habitualized response patterns. The oldest generation scored highest on the factors representing religious sanctions and need-dispositions. Thus, all in all, across the generations ego-alien reactions gradually wane: The habitualized conformity tendencies of the oldest subjects give way to a conscious awareness of superego dictates in the middle cohorts and finally are replaced by (moral and amoral) ego-syntonic responses.

A closer inspection of the exact wordings of some items may substantiate this change. Of the two items expressing self-related emotions—"I could never forgive myself" and "I'd be disappointed at myself"—only the latter is accepted by the youngest cohort. It depicts a more ego-syntonic commitment to morality inasmuch as disappointment expresses regret, which here is reflexively turned back on the person. Thereby the person is seen as being in a kind of egalitarian inner dialogue dealing with two conflicting desires (being moral vs. enjoying the profit). The feeling of disappointment indicates that the person wishes the desire to be moral had won out. In contrast, "I could never forgive myself" reflects an internal split of the self between a superior control aspect withholding forgiveness and a subjected part being denied forgiveness. Similarly, there were two items expressing a clear rejection of the transgression: "The mere thought is repulsive" and "For me this is actually unthinkable"; again, the youngest subjects could more easily identify with the second statement. The first expresses a deeply ingrained and almost physical abhorrence that seems quite inaccessible to reflection. The latter, in contrast, states that under normal conditions the behavior is beyond question but acknowledges that, in case of necessity, this might be different.

The spontaneous responses to the open-ended emotion question ("How would you feel, had you … ?") may even better illustrate the differences. In the following dialogue, three older subjects are quoted, who rejected the transgression in view of anticipated vindictive bodily or superego reactions:

TABLE 13.3

Concerns in Motivating Norm Conformity: Principal Component Results of Q-Sort Ratings

	1	2	3	4	5
Sanctions					
Religious					
Fear of God's punishment				++	
That would be a sin				++	
An awful event as God's punishment				++	
Fear of buffet of fate				++	
God sees and knows everything				++	
Formal					
Fear of being imprisoned		++			
Negative consequences at work		+			
This is a criminal offense		+			
It could be used against me		++			
If that ever became known...		++			
Informal					
Fear that others will get to know		++			
Fear of losing friends		++			
Feare of being despised		++			
They would tak behind my back		++			
People will mock at me		++			
Feeling everyone would tell it by my face		+			+
Superego					
Conscience stricken	--				+
I would never forgive myself	--		+		
Despair	-				
Hard to get over it	--				+
Considering suicide				+	
Id					
So wrong that it is unimaginable			++		
The mere thought is repulsive	-		++		
Can only think about it with repulsion	-		++		
This is actually unthinkable for me			++		
This is unnatural			+		
That could never have happened to me			++		

TABLE 13.3 (cont.)
Concerns in Motivating Norm Conformity: Principal Component Results of Q-Sort Ratings

	1	2	3	4	5
Sanctions					
Ego					
I would feel very sorry					++
I would be disappointed at myself	-				+
Consider how to make up for it					++
Confession as a relief					++
Amoral					
I would imagine I might feel relieved	++				
We would feel quite o.k. about it	++				
Would probably get over it quite soon	++				
Would not matter that much to me	++				
Glad that I had done with it	++				
% variance explained by each factor	12.4	9.7	8.6	8.1	6.0

Note. ++ and – are absolute loadings ≥ .05.
 + and – are as follows: 0.3 ≤ absolute loading < 5.

"Now, this is absolutely beyond question. ... I think it effects one's health and later on in life one might get a stomach complaint or take drugs to get over it."

"I would never have done something like that. If, however, I had ... I'd feel very miserable as if everybody could tell from my face ... very horrible, guilty in any case and shame and simply fear to live on, fear of having done something bad, well, I can't ... I think it's absolutely terrible and I don't know whether I could ever really laugh again or be happy."

"I'd have bad pangs of conscience. ... I'm absolutely obliged to respect my father's will and counteracting is a sin."

In contrast, the following quotes show that younger subjects justify their rejection of the transgression by arguments that explicate the wrongness of the act and in condemning it. They do not refer to consequences for the wrongdoer but instead mention intentions of making up to the victim:

"As far as I'm concerned—normally I could not muster the ability. I would not have the determination to do something like that, for to me that is a double breach of confidence. ... I can't really picture myself doing something like that. I can imagine that had I done it, well, I think I wouldn't feel good at all and sooner or later I'd probably. ..."

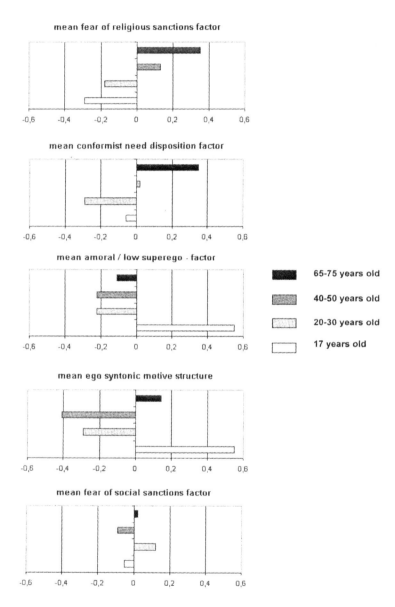

FIG. 13.1. Factors in conformity concerns.

322

"I'd feel very bad, because this is immoral. I'd have a bad self-feeling that I couldn't live with. I'd try to make up for that. Sometimes mistakes can be set right, subsequently."

"I couldn't enjoy spending the money. If that woman really looks so poor then I'd think she needs it more than I do. Although 400 Marks is a hell of a lot of money—my allowance is 60 Marks—and I could do a lot with it ... but this is out. I can't take 400 DM from an old lady who obviously needs it. And if she'd already left and I had no chance to give it back to her I'd feel very bad and probably I'd tell my parents or I'd take it to the lost and found. I'd feel: something like that is out!"

These spontaneous reactions reflect cross-generational changes in the way morality is anchored in those persons who care about it. In the traditional model the superego strictly controls the ego's conformity to preordained norms ("If I counteract—I sin") or even bars the very thought of transgression from conscious awareness by setting up strict taboos and in case of violation, threatens with lifelong retributions. In contrast, in the ego-syntonic model the individual identifies with norms he or she understands to be justified, and in case of transgressions the individual expresses regret, thus indicating that he or she experiences the lapse as a betrayal of self-chosen and willingly affirmed aspirations. The quotes by the younger subjects reflect an identity constitutive commitment to morality. Down to the wording chosen ("I couldn't muster the ability; I'd have no determination to do something like that") the statements resemble Frankfurt's (1988) explication of the concept of "volitional necessity." This self-imposed constraint is wanted inasmuch as the underlying reasons are held to be valid ("For me this is a double breach of confidence," "She needs the money more than I do"). Thus, the traditional and the modern type of moral motivation differ in two respects—the importance of autonomous moral judgment and the emotional reaction to wrongdoing, for example, fear of sanctions imposed by ego-alien instances (by the body, by third persons, and by the superego) versus ego-syntonic reactions ("I would not feel good," "bad self-feeling," "I'd feel that's out").

The sociohistoric change of the moral language game (Wittgenstein, 1984) reflects a relaxation of self-constraint. This must not be mistaken for moral disinterest. Instead, it has been shown that there is an ego-syntonic type of moral motivation. Still, the question may arise whether—overall—the weakening of internalized superego controls may lead to higher amorality. This question was not addressed in the present study that focused on the structure and not the intensity of moral motivation. Nevertheless, some speculations may be in place. At first sight, younger subjects' higher affirmation of amoral reactions seems to imply a corruption of morality; it might, however, simply mirror their greater candor. The following two quotes illustrate this possible interpretation: "I'd have a bad conscience about that. I'd start thinking why I had done it.

Could be revengefulness or ... why should someone else get it?" versus "I'd
have had good reasons ... probably I'd been treated badly by the other heirs.
I'd have felt some vindictiveness. ... They already had been overprivileged. ...
I can imagine doing something like that if I have good reasons." The quotes are
structurally similar. Both subjects see envy and jealousy ("Why should someone else get it?" and "They already had been overprivileged") as likely motives
for an act of fraud that they (pseudo-) justify: By the victim's lack of integrity
and speaking of revengefulness and vindictiveness they reinterpret an intentional transgression as a mere reaction to previous injustices. In other words,
both subjects consider cheating on one's father's last will as a conceivable option. However, only the second—the younger one—says so directly ("I could
imagine doing something like that") whereas the first—the older one—con-
ceals it by use of (conventional) moralistic phrases ("I'd have a bad conscience
about that").

Another way of addressing the issue of moral decay is looking at data of
real-life behavior of preceding generations. There are detailed analyses of the
way the Aryan law was enacted in 1938 by Nazi Germany (Bajohr, 2000). The
law ruled out Jewish ownership of firms; that is, Jewish entrepreneurs were
forced to sell their business property. The selling price was dependent not only
on state and NSDAP (the Nazi party: Nationalsozialistische Deutsche
Arbeiterpartei) approval and professional assessments but also on the behavior
of the Aryan buyer. Almost all purchasers of Jewish enterprises could be classified into one of three groups: There were unscrupulous profiteers who spared
no effort to force down the price even more (e.g., by threats or breach of con-
tract). Others accepted the profit arising from property assessments that were
too low but tried to carry out the transaction in a formally correct way. A third
group tried to adequately remunerate the owners (e.g., by secret payments or
even by illegal means). An analysis of a sample of 300 forced sales of Jewish
firms in 1938 through 1939 showed that 40% of the purchasers could be reckoned under the group of unscrupulous profiteers and 40% under the group of
unconspicuous usufructuaries, whereas 20% were fair buyers. These data do
not support a global decay hypothesis. [9]

CHANGES IN COGNITIVE MORAL UNDERSTANDING

Theoretical Considerations

The changes in motive structure correspond to changes in cognitive moral understanding (cf. Nunner-Winkler, 2000). Secularization and enlightenment
have altered the justification of moral norms. They are no longer understood as

commands preordained by God, religious authorities, or time-honored traditions. Rather, they are derived from "our common will" (Tugendhat, 1993, 2001). Rawls (1972) provided a plausible operationalization of the basic idea: Only those norms are valid that all could agree on in the original position under the veil of ignorance, that is, if unaware of any individual characteristics (e.g., membership in ethnic, religious, or generational groups; personal talents or preferences), knowing only universal features of man. Such features are man's vulnerability; his readiness to harm others for self-serving interests, and his ability to refrain from doing so; his interest to protect himself and those he cares about from being harmed (Gert, 1988). This model elucidates central aspects of a modern moral understanding. First, the principle of equality is basic. By stipulating consensus everybody is provided with the power of veto (i.e. everybody's voice is counted alike; Dworkin, 1978). Often, equality is treated as a mere procedural requirement (Habermas, 1983), but in fact it is the core substantive principle of a contractual morality (Ackerman, 1980) that strongly contrasts with previously forwarded transcendental justifications of unequal treatment (e.g., *mulier tacet in ecclesia* [women are to keep silent in church] and kingship by the grace of God). Second, all participants of the original agreement are assumed to share an interest in not being harmed or having harm done to those for whom they care. This influences the understanding of the modality of rule validity. On traditional terms, man is obliged to strictly obey divine commands—and to trustfully submit any consequences ensuing from due actions to God who will see to it that, in the long run, for the faithful, everything turns out for the best. In fact, Kant's (1959) claim that negative duties enjoy exceptionless validity still reflects a basically religious view of the world: Not even to a murderer may a man tell an untruth to save his friend's life, for "truthfulness is a strict duty that cannot be evaded. He himself does not do harm to him who suffers thereby rather the harm is caused by chance" (p. 205). According to Marquard (1981), chance may be seen as an inner worldly equivalent of divine powers that, with man's increasing self-empowerment, also became devaluated. To the extent that man sees himself as master of his fate—with God either not believed in at all or ascribed only a purely transcendental role—the concept of responsibility is expanded and he feels answerable not only for rule obedience but also for any consequences that might result therefrom. Hence, norms are ascribed only a prima facie validity, because higher import is given to harm avoidance than to strict obedience to rules. In other words, exceptions are justifiable whenever—judged from an impartial point of view—less harm is done by transgressing than by conforming.[10]

   Given the focus on harm avoidance, moral duties, and obligations (e.g., do not kill, lie, etc.; help in emergencies; and do your fair share in cooperative schemas) are more clearly differentiated from questions of a good life that increasingly come to be reckoned under the personal domain. The principle of religious tolerance provides a good illustration. Unaware of their own religious persuasion, subjects in the original position will prefer the right to religious liberty and freedom from persecution to the chance of imposing own beliefs on others. The same holds true for other personal interests and concerns: Subjects will want to be free to pursue whatever they deem worthwhile. The only constraint that is agreed on by all is the requirement that the freedom of each must be compatible with a like degree of freedom for all.

Empirical Analysis

The data from the cohort comparison show that the core elements of a modern moral understanding—equality, prima facie validity, and universal minimal morality—steadily gain importance.

Equality. The principle of equality, although declared an inviolable human right already at the end of the 18th century, had at first been interpreted rather narrowly. Thus, the right to vote was restricted to propertied men and only gradually was granted to the unpropertied, to Jews, and even to women; the right to higher education was extended to women, and there was an increase in the struggle for a greater equality of socioeconomic participation rights. Today the debate focuses on children's rights, which is reflected in the data. In the cohort comparison subjects were presented a series of proverbs and asked how often they had heard them being said during their childhood. Several proverbs expressed a hierarchical relationship between adults and children (e.g., "When adults talk children have to keep silence"; "When an adult drops something the child must pick it up"; "Greeting an adult a child must bow or curtsy to adults"; "In buses and subways children must offer their seat to adults"). The older subjects heard such admonitions repeatedly. The 20 to 30 year olds, in contrast, hardly knew them at all. In other words, special rights and duties are no longer justified in terms of ascriptive (age) status differences—prima facie even children are treated as equals.

Prima Facie Validity. Findings indicate that older subjects tend to ascribe strict validity to moral rules for two reasons. First, when asked to specify circumstances in which they might judge differently, many of them declared their judgments as unalterable. Reactions to the vignette about recycling illustrates this: "Containers for different types of refuse are situated close to the home of Family K. Family K neglects sorting its refuse." Practically all subjects (more than 90% across generations) condemned the behavior of Family K. Yet, many of the oldest subjects (62%) did so rigidly. According to their understanding norms require strict obedience, that is, there can be no exceptions (because "otherwise order is destroyed"; "that's what the containers are there for—if they set them up, I sort"; "I don't know whether they recycle the refuse—but if the containers are set up, one must sort"; "there must be order"). Most younger subjects (60%), in contrast, are willing to allow for exceptions for two reasons: if the true goal, the preservation of nature, cannot be reached (e.g., "If the containers are so far away that the harm done by riding there by car outweighs the benefit of recycling"; "If the materials are not recycled separately but thrown together again after that"), and if norms of higher valence conflict (e.g., "If a disabled person or an elderly person has problems getting to the containers").

Second, in the examples given for immoral behavior older subjects tended to simply enumerate irregularities (e.g., "lying," "committing adultery," and "swimming in the nude"). Younger subjects, in contrast, tended to embed the transgressions in concrete situational contexts (e.g., "Taking from a poor person"; "deceiving one's partner and declaring one's love"; "nudism on a Greek island—not because nakedness is immoral but it is against local customs and hurts the feelings of the people there"). More than 60% of the youngest subjects (as compared with fewer than 30% of the oldest subjects) specified context conditions for rule violations. This indicates that they ascribe a prima facie validity only to norms (e.g., stealing may be justifiable in an emergency; sexual license might be part of the partnership arrangement; and although to us nudism is a question of conventions, this might be different in other cultures). In other words, morality is no longer seen in terms of literal obedience to rules but of regard for underlying principles.

Minimal Morality. Secularization is reflected not only in a greater willingness to allow for exceptions but also in changes of the contents of moral persuasions. Thus, the obligatoriness of religious rules diminishes (e.g., about half of the oldest subjects but fewer than 10% of the youngest condemn a person who leaves the church or does not baptize his child). The same holds true of duties against the self (e.g., taking drugs or not striving to develop one's own talents is condemned by over 90% of the oldest but by only half of the youngest subjects). Older subjects tend to understand life and talents as a gift that God has entrusted to man and that man may not waste. Most of the younger subjects, in contrast, see themselves as independent owners and masters of their body and life and thus class self-destructive behaviors with personal issues (provided no harm is done to third parties). Also, the belief in the existence of natural law decreases. For example, older subjects tend to condemn working mothers, calling them "egotistic," "irresponsible," and "undutiful" (80% vs. 40% of the youngest subjects) and homosexuality, saying that it is "unnatural," "deviant," "pathological," and "sinful" (more than 60% vs. less than 20%

of the youngest subjects). Both judgments obviously rely on natural law thinking: Given that childbearing is woman's natural function, she has a duty to take
care of her offspring; given that reproduction is a natural function of sexuality,
homosexuality is unnatural. Younger subjects no longer justify norms by referring to given facts; they refer to an implicit agreement on the inner wordly
principle of harm avoidance that allows for functional equivalents in behavior.
Thus, what counts is children's well-being, which could be provided for by
others. What counts is the quality of the relationship, biological sex categories
are not of such high import.

CONCLUSION

With secularization and social differentiation morality changes come universal moral principles (e.g., equality, impartiality, harm avoidance, and respect
for the dignity of persons). These principles guide the application of a minimal
set of moral rules that substitute for a multitude of strictly obligatory rules that
used to regulate many aspects of everyday life (largely classed today with an
extended personal domain). This change has implications for the cognitive and
motivational prerequisites for an adequate moral understanding. Formerly,
morality required knowledge of concrete rules and a disposition for literal and
punctual obedience that can most reliably be secured if it is deeply ingrained in
the personality structure. The modern moral understanding, in contrast, requires situated moral judgments. Cognitively, this presupposes reasoning abilities (i.e., sociocognitive development) and complex (domain-specific)
knowledge systems. Motivationally, the context specificity of judgments presupposes a generalized commitment to the moral domain that not everybody
may develop. The sociohistorical changes in the structure of moral motivation
just described correspond to the changes in cognitive moral understanding.
Over the generations the internalization of concrete rules (in form of a strictly
controlling superego or in the form of almost automatic response habits) is being replaced by a formal type of moral motivation: a readiness to do whatever
in a given situation is judged to be right. At best, this crystallizes in the form of
a second-order moral volition—that is, a commitment the person cannot bring
himself to betray.

ENDNOTES

[1]I thank the children and parents involved in this study for their cooperation, Beate
Sodian and Angelika Weber for their participation in the development of the moral mo-
tive measure, Gus Blasi for help in coding procedures, Tina Hascher and Yvonne
Dechant for coding, and Mario Nikele for doing the statistical analyses.

[2]These findings are at variance with Kohlberg's conceptualization of the preconventional stage. The discrepancies result from different operationalizations: Turiel and Nucci explore children's understanding of the validity of moral rules. Kohlberg asked for action recommendations in dilemmas. However, before children have built up moral motivation, they will interpret Kohlberg's test question ("What should the protagonist do?") on purely pragmatic terms and recommend the person act in a way that best serves his or her interests despite their understanding of the intrinsic validity of moral rules.

[3]As children grow older emotion ascriptions no longer indicate moral motivation. Older children—like adults—expect a wrongdoer to feel bad after transgression (cf. Barden et al., 1980). Thus, at age 10 almost all LOGIC subjects attributed a negative emotion to an hypothetical wrongdoer, and even half of those who—by a different measurement procedure—were rated as low in moral motivation did so. Presumably, these seemingly moral emotion ascriptions are due to the fact that with the acquisition of self-reflexive role taking (Perner & Wimmer, 1985; Selman & Byrne, 1974) children begin to orient their answers to social desirability concerns. After all, they do know quite well that displaying regret or guilt after transgression is better than showing glee (Nunner-Winkler & Sodian, 1988).

[4]There are equivalent formulas adults sometimes use when apologizing for inadvertently hurting someone else (e.g., "Im sorry, I didn't want that," "I didn't mean to," "I didn't intend to") that express regret rather than guilt.

[5]The stories presented were devised so that the protagonist's spontaneous desires conflicted with simple rules, because only in such cases can conformity be taken to indicate moral motivation. In nonconflictual cases conformity might well be due to a spontaneous altrustic first-order desire or to lack of temptation (cf. Blasi, 1980, 1983).

[6]I thank Lucia Freuding, Barbara Frischhoz, Ute Loges, Katharina Raab, Anne Schroedter, Christian Schwabe, Anja Sommerer, and Dorothea Winkler for helping with the development of the interview schedule and the coding categories, and the staff of the institute for having conducted the interviews with the older subjects.

[7]For the three older cohorts cheating on one's father's last will was used: "You are the only one who knows that your father—shortly before he died—changed his will much to your disadvantage. You decide to keep this secret." The 17year-old LOGIC subjects were presented with a more age-appropriate story that involved not returning lost money: "You observe an elderly, poor-looking woman dropping a purse when getting up from a park bench. She just passed around the corner when you pick up the purse and find 400 DM in it. Nobody is around. You decide to keep the money." Both situations depict a neglect to filfill a norm (honesty) under aggravating conditions (betrayal of close relatives, taking from a needy person).

[8]To ease readability the signs of the factor values have been reversed in Fig. 13.1.

[9]There are counterarguments of course: For one, real-life behavior is compared with verbal assessment (and discrepancies in favor of the latter are known). Also, the analysis deals with business people (among whom persons with strategic intersts might be overrepresented). Yet, hunting after enrichment was found not only among entrepreneurs. Property of deported Jews was sold by auctions, and more than 100,000 people in Hamburg and many inhabitants of small villages (where the Jews had personally been known) participated in such public sales and without hesitation and, at low prices, took over furniture, jewelery, and so on of their former neighbors.

[10]Consensus is not necessaily reached in concrete dilemmas—after all empirical prognoses of consequences are fallible, and in pluralistic societies people legitimately differ in their evaluations of results (Nunner-Winkler, 1990).

REFERENCES

Ackerman, B. A. (1980). *Social justice in the liberal state.* New Haven, CT: Yale University Press.

Ainsworth, M. D. S., Blehar, M. C., Waters, E., & Walls, S. (1978). *Patterns of attachment: A psychological study of the strange situation.* Hillsdale, NJ: Lawrence Erlbaum Associates.

Andreoni, J. (1990). Impure altruism and donations to public goods: A theory of warm-glow giving. *The Economic Journal, 100,* 464–477.

Arsenio, W., & Kramer, R. (1992). Victimizers and their victims. *Child Development, 63,* 915–927.

Arsenio, W., & Lover, A. (1995). Children's conceptions of sociomoral affect: Happy victimizers, mixed emotions, and other expectancies. In M. Killen & D. Hart (Eds.), *Morality in everyday life* (pp. 87–128). New York: Cambridge University Press.

Asendorpf, J. B., & Nunner-Winkler, G. (1992). Children's moral motive strength and temperamental inhibition reduce their immoral tendencies in real moral conflicts. *Child Development, 63,* 1223–1235.

Bajohr, F. (2000). *Verfolgung aus gesellschafts geschichtlicher Perspektive. Die wirtschaftliche Existenzvernichtung der Juden und die deutsche Gesellschaft.* [Persecution from a socio-historic perspective. The annihilation of the economic existence of the Jews and German society.] Geschichte und Gesellschaft, 26, 629–652.

Bandura, A. (1976). *Social learning theory.* Englewood Cliffs, NJ: Prentice Hall.

Barden, R. C., Zelko, F. A., Duncan, S. W., & Masters, J. C. (1980). Children's consensual knowledge about the experiential determinants of emotion. *Journal of Personality and Social Psychology, 39,* 968-976.

Blasi, A. (1980). Bridging moral cognition and moral action: A critical review of the literature. *Psychological Bulletin, 88,* 1–45.

Blasi, A. (1983). Bridging moral cognition and moral action: A theoretical perspective. *Developmental Review, 3,* 178–210.

Blasi, A. (1984). *Autonomie im Gehorsam: Der Erwerb von Distanz im Sozialisationsprozeß.* [Autonomy in obedience. The development of distancing in the socialisation process.] In W. Edelstein & J. Habermas (Eds.), Soziale Interaktion und soziales Verstehen (pp. 300–345). Frankfurt, Germany: Suhrkamp.

Block, J. (1961). *The Q-sort method in personality assessment and psychiatric research.* Palo Alto, CA: Consulting Psychologists Press.

Bourdieu, P. (1984). *Die feinen Unterschiede: Kritik der gesellschaftlichen Urteilskraft.* [Fine differences. Critique of societal discernement.] Frankfurt, Germany: Suhrkamp.

Bowlby, J. (1986). *Bindung. Eine Analyse der Mutter-Kind-Beziehung.* [Attachment. An Analysis of mother-child-relationship.] Frankfurt, Germany: Fischer.

Colby, A., & Damon, W. (1993). The uniting of self and morality in the development of extraordinary moral commitment. In G. Noam & T.E. Wren (Eds.), *The moral self* (pp. 149–174). Cambridge, MA: MIT Press.

Colby, A., & Damon, W. (1995). The development of extraordinary moral commitment. In M. Killen & D. Hart (Eds.), *Morality in everyday life: Developmental perspectives* (pp. 342–370). New York: Cambridge University Press.

Dworkin, R. (1978). *Taking rights seriously*. Boston: Harvard University Press.

Elias, N. (1978a). *Über den Prozeß der Zivilisation. Band 1*. [The process of civilization. Vol. 1]. Frankfurt, Germany: Suhrkamp.

Elias, N. (1978b). *Über den Prozeß der Zivilisation. Band 2*. [The process of civilization. Vol. 2.]. Frankfurt, Germany: Suhrkamp.

Eysenck, H. J. (1960). The development of moral values in children: The contribution of learning theory. *British Journal of Educational Psychology, 30*, 11–21.

Eysenck, H. J. (1976). The biology of morality. In T. Lickona (Ed.), *Moral development and behavior-Theory, research, and social issues* (pp. 108–123). New York: Holt, Rinehart & Winston.

Frankfurt, H. G. (1988). *The importance of what we care about: Philosophical essays*. Cambridge, England: Cambridge University Press.

Frankfurt, H. G. (1993). On the necessity of ideals. In G. Noam & T. E. Wren (Eds.), *The moral self* (pp. 16–27). Cambridge, MA: MIT Press.

Freud, S. (1929/1989). *Civilization and its discontents*. New York: Norton.

Freud, S. (1925). Einige psychischen Folgen des anatomischen Geschlechtsunterschieds. [Some psychic consequences of anatomic sex differences.] *Gesammelte Werke, 14*. (pp. 20–30). Frankfurt, Germany: Fischer 1985.

Freud, S. (1933). Neue Folge der Vorlesungen zur Einführung in die Psychoanalyse. [New sequels of lectures on the introduction to psychoanalysis.] In S. Freud (Ed.), Studienausgabe (Vol. 1, pp. 447–608). Frankfurt, Germany: Fischer 1974.

Gert, B. (1988). Morality. A new justification of the moral rules. New York: Oxford University Press.

Habermas, J. (1983). *Moralbewußtsein und kommunikatives Handeln.* [Moral consciousness and communicative action.] Frankfurt, Germany: Suhrkamp.

Hascher, T. (1994). *Emotionsbeschreibung und Emotionsverstehen: Zur Entwicklung des Emotionsvokabulars und des Ambivalenzverstehens im Kindesalter.* [Describing and understanding emotions: Children's development of a vocabulary of emotions and of understanding ambivalence.] Münster, Germany: Waxmann.

Heckhausen, H. (1982). The development of achievement motivation. In W. W. Hartup (Ed.), *Review of child development research* (pp. 600–668). Chicago: University of Chicago Press.

Heckhausen, H. (1985). Emotionen im Leistungsverhalten aus ontogenetischer Sicht. [Emotion and motivation in achievement behaviour: An ontogenetic perspective.] In E. Chr (Ed.), *Emotionalität und Motivation im Kindes und Jugendalter* (pp. 95–131). Frankfurt, Germany: Fachbuchhandlung für Psychologie.

Helkama, K. (1979). *The development of the attribution of responsibility: A critical survey of empirical research and a theoretical outline.* Unpublished manuscript, University of Helsinki, Finland.

Jacobson, E. (1964). *The self and the object world.* New York: International Universities Press.

Kant, I. (1959). *Über ein vermeintliches Recht, aus Menschenliebe zu lügen.* [On a putative right to lie from charity.] In K. Vorländer (Ed.), Immanuel Kant: Kleinere Schriften zur Geschichtsphilosophie Ethik und Politik (pp. 199–206). Hamburg, Germany: Felix Meiner Verlag.

Kohlberg, L. (1981). *Essays on moral development: Vol 1. The philosophy of moral development: Moral stages and the idea of justice.* San Francisco: Harper & Row.

Kohlberg, L. (1984). *The psychology of moral development. The nature and validity of moral stages. Essays on Moral Development, Vol. 2.* San Francisco: Harper & Row.

Kohlberg, L., & Candee, D. (1984). The relationship of moral judgment to moral action. In L. Kohlberg (Ed.), *Essays on moral development: Vol. 2. The psychology of moral development: The nature and validity of moral stages* (pp. 498–581). San Francisco: Harper & Row.

Luhmann, N. (1998). *Die Gesellschaft der Gesellschaft.* [The society of society.] Frankfurt, Germany: Suhrkamp.

Marquard, O. (1981). *Abschied vom Prinzipiellen.* [Parting from the principled.] Stuttgart, Germany: Reclam.

Miller, N. E. (1948). Studies of fear as an acquirable drive: Fear as motivation and fear-reduction as reinforcement in the learning of new responses. *Journal of Experimental Psychology, 38,* 89–101.

Montada, L. (1993). Understanding oughts by assessing moral reasoning or moral emotions. In G. Noam & T. E. Wren (Eds.), *The moral self* (pp. 292–309). Cambridge, MA: MIT Press.

Nucci, L. P., & Turiel, E. (1993). God's word, religious rules, and their relation to Christian and Jewish children's concepts of morality. *Child Development, 64,* 1475–1491.

Nunner-Winkler, G. (1990). Moral relativism and strict universalism. In T. E. Wren (Ed.), *The moral domain. Essays on the ongoing discussion between philosophy and the social sciences* (pp. 109–126). Cambridge, MA: MIT Press.

Nunner-Winkler, G. (1998). The development of moral understanding and moral motivation. *International Journal of Educational Research, 27,* 587–603.

Nunner-Winkler, G. (1999). *Empathie, Scham und Schuld. Zur moralischen Bedeutung von Emotionen.* [Empathy, shame and guilt: The moral meaning of emotions.] In M. Grundmann (Ed.), Konstruktivistische Sozialforschung. Lebensweltliche Erfahrungskontexte, individuelle Handlungskompetenzen und die Konstruktion sozialer Strukturen (pp. 149–179). Frankfurt, Germany: Surhkamp

Nunner-Winkler, G. (2000). *Wandel in den Moralvorstellungen. Ein Generationenvergleich.* [Changes in moral understanding. An intergenerational comparison.] In W. Edelstein & G. Nunner-Winkler (Eds.), Moral im sozialen Kontext [Morality in social context] (pp. 299–336). Frankfurt, Germany: Surhkamp.

Nunner-Winkler, G. (in prep.). *Moral motivation in 17-year-olds.*

Nunner-Winkler, G., & Sodian, B. (1988). Children's understanding of moral emotions. *Child Development, 59,* 1323–1338

Oevermann, U., Allert, T., Gripp, H., Konau, E., Krambach, J., Schröder Caesar, E. (1976). *Beobachtungen zur Struktur der sozialisatorischen Interaktion: Theoretische und methodologische Fragen der Sozialisationsforschung.* [Observations concerning the structure of interaction in socialisation. Theoretical and methodological issues in research on socialisation.] In M. Auwärter, E. Kirsch, & K. Schröter (Eds.), Seminar: Kommunikation, Interaktion, Identität (pp. 371–403). Frankfurt, Germany: Suhrkamp.

Oliner, S., & Oliner, P. (1988) *The altruistic personality: Rescuers of Jews in Nazi Europe.* New York: The Free Press.

Parsons, T. (1964). *The social system.* London: The Free Press.

Perner, J., & Wimmer, H. (1985). "John thinks that Mary thinks that." Attribution of second-order beliefs by 5- to 10-year-old children. *Journal of Experimental Child Psychology, 39*, 437–447.

Rawls, J. (1972). *A theory of justice.* Cambridge, MA: Harvard University Press.

Reuband, K. H. (1988). *Von äußerer Verhaltenskonformität zu selbständigem Handeln: Über die Bedeutung kultureller und struktureller Einflüsse für den Wandel in den Erziehungszielen und Sozialisationsinhalten.* [From outward conformity to autonomous action. The relevance of cultural and structural influences for changes in the goals and contents of socialisation.] In H. O. Luthe & H. Meulemann (Eds.), Wertwandel Faktum oder Fiktion? Bestandsaufnahmen u. Diagnosen aus kultursoziologischer Sicht (pp. 73–97). Frankfurt, Germany: Campus.

Reuband, K. H. (1997). *Aushandeln statt Gehorsam. Erziehungsziele und Erziehungspraktiken in den alten und neuen Bundesländern im Wandel.* [Negotiation instead of obedience. Changes in educational goals and styles in the old and the new German countries.] In K. Lenz & L.Böhnisch (Eds.), Familien. Eine interdisziplinäre Einführung (pp. 129–153). Weinheim, Germany: Juventa.

Schneider, W., & Nunner-Winkler, G. (1989). Parent interview. In W. S. Franz & E. Weinert (Eds.), *The Munich longitudinal study on the genesis of individual competencies (LOGIC): Report No. 5. Results of wave three.* Munich, Germany: Max-Planck-Institute for Psychological Research.

Selman, R. L., & Byrne, D. F. (1974). A structural-developmental analysis of levels of role taking in middle childhood. *Child Development, 45*, 803–806.

Skinner, B. F. (1938). *The behavior of organisms: An experimental analysis.* Englewood Cliffs, NJ: Prentice-Hall.

Solomon, R. C. (1976). *The passions.* Garden City, NY: Anchor.

Taylor, G. (1985). *Pride, shame, and guilt: Emotions of self-assessment.* Oxford, England: Clarendon Press.

Tugendhat, E. (1993). *Vorlesungen über Ethik.* [Lectures on ethics.] Frankfurt, Germany: Suhrkamp.

Tugendhat, E. (2001). *Wie sollen wir Moral verstehen?* [How to understand morality.] In E. Tugendhat (Ed.), Aufsätze 1992 2000 (pp. 163–184). Frankfurt, Germany: Suhrkamp.

Turiel, E. (1983). *The development of social knowledge: Morality and convention.* Cambridge, England: Cambridge University Press.

Weinert, F. E., & Geppert, U. (1996). *Genetisch orientierte Lebensspannenstudie zur differentiellen Entwicklung (GOLD): Report No. 1. Planung der Studie.* [Genetically oriented lifespan study of differential development. Report No. 1: Planning of the study.] München, Germany: Max-Planck-Institut für Psychologische Forschung.

Weinert, F. E., & Schneider, W. (1999). *Individual development from 3 to 12: Findings from the Munich Longitudinal Study.* New York: Cambridge University Press.

White, R. W. (1959). Motivation reconsidered: The concept of competence. *Psychological Review, 66*, 297–333.

Wittgenstein, L. (1984). *Philosophische Untersuchungen.* [Philosophical investigations.] *Bd1, Werkausgabe. Frankfurt, Germany: Suhrkamp.

14

Moral Functioning: Moral Understanding and Personality

Augusto Blasi
University of Massachusetts, Boston

At least in three respects I can say that I have been fortunate in my career: I came to psychology with an interest in a field, moral development and functioning, that is of crucial importance beyond the confines of academic psychology; over 20 years ago I raised for myself the question of the relations between morality and personality, at a time when the field of moral psychology needed to expand its concern in this direction; finally, I found a congenial group of colleagues and friends that share my interest and have been willing, with great tolerance on their part, to engage in serious discussion and debate on these issues. I cannot detail here how much I learned from them over the years. Many generously contributed to the present volume by reporting important new data, extending our thinking, and also by questioning my views and assumptions—unfailingly in a spirit of dispassionate concern for the truth. I am grateful to all of them, particularly the editors of this volume, for the challenge and for the opportunity to rethink my ideas and to clarify some misunderstandings.

The central points of my position, not exactly the same through the years, could be summarized as follows: First, it seems obvious that morality, psychologically, is not a self-subsistent entity served by autonomous processes but rather a specific mode of functioning of each person as a whole; and that, therefore, moral competencies must be integrated in the overall personality system. Second, it seems also obvious that the integration of morality in personality should be conceived in such a way as to respect both the essential characteristics of morality as is understood in ordinary everyday social exchanges and also the normal characteristics of psychological functioning. It would be as inappropriate to distort morality in order to fit it with a priori and unnecessary conceptions of personality as would be inappropriate to place impossible demands on personality in order to fit a priori and unnecessary conceptions of morality. Third, it seems essential to the ordinary understanding of moral action that its intention be guided by a minimal grasp of the moral. Here, in my opinion, hinges the necessity that moral functioning be rooted in moral understanding. Fourth, because the intention to behave morally depends on some kind of personal motivation, and because motivation is one central aspect of personality, one must conceptually allow for a type of personality that is capable, in principle, of being specifically motivated by what constitutes the central characteristics of morality.

Before elaborating some of these points, I would like to broaden our perspective beyond our special concern here. In fact, this particular way of construing the issue is not limited to morality, but it should also be applied to other human ideals that share with morality the important characteristic of transcending individual self-interests. In addition to morality, there are human values and ideals—such as the ideals of beauty and truth—that make claims on us to which we feel a degree of obligation, and present objective standards that require our respect. In the ideal case, when confronted with one of these ideals, one has the experience of being at the service of a wonderful, all-important, demanding, and uncompromising aspect of humanity; one also feels privileged to serve the ideal and ready to bring one's capacities to its call. Thus, we are aware that we are not allowed to distort the truth as we know it, in order to satisfy our wishes, even if we are tempted of doing so and sometimes succeed. Likewise, a person who has acquired a degree of sensitivity for the beautiful no longer feels free to compromise it to satisfy other personal interests he or she may have. Freud (e.g., 1910, 1927) himself, in his more objective moments, recognized that psychoanalysis had no real light to bring to our understanding of what is specifically creative in art and science. Of course, he did not observe the same restraint with regard to morality, probably because he was struck by the damages inflicted on us by what could be rightly called moral pathologies. And yet there is normal morality, which, like science or art, cannot be grasped through the reductive interpretations of self-interest. In debating the question concerning the relations between morality and personality, it may be useful to keep in mind the parallels offered by the ideals of beauty and truth and how some of us may come to be guided by them.

One further point: In pursuing the inquiry concerning the relations between morality and personality, I was indeed interested in grasping the way morality actually functions; but I was also interested in approaching a conception of personality in which the subjective and agentic self is given a central role. I thought that these two threads of inquiry are closely related and depend one on the other. Personality is frequently construed as an organization of quasi-autonomous elements, dynamically interacting with each other according to impersonal principles of compensation or, worse, according to equally impersonal laws regulating the interactions among forces. In these conceptions there may be room for consciousness, but not for an agentic I that is capable of genuine choices and is not fatalistically determined by internal and external forces; in these theories there is no room for a subject self that has the potential of constructing, to some extent, the life and personality that one wishes to have. I think that only this kind of personality can integrate the demands of moral ideals (or the demands of knowledge and beauty) without distorting them; vice versa, I think that a grasp of the way moral ideals operate in people would open for us a window to understand the kind of personality we have. This perspective hopefully explains why I tried to maintain two anchor points in my work: the cognitive basis of morality and the personal agentic capacities of the self.

WHY MORALITY REQUIRES UNDERSTANDING

Starting with a terminological note, I prefer, in general, to refer to *understanding* or *grasping* also when I use the terms *cognition* or *knowledge*. *Cognition* and *cognitive* risk being construed in terms of the information processing approach, thus they may miss or distort the personal and responsible nature of the project of knowing. *Knowing* and *knowledge* may sometimes suggest the rote learning, storing, and retrieving of content information. By contrast, the term, *understanding*, brings out the assimilatory and personal aspect of knowledge.

As is well known, Piaget's (1932) theory of moral development and, even more so, Kohlberg's (e.g., 1984) were founded on the idea of moral understanding. In fact, it could be argued that all the central characteristics of Kohlberg's theory—that moral understanding is guided by a general logic, that this logic is a result of equilibratory processes, that development proceeds according to structural stages, and even the emphases on universality and justice—hinge on the momentous decision to consider understanding as the core of morality. This aspect eventually became the focus of criticism, and sometimes rejection, of Kohlberg's theory. The critical arguments are many, and several are well presented in chapters of this volume (e.g., Lapsley & Narvaez, Nisan, and Walker): Moral functioning is intrinsically affective; its nature tends to be distorted by the rationalism of the cognitive–developmental approach; people do not make moral decisions through a process of deliberation and reasoning; in fact, they seem to have an intuitive, quasi-perceptual grasp of what is right; they frequently are unaware of their reasons and incapable of representing them in words; sometimes the reasons seem to be like rationalizations, after-the-fact self-justifications and attempts at impression management; therefore, the reasons that people give tend to be inconsistent from situation to situation; in the best of cases, there is a gap between general moral criteria and concrete judgments; it is therefore impossible to predict, on the basis of stage-related criteria, which moral judgments people will formulate for different actions in different situations; and, finally, on the basis of their concrete judgments, it is difficult to predict what people actually end up doing.

It would be silly not to recognize that many of these criticisms are well taken and are based on solid observations. And yet, in the end, one is confronted with serious questions: What then? Are we going to follow those theories that, in the emotivist tradition, shed morality of all traces of genuine reasoning and rationality? (Note that the issue is not whether the processing of information through perception, attention, memory, etc. is needed: Theories do not disagree on this point.) How are we going to formulate a viable theory that differs from psychoanalysis, the various learning theories, psychobiological theories, and also from Kohlberg's theory? Can we formulate a developmental theory of moral functioning that does not give any significant role to the understanding of moral criteria?

Starting with the last question, I (e.g., 1983, 1995, 1999) consistently argued that we cannot because understanding is of the essence of morality, as is grasped in everyday language and in ordinary communication. But I also argued that the type of moral understanding that is minimally required by common social categories is very different from the theory constructed by Kohlberg. I believe that if we, as psychologists, wish to study the morality that people live and talk about, we have no choice but to minimally adopt the definition embedded in everyday language. The issue is not empirical but conceptual.

According to common understanding, moral actions belong to the very broad category of actions that can be evaluated as worthy of praise or blame. In progressively constructing this category and in focusing on it as very important for our social life, human beings also created the criteria for differentiating what is worthy of praise from what is simply worthy of admiration. These criteria are mainly three: (a) for an action to be praised, its product should be, in some sense, worthy of admiration; (b) the action should be intentional and not a result of accidental events; therefore the goal of the action should be represented, in some form, in the agent's consciousness; and (c) the agent should have specifically aimed at the admirable aspect of his or her action.

For example, a baby is not praised if, in pounding his fingers on a piano's keys, accidentally produces a nice melody. The same baby, sensitive to his parents' admiration and endowed of good memory, intentionally now, reproduces the same melody; he would not be praised for his aesthetic sense if he has no grasp of it. Praise for aesthetic actions requires some grasp of beauty in the agent as well as the intention to produce that specific aspect.

It is clear that many beneficial outcomes are produced unintentionally, for instance, by the workings of nature (e.g., all the wonderful things that are produced by our nervous or hormonal systems). Sometimes beneficial outcomes are produced by intentional actions, which, however, were not specifically aimed at the good effect, either because the agent did not understand that his or her action was good or because he or she was guided by a different motive. A child may share his or her toys with another child without realizing that what he or she did is nice, good, or moral. Another child intentionally obeys his or her mother's command but purely out of fear or by the expectation of a reward. According to our everyday understanding of morality, it would be inappropriate to consider these actions as moral just because they produced beneficial consequences and to praise these children for acting morally (Blasi, 2000).

But the type of understanding of the good that is required for moral praise may be rather limited; it may be implicit and unverbalized. As Lapsley and Narvaez (this volume—chap. 9), and Walker (this volume—chap. 1) pointed out, some people, even under questioning, may be unable to reflect on their motives and to explain the reasons for acting as they did; therefore, they would be unable to reason and deliberate. But frequently it is possible, perhaps under careful questioning, to explain one's motives, or at least to eliminate nonmoral motives. And frequently there are nonverbal indications that the agent's motive was far from being moral. Of course, this situation may create difficulties for psychologists interested in constructing empirical operations for moral behavior. Frequently, we may not know whether an action is moral or not. But we are not God; our task is not to assign praise and blame, and we should be able to live and make progress in research with this kind of uncertainty.

If we ask why, in attributing praise or blame, people tend to particularly value the intentional pursuit of motives, I tend to think that the deep reason for such a universal attitude is that a person can only own those intentional actions that are guided by conscious reasons; these actions belong to us and we are responsible for them. Praise or blame are ultimately given to the agent as recognition of his or her responsibility.

I would like to make one further comment: The type of understanding that is required for moral praise or blame concerns concrete actions, those already performed and those that are about to be performed. This brings me to Nisan's (this volume—chap. 7) distinction between abstract and concrete moral judgment. I do understand and agree with his central points, namely, that (a) people subscribe to many values in addition to moral values; (b) in any concrete decision, all or several of the relevant concerns are taken into account, including one's self-interest; and (c) people may prefer to follow nonmoral values or even self-interest, believing that the chosen course of action is overall the best. But I personally find Nisan's way of representing the judgment process somewhat confusing. Probably the process of practical judgment, in the more reflective instances, is frequently cyclical—going from a global judgment about the action being concretely considered, to an analysis of the different values and concerns involved, to an abstract consideration of each value, and not only of morality (e.g., how should this particular action be evaluated if morality were the only value or if only my career interests were at stake?), and to a final differentiated concrete judgment. I am not sure that this last judgment should be called moral, when it was ultimately guided by nonmoral values. Finally, I do not think that a person's last concrete evaluation can be identified with the action choice. Regardless of which value prevailed, one can always follow a discrepant course of action. The gap that interested me is when one's final concrete judgment emphasizes moral concerns and yet one pursues a discrepant course of action. A similar gap, I think, is possible also when the final evaluation was principally guided by nonmoral values or even self-interest. For example, a person may think that the best course of action would be to follow his or her career interests, but could not bring himself or herself to see other people being hurt by this decision.

One final comment: As I suggested, Kohlberg's theoretical understanding of moral reasoning and its development significantly differs from the minimal cognitive requirements of the ordinary concept of morality. It does not follow, however, that Kohlberg's theory is incorrect. It only means that it is not a part of conceptual requirements and that, therefore, its correctness would have to be supported by empirical evidence. I believe the evidence—pro or con—is not available yet. At the hypothetical level, the idea that a person's moral criteria naturally tend, through development, to become logically organized makes sense. Also, the enormous amount of data supporting the stages described by Kohlberg cannot be discounted so easily. But important questions remain to be answered: What is the precise nature of moral stages and of their structural properties? What are the relations between these structures and concrete moral judgments? And, most important for the present topic, what are the relations between levels of moral understanding and the degree of integration of morality in personality?

THE ROLE OF THE SELF IN MORAL MOTIVATION

My approach to moral motivation was guided by two considerations: First, the understanding of moral norms and morality in general must contain the element of intrinsic desirability; a person who knows moral norms but does not see that they are good and demand compliance for their own sake does not really understand morality. As I suggested earlier, according to common sense an action is morally praiseworthy only if it is aimed at the moral good for its own sake. But desirability is not the same as desire, and moral desires may be rather weak and ineffective in the context of other desires. Therefore—and this is the second consideration—it is not surprising to observe that frequently people know what is right but end up doing what is wrong; we allow our actions to contradict what we know and understand. There certainly are "platonic" individuals among us for whom the power of moral truths, as truths, is so great as to dominate their motivational system. But this is not the case for many others. Most of us understand moral norms, see them as desirable, are sensitive to the moral good, and are in principle motivated by it; but only sometimes (the frequency varies from person to person) the moral motivation embedded in moral understanding is effective in producing action.

It is the task of psychology to find explanations for individual differences in the ways understanding and motivation are related to each other and in the degree of congruence between these two elements of personality. In a very general sense, the answer must be found in the person's ability to translate moral understanding into moral motives, in the relative strength of moral motives relative to other motives, and in the ways different motives interact within each person's motivational system. In cases of insufficient motivation, a solution that we frequently resort to is to substitute a weak motive with a stronger one or to establish alliances with more powerful motives. Thus, a child may be able to pursue his or her school work by replacing his or her weak interest for learning with fear of being humiliated by the teacher or desire to be admired by other children. In the case of morality, however, adequate solutions are only those that respect the intrinsic desirability of moral claims. Weak moral motives may need to be reinforced, but without losing their character of desiring the moral good for its own sake.

The solution I have been elaborating relies on the self, namely (in my understanding and use of the term), that aspect of personality that underlies consciously subjective and agentic processes, in particular, processes of mastery and self-control, of ownership and appropriation, of conscious self-definition, and of internal organization and coherence. Two sets of processes, I think, are particularly important for moral functioning, both strengthening moral motivation without distorting it: the first is related to the creation and structuring of the will, as Frankfurt (e.g., 1988, 1999) understands the term; the second is related to the gradual construction of the sense of self, eventually leading to self identity. Following Frankfurt, I take the will to consist of a special desire that a desire one already has be effective in producing action. In willing, one appropriates certain desires—in our case, moral desires—and makes them especially one's own, investing oneself in and identifying oneself with them. Concretely, one prefers a moral desire over another desire in determining an intentional action, and then over another, and another, and so on. Eventually, the desire that one's moral desires be effective in one instance is generalized to many other instances; one acquires a concern for morality, cares about morality, even though one may continue to care about many other worthwhile things—perhaps more so than morality. When a person cares about morality to the point of wanting that his or her moral desires be effective not only in the present situation but also in the future, the person makes himself or herself responsible for actualizing his or her moral desires; the person becomes morally responsible. From this perspective, responsibility is a form of the will (Blasi, in press). It is important to realize that all desires are oriented to external objects, sometimes for what is intrinsically valuable in these objects. The moral will, therefore, as a result of concretely experiencing the goodness and the desirability of moral norms and values, lends possibly weak moral desires the weight, power, and authority of the agentic subject.

The second set of self processes has to do with appropriating the moral norms, principles, and values that one cares about to the developing sense of oneself and integrating them in the sense of who one is. Initially, being and wanting to be a good moral person is one self-concept among many others, and perhaps it is not more important for the sense of self than many other self-concepts. At some point and in some people, a selection takes place: Certain aspects of oneself are considered to be more "true and real" than many others from the perspective of the sense of self. Eventually, at least for many adults, the various characteristics that are recognized as elements of one's definition are hierarchically organized, and the sense of self acquires unity and depth; the person thus acknowledges that a few aspects of himself or herself are the center or the essence of his or her being. I call this special form of self-definition identity in the narrow sense or self identity. It is an identity for which one feels responsible; therefore, it inspires action and commitments. For these people new and important motives appear: the desire, indeed the need, to maintain one's identity, to exist as the person one feels to be at the core; and also the desire or the need to maintain its unity, to be internally consistent. Intentionally acting against one's core values and commitments is then experienced as self-betrayal and as a loss of one's self. Moral concerns do not need to be appropriated to the sense of oneself for a person to act morally, but frequently they are. And for some people they are the ground on which self identity is constructed. For these people, moral desires do not change, but are supported by new self motives: One continues to behave morally because moral norms and ideals are good and desirable; but, in addition, because acting against one's core commitments would be a self-betrayal and damaging to one's sense of self. The desire to maintain one's identity and to be consistent with it does not corrupt the nature of morality, because moral identity was constructed on the person's caring about morality as it objectively is. To speak of moral hedonism in this instance (as Nucci, this volume—chap. 6, seems to be doing) would be to totally misunderstand the processes by which people identify with values.

I should briefly address Nisan's objection to my view of moral identity. He argues that I try to build moral identity on "abstract moral judgments," and that this attempt is bound to fail; Because identity is essentially, by definition, concrete and individual, abstract judgments cannot be integrated in it. My reply is twofold: First, I do not think that what is integrated in the sense of self is moral judgment, whether abstract or concrete, but ideals and concerns, either about specific aspects of morality (e.g., altruism, justice, compassion, etc.) or about morality in general. Are moral ideals abstract? In one sense they are: Conceptually, any ideal (and not only moral ones) is differentiated from other ideals and other demands; in addition, it is a conception of a value in its perfection, in its pure form. It is by being a form of perfection that an ideal exercises its motivational pull. In this sense ideals are abstract. Psychologically, however, the motivational force of an ideal is far from being abstract, because it is progressively built on the accumulated effects of many concrete instances in which we actually experienced the importance, the value, and the beauty of the ideal. The ideal of justice, for instance, as psychologically felt, is neither constructed by learning the concept of justice and the various norms of fairness nor by being exposed to speeches about justice, even though all this may help; rather, it is formed by concretely experiencing in oneself and others the positive consequences of small and concrete actions of fairness and the damaging results of concrete injustices. The desire for just actions, by us and by others, is thus appropriated, and slowly is preferred to other and contrasting desires, until, in some people, the concern for justice begins to occupy the center of their concerns.

The second part of my reply is more important: The portrait of identity that Nisan draws in his chapter is a mixture of needs, desires, values, traits, and innumerable life events that we experience passively as elements existing next to each other without any particular order (Nucci seems to share this idea). I do not believe people's self-concepts, at least starting from early adolescence, can be construed in this way. Personal memory and personality perhaps can be looked at in this manner, but not self-definitions and, even less, self identity. As I mentioned, there are, on the part of the self, active processes of selection and hierarchical ordering. Only some of our own biographic data are appropriated to our sense of self; eventually, among these, only very few are seen as particularly important to the sense of who we are, as the essence of our being. Other aspects of ourselves are not rejected, but subordinated to core commitments, mainly when they create conflicts with our central values. In constructing an identity, a person does not need to give up any part of his or her richness but only needs to order it to create unity in the sense of self. Individuality is not lost as a result of centrally appropriating ideals; in fact, I believe that living one's core ideals creates a keen sense of totally being oneself and no other.

However, as I already suggested, this type of moral identity is not necessary for a person to be moral and act morally. Most people do not arrive at this level of mature identity; among those who do, many construct it around nonmoral ideals. Therefore, I agree with Nisan that most people subscribe to a variety of values; that for them moral values may be less important than others; and, in cases of conflict, may prefer to be guided by nonmoral values; and that, in doing so, they do not yield to impulses or temptations but judge their decision to be the right one or the best for them under the circumstances. However, only confusion is created when the use of the terms *right* or *best* is interpreted to mean that the decision was moral. In my view, the people Nisan has in mind may be decent moral people, but they have constructed their sense of self around ideals that are not moral.

Nucci (this volume—chap. 6) raises a more radical type of objection, questioning the basic premise of my conception. He believes that people's inconsistency in moral behavior is not a matter of moral motivation (nor, therefore, of character or personality) but of the fact that they tend to see different situations as differently related to morality. When we look at contextualized moral judgment, that is, taking into consideration the social role one is in at the moment or the different values that a specific situation elicits, then it is clear that objectively moral situations are not seen as morally relevant, and do not inspire moral action. However, Nucci argues, if we focus primarily on the moral aspects of a situation and make a moral judgment, we will act on the basis of our moral understanding. There is no need to add the sense of self or identity as a further layer. Moral understanding is all we need. I would agree with most, if not all the observations with which Nucci supports his conclusion. But Nucci may underestimate the role of motivation and, therefore, of personality in determining which of our values we concretely prefer and also the readiness to perceive situations in moral terms. He also seems to ignore what many readily recognize, namely, that, having seen in our contextualized judgment the moral relevance of an action, we still allows ourselves to be inconsistent with what we know. Many people do not simply regret what they did after the fact (the term, *regret*, suggests that they entered the action following a *mistaken* judgment); rather, and contrary to what Nucci thinks, many acknowledge that they were more or less aware, before initiating the action and during it, that they were not doing what they knew they should have done. In this case, they may experience guilt and not simply regret. The empirical evidence for this statement is frequent but informal; systematic information would be desirable.

One could raise a different question concerning the relations between morality and personality. Most psychological characteristics that determine a person's individuality and constitute the texture and background of his or her functioning are morally neutral. Some are behavioral tendencies; others are motivational orientations, cognitive styles, or emotional–expressive traits. These characteristics are the object of choice of personality psychology and of most personality measures. Their list is endless: Individuals can be classified as sociable, agreeable, field dependent, affiliative, sensitive, and insecure, or as loners, independent, self-confident, self-reliant, and dominant; as calm or excitable and needing stimulation; as courageous and daring or retreating and fearful; as emotionally stable or labile, impulsive or reflective; as ambitious, achievement oriented, and hard-working; as traditional and conservative or as innovation oriented, and so on. Each of us may relate to these traits in a passive way, as a given of our nature; we may even be unaware of our special tendencies; contrarily, we may acknowledge and appropriate them, may value or reject them, try to foster them, or control and reject them. In both cases, psychologists may wish to ask whether and how they affect moral functioning, both moral understanding and the appropriation and integration of morality in one's personality.

Norma Haan (1975, 1978) was probably the first to empirically approach these questions. Recently Walker (this volume—chap. 1) made this question the focus of an interesting program of work. Although it is too soon to draw firm conclusions, some observations can already be formulated. It is quite

plausible that personality characteristics of the type I just listed can both facilitate and inhibit moral development and moral functioning. For instance, openness to experience and to contradictions and the ability to control anxiety and
to rely on coping strategies seem indeed to facilitate the development of moral
understanding (Haan, 1978). After all, there is such a thing as moral luck (Williams, 1981). We need to remind ourselves, however, that what is psychologically difficult may not be impossible and may still be necessary. Moreover, as
Walker (this volume—chap. 1) points out, different personality dispositions
may channel moral functioning in different directions and create different
moral types.

I only would like to add a word of caution: It is easy to confuse the characteristics that are associated with moral functioning—either in people's perception
or in actual observation—with the essence of morality. When Walker's subjects–observers attribute certain traits to moral types, we do not know whether
they are trying to define (perhaps mistakenly) what is centrally required for
moral action or moral commitment, as moral, or are simply associating, in a
connotative manner, what goes with what. Similarly, in finding significant correlations between moral types and personality traits, we do not know whether
these traits are specifically moral, whether they are necessary antecedents or
consequents of moral commitment, or simply contingent correlates.

I conclude with one observation. It is risky to add variables in order to resolve new problems: The variables may have only a verbal existence; the explanations may be ad hoc, and the theorist may be unconcerned about the
effects of the new variables on the whole picture; and, most important, adding
variables tends to create new questions, particularly concerning the interactions with the other variables and the unity of the organism. From this perspective, the cognitive explanation of moral functioning is simple and elegant in its
unity. These are some of the reasons that led Nucci (this volume—chap. 6) to
go back to the explanatory power of moral understanding—this time
contextualized.

However, there is also the opposite risk: A unitary explanation may be inadequate, or may in fact rely on multiple factors, but without acknowledging them
and integrating them with the theory. Concerning the unity of the moral agent,
there are two very different ways of conceptualizing it. One relies on the functional and impersonal articulations of semiautonomous factors or on the mechanical interplay of forces; the other relies on the conscious striving of the
agentic self to make disparate elements congruent with each other and with the
person's overall goal. I always thought that only this second model is appropriate
for moral functioning. However, accustomed as we are to the scientific (or
scientistic) language of analysis and of dependent, independent, and intervening

variables, it is not easy for us to imagine the unity of the agentic self. From this perspective, in a person there is only one agent or, to use the language of medieval scholars, only one *ens quod*, one being that does this or that or acts in this or that way; personality (including cognitive) variables would be tools, instruments, or *entia quo*, qualities by which or according to which the agent operates. Only the person evaluates, judges, and acts morally; but, in doing so, he or she relies on competencies or qualities that are not self-subsistent. Among them are tools for understanding and making sense of reality, as well as qualities allowing the person to value certain ideals and not others, certain actions and not others.

REFERENCES

Blasi, A. (1983). Moral cognition and moral action: A theoretical perspective. *Developmental Review, 3*, 178–210.

Blasi, A. (1995). Moral understanding and the moral personality: The process of moral integration. In W. M. Kurtines and J. L. Gewirtz (Eds.), *Moral development: An introduction* (pp. 229–253). Boston: Allyn and Bacon.

Blasi, A. (1999). Emotions and moral motivation. *Journal for the Theory of Social Behaviour, 29*, 1–19.

Blasi, A. (2000). Was sollte als moralisches Verhalten gelten? Das Wesen der 'frühen Moral' in der kindlichen Entwicklung [What should count as moral behavior. The nature of "early morality" in children's development]. In W. Edelstein and G. Nunner-Winkler (Eds.), *Moral im sozialen Kontent* [Morality in context] (pp. 116–145). Frankfurt, Germany: Suhrkamp.

Blasi, A. (in press 2004). Character, moral development, and the self. In D. K. Lapsley and F. C. Power (Eds.), *Character psychology and character education*. Notre Dame, IN: University of Notre Dame Press.

Frankfurt, H. G. (1988). *The importance of what we care about*. New York: Cambridge University Press.

Frankfurt, H. G. (1999). *Necessity, volition, and love*. Cambridge, UK: Cambridge University Press.

Freud, S. (1910). *Leonardo da Vinci and a memory of his childhood. The standard edition of the complete psychological works of Sigmund Freud* (vol. 11, pp. 63–137). London: The Hogarth Press.

Freud, S. (1927). *The future of an illusion. The standard edition of the complete psychological works of Sigmund Freud* (Vol. 21, pp. 5–56). London: The Hogarth Press.

Haan, N. (1975). Moral reasoning in hypothetical and in actual situation of civil disobedience. *Journal of Personality and Social Psychology, 32*, 255–270.

Haan, N. (1978). Two moralities in action contexts: Relationships to thought, ego regulation, and development. *Journal of Personality and Social Psychology, 36*, 286–305.

Kohlberg, L. (1984). *The psychology of moral development: The nature and validity of moral stages*. San francisco, CA: Harper and Row.

Piaget, J. (1965). *Moral judgment of the child*. New York: Free Press.

Williams, B. (1981). *Moral luck*. Cambridge, UK: Cambridge University Press.

Author Index

Subject Index

Self-understanding, 66
Self-worth, 60, 118, *see also* Self-esteem
Social class, 68
Social development, 65
Social learning theory, 136, 168
Socialization, 114, 302
Social cognitive theory, 195
Socio-moral environment, 53
Spirituality, 7
Spontaneous trait inference, 204
Structuralism, 116
Subjectivity, 177–178
Superego, 153, 304, 309–311

T
Traits, *see also* Personality
   character, 114, 183, 194
   personality, 114, 168, 193, 196
Truth Commission, 106
Type A reasoning, 308
Type B reasoning, 217, 308

U
Universalizability, 106
Utilitarians, 166

V
Values, 7
Veil of ignorance, 139, 157, 327
Virtues, 10, 15, 168, 182–183, 185, 195–196
Virtue theory, 113
Virtue ethics, 152, 167
Voluntarism, 120

W
Washington University Sentence Completion
      Test, 227
Willpower, 182, 184–188, 194